The Poets' Dante

Ezra Pound • William Butler Yeats •

Charles Williams • T. S. Eliot • Osip Mandelstam

• Eugenio Montale • Jorge Luis Borges •

W. H. Auden • Robert Fitzgerald •

Robert Lowell • Robert Duncan •

Howard Nemerov • James Merrill • Seamus Heaney

• Charles Wright • Jacqueline Osherow •

J. D. McClatchy • W. S. Merwin • Robert Pinsky

• Geoffrey Hill • Rosanna Warren • W. S. Di Piero

• Daniel Halpern • Alan Williamson • Mark Doty

• C. K. Williams • Mary Baine Campbell •

Edward Hirsch

The Poets' Dante

Edited

by

Peter S. Hawkins

and

Rachel Jacoff

Farrar, Straus and Giroux

New York

Farrar, Straus and Giroux
19 Union Square West, New York 10003

Distributed in Canada by Douglas & McIntyre Ltd.
Printed in the United States of America
Published in 2001 by Farrar, Straus and Giroux
First paperback edition, 2002

Owing to limitations of space, all acknowledgments for permission to reprint
previously published material can be found on pages 405–6.

Library of Congress Cataloging-in-Publication Data
The poets' Dante / edited by Peter S. Hawkins and Rachel Jacoff.
    p.   cm.
    ISBN 0-374-52840-3 (pbk.)
    1. Dante Alighieri, 1265–1321. Divina commedia.   2. Dante Alighieri,
1265–1321—Appreciation.   3. Dante Alighieri, 1265–1321—Influence.
4. Poetry, Modern—20th century—Sources.   I. Jacoff, Rachel.   II. Hawkins, Peter S.

PQ4381.2 .P64 2001
851'.1—dc21

                                                    00-033552

Designed by Abby Kagan

www.fsgbooks.com

1 3 5 7 9 10 8 6 4 2

In memory of
David Kalstone and James Merrill

NOW DO U UNDERSTAND WHAT HEAVEN IS

IT IS THE SURROUND OF THE LIVING

James Merrill, *The Changing Light at Sandover*

Contents

Preface ix
Introduction xiii

Part I

Ezra Pound
  from *Dante* 3
William Butler Yeats
  from *A Vision* 12
Charles Williams
  from *The Figure of Beatrice* 16
T. S. Eliot
  What Dante Means to Me 28
Osip Mandelstam
  Conversation about Dante 40
Eugenio Montale
  Dante, Yesterday and Today 94
Jorge Luis Borges
  The Divine Comedy 118
W. H. Auden
  from *The Vision of Eros* 136
Robert Fitzgerald
  Mirroring the Commedia: *An Appreciation of*
    Laurence Binyon's Version 144
Robert Lowell
  Dante's Actuality and Fecundity in the Anglo-Saxon World 171
  Epics 176
Robert Duncan
  The Sweetness and Greatness of Dante's Divine Comedy 186
Howard Nemerov
  The Dream of Dante 210

James Merrill
   Divine Poem   227

Part II

Seamus Heaney
   Envies and Identifications: Dante and the Modern Poet   239
Charles Wright
   Dantino Mio   259
Jacqueline Osherow
   She's Come Undone: An American Jew Looks at Dante   265
J. D. McClatchy
   His Enamel   277
W. S. Merwin
   Poetry Rising from the Dead   292
Robert Pinsky
   The Pageant of Unbeing   306
Geoffrey Hill
   Between Politics and Eternity   319
Rosanna Warren
   Words and Blood   333
W. S. Di Piero
   Our Sweating Selves   344
Daniel Halpern
   Dante in Perpignan   354
Alan Williamson
   The Tears of Cocytus   359
Mark Doty
   Rooting for the Damned   370
C. K. Williams
   Souls   380
Mary Baine Campbell
   Wrath, Order, Paradise   383
Edward Hirsch
   Summoning Shades   395

Preface

Like most American readers of Dante, we first came to the poet through Ezra Pound and T. S. Eliot. By virtue of his presence in the *Cantos* and *The Waste Land*, the *Divine Comedy* was required reading for us—undergraduates who noticed footnotes and wanted to read what the masters had read. Somewhere late in our respective graduate studies in English, however, Italian became the language to learn and Dante the literary imagination we wanted to inhabit. He was without rival "l'altissimo poeta." Nevertheless, we each kept on reading the poetry of our climate, loving especially James Merrill, Gjertrud Schnackenberg, Charles Wright, Seamus Heaney—poets who had, we felt, a powerful affinity for Dante, if not outright debts to pay. Curiosity about these connections led us to some excellent secondary literature: volumes edited by Stuart McDougal and Nick Havely; pioneering work by Paget Toynbee and Angelina La Piana; and a number of very fine essays by John Ahern, Ted Cachey, Matthew Pearl, David Wallace, and others. What we wanted, however, was something more primary than the thoughts of literary critics.

During one early morning conversation, we came up with the idea of a collection of essays on Dante written by the poets we admired. In the first instance, this would mean bringing together published but often difficult to find prose work produced by our Modernist heroes and their earlier twentieth-century contemporaries. The longer we spoke, the more intriguing it became also to imagine a variety of living poets giving their thoughts on Dante: telling how they first encountered him, what drew them in, what kept them at a distance, whether his writing had any direct influence on their own. No doubt, there would be some who avoided prose altogether and others who had projects that already claimed their attention. Yet, what might we find if we asked?

This conversation eventually led to a talk with Jonathan Galassi at Farrar, Straus and Giroux. He responded with enthusiasm to the idea that has now become *The Poets' Dante* and put us immediately into the capable hands of his assistants, Phoebe Nobles, Lorin Stein, James Wilson, and Chandra Wohleber. J. D. McClatchy and Rosanna Warren gave us helpful advice at various points in our work, as did Maxine Groffsky, Michael Hendrickson, Andrea Nightingale, and Diana and Douglas Wilson.

Although much of our labor on this volume took place on the telephone or over weekends, we were afforded one unforgettable month to be in the same place, thanks to the generosity of the Bogliasco Foundation. Its Liguria Study Center, perched in a little pine forest above the Mediterranean, gave us the chance to read widely and learn how to write together. The staff of the Center, as well as the company of other fellows—especially graphic artist Lynda Frese and composer Steven Everett—greatly enriched our time on the aptly named Golfo Paradiso.

Dante made communication with the dead the substance of his poetry. More than any other writer, he showed literature to be an ongoing conversation with the past—a ghost story for the living. We hope that these twentieth-century essays will demonstrate how our poets remain haunted by his presence and are, to one degree or another, sojourners in his literary afterlife. In a line with unmistakable echoes of the *Comedy*, Eugenio

Montale wrote, "Ma è possibile, lo sai, amare un ombra, ombre noi stessi" (But it is possible, you know, to love a shade, being shades ourselves). This collection explores the particular shadowland where poets love (and quarrel with) Dante's shade—we who are shades ourselves.

Introduction

During the dog days of summer 1999, the *New York Times* "Bookend" was given over entirely to Seymour Chwast's cartoon, "Dante's *Divine Comedy*: The Diagram." This playful rendering of the three realms of the afterlife (in full color, and with subdivisions duly labeled) offered the Sunday *Book Review* reader a peppier version of the schematic overview provided in most editions of Dante's poem. In recognition of popular taste for the last six centuries, Hell took up two thirds of the page, with Purgatory and Paradise discreetly tucked away into corners. Any Dante expert would be quick to note particular mistakes—how could the artist have left the Primum Mobile out of the picture?—but the larger question was why the cartoon was there, without explanation, in the first place. Why should the newspaper of record have assumed that an ordinary reader would recognize the poem being diagrammed, let alone find the recognition entertaining? Was this a summertime reward for having long ago "done" the Great Books, or did it all have to do with global warming, the Balkans, and the approach of the new millennium—with apocalypse now?

The fact is that Dante is known not only by people who once read his poem, but also by the far larger number who have never turned a page. He is a figure in contemporary popular culture as well as in the academy's "selva oscura." For instance, several recent American movies—*Clerks* (1994), *Seven* (1995), and *Dante's Peak* (1997)—allude more or less openly to the poem, as does a rock group that took its name, "Divine Comedy," presumably in a bid to be remembered. The United States is studded with restaurants and bars called "Dante's Inferno"—a phrase also routinely used by journalists to describe any number of social or political hells. The *New Yorker's* cartoonists would be lost without Dante's pitchfork-wielding demons or classifications of punishment. Nor is his favor with humorists limited to the United States. A recent Japanese novel, *The Ruin of the Divine Comedy*, has the poet appear to the author of the book at the very moment of nuclear holocaust. With Dante as guide, the two explore a burlesque inferno replete with prominent Japanese politicians, both living and dead. Within the Western canon, only Shakespeare has similar international currency or crossover appeal.

Given Dante's present-day "niche" in the English-speaking world, it may seem that he must long have been a powerful presence in our poetry—his work (in Shelley's words) "the bridge thrown over the stream of time, uniting the modern and the ancient world." Yet this is not the case. True, Chaucer knew his poetry well enough to parody it; Milton quotes Dante's prose in his polemical writings, and in *Paradise Lost* carries on an intermittent dialogue with the *Comedy*. But between Chaucer and Milton, there is little evidence of Dante's importance to poets; after Milton, his fortune reaches its nadir. For the eighteenth century, he was the quintessence of everything "Gothick"—"extravagant, absurd, disgusting" in Horace Walpole's 1782 estimation. Yet less than one hundred years later, Ruskin could celebrate him as a cultural touchstone, "the central man in all the world." Dante was a nineteenth-century phenomenon throughout Europe and in the United States, esteemed by Coleridge, Byron, and Shelley, by Browning and the Rossettis, as well as by Emerson, Longfellow, and Whitman. Starting with Henry Cary's 1814 version of the

Comedy, a spate of translations on both sides of the Atlantic suddenly made his poetry readily available. The illustrations of John Flaxman, William Blake, and Gustave Doré turned a poem replete with images into unforgettable, mass-produced pictures.

Nor was this nineteenth-century Dante any less multifaceted than his own great work. Depending on the admirer, he was considered the father of modern poetry, the liberator of vernacular speech, the civic poet, the exile and wanderer, the prophet of nationalism or of world government, the adoring lover, the exacting craftsman. As *pater patriae* of the Risorgimento, Dante not only became required reading in Italian schools but a runaway best-seller. Simultaneously in the United States, he was Emerson's model for a distinctly American genius who could write autobiography "in colossal cipher," whose eloquence was capacious enough to include the rough and ready of the American frontier: "he knows 'God damn,' and can be rowdy if he pleases, and does please." No less rough a rider than Teddy Roosevelt, writing in 1911, saw that Dante had caught the true grit of American life. "The Bowery is one of the great highways of humanity, a highway of varied interest, of fun, of work, of sordid and terrible tragedy; and it is haunted by demons, as horrible as any that stalk through the pages of the 'Inferno.' But no man of Dante's art and Dante's soul would write of it nowadays, and he would hardly be understood if he did."

Since a new century predictably turns against the tastes of its predecessor, one would expect that the Dante beloved of Romantics, Victorians, and Pre-Raphaelites would fall out of favor with writers self-conscious about "making it new." Yet, quite the contrary, it is in the English-speaking twentieth century that Dante has become the great Poet Interlocutor, the master of *poetando*. The list of those who have been in sustained dialogue with him is both diverse and long; it is also full of Americans, whether by birth or long-term residence. Pound and Eliot come immediately to mind; after them, Merrill, Heaney, Derek Walcott, and Charles Wright, followed by many others at the beginning of the twenty-first century, as this volume aims to show. A recent surge in translation is also part of the picture. In 1993, Daniel Halpern mobilized twenty poets to produce a multi-voiced *Inferno*; this venture in turn led to Robert Pinsky's immensely successful *Inferno* in 1995 and to W. S. Merwin's 2000 *Purgatorio*.

Why should a medieval Catholic visionary exert such appeal to writers living in so different a world? Perhaps it is the extraordinary breadth of his intellect and the range of emotions he explores; or the cultural richness of Italy, which has so long appealed to the Northern imagination; or a religious vision that manages somehow to speak eloquently to people who do not share its dogmas? What has often been celebrated as Dante's "universality"—the sheer scope of the *Comedy*—seems to have made it possible to engage his work on many different levels, and often on utterly divergent terms. He was venerated by Pound and Eliot, in Heaney's phrase, as "the aquiline patron of international Modernism," but during the same period treated quite playfully by Samuel Beckett, James Joyce, and Wallace Stevens. For some, the *Inferno* is the canticle of choice, while others gravitate toward the *Purgatorio* or *Paradiso*. Poets are drawn to the *Comedy*'s vivid dramatic encounters, its clusters of metaphor, its linguistic and metrical inventiveness. Finally, Dante's intense interest in the relationship of poets to one another—and thus to questions of origin and descent, poetic paternity and filiation—has offered several models for writers eager to position themselves within and against literary tradition.

Dante's afterlife in English-language poetry has already been well studied by literary critics. What we are presenting here, however, is a more primary discourse, one in which poets speak for themselves. We begin with a series of essays (or, on occasion, excerpts from longer prose works) written by the Illustrious Dead: all have been previously published but never before "bound in one volume." This sequence stretches chronologically from Pound's immensely influential *Spirit of Romance* (1910) to Merrill's "Divine Poem" (1980). Despite our English-language focus, we also include translated essays by Osip Mandelstam, Eugenio Montale, and Jorge Luis Borges. These earlier twentieth-century poets share Mandelstam's desire "to wrench Dante from classroom rhetoric," to recuperate the poet's "inexhaustible contemporaneity" in our time.

The second section of the book presents new essays commissioned from living poets who are writing at different stages of their careers and who represent varying degrees of involvement with the *Comedy* and its author. Some have clearly been influenced by Dante and are in open dialogue with him; we asked others to write simply because we wanted to know what they would have to say on the subject. The essays gathered here are widely different in scope, format, and style, and it is precisely this range and diversity of response that reinforces our sense of how pluralistic Dante's influence remains.

In a collection of some thirty essays, each with its distinct "take" on Dante's importance, it may be useful to elaborate upon those aspects of his life and work that have proved most compelling to twentieth-century writers. Here we must begin with the intrinsic power of Dante's personal story: his love for Beatrice, his involvement not only in Florentine politics, but in the larger European scene, the reversals of fortune that turned him into a wanderer, his transformation of personal and political disaster into poetic triumph. The major source for this biography, Boccaccio's mid-fourteenth-century *Vita di Dante*, captivated the English Romantics, who judged Dante, in Shelley's words, as "the most glorious imagination of modern poetry," and saw him as a brooding Byronic figure, the Bard of Hell. In reaction to the nineteenth century's preoccupation with Dante the man, Eliot stressed poetic and religious Tradition against the particularity of the Individual Talent: a poet's work was what mattered, not the historical self and its private drama. Nonetheless, despite Eliot's critical sway, the details of Dante's biography and his vivid self-presentation in the *Comedy* proved too compelling to be ignored by subsequent writers. Indeed, the autobiographical and even confessional nature of the poem have made Dante a congenial model for lyric poets, many of whom become the protagonists of their own stories. As Pound noted, the *Comedy* "is in a sense lyric, the tremendous lyric of the subjective Dante."

Arguably, the single most important preoccupation of the poet's life story is love in all its forms—the force that "moves the sun and the other stars" and propels Dante's imagination from the early *Vita Nuova* to the final canticle of the *Comedy*. Throughout this career-long meditation on the nature of *amore*, Beatrice serves as his focus, as the figure through which he imagines his fulfillment. Behind her stretches a long-established medieval tradition, rediscovered by the English Romantics and, around mid-century, by major poets in America. At the bidding of Margaret Fuller, Emerson made the first English translation of the *Vita Nuova* in 1843 (although this work was lost until roughly one hundred years later). In England, the pale lover of Dante's earliest work was taken up first by Rossetti's Pre-Raphaelite Brotherhood and then by Yeats, who made the author of the *Comedy* a "mask" for himself—a poet wounded by love and politics, who nonetheless turned disappointment into art. Pound saw Dante as the culmination of the rich lineage of Provençal and earlier Italian lyric poets, as *il miglior fabbro*—the master craftsman of Romance.

Yet none of these "rediscoveries" took note of what was truly innovative in Dante's treatment of love: the theological depth he accorded to human *amore*, the possibility that the beloved might actually become the way to God. Eliot was interested in this vision but could not take it beyond the enigmatic Lady of *Ash-Wednesday*. Instead, it was Charles Williams in his 1943 study, *The Figure of Beatrice*, who put into circulation an intensely Christian reading of the *Comedy*. Whereas Eliot had claimed that the *Vita Nuova* was anti-romantic, teaching us "not to expect more from *life* than it can give or more from *human* beings than they can give," Williams viewed Dante as the great exemplar of his theology of Romantic Love and the *Comedy* as its scripture. In this understanding of Dante's incarnational poetics, human love is fully embodied, its goal nothing short of the "coinherence" of flesh and spirit, of the human in the divine. Perhaps speaking to Pound and Eliot as much as to the scholarly keepers of the flame, Williams argued the relevance of personal life as the source book for theological as well as literary interpretation. "We have looked everywhere for enlightenment on Dante," he wrote, "except in our lives and love-affairs." To read the poet aright was to learn to take one's own loves more seriously; it was to learn how to love.

Two other writers took up Williams's understanding of Dante in the late 1940s. Dorothy Sayers's *terza rima* translation of the *Comedy* appeared in the new Penguin paperback series; its commentary on the poem was heavily indebted to *The Figure of Beatrice* and made Williams's theological interpretation available to a mass-market audience. No less a champion was W. H. Auden, who counted Williams (along with Kierkegaard) as a primary spiritual mentor, and whose interpretation of Dante, not to mention of love, was greatly influenced by what he read in *The Figure of Beatrice*. In more than one discussion of Eros as "intended to lead the lover towards the love of the uncreated source of all beauty," he expands both the *Vita Nuova* and Williams's "Romantic Theology" to include the same-sex love he had himself experienced. "When the vision of Eros is genuine," he wrote, "I do not think it makes sense to apply to it terms like heterosexual or homosexual." Auden brought to considerations of love a refreshing sense of humor inevitable in any descent from the Empyrean to the reality of a carnal lover. This meant including the comic within the divine, allowing playfulness to lighten the *poema sacro*.

Almost as important as the experience of love in Dante's work is his passionate involvement in the often tragic world of politics. Just as his relationship with Beatrice provided an autobiographical foundation for his lifelong meditation on the nature of *amore*, so too his banishment from Florence compelled him to deal with questions of justice from the painful perspective of the disenfranchised outsider. This exilic figure bemoaning the fate of "serva Italia"—Italy enslaved—became a rallying point for Risorgimento Italy, as well as for Byron in "The Prophecy of Dante." At the same time, Dante also appealed to Americans such as Emerson, Longfellow, and other members of the Cambridge "Dante Club": James Russell Lowell, Charles Eliot Norton, and Oliver Wendell Holmes. All of these New Englanders saw the poet as properly belonging to their New World rather than to the old. As Holmes wrote in a sonnet addressed to the city of Florence,

> Thine exile's shrine, thy sorrowing love embowers,
>   Yet none with truer homage bends the knee,
>   Or stronger pledge of fealty brings, than we,
> Whose poets make thy dead immortal ours.

Florence's loss was Boston's gain, not as some European antiquity transported to these shores, but as a model for a genuinely American poetry, for a new English vernacular.

It is remarkable how the dated specificity of Dante's political concerns—the bewildering struggles between Guelph and Ghibelline or the suspect dream of empire—was transformed by his bitter experience of exile into powerful personal witness. Indeed, his loss of "everything held most dear" has become poignant in the wake of two world wars and in the midst of today's internecine conflicts. Especially evocative is Dante's identity as a displaced person who finds a powerful voice in the experience of being uprooted or silenced. Here one thinks most dramatically of a number of Russian writers who took the exiled Dante as one of their own—Mandelstam, Anna Akhmatova, Alexander Solzhenitsyn, and Joseph Brodsky—as well as of those others (Pound and Eliot, Beckett and Joyce) for whom leaving home was a choice rather than a necessity. Dante's example of spiritual and cultural isolation also inflects the complex relations to "homeland" found in the poetry of Seamus Heaney and Derek Walcott.

In addition to the interest of his life story and the themes of love and politics rooted in that personal experience, Dante has been highly attractive to writers for more purely literary reasons. The *Comedy*'s architectural complexity and extraordinary structural symmetries have been important for later poets, who found in his work perhaps the greatest statement of coherence, the most Supreme Fiction. In the final canto of the *Paradiso*, Dante speaks of seeing all that is scattered throughout the universe "bound with love in one volume": in so doing, he provides an inclusive image that has come to stand for the comprehensiveness of the poem itself. Twentieth-century poets understood the impossibility of creating such an all-encompassing artifact in their own time but remained intrigued by the prospect nonetheless. Pound set out to make his *Cantos* a summation of everything that had been known since Dante's time, and for over fifty years tried to bring diverse materials into an order that he admitted he could not achieve: "I am not a demigod, I cannot make it cohere." Eliot's *The Waste Land* is a bricolage of earlier texts that announces itself as shoring up fragments against its ruins. In the early 1930s, Auden attempted a mock-epic journey from capitalist hell to Communist paradise, but was never able to complete the work. Although Merrill's *The Changing Light at Sandover* produces a comprehensive cosmology that rivals Yeats, if not Dante, for most readers, it succeeds best in its lyrical moments. In lieu of the *Comedy*'s unified, even totalizing story, many contemporary poets have chosen to write sequences, collections of short but related poems that privilege what is partial and implied over any developed master narrative.

Dante's great metrical innovation—*terza rima*—has proved to be yet another source of fascination. Merrill described it as writing

on water: "No verse form *moves* so wonderfully. Each tercet's first
and third line rhyme with the middle one of the preceding set,
and enclose the new rhyme-sound of the next, the way a scull
outstrips the twin, already dissolving oarstrokes that propel it. As
rhymes interlock throughout a canto, so do incidents and images
throughout the poem." Mandelstam chose another metaphor and
called attention to the waltz-like rhythm of the meter. In *terza
rima*, the central line of each tercet rhymes with the first and third
lines of the subsequent *terzina*, thereby establishing an interlocking
rhythmic continuity. Two steps forward, one step back.

Despite the great difficulty of writing this verse form in English, poets from Shelley on have taken up the challenge. Usually,
as in *The Changing Light at Sandover*, the presence of *terza rima* is
intermittent and strategic, always quite deliberately recalling
Dante's presence and in that way implicating him in the new text.
Along with strict imitation, there have been many adaptations
of the rhyme. Eliot's much-praised rewriting in "Little Gidding" of
the *Inferno* 15 encounter with Brunetto Latini offers a version of
the form through an alternation of masculine and feminine endings. Other approximations abound in modern poetry, with even
partially rhymed or unrhymed tercets—as in Yeats's "Cuchulain
Comforted" and Stevens's *Notes Toward a Supreme Fiction*—carrying with them the echo, as well as the energy, of Dante's *terzinas*.

The *Comedy* has also provided twentieth-century poets with
additional sources of literary inspiration. What Gianfranco Contini
celebrated as Dante's "plurilinguismo," his extraordinary range of
language and tone, helped expand the notion of what "the poetic"
could properly include. In Dante's freedom from classical notions
of stylistic decorum, he moved with ease from the sublime to the
scatological, from prayer to invective, from the abstractions of light
metaphysics to the grotesque specificity of anatomy. This poetic license has not always been appreciated: the hybrid identity of the
Comedy—its refusal to be one thing or another, whether on
the level of genre or of style—consistently offended readers from

the Renaissance to the eighteenth century. However, it is precisely this "transgressive" aspect of Dante's work that has been liberating for many modern poets. His multiplicity of lexical and tonal registers, his openness to dialect and to the particularity of a local scene, have authorized experiments of many different kinds.

One aspect of Dante's "plurilinguismo" is his incorporation of other languages within his own vernacular. Dante felt free to introduce the entire linguistic world as he knew it into the *Comedy*, including lines or phrases of Latin, Provençal, Hebrew, and Greek, a smattering of Italian dialects, even the occasional outburst of gibberish—all subjected to the rigors of his *terza rima*. Eliot's inclusion of bits of French, German, Italian, Latin, and Sanskrit in *The Waste Land* made this "polyglossia" a feature of Modernism, albeit one that suggested global incoherence rather than universality. Pound went further with this proliferation of tongues, at times carrying it beyond the bounds of readability: in some of the *Cantos*, for instance, Chinese ideograms jostle against swatches of ancient Greek and a host of vernaculars. Without Pound's sacrifice of intelligibility, Walcott brings Homer and Dante to the Caribbean, joining the Creole of his native region to the British English he learned at home and spoke at school and in church.

A few of the poets gathered in this collection may share the fundamentals of Dante's Christianity, but largely they do not. Nonetheless, the poet's profoundly theological imagination continues to appeal, if only as something to be demythologized or reinterpreted. For many, Dante's vision of Paradise as a realm of increasing luminosity is especially engaging. Indeed, it is as the poet of radiance that Dante has been cherished (and his *Paradiso* become the favored canticle) of the later Eliot, of Merrill, Wright, and Schnackenberg. Twentieth-century poetry is full of epiphanic moments, glimpses of illumination. These sporadic "spots of time" have supplanted Dante's sustained vision of eternity; and when they do occur, such moments are often undercut or made ironic, exposed as ephemeral, their heightened diction deflated with humor. Nonetheless, contemporary language of the sublime owes much to Dante, who continues to inspire theologically haunted poets drawn to the power of visionary language even in the absence of vision itself.

The *Comedy*—a sustained conversation between the mortal Dante and a host of immortal shades—also provides a model, in the tradition of Homer and Virgil, for how a living poet may speak with the dead. It is striking how deep this impulse remains in modern poetry, in an age when the afterlife, let alone communication with it, is hardly otherwise credible to most intellectuals. Is this because the *Comedy* is a fiction, so that one can "believe" in its formulations without having to subscribe to its theology? Or is the poem as close as many writers can come to theology of any kind, discovering in it a motive (or excuse) for religious metaphor? In any event, Dante's tripartite landscape of eternity and the dramatic encounters that take place there have provided twentieth-century poets with imaginative material to be recalled and transformed.

The "familiar compound ghost" of Eliot's "Little Gidding," based on Dante's charged encounter with the "paternal" Brunetto Latini, made the meeting with a dead poetic mentor one of the most enduring "scenes" in modern poetry. Robert Lowell, Merrill, Heaney, Walcott, and Wright have all rewritten this exchange, making it an opportunity to reflect on poetic tradition and one's place within it. Heaney's *Station Island*, set in St. Patrick's Purgatory (a traditional site for the intersection of this world and the next), provides the most extended reworking. Against the background of the Irish "Troubles," the poet meets with friends, relatives, and teachers in an attempt to both honor their sufferings and authorize himself for taking a different path. Merrill bypasses Christianity entirely and adopts the Ouija board as a means of conversing with the dead. For him, Auden becomes the key voice

of poetic tradition speaking from the "other side." Whereas Dante
had imagined Virgil granting him in *Inferno* 4 a place alongside the
great poets of antiquity, Merrill gives Auden the task of ratifying
his own endeavors as a player in the "greenwood perspectives of
the mother tongue." Montale imagines poignant encounters with
the shades of both mother and father, as poems about cemetery
visits turn into the occasions of epiphany and exchange. Likewise,
Walcott's *Omeros* includes meetings not only with such poetic father figures as Homer and Joyce, but also with Walcott's actual father, Warwick. In Charles Wright's "A Journal in the Year of the
Ox," there is even an encounter with Dante himself, who counsels
the poet

> *Brother, remember the way it was*
> *In my time: nothing has changed:*
> *Penitents terrace the mountainside, the stars hang in their bright courses*
> *And darkness is still the dark:*
> *concentrate, listen hard,*
> *Look to the nature of all things . . .*

In all these ways, then, the notion of communication with the
shades remains a poetic option throughout the twentieth century,
with the *Comedy* making viable the afterlife conversation quite
apart from questions of belief.

Looking back at the various unexpected roles Dante has played in
twentieth-century poetry, we also look forward to the unpredictable continuation of this story. Near the beginning of the
nineteenth-century Dante revival, Shelley characterized the *Comedy* and its author as buried fire ready to burst into flame: "his very
words are instinct with spirit; each is a spark, a burning atom of
inextinguishable thought; and many yet lie covered in the ashes of
their birth, and pregnant with a lightning which has yet found no

conductor." Over a hundred years later, in the 1930s, Mandelstam employed a Futurist lexicon to claim that this medieval poem was in fact a rocket about to be launched: "It is unthinkable to read the cantos of Dante without aiming them in the direction of the present day. They were made for that. They are missiles for capturing the future." Given Dante's preoccupation with precursors and peers, he would not have been surprised to learn that, among "la futura gente," it would be poets who most forcibly recognized him as their contemporary. Could even he, however, have guessed that his Florentine vernacular would have so fired the imagination of the Western world, or enjoyed so long a poetic afterlife in English?

Part I

Ezra Pound

from *Dante*

The *Divina Commedia* must not be considered as an epic; to compare it with epic poems is usually unprofitable. It is in a sense lyric, the tremendous lyric of the subjective Dante; but the soundest classification of the poem is Dante's own, "as a comedy which differs from tragedy in its content,"[1] for "tragedy begins admirably and tranquilly," and the end is terrible, "whereas comedy introduces some harsh complication, but brings the matter to a prosperous end." The *Commedia* is, in fact, a great mystery play, or better, a cycle of mystery plays.

. . . Any sincere criticism of the highest poetry must resolve itself into a sort of profession of faith. The critic must begin with a "credo," and his opinion will be received in part for the intelligence he may seem to possess, and in part for his earnestness. Certain of Dante's supremacies are comprehensible only to such as know Italian and have themselves attained a certain proficiency in the poetic art. An *ipse dixit* is not necessarily valueless. The penalty for remaining a layman is that one must at times accept a specialist's opinion. No one ever took the trouble to become a specialist for the bare pleasure of ramming his *ipse dixit* down the general throat.

There are two kinds of beautiful painting one may perhaps illustrate by the works of Burne-Jones and Whistler; one looks at the first kind of painting and is immediately delighted by its beauty; the second kind of painting, when first seen, puzzles one, but on leaving it, and going from the gallery one finds new beauty in natural things—a Thames fog, to use the hackneyed example. Thus, there are works of art which are beautiful objects and works of art which are keys or passwords admitting one to a deeper knowledge, to a finer perception of beauty; Dante's work is of the second sort.

Presumably critical analysis must proceed in part by comparison; Wordsworth is, we may say, the orthodox sign for comprehension of nature, yet where has Wordsworth written lines more instinct with "nature-feeling" than those in the twenty-eight of the *Purgatorio*?

l' aqua, diss' io, e il suon della foresta
impugnan dentro a me novella fede.

The water, quoth I, and the woodland murmuring
drive in new faith upon my soul.

So one is tempted to translate it for the sake of the rhythm, but Dante has escaped the metaphysical term, and describes the actual sensation with more intensity. His words are: "indrive new faith within to me."

Wordsworth and the Uncouth American share the palm for modern "pantheism," or some such thing; but weigh their words with the opening lines of the *Paradiso*:

La gloria di colui che tutto move
Per l' universo penetra e risplende
In una parte più, e meno altrove.

The glory of him who moveth all
Penetrates and is resplendent through the all
In one part more and in another less.

The disciples of Whitman cry out concerning the "cosmic sense," but Whitman, with all his catalogues and flounderings, has never so perfectly expressed the perception of cosmic consciousness as does Dante in the canto just quoted:[2]

Qual si fe' Glauco nel gustar dell' erba
Che il fe' consorto in mar degli altri dei.

As Glaucus, tasting of the grass which made him
sea-fellow of the other gods.

Take it as simple prose expression, forget that it is told with matchless sound, discount the suggestion of the parallel beauty in the older myth, and it is still more convincing than Whitman.

Shelley, I believe, ranks highest as the English "transcendental" poet, whatever that may mean. Shelley is honest in his endeavor to translate a part of Dante's message into the more northern tongue. He is, in sort, a faint echo of the *Paradiso*, very much as Rossetti is, at his best, an echo of the shorter Tuscan poetry. I doubt if Shelley ever thought of concealing the source of much of this beauty, which he made his own by appreciation. Certainly few men have honored Dante more than did Shelley. His finest poem, the *Ode to the West Wind*, bears witness to his impressions of the earlier canti; thus to the host under the whirling ensign in canto 3 of the *Inferno*, and especially to lines 112–14:

Come d' autunno si levan le foglie
L' uno appreso dell' altra infin che il ramo
Vede alla terra tutte le sue spoglie.

As leaves of autumn fall one after one
Till the branch seeth all its spoils upon
The ground . . .

The full passage from which this is taken foreshadows Shelley's "pestilence-stricken multitudes." In the fifth canto "shadows borne upon the aforesaid strife,"[3] and the rest, with the movement of the wind, is pregnant with suggestions for the splendid English ode. I detract nothing from Shelley's glory, for of the tens of thousands who have read these canti, only one has written such an ode.

This is not an isolated or a chance incident; the best of Shelley is filled with memories of Dante.

The comparison of Dante and Milton is at best a stupid convention. Shelley resembles Dante afar off, and in a certain effect of clear light which both produce.

Milton resembles Dante in nothing; judging superficially, one might say that they both wrote long poems which mention God and the angels, but their gods and their angels are as different as their styles and abilities. Dante's god is ineffable divinity. Milton's god is a fussy old man with a hobby. Dante is metaphysical, where Milton is merely sectarian. *Paradise Lost* is conventional melodrama, and later critics have decided that the Devil is intended for the hero, which interpretation leaves the whole without significance. Dante's Satan is undeniably and indelibly evil. He is not "Free Will" but stupid malignity. Milton has no grasp of the superhuman. Milton's angels are men of enlarged power, plus wings. Dante's angels surpass human nature, and differ from it. They move in their high courses inexplicable.

> ma fé sembiante
> d' uomo, cui altra cura stringa. (101–2)

Appeared as a man whom other care incites.[4]

Milton, moreover, shows a complete ignorance of the things of the spirit. Any attempt to compare the two poets as equals is bathos, and it is, incidentally, unfair to Milton, because it makes one forget all his laudable qualities.

Shakespear alone of the English poets endures sustained comparison with the Florentine. Here are we with the masters; of neither can we say, "He is the greater"; of each we must say, "He is unexcelled."

It is idle to ask what Dante would have made of writing stage plays, or what Shakespear would have done with a "Paradise."

There is almost an exact three centuries between their dates of birth [Dante was born in 1265; Shakespear in 1564]. America had been discovered, printing, the Reformation, the Renaissance were new forces at work. Much change had swept over the world; but art and humanity, remaining ever the same, gave us basis for comparison.

Dante would seem to have the greater imaginative "vision," the greater ability to see the marvellous scenery through which his action passes; but Shakespear's vision is never deficient, though his expression of it be confined to a few lines of suggestion and the prose of the stage directions.

Shakespear would seem to have greater power in depicting various humanity, and to be more observant of its foibles; but recalling Dante's comparisons to the gamester leaving the play, to the peasant at the time of hoar-frost, to the folk passing in the shadow of evening, one wonders if he would have been less apt at fitting them with speeches. His dialogue is comparatively symbolic, it serves a purpose similar to that of the speeches in Plato, yet both he and Plato convey the impression of individuals speaking.

If the language of Shakespear is more beautifully suggestive, that of Dante is more beautifully definite; both men are masters of the whole art. Shakespear is perhaps more brilliant in his use of epithets of proper quality; thus I doubt if there be in Dante, or in all literature, any epithet so masterfully-placed as is Shakespear's in the speech of the Queen-mother to Hamlet where she says "And with the incorporal air do hold discourse," suggesting both the common void of the air which she sees and the ghostly form at which Hamlet stands aghast; on the other hand, Dante is, perhaps, more apt in "comparison."

"The apt use of metaphor, arising, as it does, from a swift perception of relations, is the hall-mark of genius": thus says Aristotle. I use the term "comparison" to include metaphor, simile (which is a more leisurely expression of a kindred variety of thought), and the "language beyond metaphor," that is, the more compressed or elliptical expression of metaphorical perception, such as antithesis suggested or implied in verbs and adjectives; for we find adjectives of two sorts, thus, adjectives of pure quality, as: white, cold, ancient; and adjectives which are comparative, as: lordly. Epithets may also be distinguished as epithets of primary and secondary apparition. By epithets of primary apparition I mean those which describe what is actually presented to the sense or vision. Thus in "selva oscura," ("shadowy wood"); epithets of secondary apparition or afterthought are such as in "*sage* Hippotades" or "*forbidden* tree." Epithets of primary apparition give vividness to description and stimulate conviction in the actual vision of the poet. There are likewise clauses and phrases of "primary apparition." Thus, in canto 10 of the *Inferno*, where Cavalcante de' Cavalcanti's head appears above the edge of the tomb, "I believe he had risen on his knees,"[5] has no beauty in itself, but adds greatly to the verisimilitude.

There are also epithets of "emotional apparition," transensuous, suggestive as in Yeats' line, "Under a bitter *black* wind that blows from the left hand." Dante's coloring and qualities of the infernal air, although they are definitely symbolical and not indefinitely suggestive, foreshadow this sort of epithet. The modern symbolism is more vague, it is sometimes allegory in three dimensions instead of two, sometimes merely atmospheric suggestion.

It is in the swift forms of comparison, however, that Dante sets much of his beauty. Thus: "dove il sol tace," ("where the sun is silent,") or, "l'aura morta," ("the dead air."). In this last the comparison fades imperceptibly into emotional suggestion.

His vividness depends much on his comparison by simile to particular phenomena; . . . thus Dante, following the Provençal, says, not "where a river pools itself," but "As at Arles, where the Rhone pools itself."[6] Or when he is describing not a scene but a feeling, he makes such comparison as in the matchless simile to Glaucus.

Dante's temperament is austere, patrician; Shakespear, as nature, combines refinement with profusion; it is as natural to compare Dante to a cathedral as it is to compare Shakespear to a forest; yet Shakespear is not more enamored of out-of-door beauty than is Dante. Their lands make them familiar with a different sort of out-of-doors. Shakespear shows his affection for this beauty as he knows it in—

—the morn, in russet mantle clad,
Walks o'er the dew of yon high eastward hill;

and Dante, when the hoar-frost

paints her white sister's image on the ground.

It is part of Dante's aristocracy that he conceded nothing to the world, or to opinion—like Farinata, he met his reverses "as if he held Hell in great disdain";[7] Shakespear concedes, succeeds, and repents in one swift, bitter line: "I have made myself a motley to the view."

Shakespear comes nearer to most men, partly from his habit of speaking from inside his characters instead of conversing with them. He seems more human, but only when we forget the intimate confession of the *Vita Nuova* or such lines of the *Commedia* as

col quale il fantolin corre alla mamma
quand' ha paura o quando egli è aflitto.

as the little child runs to its mother when it
has fear, or when it is hurt.

Dante has the advantage in points of pure sound; his ono-
matopoeia is not a mere trick of imitating natural noises, but is a
mastery in fitting the inarticulate sound of a passage to the mood
or to the quality of voice which expresses that mood or passion
which the passage describes or expresses. Shakespear has a language less apt for this work in pure sound, but he understands the
motion of words, or, if the term be permitted, the overtones and
undertones of rhythm, and he uses them with a mastery which no
one but Burns has come reasonably near to approaching. Other
English poets master this part of the art occasionally, or as if by accident; there is a fine example in a passage of Sturge Moore's *De-
feat of the Amazons*, where the spirit of his faun leaps and scurries,
with the words beginning: "Ahi! ahi! ahi! Laomedon."

. . . That Shakespear, as Dante, is the conscious master of his art
is most patent from the manner in which he plays with his art
in the sonnets, teasing, experimenting, developing that technique
which he so marvellously uses and so cunningly conceals in the
later plays. To talk about "wood-notes wild" is sheer imbecility.

Did Shakespear know his Tuscan poetry directly or through
some medium, through Petrarch, or through some Italianized
Englishman? Why did he not write a play on Francesca da Rimini? There are a number of subjects for amusing speculation; theo-
ries will be built from straws floating in the wind; thus Francis
Meres, when in 1598 he writes of Shakespear's "fine-filed phrase,"
may or may not have some half memory of Dante's "amorosa
lima," the "loving file" that had "polished his speech."

Our knowledge of Dante and of Shakespear interacts; intimate

acquaintance with either breeds that discrimination which makes
us more keenly appreciate the other.

(1910)

Notes

1. *Epistle to Can Grande.*
2. *Paradiso* 1.68–69.
3. Ombre portate della detta briga.
4. *Inferno* 9.101–102.
5. Credo che s'era in ginocchie levata.
6. Si come ad Arli, ove il Rodano stagna.
7. Si come avesse l' inferno in gran dispetto.

William Butler Yeats

from *A Vision*

Will—The *Daimonic* Man.

     Mask (from Phase 3). *True*—Simplification through intensity. *False*—Dispersal.

Creative Mind (from Phase 13). *True*—Creative imagination through *antithetical* emotion. *False*—Enforced self-realization.

Body of Fate (from Phase 27)—Loss.

Examples: Dante, Shelley, Landor.

He is called the *Daimonic* man because Unity of Being, and consequent expression of *Daimonic* thought, is now more easy than at any other phase. As contrasted with Phase 13 and Phase 14, where mental images were separated from one another that they might be subject to knowledge, all now flow, change, flutter, cry out, or mix into something else; but without, as at Phase 16, breaking and bruising one another, for Phase 17, the central phase of its triad, is without frenzy. The *Will* is falling asunder, but without explosion and noise. The separated fragments seek images rather than ideas, and these the intellect, seated in Phase 13, must synthesise in vain, drawing with its compass-point a line that shall but represent the outline of a bursting pod. The being has for its supreme aim, as it had at Phase 16 (and as all subsequent *antithetical* phases shall have), to hide from itself and others this separation and disorder, and it conceals them under the emotional *Image* of Phase 3; as Phase 16 concealed its greater violence under that of Phase 2. When true to phase the intellect must turn all its synthetic power to this task. It finds, not the impassioned myth that Phase 16 found, but a *Mask* of simplicity that is also intensity. This *Mask* may represent intellectual or sexual passion; seem some Ahasuerus or Athanase; be the gaunt Dante of the *Divine Comedy*; its corresponding Image may be Shelley's Venus Urania, Dante's Beatrice, or even the Great Yellow Rose of the *Paradiso*. The *Will*, when true to phase, assumes, in assuming the *Mask*, an intensity which is never dramatic but always lyrical and personal, and this intensity, though always a deliberate assumption, is to others but the charm of the being; and yet the *Will* is always aware of the *Body of Fate*, which perpetually destroys this intensity, thereby leaving the *Will* to its own "dispersal."

At Phase 3, not as *Mask* but as phase, there should be perfect physical well-being or balance, though not beauty or emotional intensity, but at Phase 27 are those who turn away from all that Phase 3 represents and seek all those things it is blind to. The *Body of Fate*, therefore, derived from a phase of renunciation, is "loss," and works to make impossible "simplification by intensity." The being, through the intellect, selects some object of desire for a representation of the *Mask* as Image, some woman perhaps, and the *Body of Fate* snatches away the object. Then the intellect (*Creative Mind*), which in the most *antithetical* phases were better described as imagination, must substitute some new image of desire; and in the degree of its power and of its attainment of unity, relate that which is lost, that which has snatched it away, to the new image of desire, that which threatens the new image to the being's unity. If its unity be already past, or if unity be still to come, it may for all that be true to phase. It will then use its intellect merely to isolate *Mask* and Image, as chosen forms or as conceptions of the mind.

If it be out of phase it will avoid the subjective conflict, acquiesce, hope that the *Body of Fate* may die away; and then the *Mask*

will cling to it and the Image lure it. It will feel itself betrayed, and
persecuted till, entangled in *primary* conflict, it rages against all that
destroys *Mask* and Image. It will be subject to nightmare, for its
Creative Mind (deflected from the *Image* and *Mask* to the *Body of
Fate*) gives an isolated mythological or abstract form to all that excites its hatred. It may even dream of escaping from ill-luck by
possessing the impersonal *Body of Fate* of its opposite phase and of
exchanging passion for desk and ledger. Because of the habit of
synthesis, and of the growing complexity of the energy, which
gives many interests, and the still faint perception of things in their
weight and mass, men of this phase are almost always partisans,
propagandists and gregarious; yet because of the *Mask* of simplification, which holds up before them the solitary life of hunters and
of fishers and "the groves pale passion loves," they hate parties,
crowds, propaganda. Shelley out of phase writes pamphlets, and
dreams of converting the world, or of turning man of affairs and
upsetting governments, and yet returns again and again to these
two images of solitude, a young man whose hair has grown white
from the burden of his thoughts, an old man in some shell-strewn
cave whom it is possible to call, when speaking to the Sultan, "as
inaccessible as God or thou." On the other hand, how subject he is
to nightmare! He sees the devil leaning against a tree, is attacked
by imaginary assassins, and, in obedience to what he considers a
supernatural voice, creates *The Cenci* that he may give to Beatrice
Cenci her incredible father. His political enemies are monstrous,
meaningless images. And unlike Byron, who is two phases later, he
can never see anything that opposes him as it really is. Dante, who
lamented his exile as of all possible things the worst for such as he,
and sighed for his lost solitude, and yet could never keep from politics, was, according to a contemporary, such a partisan, that if a
child, or a woman, spoke against his party he would pelt this child
or woman with stones. Yet Dante, having attained, as poet, to
Unity of Being, as poet saw all things set in order, had an intellect
that served the *Mask* alone, that compelled even those things that

opposed it to serve, and was content to see both good and evil. Shelley, upon the other hand, in whom even as poet unity was but in part attained, found compensation for his "loss," for the taking away of his children, for his quarrel with his first wife, for later sexual disappointment, for his exile, for his obloquy—there were but some three or four persons, he said, who did not consider him a monster of iniquity—in his hopes for the future of mankind. He lacked the Vision of Evil, could not conceive of the world as a continual conflict, so, though great poet he certainly was, he was not of the greatest kind. Dante suffering injustice and the loss of Beatrice, found divine justice and the heavenly Beatrice, but the justice of *Prometheus Unbound* is a vague propagandist emotion and the women that await its coming are but clouds. This is in part because the age in which Shelley lived was in itself so broken that true Unity of Being was almost impossible, but partly because, being out of phase so far as his practical reason was concerned, he was subject to an *automatonism* which he mistook for poetical invention, especially in his longer poems. *Antithetical* men (Phase 15 once passed) use this *automatonism* to evade hatred, or rather to hide it from their own eyes; perhaps all at some time or other, in moments of fatigue, give themselves up to fantastic, constructed images, or to an almost mechanical laughter.

Landor has been examined in *Per Amica Silentia Lunae*. The most violent of men, he uses his intellect to disengage a visionary image of perfect sanity (*Mask* at Phase 3) seen always in the most serene and classic art imaginable. He had perhaps as much Unity of Being as his age permitted, and possessed, though not in any full measure, the Vision of Evil.

(1925)

Charles Williams

from *The Figure of Beatrice*

The figure of Beatrice is presented at the beginning of Dante's first book, for Dante is one of those poets who begin their work with what is declared to be an intense personal experience. That experience is, as such, made part of the poetry; and it is not only so, with Dante, at the beginning, but also when, in his later and greater work, the experience is recalled and confirmed.

He defined the general kind of experience to which the figure of Beatrice belongs in one of his prose books, the *Convivio* (4.25). He says there that the young are subject to a "stupor" or astonishment of the mind which falls on them at the awareness of great and wonderful things. Such a stupor produces two results—a sense of reverence and a desire to know more. A noble awe and a noble curiosity come to life. This is what had happened to him at the sight of the Florentine girl, and all his work consists, one way or another, in the increase of that worship and that knowledge.

The image of Beatrice existed in his thought; it remained there and was deliberately renewed. The word image is convenient for two reasons. First, the subjective recollection within him was of something objectively outside him; it was an image of an exterior fact and not of an interior desire. It was sight and not invention. Dante's whole assertion was that he could not have invented Beatrice. Secondly, the outer exterior shape was understood to be an image of things beyond itself. Coleridge said that a symbol must have three characteristics: (i) it must exist in itself, (ii) it must derive from something greater than itself, (iii) it must represent in itself that greatness from which it derives. I have preferred the word image to the word symbol, because it seems to me doubtful if the word symbol nowadays sufficiently expresses the vivid individual existence of the lesser thing. Beatrice was, in her degree, an image of nobility, of virtue, of the Redeemed Life, and in some sense of Almighty God himself. But she also remained Beatrice right to the end; her derivation was not to obscure her identity any more than her identity should hide her derivation. Just as there is no point in Dante's thought at which the image of Beatrice in his mind was supposed to exclude the actual objective Beatrice, so there is no point at which the objective Beatrice is to exclude the Power which is expressed through her. But as the mental knowledge or image of her is the only way by which she herself can be known, so she herself is (for Dante) the only way by which that other Power can be known—since, in fact, it was known so. The maxim of his study, as regards the final Power, was: "This also is Thou, neither is this Thou."

I say "the only way," but only to modify it. There were, in his mind, many other shapes—of people and places, of philosophies and poems. All these had their own identities and were each autonomous. But in his poetry Dante determined to relate them all to the Beatrician figure, and he brought that figure as near as he could to the final image, so far as he could express it, of Almighty God. It is, we all agree, one of the marks of his poetic genius. But it is something else also. It is the greatest expression in European literature of the way of approach of the soul to its ordained end through the affirmation of the validity of all those images, beginning with the image of a girl.

It is an accepted fact that there have, on the whole, been two chief ways of approach to God defined in Christian thought. One, which is most familiar in the records of sanctity, has been known as the Way of Rejection. It consists, generally speaking, in the renunciation of all images except the final one of God himself, and even—sometimes but not always—of the exclusion of that only Image of all human sense. The great intellectual teacher of that Way was Dionysius the Areopagite; its conclusion was summed in a paragraph:

"Once more, ascending yet higher, we maintain that It is not soul, or mind, or endowed with the faculty of imagination, conjecture, reason, or understanding; nor can It be described by the reason or perceived by the understanding, since It is not number, or order, or greatness, or littleness, or equality, or inequality, and since It is not immovable nor in motion, or at rest, and has no power, and is not power or light, and does not live, and is not life; nor is It personal essence, or eternity, or time; nor can It be grasped by the understanding, since It is not knowledge or truth; nor is It kingship or wisdom; nor is It one, nor is It unity, nor is It Godhead or Goodness; nor is It a Spirit, as we understand the term, since It is not Sonship or Fatherhood; nor is It any other thing such as we or any other being can have knowledge of; nor does It belong to the category of non-existence or to that of existence; nor do existent beings know It as it actually is, nor does It know them as they actually are; nor can the reason attain to It to name It or to know It; nor is It darkness, nor is It light, or error, or truth; nor can any affirmation or negation apply to It; for while applying affirmations or negations to those orders of being that come next to It, we apply not unto It either affirmation or negation, inasmuch as it transcends all affirmation by being the perfect and unique Cause of all things, and transcends all negation by the pre-eminence of Its simple and absolute nature—free from every limitation and beyond them all."

The other Way is the Way of Affirmation, the approach to God through these images. The maxim of this Way is in the creed of St. Athanasius: "Not by conversion of the Godhead into flesh, but by taking of the Manhood into God." That clause was primarily a definition of the Incarnation, but, being that, it necessarily involved much beside. Other epigrams of the sort are, no doubt, scattered through the history of the Church. But for any full expression of it, the Church had to wait for Dante. It may be that that Way could not be too quickly shown to the world in which the young Church lived. It was necessary first to establish the awful difference between God and the world before we could be permitted to see the awful likeness. It is, and will always remain, necessary to remember the difference in the likeness. Neither of these two Ways indeed is, or can be, exclusive. The most vigorous ascetic, being forbidden formally to hasten his death, is bound to attend to the actualities of food, drink, and sleep which are also images, however brief his attention may be. The most indulgent of Christians is yet bound to hold his most cherished images—of food, drink, sleep, or anything else—negligible beside the final Image of God. And both are compelled to hold their particular Images of God negligible beside the universal Image of God which belongs to the Church, and even that less than the unimaged reality.

Our sacred Lord, in his earthly existence, deigned to use both methods. The miracle of Cana and all the miracles of healing are works of the affirmation of images; the counsel to pluck out the eye is a counsel of the rejection of images. It is said that he so rejected them for himself that he had nowhere to lay his head, and that he so affirmed them by his conduct that he was called a glutton and a wine bibber. He commanded his disciples to abandon all images but himself and promised them, in terms of the same images, a hundred times what they had abandoned. The Crucifixion and the Death are rejection and affirmation at once, for they affirm death only to reject death; the intensity of that death is the opportunity of its own dissolution; and beyond that physical rejection of earth lies the re-affirmation of earth which is called the Resurrection.

As above, so below; as in him, so in us. The tangle of affirmation and rejection which is in each of us has to be drawn into some kind of pattern, and has so been drawn by all men who have ever lived. The records of Christian sanctity have on the whole stressed the rejection. This indeed can hardly be avoided in any religion—nor perhaps outside all religion; the mere necessities of human life—change, misadventure, folly, age, and death—everywhere involve it. But even more within religion the discipline of the soul, ordinary or extraordinary, enforces it. The general praise of ascetic life and even the formal preference of one good (such as virginity) to another good (such as marriage) have themselves imaged that enforcement. On the other hand such great doctrines as the Resurrection of the Body and the Life Everlasting have continually recalled the Affirmation; with every act of charity towards others, every courtesy towards others, and even permissibly towards ourselves. The very equalling of ourselves with others and of others with ourselves is a declaration of the republic of images. No doubt these doctrines, metaphysical or moral, are to be understood after a great manner and towards God. But no doubt also every way of understanding leaves them exact in themselves. After the affirmations we may have to discover the rejections, but we must still believe that after the rejections the greater affirmations are to return.

In the literature of Europe the greatest record of the Way of Affirmation of Images is contained in the work of Dante Alighieri. There the facts of existence are translated into the actualities of poetry; they are all drawn, in Hippolyta's admirable definition of poetry (*Midsummer Night's Dream*, 5.1), into

> something of great constancy,
> But howsoever, strange and admirable.

The "constancy" of this work is its most remarkable characteristic—both in the sense of lastingness and in the sense of consistency. The greater, the most important, part of that work is poetry, and we must not, of course, confuse poetry with religion. We do not know if, or how far, Dante himself in his own personal life cared or was able to follow the Way he defined, nor is it our business. We do not know if he was a "mystic," nor is it our business; and the word, having been mentioned, may now be dismissed. The present point about the work of this great poet is that it refers us not to a rare human experience but to a common; or rather it begins with one that is common and continues on a way which might be more common than it is. What we can say about Dante, and almost all that we can say about him, is that he had the genius to imagine the Way of Affirmation wholly—after a particular manner indeed, but then that is the nature of the way of the Images. If a man is called to imagine certain images, he must work in them and not in others. The record of the Dantean Way begins with three things—an experience, the environment of that experience, and the means of understanding and expressing that experience; say—a woman, a city, and intellect or poetry; say again—Beatrice, Florence, and Virgil. These images are never quite separated, even in the beginning; towards the end they mingle and become a great complex image. They end with the inGodding of man.

This, to Dante, necessary (but also voluntary) choice of images is not, of course, the only choice; it is not the only method of that Way. On the whole, the nearest thing to it which we have in English literature is in the *Prelude* of Wordsworth, and in his other lesser poems. The *Prelude* begins also with the affirmation of images, but this time of "fountains, meadows, hills and groves." Had Wordsworth been of the stature of Dante, we should have had in English an analysis and record of a Way of Affirmation comparable to the Italian. He was not; he ceased even while he spoke of those "hiding-places of man's power" of which he desired to write. Yet the very title of the poem reminds us that he had intended no less a task; he was precisely aiming to enter into an understanding, in poetry, of "the two great ends of liberty and power"; "la potestate,"

says Virgil to Dante (*Purg.* 18.70–75), ". . . la nobile virtù . . . lo
libero arbitrio." "This power . . . this noble virtue . . . (is) the liberty
of the will." Wordsworth rather reminded us of the Way than defined it for us. But he did remind us of the business of the Imagination which is the faculty by which images, actual or poetic, are
understood.

> Imagination—here the power so-called
> Through sad incompetence of human speech,
> That awful Power, rose from the mind's abyss;

and again:

> This spiritual love acts not nor can exist
> Without Imagination; which, in truth,
> Is but another name for absolute power,
> And keenest insight, amplitude of mind,
> And Reason in her most exalted mood;

and again:

> Imagination having been our theme,
> So also hath this spiritual love,
> For they are each in each, and cannot stand
> Dividually. Here must thou be, O man,
> Power to thyself; no helper hast thou here;
> Here keepest thou in singleness thy state.
> No other can divide with thee this work.
> No secondary hand can intervene
> To fashion this ability; 'tis thine,
> The prime and vital principle is thine,
> In the recesses of thy nature, far
> From any reach of outward fellowship,
> Else is not thine at all. But joy to him,

Oh, joy to him who here hath sown, hath laid
Here, the foundation of his future years!
For all that friendship, all that love can do,
All that a darling countenance can look,
Or dear voice utter, to complete the man,
Perfect him, made imperfect in himself,
All shall be his; and he whose soul hath risen
Up to the height of feeling intellect
Shall want no humbler tenderness.

It has seemed worth while to quote at this length for two reasons: (i) because the whole passage is a description of the difficulty of the Way of the Images, (ii) because a number of the phrases are, as might have been expected, exactly applicable to that other Dantean Way. It is not to be rashly assumed that the Way of Affirmation is much easier than the Way of Rejection. To affirm the validity of an image one does not at the moment happen to like or want—such as that of one's next door neighbour—is as harsh as to reject an image—such as oneself as successful—which one does happen to like and want. "To fashion this ability" is a personal, secret, and arduous business. It is the Purgatory of the *Divine Comedy*; just as "the dear voice" of Beatrice assists in the *New Life*, as in the *Paradise*, in the perfecting of Dante. That Wordsworth wrote like Wordsworth and not like Dante may be a criticism of his verse but does not alter the application of the maxims.

The great resemblance between Dante and Wordsworth rather than any other of the English poets is that the work of each of these pretends to start from a definite and passionate personal experience. In that sense their work has something in common which is not, for example, in either Shakespeare or Milton, the throb in their poetry of a personal discovery. The Shakespearian world becomes gradually full of human capacities; the Miltonic is ritually aware (in the *Ode on the Nativity*) of the moment following the victory of one capacity over the others. But Dante, even in the first—call it an anecdote, is aware of three kinds of capacity all overwhelmed by a power; and Wordsworth has a similar, though less analysed, sense. The next to nearest is Patmore, but the entry of Patmore on this Way is more graceful and delicate; he delays, as it were, poetically, before the revelation of an "unknown mode of being." This "unknown mode" which in Wordsworth is "Nature" is in Dante Romantic Love. I keep the word Romantic for three reasons. The first is that there is no other word so convenient for describing that particular kind of sexual love. The second is that it includes other loves besides the sexual. The third is that in following the Dantean record of his love it may be possible to understand something more of Romanticism itself, and of its true and false modes of being. The word should not be too narrowly confined to a literary manner. It defines an attitude, a manner of receiving experience. I do not see any grounds on which, if we are to call the young Wordsworth a Romantic, we can deny the term to the young Dante. That there is a false Romanticism I willingly concede; that Dante denounced it I hope to suggest. But the false does not abolish the true or the value of the true, any more than the cheap use of the word Romantic spoils the intellectual honour which properly accompanies it.

Romantic Love then was the personal experience with which Dante's poetry ostensibly began; that is, the love which has been described in so many exalted terms by so many poets. Since one of the purposes of this book is to examine its nature as Dante revealed it, there is no need to delay to do so outside Dante. A question debated is whether it is, in varying degrees, a normal human experience. Those who suppose it not to be will naturally deny that an examination of the pattern of the work dealing with that abnormal state can have any general value. Those who believe that it is may agree that such an examination of a normal state may perhaps have some such value. I am not suggesting that Dante confined his attention to Beatrice alone. Beatrice, as was said above, was met in Florence; and Florence was a city; and images of cities, human and indeed divine, are part of Dante's affirmation. That affirmation was made, by him, in prose and verse; and such prose and verse was the means of his poetic images, and formed in itself an actuality of his life; that is, literature was an image, of which the greatest expression in his own work was the shape of Virgil. It is because Dante knew that there was a great deal other than Beatrice to which he must attend that his attention to Beatrice is valuable. It is that inclusion which prevents his Way of Affirmation being either a mere sentimentality or a disguised egotism. He was, it must be admitted, moral, for he perceived that images existed in their own right and not merely in his.

The image of the woman was not new in him, nor even the mode in which he treated it. What was new was the intensity of his treatment and the extreme to which he carried it. In his master's great poem—in Virgil's *Aeneid*—the image of the woman and the image of the city had both existed, but opposed. Dido had been the enemy of Rome, and morality had carried the hero away from Dido to Rome. But in Dante they are reconciled; the appearance of Virgil at the opening of the *Commedia* has about it this emphasis also. Virgil could not enter the paradise of that union, for his poem had refused it. But after Virgil the intellect had had visions which it communicated to the heart, if indeed they are so far separate. Since Dante the corrupt following of his way has spoiled the repute of the vision. But the vision has remained. People still fall in love, and fall in love as Dante did. It is not unusual to find them doing it.

There are two other matters which should be touched on in relation to this particular romantic vision and marriage. The first is the error that it is, or should be, the only basis for marriage. It would be as ridiculous to assert this as it is foolish to deny that it often forms such a basis. The "falling in love" often happens, but it is not to be either demanded or denied. There are many modulations and combinations of vision, affection, and appetite, and none of these modulations is necessarily an improper beginning for that great experiment which we call marriage.

The second, and opposite, error is that it necessarily involves marriage; it may indeed exist—as it seems to have done in Dante's own case—where, for one reason or another, marriage is not only impossible but is never even contemplated. Adoration, and it is adoration of its own proper kind which is involved, may exist between all kinds of people; that kind of secondary worship permitted, under the name of *dulia*, to saints and angels and other express vehicles of the Glory. Where this romantic adoration exists, there this proper intellectual investigation of it ought to exist. The clearest possibility of this Way, and perhaps the most difficult, may be in marriage, but the suggestion of it is defined wherever the suggestion of adoration is present. "Hero-worship," and even more sentimental states, are only vaguer and less convincing images of the quality which this love is. They are often foolish, but they are apt also to have that kind of sincerity which may, one way or another, become fidelity to the image or to the principle within and beyond the image. One way or another this state is normal; what is not yet normal is the development of that state to its proper end.

It may be thought that the death of Beatrice interferes with the proposition that the way of Dante's imagination can be an image of the normal way of romantic love, whether with marriage or without. There are two answers. The first is that the death of Beatrice corresponds to a not uncommon stage in the sensible development in the Way. The second is that the death of Beatrice, or (let us say) the disappearance of Beatrice, does not mean the abandonment of her image; and that the *Commedia*, by its maintenance of that image, exhibits the definitions of the Way in their general application . . .

The general maxim of the whole way in Dante is *attention*; "look," "look well." At the beginning he is compelled to look by the shock of the vision; later his attention is enforced by command

and he obeys by choice. At the beginning, two of the three images—poetry and the city—are habitual to him though still fresh
and young; they do not astonish him. But Beatrice does. *Incipit Vita
Nova*. It was, with Dante as with Wordsworth,

> the bodily eye . . .
> Which spake perpetual logic to my soul,
> And by the unrelenting agency
> Did bind my feelings even as in a chain.

. . . Beatrice is his Knowing. To say so is not to reduce her actuality nor her femininity. The reason for the insistence on her
femininity is simple—it is that this is what Dante insisted on, and
that we ought perhaps to take Dante's poetry as relevant to our
own affairs. Perhaps also we ought not. But if we ought, then the
whole of his work is the image of a Way not confined to poets.
That Way is not only what the poem is "about"; it is (according to
it) what Love is "about." It is what Love is "up to," and the only
question is whether lovers are "up to" Love. Were they, the *Vita*
and the *Paradiso* would be the only way. The complex art of this
knowledge is certainly not confined to romantic love of the male-
female kind. Wherever the "stupor" is, there is the beginning of
the art. Wherever any love is—and some kind of love in every man
and woman there must be—there is either affirmation or rejection
of the image, in one or other form. If there is rejection—of that
Way there are many records. Of the affirmation, for all its greater
commonness, there are fewer records. "Riguarda qual son io"—we
have hardly yet begun to be looked at or to look.

(1943)

T. S. Eliot

What Dante Means to Me

May I explain first why I have chosen, not to deliver a lecture about Dante, but to talk informally about his influence upon myself? What might appear egotism, in doing this, I present as modesty; and the modesty which it pretends to be is merely prudence. I am in no way a Dante scholar; and my general knowledge of Italian is such, that on this occasion, out of respect to the audience and to Dante himself, I shall refrain from quoting him in Italian. And I do not feel that I have anything more to contribute, on the subject of Dante's poetry, than I put, years ago, into a brief essay. As I explained in the original preface to that essay, I read Dante only with a prose translation beside the text. Forty years ago I began to puzzle out the *Divine Comedy* in this way; and when I thought I had grasped the meaning of the passage which especially delighted me, I committed it to memory; so that, for some years, I was able to recite a large part of one canto or another to myself, lying in bed or on a railway journey. Heaven knows what it would have sounded like, had I recited it aloud; but it was by this means that I steeped myself in Dante's poetry. And now it is twenty years since I set down all that my meager attainments qualified me to say about Dante. But I thought it not uninteresting to myself, and possibly to others, to try to record in what my own debt to Dante consists. I do not think I can explain everything, even to myself; but as I still, after forty years, re-gard his poetry as the most persistent and deepest influence upon my own verse, I should like to establish at least some of the rea-sons for it. Perhaps confessions by poets, of what Dante has meant to them, may even contribute something to the appreciation of Dante himself. And finally, it is the only contribution I can make.

The greatest debts are not always the most evident; at least, there are different kinds of debt. The kind of debt that I owe to Dante is the kind which goes on accumulating, the kind which is not the debt of one period or another of one's life. Of some poets I can say I learned a great deal from them at a particular stage. Of Jules Laforgue, for instance, I can say that he was the first to teach me how to speak, to teach me the poetic possibilities of my own idiom of speech. Such early influences, the influences which, so to speak, first introduce one to oneself, are, I think, due to an impres-sion which is in one aspect, the recognition of a temperament akin to one's own, and in another aspect the discovery of a form of expression which gives a clue to the discovery of one's own form. These are not two things, but two aspects of the same thing. But the poet who can do this for a young writer, is unlikely to be one of the great masters. The latter are too exalted and too re-mote. They are like distant ancestors who have been almost dei-fied; whereas the smaller poet, who has directed one's first steps, is more like an admired elder brother.

Then, among influences, there are the poets from whom one has learned some one thing, perhaps of capital importance to one-self, though not necessarily the greatest contribution these poets have made. I think that from Baudelaire I learned first, a precedent for the poetical possibilities, never developed by any poet writing in my own language, of the more sordid aspects of the modern metropolis, of the possibility of fusion between the sordidly realis-tic and the phantasmagoric, the possibility of the juxtaposition of the matter-of-fact and the fantastic. From him, as from Laforgue, I learned that the sort of material that I had, the sort of experience that an adolescent had had, in an industrial city in America, could be the material for poetry; and that the source of new poetry might be found in what had been regarded hitherto as the impossible, the sterile, the intractably unpoetic. That, in fact, the business of the poet was to make poetry out of the unexplored resources of the unpoetical; that the poet, in fact, was committed by his profession to turn the unpoetical into poetry. A great poet can give a younger poet everything that he has to give him, in a very few lines. It may be that I am indebted to Baudelaire chiefly for half a dozen lines out of the whole of *Fleurs du Mal*; and that his significance for me is summed up in the lines:

Fourmillante Cité, cité pleine de rêves,
Où le spectre en plein jour raccroche le passant.

I knew what *that* meant, because I had lived it before I knew that I wanted to turn it into verse on my own account.

I may seem to you to be very far from Dante. But I cannot give you any approximation of what Dante has done for me, without speaking of what other poets have done for me. What I have written about Baudelaire, or Dante, or any other poet who has had a capital importance in my own development, I have written *because* that poet has meant so much to me, but not about myself, but *about* that poet and his poetry. That is, the first impulse to write about a great poet is one of gratitude; but the reasons for which one is grateful may play a very small part in a critical appreciation of that poet.

One has other debts, innumerable debts, to poets, of another kind. There are poets who have been at the back of one's mind, or perhaps, consciously there, when one has had some particular problem to settle, for which something they have written suggests the method. There are those from whom one has consciously borrowed, adapting a line of verse to a different language or period or context. There are those who remain in one's mind as having set the standard for a particular poetic virtue, as Villon for honesty, and Sappho for having fixed a particular emotion in the right and the minimum number of words, once and for all. There are also the great masters, to whom one slowly grows up. When I was young I felt much more at ease with the lesser Elizabethan dramatists than with Shakespeare: the former were, so to speak, playmates nearer my own size. One test of the great masters, of whom Shakespeare is one, is that the appreciation of their poetry is a lifetime's task, because at every stage of maturing—and that should be one's whole life—you are able to understand them better. Among these are Shakespeare, Dante, Homer and Virgil.

I have ranged over some varieties of "influence" in order to approach an indication, by contrast, of what Dante has meant to me. Certainly I have borrowed lines from him, in the attempt to reproduce, or rather to arouse in the reader's mind the memory of some Dantesque scene, and thus establish a relationship between the medieval inferno and modern life. Readers of my "Waste Land" will perhaps remember that the vision of my city clerks trooping over London Bridge from the railway station to their offices evoked the reflection "I had not thought death had undone so many"; and that in another place I deliberately modified a line of Dante by altering it—"sighs, short and infrequent, were exhaled." And I gave the references in my notes, in order to make the reader who recognized the allusion, know that I meant him to recognize it, and know that he would have missed the point if he did not recognize it. Twenty years after writing "The Waste Land," I wrote, in "Little Gidding," a passage which is intended to be the nearest equivalent to a canto of the *Inferno* or the *Purgatorio*, in style as well as content, that I could achieve. The intention, of course, was the same as with my allusions to Dante in "The Waste Land": to present to the mind of the reader a parallel, by means of contrast, between the *Inferno* and the *Purgatorio*, which Dante visited, and a hallucinated scene after an air-raid. But the method is different: here I was debarred from quoting or adapting at length—I borrowed and adapted freely only a few phrases—because I was *imitating*. My first problem was to find an approximation to the *terza rima* without rhyming. English is less copiously provided with rhyming words than Italian; and those rhymes we have are in a way more emphatic. The rhyming words call too much attention to themselves: Italian is the one language known to me in which exact rhyme can always achieve its effect—and what the effect of rhyme is, is for the neurologist rather than the poet to investigate—without the risk of obtruding itself. I therefore adopted, for my purpose, a simple alternation of unrhymed masculine and feminine terminations, as the nearest way of giving the light effect of the rhyme in Italian. In saying this, I am not attempting to lay down a law, but merely explaining how I was directed in a particular situation. I think that rhymed *terza rima* is probably less unsatisfactory for translations of the *Divine Comedy* than is blank verse. For, unfortunately for this purpose, a different meter is a different mode of thought; it is a different kind of *punctuation*, for the emphases and the breath pauses do not come in the same place. Dante *thought* in *terza rima*, and a poem should be translated as nearly as possible in the same thought-form as the original. So that, in a translation into blank verse, something is lost; though on the other hand, when I read a *terza rima* translation of the *Divine Comedy* and come to some passage of which I remember the original pretty closely, I am always worried in anticipation, by the inevitable shifts and twists which I know the translator will be obliged to make, in order to fit Dante's words into English rhyme. And no verse seems to demand greater literalness in translation than Dante's, because no poet convinces one more completely that the word he has used is the word he wanted, and that no other will do.

I do not know whether the substitute for rhyme that I used in the passage referred to would be tolerable for a very long original poem in English: but I do know that I myself should not find the rest of my life long enough time in which to write it. For one of the interesting things I learnt in trying to imitate Dante in English, was the extreme difficulty. This section of a poem—not the length of one canto of the *Divine Comedy*—cost me far more time and trouble and vexation than any passage of the same length that I have ever written. It was not simply that I was limited to the Dantesque type of imagery, simile and figure of speech. It was chiefly that in this very bare and austere style, in which every word has to be "functional," the slightest vagueness or imprecision is immediately noticeable. The language has to be very direct; the line, and the single word, must be completely disciplined to the purpose of the whole; and, when you are using simple words and simple phrases, any repetition of the most common idiom, or of the most frequently needed word, becomes a glaring blemish.

I am not saying that *terza rima* is to be ruled out of original English verse composition; though I believe that to the modern ear—that is, the ear trained during this century, and therefore accustomed to much greater exercise in the possibilities of unrhymed verse—a modern long poem in a set rhymed form is more likely to sound monotonous as well as artificial, than it did to the ear of a hundred years ago. But I am sure that it is only possible in a long poem, if the poet is borrowing only the form, and not attempting to remind the reader of Dante in every line and phrase. There is one poem in the 19th Century which, at moments, seems to contradict this. This is *The Triumph of Life*. I should have felt called upon today to refer to Shelley in any case, because Shelley is the English poet, more than all others, upon whom the influence of Dante was remarkable. It seems to me that Shelley confirms also my impression that the influence of Dante, where it is really powerful, is a *cumulative* influence: that is, the older you grow, the stronger the domination becomes. *The Triumph of Life*, a poem which is Shelley's greatest tribute to Dante, was the last of his great poems. I think it was also the greatest. It was left unfin-

ished; it breaks off abruptly in the middle of a line; and one wonders whether even Shelley could have carried it to successful completion. Now the influence of Dante is observable earlier; most
evident in the *Ode to the West Wind*, in which, at the very beginning, the image of the leaves whirling

> Like driven ghosts from an enchanter fleeing

would have been impossible but for the *Inferno*—in which the
various manifestations of *wind*, and the various sensations of *air*, are
as important as are the aspects of *light* in the *Paradiso*. In *The Triumph of Life* however I do not think that Shelley was setting himself to aim at such a close approximation to the spareness of Dante
as I was; he had left open for himself all of his copious resources of
English poetical speech. Nevertheless, because of a natural affinity
with the poetic imagination of Dante, a saturation in the poetry
(and I need not remind you that Shelley knew Italian well, and
had a wide and thorough knowledge of all Italian poetry up to his
time), his mind is inspired to some of the greatest and most Dantesque lines in English. I must quote one passage which made an
indelible impression upon me over forty-five years ago:

> Struck to the heart by this sad pageantry,
> Half to myself I said—"And what is this?
> Whose shape is that within the car? And why—"
>
> I would have added—"is all here amiss?"
> But a voice answered—"Life!"—I turned, and knew
> (O Heaven, have mercy on such wretchedness!)
>
> That what I thought was an old root which grew
> To strange distortion out of the hill side,
> Was indeed one of those deluded crew,

And that the grass, which methought hung so wide
And white, was but his thin discoloured hair,
And that the holes he vainly sought to hide,

Were or had been eyes:—"If thou canst, forbear
To join the dance, which I had well forborne!"
Said the grim Feature (of my thought aware).

"I will unfold that which to this deep scorn
Led me and my companions, and relate ·
The progress of the pageant since the morn;

If thirst of knowledge shall not then abate,
Follow it thou even to the night, but I
Am weary."—Then like one who with the weight

Of his own words is staggered, wearily
He paused; and ere he could resume, I cried:
"First, who art thou?"—"Before thy memory,

"I feared, loved, hated, suffered, did and died,
And if the spark with which Heaven lit my spirit
Had been with purer nutriment supplied,

"Corruption would not now thus much inherit
Of what was once Rousseau,   nor this disguise
Stain that which ought to have disdained to wear it . . ."

Well, this is better than I could do. But I quote it, as one of the
supreme tributes to Dante in English, for it testifies to what Dante
has done, both for the style and for the soul of a great English
poet. And incidentally, a very interesting comment on Rousseau.
It would be interesting, but otiose, to pursue the evidence of

Shelley's debt to Dante further; it is sufficient, to those who
know the source, to quote the first three of the prefatory lines to
Epipsychidion—

> My Song, I fear that thou wilt find but few
> Who fitly shall conceive thy reasoning,
> Of such hard matter does thou entertain.

I think I have already made clear, however, that the important
debt to Dante does not lie in a poet's borrowings, or adaptations
from Dante; nor is it one of those debts which are incurred only
at a particular stage in another poet's development. Nor is it found
in those passages in which one has taken him as a model. The important debt does not occur in relation to the number of places in
one's writings to which a critic can point a finger, and say, here
and there he wrote something which he could not have written
unless he had Dante in mind. Nor do I wish to speak now of any
debt which one may owe to the thought of Dante, to his view of
life, or to the philosophy and theology which give shape and content to the *Divine Comedy*. That is another, though by no means
unrelated question. Of what one learns, and goes on learning,
from Dante I should like to make three points.

The first is, that of the very few poets of similar stature there is
none, not even Virgil, who has been a more attentive student of
the *art* of poetry, or a more scrupulous, painstaking and *conscious*
practitioner of the *craft*. Certainly no English poet can be compared with him in this respect, for the more conscious crafts-
men—and I am thinking primarily of Milton—have been much
more limited poets, and therefore more limited in their craft also.
To realize more and more what this means, through the years of
one's life, is itself a moral lesson; but I draw a further lesson from it
which is a moral lesson too. The whole study and practice of
Dante seems to me to teach that the poet should be the servant of
his language, rather than the master of it. This sense of responsibil-

ity is one of the marks of the *classical poet*, in the sense of "classical" which I have tried to define elsewhere, in speaking of Virgil. Of some great poets, and of some great English poets especially, one can say that they were privileged by their genius to *abuse* the English language, to develop an idiom so peculiar and even eccentric, that it could be of no use to later poets. Dante seems to me to have a place in Italian literature which, in this respect, only Shakespeare has in ours; that is, they give body to the soul of the language, conforming themselves, the one more and the other less consciously, to what they divined to be its possibilities. And Shakespeare himself takes liberties which only his genius justifies; liberties which Dante, with an equal genius, does not take. To pass on to posterity one's own language, more highly developed, more refined, and more precise than it was before one wrote it, that is the highest possible achievement of the poet as poet. Of course, a really supreme poet makes poetry also more difficult for his successors, by the simple fact of his supremacy, and the price a literature must pay, for having a Dante or a Shakespeare, is that it can have only *one*. Later poets must find something else to do, and be content if the things left to do are lesser things. But I am not speaking of what a supreme poet, one of those few without whom the current speech of a people with a great language would not be what it is, does for later poets, or of what he prevents them from doing, but of what he does for everybody after him who speaks that language, whose mother tongue it is, whether they are poets, philosophers, statesmen or railway porters.

That is one lesson: that the great master of a language should be the great servant of it. The second lesson of Dante—and it is one which no poet, in any language known to me, can teach—is the lesson of *width of emotional range*. Perhaps it could be best expressed under the figure of the spectrum, or of the gamut. Employing this figure, I may say that the great poet should not only perceive and distinguish more clearly than other men, the colors or sounds within the range of ordinary vision or hearing; he should perceive vibrations beyond the range of ordinary men, and be able to make men see and hear more at each end than they could ever see without his help. We have for instance in English literature great religious poets, but they are, by comparison with Dante, *specialists*. That is all they can do. And Dante, because he could do everything else, is for that reason the greatest "religious" poet, though to call him a "religious poet" would be to abate his universality. The *Divine Comedy* expresses everything in the way of emotion, between depravity's despair and the beatific vision, that man is capable of experiencing. It is therefore a constant reminder to the poet, of the obligation to explore, to find words for the inarticulate, to capture those feelings which people can hardly even feel, because they have no words for them; and at the same time, a reminder that the explorer beyond the frontiers of ordinary consciousness will only be able to return and report to his fellow-citizens, if he has all the time a firm grasp upon the realities with which they are already acquainted.

These two achievements of Dante are not to be thought of as separate or separable. The task of the poet, in making people comprehend the incomprehensible, demands immense resources of language; and in developing the language, enriching the meaning of words and showing how much words can do, he is making possible a much greater range of emotion and perception for other men, because he gives them the speech in which more can be expressed. I only suggest as an instance what Dante did for his own language—and for ours, since we have taken the word and anglicized it—by the verb *trasumanare*.

What I have been saying just now is not irrelevant to the fact—for to me it appears an incontestable fact—that Dante is, beyond all other poets of our continent, the most *European*. He is the least provincial—and yet that statement must be immediately protected by saying that he did not become the "least provincial" by ceasing to be local. No one is more local; one never forgets that there is much in Dante's poetry which escapes any reader whose native language is not Italian; but I think that the foreigner is less *aware* of any residuum that must for ever escape him, than any of us in reading any other master of a language which is not our own. The Italian of Dante is somehow *our* language from the moment we begin to try to read it; and the lessons of craft, of speech and of exploration of sensibility are lessons which any European can take to heart and try to apply in his own tongue.

(1950)

Osip Mandelstam

Conversation about Dante

Così gridai cola faccia levata . . .

Inferno 16.76

– I –

Poetic discourse is a hybrid process, one which crosses two sound modes: the first of these is the modulation we hear and sense in the prosodic instruments of poetic discourse in its spontaneous flow; the second is the discourse itself, i.e. the intonational and phonological performance of these instruments.

Understood in this way, poetry is not a part of nature, not even its best or choicest part, let alone a reflection of it—this would make a mockery of the axioms of identity; rather, poetry establishes itself with astonishing independence in a new extra-spatial field of action, not so much narrating as acting out in nature by means of its arsenal of devices, commonly known as tropes.

It is only with the severest qualifications that poetic discourse or thought may be referred to as "sounding"; for we hear in it only the crossing of two lines, one of which, taken by itself, is completely mute, while the other, abstracted from its prosodic transmutation, is totally devoid of significance and interest, and is susceptible of paraphrasing, which, to my mind, is surely a sign of non-poetry. For where there is amenability to paraphrase, there the sheets have never been rumpled, there poetry, so to speak, has never spent the night.

Dante is a master of the instruments of poetry; he is not a manufacturer of tropes. He is a strategist of transmutation and hybridization; he is least of all a poet in the "general European" sense or in the usage of cultural jargon.

Wrestlers tying themselves into a knot in the arena may be viewed as an instance of the mutation of instruments into harmony:

> These naked, glistening wrestlers who walk
> Back and forth, strutting about
> And showing off their physical
> Prowess before grappling in the decisive
> Fight . . .
>
> (*Inf.* 16.22–24)

whereas the modern film, metamorph of the tapeworm, turns into the wickedest parody of the use of prosodic instruments in poetic discourse, for its frames simply move forward without conflict, merely replacing one another.

Imagine something intelligible, grasped, wrested from obscurity, in a language voluntarily and willingly forgotten immediately after the act of intellection and realization is completed . . .

What is important in poetry is only the understanding which brings it about—not at all the passive, reproducing, or paraphrasing understanding. Semantic adequacy is equivalent to the feeling of having fulfilled a command.

The signal waves of meaning vanish, having completed their work; the more potent they are, the more yielding, and the less inclined to linger.

Otherwise stereotypes are inevitable, the hammering in of those manufactured nails known as images of cultural history.

Superficial explanatory imagery is incompatible with suitability as an instrument of poetic discourse.

The quality of poetry is determined by the speed and decisiveness with which it embodies its schemes and commands in diction, the instrumentless, lexical, purely quantitative verbal mat-

ter. One must traverse the full width of a river crammed with
Chinese junks moving simultaneously in various directions—this
is how the meaning of poetic discourse is created. The meaning, its
itinerary, cannot be reconstructed by interrogating the boatmen:
they will not be able to tell how and why we were skipping from
junk to junk.

Poetic discourse is a carpet fabric containing a plethora of
textile warps differing from one another only in the process of
coloration, only in the partitura of the perpetually changing commands of the instrumental signaling system.

It is an extremely durable carpet, woven out of fluid: a carpet
in which the currents of the Ganges, taken as a fabric theme, do
not mix with the samples of the Nile or the Euphrates, but remain
multicolored, in braids, figures, and ornaments—not in patterns,
though, for a pattern is the equivalent of paraphrase. Ornament is
good precisely because it preserves traces of its origin like a piece
of nature enacted. Whether the piece is animal, vegetable, steppe,
Scythian or Egyptian, indigenous or barbarian, it is always speaking, seeing, acting.

Ornament is stanzaic. Pattern is of the line.

The poetic hunger of the old Italians is magnificent, their
youthful, animal appetite for harmony, their sensual lust after
rhyme—*il disio!*

The mouth works, the smile nudges the line of verse, cleverly
and gaily the lips redden, the tongue trustingly presses itself against
the palate.

The inner form of the verse is inseparable from the countless
changes of expression flitting across the face of the narrator who
speaks and feels emotion.

The art of speech distorts our face in precisely this way; it dis-
rupts its calm, destroys its mask . . .

When I began to study Italian and had barely familiarized myself with its phonetics and prosody, I suddenly understood that the

center of gravity of my speech efforts had been moved closer to my lips, to the outer parts of my mouth. The tip of the tongue suddenly turned out to have the seat of honor. The sound rushed toward the locking of the teeth. And something else that struck me was the infantile aspect of Italian phonetics, its beautiful child-like quality, its closeness to infant babbling, to some kind of eternal dadaism.

> E consolando, usava l'idioma
> Che prima i padri e le madri trastulla;
> ... Favoleggiava con la sua famiglia
> De' Troiani, de Fiesole, e di Roma.
>   (*Par.* 15.122–26)

Would you like to become acquainted with the dictionary of Italian rhymes? Take the entire Italian dictionary and leaf through it as you will ... Here every word rhymes. Every word begs to enter into *concordanza*.

The abundance of marriageable endings is fantastic. The Italian verb increases in strength toward its end and only comes to life in the ending. Each word rushes to burst forth, to fly from the lips, to run away, to clear a place for the others.

When it became necessary to trace the circumference of a time for which a millennium is less than a wink of an eyelash, Dante introduced infantile "trans-sense" language into his astronomical, concordant, profoundly public, homiletic lexicon.

Dante's creation is above all the entrance of the Italian language of his day onto the world stage, its entrance as a totality, as a system.

The most dadaist of the Romance languages moves forward to take the first place among nations.

- I I -

We must give some examples of Dante's rhythms. People know nothing about this, but they must be shown. Whoever says, "Dante is sculptural," is influenced by the impoverished definitions of that great European. Dante's poetry partakes of all the forms of energy known to modern science. Unity of light, sound and matter form its inner nature. Above all, the reading of Dante is an endless labor, for the more we succeed, the further we are from our goal. If the first reading brings on only shortness of breath and healthy fatigue, then equip yourself for subsequent readings with a pair of indestructible Swiss hobnailed boots. In all seriousness the question arises: how many shoe soles, how many oxhide soles, how many sandals did Alighieri wear out during the course of his poetic work, wandering the goat paths of Italy.

Both the *Inferno* and, in particular, the *Purgatorio* glorify the human gait, the measure and rhythm of walking, the footstep and its form. The step, linked with breathing and saturated with thought, Dante understood as the beginning of prosody. To indicate walking he utilizes a multitude of varied and charming turns of phrase.

In Dante philosophy and poetry are constantly on the go, perpetually on their feet. Even a stop is but a variety of accumulated movement: a platform for conversations is created by Alpine conditions. The metrical foot is the inhalation and exhalation of the step. Each step draws a conclusion, invigorates, syllogizes.

Education is schooling in the swiftest possible associations. You grasp them on the wing, you are sensitive to allusions—therein lies Dante's favorite form of praise.

The way Dante understands it, the teacher is younger than the pupil, for he "runs faster."

When he turned aside he appeared to me
like one of those runners who chase each other
over the green meadows around Verona,

and his physique was such that
he struck me as belonging to the host of winners, not to
the losers . . .

The metaphor's rejuvenating power brings the educated old
man, Brunetto Latini, back to us in the guise of a youthful victor
at a Veronese track meet.

What is Dantean erudition?

Aristotle, like a double-winged butterfly, is edged with the
Arabian border of Averroes.

Averois, che il gran comento feo
(*Inf.* 4.144)

Here the Arab Averroes accompanies the Greek Aristotle. They
are both components of the same drawing. They can both find
room on the membrane of a single wing.

The conclusion of canto 4 of the *Inferno* is truly an orgy of
quotations. I find here a pure and unalloyed demonstration of
Dante's keyboard of references.

A keyboard stroll around the entire horizon of Antiquity. Some
Chopin polonaise in which an armed Caesar with a gryphon's
eyes dances alongside Democritus, who had just finished splitting
matter into atoms.

A quotation is not an excerpt. A quotation is a cicada. Its natural state is that of unceasing sound. Having once seized hold of
the air, it will not let it go. Erudition is far from being equivalent
to a keyboard of references for the latter comprises the very
essence of education.

By this I mean that a composition is formed not as a result of
accumulated particulars, but due to the fact that one detail after
another is torn away from the object, leaves it, darts out, or is
chipped away from the system to go out into a new functional
space or dimension, but each time at a strictly regulated mo-

ment and under circumstances which are sufficiently ripe and unique.

We do not know things themselves; on the other hand, we are highly sensitive to the facts of their existence. Thus, in reading Dante's cantos we receive communiqués, as it were, from the battlefield and from that data make superb guesses as to how the sounds of the symphony of war are struggling with each other, although each bulletin taken by itself merely indicates some slight shift of the flags for strategic purposes or some minor changes in the timbre of the cannonade.

Hence, the thing emerges as an integral whole as a result of the simple differentiating impulse which transfixed it. Not for one instant does it retain any identity with itself. If a physicist, having once broken down an atomic nucleus, should desire to put it back together again, he would resemble the partisans of descriptive and explanatory poetry for whom Dante represents an eternal plague and a threat.

If we could learn to hear Dante, we would hear the ripening of the clarinet and the trombone, we would hear the transformation of the viola into a violin and the lengthening of the valve on the French horn. And we would be able to hear the formation around the lute and the theorbo of the nebulous nucleus of the future homophonic three-part orchestra.

Furthermore, if we could hear Dante, we would be unexpectedly plunged into a power flow, known now in its totality as a "composition," now in its particularity as a "metaphor," now in its indirectness as a "simile," that power flow which gives birth to attributes so that they may return to it, enriching it with their own melting and, having barely achieved the first joy of becoming, they immediately lose their primogeniture in merging with the matter which is rushing in among the thoughts and washing against them.

The beginning of canto 10 of the *Inferno*. Dante urges us into the inner blindness of the compositional clot:

We now climbed up the narrow
path between the craggy
wall and the martyrs—my teacher
and I right at his back . . .

All our efforts are directed toward the struggle against the density and darkness of the place. Illuminated shapes cut through it like teeth. Here strength of character is as essential as a torch in a cave.

Dante never enters into single combat with his material without having first prepared an organ to seize it, without having armed himself with some instrument for measuring concrete time as it drips or melts. In poetry, where everything is measure and everything derives from measure, revolves about it and for its sake, instruments of measure are tools of a special kind, performing an especially active function. Here the trembling hand of the compass not only indulges the magnetic storm, but makes it itself.

And thus we can see that the dialogue of canto 10 of the *Inferno* is magnetized by the forms of verb tenses: the perfective and imperfective past, the subjunctive past, even the present and the future are all categorically and authoritatively presented in the tenth canto.

The entire canto is constructed on several verbal thrusts which leap boldly out of the text. Here the table of conjugations opens like a fencing tournament, and we literally hear how the verbs mark time.

First thrust:

La gente che per li sepolcri giace
Potrebbesi veder? . . .

"May I be permitted to see those people laid in open graves?"
Second thrust:

. . .Volgiti: che fai?

The horror of the present tense is given here, some kind of *terror praesentis*. Here the unalloyed present is taken as a sign introduced to ward off evil. The present tense, completely isolated from both the future and the past, is conjugated like pure fear, like danger.

Three nuances of the past tense (which has absolved itself of any responsibility for what has already occurred) are given in the following tercet:

I fixed my eyes on him,
And he drew himself up to his full height,
As if his great disdain could disparage Hell.

And then, like a mighty tuba, the past tense explodes in Farinata's question:

. . . Chi fuor li maggior tui?—

"Who were your forefathers?"
How that auxiliary verb is stretched out here, that little truncated *fuor* instead of *furon*! Wasn't it through the lengthening of a valve that the French horn was formed?

Next comes a slip of the tongue in the form of the past perfect. This slip felled the elder Cavalcanti: from Alighieri, a comrade and contemporary of his son, the poet Guido Cavalcanti, still thriving at the time he heard something—it little matters what—about his son using the fatal past perfect: *ebbe*.

And how astonishing that precisely this slip of the tongue opens the way for the main stream of the dialogue: Cavalcanti fades away like an oboe or clarinet, having played its part, while Farinata, like a deliberate chess player, continues his interrupted move, and renews the attack:

"E se," continuando al primo detto,
  "S'egli han quell'arte," disse, "male appresa,
  Ciò mi tormenta più che questo letto."

The dialogue in the tenth canto of the *Inferno* is an unanticipated explicator of the situation. It flows out all by itself from the interstices of the rivers.

All useful information of an encyclopedic nature turns out to have been already communicated in the opening lines of the canto. Slowly but surely the amplitude of the conversation broadens; mass scenes and crowd images are obliquely introduced.

When Farinata rises up contemptuous of Hell, like a great nobleman who somehow landed in jail, the pendulum of the conversation is already swinging across the full diameter of the gloomy plain now invaded by flames.

The scandal in literature is a concept going much further back than Dostoevsky; however, in the thirteenth century and in Dante's writings it was much more powerful. Dante collides with Farinata in this undesirable and dangerous encounter just as Dostoevsky's rogues run into their tormentors in the most inopportune places. A voice floats forward; it remains unclear to whom it belongs. It becomes more and more difficult for the reader to conduct the expanding canto. This voice—the first theme of Farinata—is the minor Dantean *arioso* of the suppliant type—extremely typical of the *Inferno*.

O Tuscan, who travels alive through
this fiery city and speaks so
eloquently! Do not refuse to
stop for a moment . . . Through
your speech I recognized you
as a citizen of that noble

region to which I, alas! was
too much of a burden . . .

Dante is a poor man. Dante is an internal *raznochinets*, the descendant of an ancient Roman family. Courtesy is not at all characteristic of him, rather something distinctly the opposite. One
would have to be a blind mole not to notice that throughout the
Divina Commedia Dante does not know how to behave, does not
know how to act, what to say, how to bow. I am not imagining
this; I take it from the numerous admissions of Alighieri himself,
scattered throughout the *Divina Commedia*.

The inner anxiety and painful, troubled gaucheries which accompany each step of the diffident man, as if his upbringing were
somehow insufficient, the man untutored in the ways of applying
his inner experience or of objectifying it in etiquette, the tormented and downtrodden man—such are the qualities which
both provide the poem with all its charm, with all its drama, and
serve as its background source, its psychological foundation.

If Dante had been sent forth alone, without his *dolce padre*,
without Virgil, scandal would have inevitably erupted at the very
start, and we would have had the most grotesque buffoonery
rather than a journey amongst the torments and sights of the underworld!

The gaucheries averted by Virgil serve to systematically amend
and redirect the course of the poem. The *Divina Commedia* takes
us into the inner laboratory of Dante's spiritual qualities. What for
us appears as an irreproachable Capuchin and a so-called aquiline
profile was, from within, an awkwardness surmounted by agony, a
purely Pushkinian, *Kammerjunker* struggle for social dignity and a
recognized social position for the poet. The shade which frightens
children and old women took fright itself, and Alighieri suffered
fever and chills: all the way from miraculous bouts of self-esteem
to feelings of utter worthlessness.

Dante's fame has up to now been the greatest obstacle to understanding him and to a profound study of his work, and this situation shall continue for a long time to come. His lapidary quality is no more than a product of the enormous inner imbalance which expressed itself in dream executions, in imagined encounters, in elegant retorts prepared in advance and fostered on bile, aimed at destroying his enemy once and for all and invoking the final triumph.

How often did the kindest of fathers, the preceptor, reasonable man, and guardian snub the internal *raznochinets* of the fourteenth century who found it such agony to be a part of the social hierarchy, while Boccaccio, practically his contemporary, delighted in the same social system, plunged into it, gamboled about in it?

"Che fai?" (What are you doing?) sounds literally like a teacher's cry: you've lost your mind! . . . Then the sounds of the organ come to the rescue, drowning out the shame and concealing the embarrassment.

It is absolutely false to perceive Dante's poem as some extended single-line narrative or even as having but a single voice. Long before Bach and at a time when large monumental organs were not yet being built and only the modest embryonic prototypes of the future wonders existed, when the leading instrument for voice accompaniment was still the zither, Alighieri constructed in verbal space an infinitely powerful organ and already delighted in all its conceivable stops, inflated its bellows, and roared and cooed through all its pipes.

Come avesse lo inferno in gran dispitto
(*Inf.* 10.36)

is the line which gave birth to the entire European tradition of demonism and Byronism. Meanwhile, instead of raising his sculpture on a pedestal as Hugo, for instance, might have done, Dante envelops it in a sordine, wraps it round with gray twilight, and conceals it at the very bottom of a sack of mute sounds.

It is presented in the diminuendo stop, it falls to the ground out of the window of the hearing.

In other words, its phonetic light is turned off. The gray shadows have blended.

The *Divina Commedia* does not so much take up the reader's time as augment it, as if it were a musical piece being performed.

As it becomes longer, the poem moves further away from its end, and the very end itself approaches unexpectedly and sounds like the beginning.

The structure of the Dantean monologue, built like the stop mechanism of an organ, can be well understood by making use of an analogy with rock strata whose purity has been destroyed by the intrusion of foreign bodies.

Granular admixtures and veins of lava indicate a single fault or catastrophe as the common source of the formation.

Dante's poetry is formed and colored in precisely this geological manner. Its material structure is infinitely more significant than its celebrated sculptural quality. Imagine a monument of granite or marble whose symbolic function is intended not to represent a horse or a rider, but to reveal the inner structure of the marble or granite itself. In other words, imagine a granite monument erected in honor of granite, as if to reveal its very idea. Having grasped this, you will then be able to understand quite clearly just how form and content are related in Dante's work.

Any unit of poetic speech, be it a line, a stanza or an entire lyrical composition, must be regarded as a single word. For instance, when we enunciate the word "sun," we do not toss out an already prepared meaning—this would be tantamount to semantic abortion—rather we are experiencing a peculiar cycle.

Any given word is a bundle, and meaning sticks out of it in various directions, not aspiring toward any single official point. In pronouncing the word "sun," we are, as it were, undertaking an enormous journey to which we are so accustomed that we travel in our sleep. What distinguishes poetry from automatic speech is that it rouses us and shakes us into wakefulness in the middle of a word. Then it turns out that the word is much longer than we thought, and we remember that to speak means to be forever on the road.

The semantic cycles of Dantean cantos are constructed in such a way that what begins, for example, as "honey" (*med*), ends up as "bronze" (*med'*), what begins as "a dog's bark" (*lai*), ends up as "ice" (*led*).

Dante, when he feels the need, calls eyelids "the lips of the eye." This is when ice crystals of frozen tears hang from the lashes and form a shield which prevents weeping.

> Gli occhi lor, ch'eran pria pur dentro molli,
> Gocciar su per le labbra . . .
> <div align="right">(<i>Inf.</i> 32.46–47)</div>

Thus, suffering crosses the sense organs, producing hybrids, and bringing about the labial eye.

There is not just one form in Dante, but a multitude of forms. One is squeezed out of another and only by convention can one be inserted into another.

He himself says:

> Io premerei di mio concetto il suco—
> <div align="right">(<i>Inf.</i> 32.4)</div>

"I would squeeze the juice out of my idea, out of my conception"—that is, he considers form as the thing which is squeezed out, not as that which serves as a covering.

In this way, strange as it may seem, form is squeezed out of the content-conception which, as it were, envelops the form. Such is Dante's precise thought.

But whatever it may be, we cannot squeeze something out of anything except a wet sponge or rag. Try as we may to twist the conception even into a plait, we will never squeeze any form out of it unless it is already a form itself. In other words, any process involving the creation of form in poetry presupposes lines, periods, or cycles of sound forms, as is the case with individually pronounced semantic units.

A scientific description of Dante's *Commedia*, taken as a flow, as a current, would inevitably assume the look of a treatise on metamorphoses, and would aspire to penetrate the multitudinous states of poetic matter, just as a doctor in making his diagnosis listens to the multitudinous unity of the organism. Literary criticism would then approach the method of living medicine.

– I I I –

Examining the structure of the *Divina Commedia* as best I can, I come to the conclusion that the entire poem is but one single unified and indivisible stanza. Rather, it is not a stanza, but a crystallographic figure, that is, a body. Some incessant craving for the creation of form penetrates the entire poem. It is strictly a stereometric body, one continuous development of the crystallographic theme. It is inconceivable that anyone could grasp with the eye alone or even visually imagine to oneself this form of thirteen thousand facets, so monstrous in its exactitude. My lack of even the most obvious information about crystallography, an ignorance in this field as in many others common in my circle, deprives me of the pleasure of grasping the true structure of the *Divina Commedia*, but such is the marvelously stimulating power of Dante that he has awakened in me a concrete interest in crystallography, and as a grateful reader—*lettore*—I shall try to satisfy him.

The process of creating this poem's form transcends our conceptions of literary invention and composition. It would be much more correct to recognize instinct as its guiding principle. The exemplary definitions proposed here are hardly intended to show off my own metaphorical capacity. Rather, I am engaged in a struggle to make the work comprehensible as an entity, to graphically demonstrate that which is conceivable. Only through metaphor is it possible to find a concrete sign to represent the instinct for form creation by which Dante accumulated and poured forth his *terza rima*.

We must try to imagine, therefore, how bees might have worked at the creation of this thirteen-thousand-faceted form, bees endowed with the brilliant stereometric instinct, who attracted bees in greater and greater numbers as they were required. The work of these bees, constantly keeping their eye on the whole, is of varying difficulty at different stages of the process. Their cooperation expands and grows more complicated as they participate in the process of forming the combs, by means of which space virtually emerges out of itself.

The bee analogy is suggested, by the way, by Dante himself. Here are three lines, the opening of canto 16 of the *Inferno*:

Già era in loco ove s'udia il rimbombo
  Dell' acqua che cadea nell' altro giro,
  Simile a quel che l'arnie fanno rombo . . .

Dante's comparisons are never descriptive, that is, purely representational. They always pursue the concrete task of presenting the inner form of the poem's structure or driving force. Let us take the very large group of "bird" similes—all of them extensive caravans now of cranes, now of grackles, now of swallows in classical military phalanxes, now the anarchically disorderly crows so unsuited to the Latin military formation—this entire group of extended similes always corresponds to the instinct for the pilgrimage, the journey, colonization, migration. Or, for example, let us take the equally large group of river similes, portraying the rise in the

Apennines of the river Arno which irrigates the valley of Tuscany, or the descent of the Alpine wet nurse, the river Po, into the valley of Lombardy. This group of similes is distinguished by its extraordinary breadth and its graduated descent from tercet to tercet, always leading to a complex of culture, homeland and settled civilization, to a political and national complex, so conditioned by the watersheds and, in addition, by the power and the direction of the rivers.

The force of a Dantean simile, strange as it may seem, operates in direct proportion to our ability to do without it. It is never dictated by some beggarly logical necessity. Tell me, if you can, what necessitated Dante's comparing the poem as it was being concluded with part of a *donna*'s attire (what we call a "skirt" nowadays, but in old Italian would, at best, have been called a "cloak" or in general, a "dress"), or comparing himself with a tailor who had, excuse the expression, exhausted his material?

-IV-

In succeeding generations, as Dante moved further and further beyond the reach of the public and even of the artists themselves, he became shrouded in ever greater mystery. Dante himself was striving for clear and precise knowledge. He was difficult for contemporaries, exhausting, but he rewarded their efforts with knowledge. Later everything became much worse. An ignorant cult of Dantean mysticism was elaborately developed, devoid, like the very concept of mysticism, of any concrete substance. There also appeared the "mysterious" Dante of the French engravings, consisting of a monk's hood, an aquiline nose, and his procuring of something among the mountain crags.

Among us in Russia none other than Alexander Blok fell victim to this voluptuous ignorance on the part of the ecstatic adepts of Dante who never read him:

Dante's shade with his aquiline profile
Sings to me of the New Life . . .

The inner illumination of Dantean space derived from structural elements alone was of absolutely no interest to anyone.

I will now show how little concern Dante's early readers indicated for his so-called mysticism. I have in front of me a photograph of a miniature from one of the very earliest copies of Dante, dating from the middle of the 14th century (from the collection of the Perugia library). Beatrice is showing Dante the Trinity. There is a bright background with peacock designs, like a gay calico hanging. The Trinity in a willow frame is ruddy, rose-cheeked, and round as merchants. Dante Alighieri is depicted as a dashing young man, and Beatrice as a vivacious, buxom young girl. Two absolutely ordinary figures, a scholar brimming over with health courts a no less flourishing city maiden.

Spengler, who dedicated some superb pages to Dante, nevertheless viewed him from his loge at the German State Opera Theater, and when he says "Dante," we must nearly always understand "Wagner" on the Munich stage.

The purely historical approach to Dante is just as unsatisfactory as the political or theological approach. The future of Dante criticism belongs to the natural sciences when they will have achieved a sufficient degree of refinement and developed their capacity for thinking in images.

With all my might I would like to refute that loathsome legend which depicts Dante's coloring as either indisputably dull or of an infamous Spenglerian brownish hue. First of all, I will cite the testimony of a contemporary, an illuminator. This miniature is from the same collection of the museum in Perugia. It belongs to canto 1: "I saw a beast and turned back."

Here is a description of the coloring of that remarkable miniature, of a higher quality than the preceding one, and fully in accord with the text:

"Dante's clothing is *bright blue (adzhura chiara)*. Virgil's beard is long and his hair is gray. His toga is also gray; his cloak is *rose colored*; the denuded mountains are gray."

In other words, we see here bright azure and rosy flecks against smoky-gray nature.

In canto 17 of the *Inferno* there is a monster of conveyances by the name of Geryon, something on the order of a super tank equipped with wings.

He offers his services to Dante and Virgil, having obtained from the ruling hierarchy proper orders for transporting the two passengers to the lower, eighth circle.

> Due branche avea pilose infin l'ascelle;
>   Lo dosso e il petto ed ambedue le coste
>   Dipinte avea di nodi e di rotelle.
> Con più color, sommesse e soprapposte,
>   Non fer mai drappo Tartari né Turchi,
>   Né fur tai tele per Aragne imposte.
>   (*Inf.* 17.13–18)

Here the subject is the color of Geryon's skin. His back, chest and sides are variously colored, ornamented with small knots and shields. Dante explains that neither the Turkish nor Tartar weavers ever used brighter colors for their carpets ...

The textile brilliance of this comparison is blinding, but the commercial perspectives of textiles revealed in it are completely unexpected.

With respect to its theme, canto 17 of the *Inferno*, devoted to usury, is very close to both the commercial inventory and to the turnover of the banking system. Usury, which made up for a deficiency in the banking system where a constant demand was already being experienced, was a crying evil of that age; however, it was also a necessity which eased the flow of goods in the Mediterranean region. Usurers were condemned both in the church and in literature; nevertheless, people still ran to them. Even the noble families practiced usury, peculiar bankers with major landholdings and an agrarian base—this especially peeved Dante.

Scorching hot sands make up the landscape of canto 17, that is, something reminiscent of the Arabian caravan routes. The most exalted usurers are sitting on the sand: the Gianfigliacci and the Ubbriachi from Florence, the Scrovegni from Padua. Each one wears a small sack around his neck or an amulet or little purse embroidered with the family coat-of-arms outlined against a colored background: one wears an azure lion on a gold ground; another wears a goose, whiter than freshly churned butter, against a blood-red background; the third bears a blue swine on a white background.

Before plunging into the abyss, gliding down on Geryon's back, Dante examines this strange exhibit of family crests. I call your attention to the fact that the usurers' sacks are presented as emblems of color. The energy of the color epithets and the way in which they are placed in the verse line muffles the heraldry. The colors are listed with a kind of professional harshness. In other words, the colors are presented at that stage when they are still found on the artist's palette, in his studio. And what is so astonishing about that? Dante felt right at home in the world of painting; he was a friend of Giotto, and attentively followed the struggle between the various schools of painting and the fashionable trends.

Credette Cimabue nella pittura ...
(*Purg.* 11.94)

Having observed the usurers long enough, they embarked on Geryon. Virgil threw his arms around Dante's neck and cried out to the official dragon: "Descend in broad, flowing circles: remember your new burden ..."

The craving to fly tormented and exhausted the men of Dante's era no less than alchemy. A hunger after cloven space. All sense of direction vanished. Nothing was visible. Only the Tartar's back lay before them, that terrifying silk dressing gown of Geryon's skin. Speed and direction can be judged only by the air whipping across the face. The flying machine was not yet invented, Leonardo's plans did not yet exist, but the problem of gliding to a safe landing was already resolved.

Then at last, falconry bursts in with an explanation. Geryon's maneuvers in slowing down his descent resemble the return of a falcon from an unsuccessful flight, who having flown up in vain, slowly returns at the call of the falconer and having landed, flies away offended, assuming a perch somewhere off in the distance.

Now let's try to grasp all of canto 17 as a whole, but from the point of view of the organic chemistry of Dantean imagery, which has nothing in common with allegory. Instead of merely retelling the so-called content, we will look at this link in Dante's work as a continuous transformation of the substratum of poetic material, which preserves its unity and aspires to pierce its own internal self.

Dante's thinking in images, as is the case in all genuine poetry, exists with the aid of a peculiarity of poetic material which I propose to call its convertibility or transmutability. Only in accord with convention is the development of an image called its development. And indeed, just imagine an airplane (ignoring the technical impossibility) which in full flight constructs and launches another machine. Furthermore, in the same way, this flying machine, while fully absorbed in its own flight, still manages to assemble and launch yet a third machine. To make my proposed comparison more precise and helpful, I will add that the production and launching of these technically unthinkable new machines which are tossed off in mid-flight are not secondary or extraneous functions of the plane which is in motion, but rather comprise a most essential attribute and part of the flight itself, while assuring its feasibility and safety to no less a degree than its properly operating rudder or the regular functioning of its engine.

Of course, only by stretching the point can one apply the term "development" to this series of projectiles constructed in flight, which fly away, one after the other, in order to maintain the integrity of movement itself.

Canto 17 of the *Inferno* is a brilliant confirmation of the transmutability of poetic material in the above-mentioned sense of the term. The figures of this transmutability may be drawn approximately as follows: the little flourishes and shields on Geryon's mottled Tartar skin—silken carpets woven with ornaments, spread out on Mediterranean counters—a perspective of maritime commerce, of banking and piracy—usury and the return to Florence via the heraldic sacks with specimens of fresh colors that had never been used—the craving for flight underscored by Eastern ornament, which turns the material of the canto toward the Arabic fairytale with its technique of the flying carpet—and, finally, the second return to Florence with the aid of the falcon, irreplaceable precisely because he is unnecessary.

Not being satisfied with this truly miraculous demonstration of the transmutability of poetic material, which leaves all the associative gambits of modern European poetry far behind, Dante, as if to mock his slow-witted reader, after everything has been unloaded, played out, given away, brings Geryon down to earth and graciously equips him for a new journey, like the tuft of an arrow released from a bowstring.

- V -

Dante's drafts, of course, have not come down to us. There is no opportunity for us to work on the history of his text. But it does not follow, of course, that there were no inkstained manuscripts or that the text hatched out full grown like Leda out of the egg or Pallas Athena out of the head of Zeus. But the unfortunate interval of six centuries plus the quite excusable fact of the absence of rough drafts have played a dirty trick on us. For how many centuries have people been talking and writing about Dante as if he had expressed his thoughts directly on official paper?

Dante's laboratory? That does not concern us! What can ignorant piety have to do with that? Dante is discussed as if he had the completed whole before his eyes even before he had begun work and as if he had utilized the technique of moulage, first casting in plaster, then in bronze. At best, he is handed a chisel and allowed to carve or, as they love to call it, "to sculpt." However, one small detail is forgotten: the chisel only removes the excess, and a sculptor's draft leaves no material traces (something the public admires). The stages of a sculptor's work correspond to the writer's series of drafts.

Rough drafts are never destroyed.

There are no ready-made things in poetry, in the plastic arts or in art in general.

Our habit of grammatical thinking hinders us here—putting the concept of art in the nominative case. We subordinate the very process of creation to the purposeful prepositional case, and we reason like some robot with a lead heart, who having swung about as required in a variety of directions, and having endured various jolts as he answered the questionnaire—about what? about whom? by whom and by what?—finally established himself in the Buddhist, schoolboy calm of the nominative case. Meanwhile, a finished thing is just as subject to the oblique cases as to the nominative case. Moreover, our entire study of syntax is the most powerful survival of scholasticism and, by being in philosophy, in epistemology, it is put in its proper subordinate position, and completely overwhelmed by mathematics which has its own independent, original syntax. In the study of art this scholasticism of syntax still reigns supreme, causing colossal damage by the hour.

Precisely those who are furthest from Dante's method in European poetry and, bluntly speaking, in polar opposition to him, go by the name Parnassians: Heredia, Leconte de Lisle. Baudelaire is much closer. Verlaine is still closer, but the closest of all the French poets is Arthur Rimbaud. Dante is by his very nature one who shakes up meaning and destroys the integrity of the image. The composition of his cantos resembles an airline schedule or the indefatigable flights of carrier pigeons.

Thus the safety of the rough draft is the statute assuring preservation of the power behind the literary work. In order to arrive on target one has to accept and take into account winds blowing in a somewhat different direction. Exactly the same law applies in tacking a sailboat.

Let us remember that Dante Alighieri lived during the heyday of sailing ships and that sailing was a highly developed art. Let us not reject out of hand the fact that he contemplated models of tacking and the maneuvering of sailing vessels. He was a student of this most evasive and plastic sport known to man since his earliest days.

Here I would like to point out one of the remarkable peculiarities of Dante's psyche: he was terrified of the direct answer, perhaps conditioned by the political situation in that extremely dangerous, enigmatic and criminal century.

While as a whole the *Divina Commedia* (as we have already stated) is a questionnaire with answers, each of Dante's direct responses is literally hatched out, now with the aid of his midwife, Virgil, now with the help of his nurse, Beatrice, and so on.

The *Inferno*, canto 16. The conversation is conducted with that intense passion reserved for the prison visit: the need to utilize, at whatever cost, the tiny snatches of a meeting. Three eminent Florentines conduct an inquiry. About what? About Florence, of course. Their knees tremble with impatience, and they are terrified of hearing the truth. The answer, lapidary and cruel, is received in the form of a cry. At this, even Dante's chin quivers, although he made a desperate effort to control himself, and he tosses back his head, and all this is presented in no more nor less than the author's stage direction:

Così gridai colla faccia levata
                    (*Inf.* 16.76)

Sometimes Dante is able to describe a phenomenon so that
not the slightest trace of it remains. To do this he uses a device
which I would like to call the Heraclitean metaphor; it so strongly
emphasizes the fluidity of the phenomenon and cancels it out
with such a flourish, that direct contemplation, after the metaphor
has completed its work, is essentially left with nothing to sustain it.
I have already taken the opportunity several times to state that
Dante's metaphorical devices exceed our conception of composition inasmuch as our critical studies, fettered by the syntactic
mode of thinking, are powerless before them.

When the peasant, climbing up the hill
During that season when the being who illuminates the
    world,
Is least reticent to show his face to us,
And the water midges yield their place to the mosquitoes,
Sees the dancing fireflies in the hollow,
In the same spot, perhaps, where he labored as a reaper or
    plowman—
So with little tongues of flame the eighth circle gleamed,
Completely visible from the heights where I had climbed;
And as the one who took his revenge with the aid of bears,
Upon seeing the departing Chariot of Elijah,
When the team of horses tore away into the heavens,
Stared as best he could but could make out nothing
Except one single flame
Wasting away, like a small cloud rising in the sky—
So the tongue-like flame filled the chinks in the tombs,
Appropriating the wealth of the graves as their profit,
While enveloped in each flame a sinner was concealed.
                    (*Inf.* 26.25–42)

If your head is not spinning from this miraculous ascent, worthy of Sebastian Bach's organ music, then try to indicate where the first and second members of the comparison are to be found, what is compared with what, and where the primary and secondary explanatory elements are located.

An impressionistic preparatory introduction awaits the reader in a whole series of Dante's cantos. Its purpose is to present in the form of a scattered alphabet, in the form of a leaping, sparkling, well-splashed alphabet the very elements which, in accord with the laws of the transformability of poetic material, will be united into formulas of meaning.

Thus, in this introduction, we see the extraordinarily light, glittering Heraclitean dance of the summer midges which prepares us to apprehend the serious and tragic speech of Odysseus.

Canto 26 of the *Inferno* is the most oriented toward sailing of all Dante's compositions, the most given to tacking, and by far the best at maneuvering. It has no equals in versatility, evasiveness, Florentine diplomacy and Greek cunning.

Two basic parts are clearly distinguishable in this canto: the luminous, impressionistic preparatory introduction and the well-balanced, dramatic tale, which Odysseus tells about his last voyage, about his journey out into the deeps of the Atlantic and his terrible death under the stars of an alien hemisphere.

In the free flow of its thought this canto comes very close to improvisation. But if you listen more attentively, you will see that the poet is improvising inwardly in his beloved, secret Greek, using only the phonetics and the fabric of his native Italian idiom to carry out his purpose.

If you give a child a thousand rubles and then suggest that he make a choice of keeping either the coins or the banknotes, he will of course choose the coins, and in this way you can retrieve the entire sum by giving him some small change. Exactly the same experience has befallen European literary criticism which nailed Dante to the landscape of Hell familiar from the engravings. No one has yet approached Dante with a geologist's hammer to ascertain the crystalline structure of his rock, to study its phenocryst, its smokiness, or its patterning, or to judge it as rock crystal subject to the most varied of nature's accidents.

Our criticism tells us: distance the phenomenon and I will deal with it and absorb it. "Holding something at a distance" (Lomonosov's expression) and cognoscibility are almost identical for our criticism.

Dante has images of parting and farewell. It is most difficult to descend through the valleys of his verses of parting.

We have still not succeeded in tearing ourselves away from that Tuscan peasant admiring the phosphorescent dance of the fireflies, nor in closing our eyes to the impressionistic dazzle of Elijah's chariot as it fades away into the clouds before the pyre of Eteocles has been cited, Penelope named, the Trojan horse flashed by, Demosthenes lent Odysseus his republican eloquence, and the ship of old age fitted out.

Old age, in Dante's conception of the term, means, above all, breadth of vision, heightened capacity, and universal interests. In Odysseus's canto the earth is already round.

It is a canto concerned with the composition of human blood which contains in itself the salt of the ocean. The beginning of the voyage is located in the system of blood vessels. The blood is planetary, solar and salty . . .

With all the convolutions of his brain Dante's Odysseus despises sclerosis just as Farinata despised Hell.

> Is it possible that
> we are born merely to enjoy
> animal comforts and
> that we will not devote
> the remaining portion of our
> vanishing senses to an act

of boldness—to Westward
sailing, beyond the Gates of
Hercules, where the world
unpopulated, continues on?

The metabolism of the planet itself takes place in the blood, and the Atlantic sucks in Odysseus, swallowing up his wooden ship.

It is inconceivable to read Dante's cantos without directing them toward contemporaneity. They were created for that purpose. They are missiles for capturing the future. They demand commentary in the *futurum*.

For Dante time is the content of history understood as a simple synchronic act; and vice-versa: the contents of history are the joint containing of time by its associates, competitors, and co-discoverers.

Dante is an antimodernist. His contemporaneity is continuous, incalculable and inexhaustible.

That is why Odysseus's speech, as convex as the lens of a magnifying glass, may be turned toward the war of the Greeks and Persians as well as toward Columbus's discovery of America, the bold experiments of Paracelsus, and the world empire of Charles V.

Canto 26, dedicated to Odysseus and Diomed, is a marvelous introduction to the anatomy of Dante's eye, so perfectly adjusted alone for the revelation of the structure of future time. Dante had the visual accommodation of predatory birds, but it was unadjusted to focussing in a narrow radius: his hunting grounds were too large.

The words of the proud Farinata may be applied to Dante himself:

Noi veggiam, come quei ch'ha mala luce.
(*Inf.* 10.100)

That is, we, the souls of sinners, are capable of seeing and distin-
guishing only the distant future, but for this we have a special gift.
We become absolutely blind as soon as the doors to the future
slam shut before us. And in this respect we resemble those who
struggle with the twilight, and, in discerning distant objects, fail to
make out what is close by.

In canto 26 dance is strongly expressed as the origin of the
rhythms of the *terza rima*. Here one is struck by the extraordinary
light-heartedness of the rhythm. The meter is organized according
to waltz time:

> E se già fosse, non saria per tempo.
> Così foss' ei, da che pure esser dee;
> Chè più mi graverà com' più m'attempo.
>   (*Inf.* 26.10–12)

It is difficult for us as foreigners to penetrate the ultimate secret of foreign poetry. We cannot be judges, we cannot have the
last word. But it seems to me that it is precisely here that we find
the enchanting pliability of the Italian language which only the
ear of a native Italian can perceive completely.

Here I am quoting Marina Tsvetaeva, who once mentioned
the "pliability of the Russian language . . ."

If you attentively watch the mouth of an accomplished poetry
reader, it will seem as if he were giving a lesson to deaf-mutes, that
is, he works with the aim of being understood even without
sounds, articulating each vowel with pedagogical clarity. And thus
it is enough to see how canto 26 sounds in order to hear it. I
would say that in this canto the vowels are anxious and twitching.

The waltz is primarily a dance of undulation. Nothing even
remotely resembling it was possible in Hellenic or Egyptian culture. (I am indebted to Spengler for this juxtaposition.) The very
foundation of the waltz is the purely European passion for peri-

odic undulating movements, the very same close listening to sound and light waves found in all our theory of sound and light, in all our scientific study of matter, in all our poetry and music.

- V I -

O Poetry, envy crystallography, bite your nails in anger and impotence! For it is recognized that the mathematical formulas necessary for describing crystal formation are not derivable from three-dimensional space. You are denied even that element of respect which any piece of mineral crystal enjoys.

Dante and his contemporaries did not know geological time. Paleontological clocks were unknown to them: the clock of coal, the clock of infusorial limestone, the clocks of sand, shale and schist. They circled round in the calendar, dividing up days into quarters. However, the Middle Ages did not fit into the Ptolemaic system: they found shelter in it.

Aristotle's physics were added to Biblical genetics. These two poorly matched things did not want to merge. The enormous explosive power of the Book of Genesis (the idea of spontaneous generation) fell upon the tiny island of the Sorbonne from all sides, and we will not be mistaken if we say that the men of Dante's age lived in an antiquity which was completely awash in modernity, like the globe embraced by Tyutchev's ocean. It is already very difficult for us to imagine how things which were familiar to absolutely everyone—school trots, which became a part of the obligatory elementary school program—how the entire Biblical cosmogony with its Christian appendages could have been accepted by the educated people of that time so literally, as if it were a special edition of the daily newspaper.

And if we approach Dante from this point of view, it will appear that he saw in Biblical tradition not so much its sacred, daz-

zling aspects as subject matter which, with the help of zealous re-
porting and passionate experimentation, could be turned to his
advantage.

In canto 26 of the *Paradiso*, Dante goes so far as to have a private conversation with Adam, to conduct a real interview. St. John
the Divine, the author of the Apocalypse, acts as his assistant.

I maintain that every element of the modern experimental
method may be found in Dante's approach to Biblical tradition.
These include the creation of specially contrived conditions for
the experiment, the use of instruments of such precision that there
is no reason to doubt their validity, and clear verification of the results.

The situation in canto 26 of the *Paradiso* can be defined as a
solemn examination performed on optical instruments in concert
hall surroundings. Music and optics create the basis of the situation.

The major antinomy of Dante's experience is to be found in
his rushing back and forth between the example and the experiment. Examples are extracted from the patriarchal bag of ancient
consciousness with the understanding that they be returned as
soon as they are no longer needed. Experiments, the drawing of
certain required facts out of the total sum of experience, no longer
return them in accord with some promissory note, but rather
launch them into orbit.

The Evangelical parables and the little examples of the scholastics are but cereal grains to be consumed and destroyed. Experimental science, on the other hand, drawing facts out of coherent
reality, forms a kind of seed-fund out of them, an inviolable preserve, which comprises, as it were, the property of a time as yet
unborn but already indebted.

The position of the experimenter with respect to factology,
insofar as he aspires toward a trusting union with it, is by nature
unstable, agitated and off balance. It brings to mind the above-
mentioned figure of the waltz, because after each half-turn on the

toes, in coming together the dancer's heels always meet on a new square of the parquetry and in a qualitatively different way. The dizzying Mephisto Waltz of experimentation originated in the Trecento, or perhaps even long before that; furthermore, it originated in the process of poetic formation, in the undulations of formulating procedure, in the transformability of poetic matter, the most precise, prophetic and indomitable of all matter.

Because of theological terminology, scholastic grammar, and our ignorance of allegory, we have overlooked the experimental dances in Dante's *Commedia*. In keeping with the formulas of outmoded scholarship, we made Dante look better, and at the same time used his theology as a vessel for the dynamics of his poetry.

To the sensitive palm placed on the neck of a warm pitcher, the pitcher gains form precisely because of its warmth. Warmth in this case is felt before form, thus it fulfills the sculptural function. In its cold state, forcibly torn from its incandescence, Dante's *Commedia* is suitable only for analyses by mechanistic tweezers; it is unsuitable for reading, for performing.

> Come quando dall'acqua o dallo specchio
>   Salta lo raggio all' opposita parte,
>   Salendo su per lo modo parecchio
> A quel che scende, e tauto si diparte
>   Dal cader della pietra in egual tratta,
>   Sì come mostra esperienza ed arte . . .
>   (*Purg.* 15.16–21)

"Just as a ray of sunlight striking the surface of water or a mirror is reflected back at an angle corresponding to the angle of incidence, which differentiates it from a falling stone bouncing up at a perpendicular from the earth—a fact attested by both science and art . . ."

When the need for empirical verification of Biblical tradition first dawned on Dante, when he first indicated a taste for what I propose to call a "sacred induction," the conception of the *Divina Commedia* had already taken shape, and its success was virtually assured.

The poem, when most densely covered with foliage, is directed toward authority; its sound is fullest; it is most concert-like at that point when it is caressed by dogma, by canon, by the firm eloquent word. But therein lies the problem: in authority, or to be more exact, in authoritativeness, we can see only insurance against error and we are not at all equipped to understand that grandiose music of trustfulness, of trust, to make out those nuances of probability and conviction as delicate as an Alpine rainbow, which Dante has under his control.

Col quale il fantolin corre alla mamma—
(*Purg.* 30.44)

So Dante fawns upon authority.

A number of the cantos of the *Paradiso* are enclosed in the hard capsule of an examination. In certain passages one can clearly make out the examiner's basso and the candidate's shy tinkling response. The insertion of the grotesque and the genre picture ("the examination of a candidate for the Baccalaureate") comprises a necessary attribute of the elevated and concert-like composition of the third part. However, the first example of it is presented as early as the second canto of the *Paradiso* (Beatrice's argument about the origin of spots on the moon).

In order to grasp the very nature of Dante's intercourse with the authorities, that is, the forms and methods of his cognition, it is necessary to take into account both the concert-like circumstances of the scholastic cantos of the *Commedia* and the very preparation of the organs of perception. Here I am not even speaking about that most remarkably staged experiment with the candle and three mirrors, where it is proven that the reverse path of light has as its source the refraction of the ray, but I must not fail to mention the preparation of the eye for the apperception of new things.

This preparation is developed into an actual dissection: Dante divines the layered structure of the retina: *di gonna in gonna* . . .

Music here is not merely a guest invited to step indoors, but a full participant in the argument; or to be more precise, it promotes the exchange of opinions, coordinates it, and encourages syllogistic digestion, stretches premises and compresses conclusions. Its role is both absorptive and resorptive: it is a purely chemical role.

When you read Dante with all your powers and with complete conviction, when you transplant yourself completely to the field of action of the poetic material, when you join in and coordinate your own intonations with the echoes of the orchestral and thematic groups continually arising on the pocked and undulating semantic surface, when you begin to catch through the smoky-crystalline rock the sound-forms of phenocryst inserted into it, that is, additional sounds and thoughts conferred on it no longer by a poetic but by a geological intelligence, then the purely vocal, intonational and rhythmical work is replaced by a more powerful coordinating force—by the conductor's function—and the hegemony of the conductor's baton comes into its own, cutting across orchestrated space and projecting from the voice like some more complex mathematical measure out of a three-dimensional state.

Which comes first, listening or conducting? If conducting is no more than the nudging along of music which rolls forth of its own accord, then of what use is it when the orchestra is good in itself, when it performs impeccably by itself? An orchestra without a conductor, as a long-cherished hope, belongs to the same order of vulgar pan-European "ideals" as the international language Esperanto, symbolizing the linguistic teamwork of all mankind.

Let us investigate how the conductor's baton first appeared and we will see that it arrived neither sooner nor later than when it was needed; what is more, it arrived as a new and original form of activity, creating in the air its own new domain.

Let us listen to how the conductor's baton was born, or better, how it was hatched out of the orchestra.

1732: Time (tempo or beat)—formerly tapped out with the foot, now usually with the hand. Conductor—*conducteur, der Anführer* (Walther, *Musical Dictionary*).

1753: Baron Grimm calls the conductor of the Paris Opera a woodcutter due to his habit of beating time aloud, a habit which since the time of Lully has reigned at the Paris Opera (Shunemann, *Geschichte des Dirigierens*, 1913).

1810: At the Frankenhausen musical festival Spohr conducted with a baton made of rolled-up paper, "without the least noise and without any grimaces" (Spohr, *Autobiography*).

The conductor's baton was badly overdue when it was born: the chemically radioactive orchestra anticipated it. The usefulness of the conductor's baton is far from being its only justification. The chemical nature of orchestral sounds finds its expression in the dance of the conductor who stands with his back to the audience. And this baton is far from being an external, administrative accessory or a distinctive symphonic police which could be done away with in an ideal state. It is no less than a dancing chemical formula which integrates reactions perceptible to the ear. I beg of you not to regard it merely as a supplementary mute instrument, invented for greater visibility and to provide additional pleasure. In a certain sense this invulnerable baton qualitatively contains in itself all the elements in the orchestra. But how does it contain them? It gives off no smell of them, nor can it. It does not smell of chlorine, as the formula of ammonium chloride or ammonia does not smell of ammonium chloride or of ammonia.

Dante was chosen as the theme of this conversation not because I wanted to focus attention on him as a means to studying the classics and to seat him alongside of Shakespeare and Lev Tolstoi, as some kind of Kirpotin-style *table d'hôte*, but because he is the greatest, the unrivaled master of transmutable and convertible poetic material, the earliest and simultaneously the most powerful chemical conductor of the poetic composition existing only in the swells and waves of the ocean, only in the raising of the sails and in the tacking.

- V I I -

Dante's cantos are scores for a particular chemical orchestra in which the external ear can easily distinguish comparisons identical with the impulses and solo parts, that is, the arias and ariosos, peculiar self-avowals, self-flagellations or autobiographies, sometimes brief and capable of fitting into the palm of the hand, sometimes lapidary, like a tombstone inscription, sometimes unrolled like a certificate awarded by some medieval university, sometimes well-developed, articulated, and capable of achieving a dramatic, operatic fullness, as, for instance, Francesca's famous cantilena.

Canto 33 of the *Inferno*, containing Ugolino's tale about how he and his three sons died of starvation in the prison tower of Archbishop Ruggieri of Pisa, is enveloped in the dense and heavy timbre of a cello like rancid, poisoned honey.

The density of the cello timbre is best for communicating expectation and agonizing impatience. There is no power on earth which can hasten the movement of honey pouring out of a tilted jar. Hence, the cello could only take shape and be given form when the European analysis of time had made sufficient progress, when sundials were superseded and the ancient observer of the shadow stick moving around Roman numerals drawn in the sand had been transformed into an impassioned participant of differential torture, into a martyr to the infinitesimal. A cello retards sound, no matter how it hurries. Ask Brahms—he knew it. Ask Dante—he heard it.

Ugolino's tale is one of the most remarkable of Dante's arias, one of those events when a man, who has been offered some singular never-to-be-repeated opportunity to audition, is completely transformed right in front of his audience; he plays on his unhappiness like a virtuoso, and draws out of his misfortune a timbre completely unheard of before and unknown even to himself.

We must remember that timbre is a structural principle much like the alkalinity or acidity of some chemical compound. However, the chemical retort is not the space in which the chemical reaction takes place. That would be far too simple.

Ugolino's cello-like voice, overgrown with a prison beard, starving and locked up with his three fledgling sons, one of whom bears the sharp, violin-like name of Anselmuccio, flows out of a narrow crack:

Breve pertugio dentro dalla muda

It matures in the box of the prison resonator, and thus, in this instance, the cello fraternizes in all seriousness with the prison.

Il carcere—the prison—supplements and acoustically conditions the vocal work of the autobiographical cello.

In the subconscious of the Italian people prison played a prominent role. Nightmares of prison life were imbibed with the mother's milk. The Trecento tossed men into prison with astonishing unconcern. Ordinary prisons were open for viewing, like our churches and museums. The interest in prisons was exploited by the prison wardens as well as by the fear-inspiring machinery of the small states. There was a lively intercourse between the prisons and the free world outside resembling diffusion, mutual infiltration.

And thus Ugolino's story is one of those migratory anecdotes, one of those horror stories which mothers used to frighten their children, one of those entertaining horror tales which are mumbled with great satisfaction as a remedy for insomnia while tossing and turning in bed. It is well known as a ballad, like Bürger's *Lenore*, the *Lorelei*, or the *Erlkönig*.

It thus corresponds to a glass retort; it is so accessible and comprehensible, irrespective of the quality of the chemical process taking place within it.

However, the largo for cello presented by Dante in Ugolino's name has its own space, its own structure as revealed in the timbre. The ballad-retort with its familiar motif is smashed to smithereens. Chemistry with its architectonic drama takes over.

> I 'non so chi tu sei, nè per che modo
>   Venuto se' quaggiù; ma Fiorentino
>   Mi sembri veramente quand' io t'odo.
> Tu dei saper ch'io fui Conte Ugolino . . .
>   (*Inf.* 33.10–13)

> . . . I know not who thou art, or how thou camest here, but by your speech it seems thou must be a true Florentine. Thou must know that I was Count Ugolino . . .

"Thou must know"—*tu dei saper*—the first note on the cello, the first thrust of the theme.

The second note on the cello: "if thou dost not weep now, I know not what can wring tears from thine eyes." Here are revealed the truly boundless horizons of compassion. Moreover, the compassionate one is invited to enter as a new partner, and we already hear his quavering voice from the distant future.

Nevertheless, I did not make mention of the ballad accidentally. Ugolino's story is a ballad precisely because of its chemical properties, despite its being incarcerated in the prison retort. The following elements of the ballad are to be found: the conversation between the father and his sons (remember the *Erlkönig*); the chase after time which is slipping away, that is, continuing the parallel with the *Erlkönig*—in that case, the father's mad dash with his trembling son in his arms, in the other, the prison situation, that is, counting the dripping of the water as a measure of time which brings the father and his three sons closer to the mathematically conceivable threshold of death by starvation, no matter how impossible it may seem to the father's consciousness. The same rhythm of the mad dash emerges here in disguise, in the mute wailing of the cello, which strives with all its might to break out of the situation and gives a sound picture of a still more terrifying, slow chase, breaking speed down into the most delicate fibers.

Finally, just as the cello is wildly conversing with itself and squeezing out of itself questions and answers, Ugolino's story is interpolated with the touching and helpless rejoinder of his sons:

... ed Anselmuccio mio
Disse: "Tu guardi sì, padre! Che hai?"
                    (*Inf.* 33.50–51)

...And my Anselmuccio said: "Father,
where art thou looking? What is
the matter?"

That is, the dramatic structure of the story flows out of the timbre itself, for the timbre is in no way sought after and stretched over the story as over the last of a shoe.

- V I I I -

It seems to me that Dante made a careful study of all speech defects, listening closely to stutterers and lispers, to nasal twangs and inarticulate pronunciation, and that he learned much from them.

I would very much like to speak about the auditory coloration of canto 32 of the *Inferno.*

A peculiar labial music: "abbo"—"gabbo"—"babbo"—

"Tebe"—"plebe"—"zebe"—"converrebbe." It's as if a nurse had participated in the creation of phonetics. Now the lips protrude in a childish manner, now they extend into a proboscis.

The labials form some kind of "numbered bass"—*basso continuo*, namely, the chordal basis of harmonization. They are joined by smacking, sucking and whistling sounds, and also by dental "zz" and "dz" sounds.

I pulled out a single thread at random: *cagnazzi—riprezzo—guazzi—mezzo—gravezza.*

The tweaking, smacking and labial explosives do not cease for a single second.

The canto is interlarded with a vocabulary which can best be termed an assortment of seminary student insults and cruel schoolboy taunts: *coticagna* (nape); *dischiomi* (to pull out hair, locks); *sonar con le mascelle* (to bawl, to bark); *pigliare a gabbo* (to brag, to loaf about). With the aid of this blatantly shameless, intentionally infantile orchestration, Dante grows the crystals for his auditory landscapes of Giudecca (the circle of Judas) and Caina (the circle of Cain).

> Non fece al corso suo sì grosso velo
>   D'inverno la Danoia in Osteric,
>   Nè Tanaï la sotto il freddo cielo,
> Com'era quivi; chè, se Tambernic
>   Vi fosse su caduto, o Pietrapana,
>   Non avria pur dall'orlo fatto cric.

Suddenly, for no apparent reason, a Slavic duck begins quacking: *Osteric, Tambernic, cric* (the onomatopoeic word for crackling).

The ice explodes phonetically and is scattered across the names of the Danube and the Don. The cold-generating tendency of canto 32 arises from the intrusion of physics into a moral idea—betrayal, a frozen conscience, the ataraxia of shame, absolute zero.

Canto 32 is written in the tempo of a modern scherzo. But what is that? An anatomical scherzo which is studying the degeneration of speech based on onomatopoeic infantilisms.

A new link is revealed here between food and speech. Shameful pronunciation is turned back to where it came from; it is turned back to champing, biting, gurgling and chewing.

The articulation of food and speech almost coincide. A strange locust-like phonetics is created:

Mettendo i denti in nota di cicogna—

"Working with their teeth like grasshopper's jaws."

Finally, we must note that canto 32 is overflowing with anatomical lust.

"That same famous blow which simultaneously destroyed the wholesomeness of the body and injured its shade . . ." There is also purely surgical satisfaction: "The one whose gorget was sawed by Florence . . ."—

Di cui segò Fiorenza la gorgiera . . .

And further: "Just as a hungry man greedily falls upon bread, so one of them fell on the other, sinking his teeth into the very place where the nape becomes the neck . . ."—

Là 've il cervel s'aggiunge con la nuca . . .

All this danced about like a Dürer skeleton on hinges and leads you off to German anatomy.

After all, isn't a murderer something of an anatomist?

Didn't an executioner in the Middle Ages slightly resemble a scientific worker?

The art of war and the art of execution remind you a bit of the threshold of a dissecting room.

- I X -

The *Inferno* is a pawnshop in which all the countries and cities known to Dante were left unredeemed. This extremely powerful construct of the infernal circles has a framework. It cannot be conveyed in the form of a crater. It cannot be portrayed on a relief map. Hell hangs suspended on the wire of urban egoism.

It is incorrect to think of the *Inferno* as something with three dimensions, as some combination of enormous circuses, of deserts with scorching sands, of stinking swamps, of Babylonian capitals with mosques burning red-hot. Hell contains nothing inside itself and has no dimensions; like an epidemic, an infectious disease or the plague, it spreads like a contagion, even though it is not spatial.

Love of the city, passion for the city, hatred for the city—these serve as the materials of the *Inferno*. The rings of Hell are no more than Saturn's circles of emigration. To the exile his sole, forbidden and irretrievably lost city is scattered everywhere—he is surrounded by it. I would like to say that the *Inferno* is surrounded by Florence. Dante's Italian cities—Pisa, Florence, Lucca, Verona— these precious civic planets, are drawn out into monstrous rings, stretched into belts, restored to a nebulous, gasiform state.

The anti-landscape nature of the *Inferno* forms, as it were, the conditions of its graphic character.

Imagine Foucault's grandiose experiment carried out not with one pendulum, but with a multitude of pendulums all swinging past one another. Here space exists only insofar as it is a receptacle for amplitudes. To make Dante's images more precise is as unthinkable as listing the names of all the individuals who participated in the migration of peoples.

> Just as the Flemish between
> Wissant and Bruges, protecting
> themselves from the sea's floodtide,
> erect dikes to push the sea back;

and just as the Paduans construct
embankments along the shores of
the Brenta to assure the safety of
their cities and castles in
the expectation of spring with its
melting snows on the Chiarentana
[part of the snowy Alps]—so these
dams were built, though not so
monumental, almost despite the engineer . . .

(Inf. 15.4–12)

Here the moons of the polynomial pendulum swing from Bruges to Padua, teaching a course in European geography, lecturing on the art of engineering, on the techniques of urban safety, on the organization of public works, and on the significance of the Alpine watershed for the Italian state.

What have we, who crawl on our knees before a line of verse, preserved from these riches? Where are its godfathers, where are its enthusiasts? What will become of our poetry which lags so disgracefully behind science?

It is terrifying to think that the blinding explosions of contemporary physics and kinetics were used 600 years before their thunder sounded. Indeed, words do not suffice to brand the shameful, barbarous indifference shown toward them by the pitiful compositors of clichéd thought.

Poetic speech creates its own instruments on the move and cancels them out without halting.

Of all our arts painting alone, and in particular modern French painting, has not yet ceased to hear Dante. This is the painting which elongates the bodies of horses as they approach the finish line at the hippodrome.

Whenever a metaphor raises the vegetable colors of existence to an articulate impulse, I gratefully remember Dante.

We describe the very thing that cannot be described. That is, nature's text comes to a standstill, but we have unlearned how to describe the single thing which, by its structure, yields to poetic representation, that is, the impulses, intentions and amplitudes of fluctuation.

Ptolemy has returned via the back door. Giordano Bruno was burned in vain! ...

While still in the womb our creations become known to everyone, but Dante's multinomial, multi-sailed and kinetically kindled comparisons preserve to this day the charm of the as-yet-unsaid.

His "reflexology of speech" is astonishing—a science, still not completely established, of the spontaneous psycho-physiological influence of the word on those who are conversing, on the audience surrounding them, and on the speaker himself, as well as on the means by which he communicates his urge to speak, that is, by which he signals with a light his sudden desire to express himself.

Here he comes closest to approaching the wave theory of sound and light, determining their relationship.

> Just as an animal covered
> with a cloth grows nervous and
> irritable, only the moving
> folds of the material indicating
> his displeasure, so the first
> created soul [Adam's] expressed
> to me through the covering
> [light] the extent of its
> pleasure and sense of joy in
> answering my question ...
> (*Par.* 26.97–102)

In the third part of the *Commedia* (the *Paradiso*), I see a genuine kinetic ballet. Here we see every possible kind of luminous figure and dance, down to the tapping of heels at a wedding celebration.

Four torches glowed before me,
and the nearest one suddenly came
to life and grew as rosy as if Jupiter
and Mars were suddenly
transformed into birds and were
exchanging feathers.
                    (*Par.* 27.10–15)

Isn't it strange that a man who is preparing to speak should
arm himself with a tautly strung bow, a full supply of feathered ar-
rows, prepare mirrors and convex lenses, and squint at the stars like
a tailor threading a needle? . . .

I devised this composite quotation, merging various passages
from the *Commedia*, in order to best exhibit the characteristics of
the speech-preparatory moves of Dante's poetry.

Speech preparation is even more within his sphere than articulation, that is, than speech itself.

Remember Virgil's marvelous supplication to the wiliest of the
Greeks.

It is completely suffused with the softness of Italian diph-
thongs.

These are the writhing, ingratiating and sputtering tongues of
small unprotected oil lamps, muttering about the greasy wick . . .

O voi, che siete due dentro ad un foco,
    S'io meritai di voi, mentre ch'io vissi,
    S'io meritai di voi assai o poco . . .
                    (*Inf.* 26.79–81)

Dante ascertains the origin, fate and character of a man according to his voice, just as the medicine of his day diagnosed a
man's health according to the color of his urine.

- X -

He is filled with a sense of the ineffable gratitude toward the copious riches falling into his hands. For he has no small task: space
must be prepared for the influx, the cataract must be removed
from the rigid vision, care must be taken that the bounty of poetic
material pouring out of the cornucopia does not flow through the
fingers, does not flow away through an empty sieve.

> Tutti dicean:"Benedictus qui venis!"
>   E, fior gittando di sopra e d'intorno:
> "Manibus o date lilia plenis!"
>   (*Purg.* 30.19–21)

The secret of Dante's capacity resides in the fact that he introduces not a single word of his own fabrication. Everything sets
him going except fabrication, except invention. Indeed, Dante and
fantasy are incompatible! . . . You should be ashamed of yourselves,
O French Romantics, you unfortunate *incroyables* in red vests, for
slandering Alighieri! What fantasy can you find in him? He writes
to dictation, he is a copyist, he is a translator . . . He is completely
bent over in the posture of a scribe casting a frightened sidelong
glance at the illuminated original he borrowed from the prior's
library.

It seems that I have forgotten to say that preceding the *Commedia* there was some presage, some kind of hypnotic séance, as it
were. But this, I suppose, is too implausible. If one considers this
astonishing work from the angle of written language, from the
viewpoint of the independent art of writing which in the year
1300 was on an equal footing with painting and music, and was
regarded as among the most venerated professions, then we may
add yet one more analogy to all the analogies proposed above—
taking dictation, copying, transcribing.

Sometimes, but very rarely, Dante shows us his writing tools.

His pen is termed *penna*, that is, it participates in a bird's flight; his inks are called *inchiostro*, that is, monastery accessories; his verse lines are also called *inchiostri*, although sometimes they are designated as Latin school *versi*, or even more modestly, *carte*, which is an astonishing substitution, "pages" instead of "verse lines."

But even when written down and ready, this is still not the end of the process, for then the written object must be taken somewhere, must be shown to someone to be checked and "praised."

It is not enough to say "copying," for what we are involved with here is calligraphy in response to dictation by the most terrifying and impatient dictators. The dictator-overseer is far more important than the so-called poet.

> . . . Now I must labor a little longer,
> and then I must show my
> notebook, bathed in the tears of
> a bearded schoolboy, to my most
> severe Beatrice, who radiates not
> only beauty but literacy.

Long before Arthur Rimbaud's alphabet of colors, Dante linked color with the pleophany of articulate speech. But he is a dyer, a textile-maker. His ABC is the alphabet of fluttering fabrics dyed with chemical powders and vegetable dyes:

> Sopra candido vel cinta d'oliva
>   Donna m'apparve, sotto verde manto,
>   Vestita di color di fiamma viva.
>   (*Purg.* 30.31–33)

His impulses toward color may sooner be called textile than alphabet impulses. Color is for him only in the fabric. For Dante the greatest intensity of material nature as a substance defined by color is found in textiles. And weaving is the occupation closest to qual-itativeness, to quality.

Now I will attempt to describe one of the innumerable conductorial flights of Dante's baton. We shall take this flight as if immersed in the actual setting of precious and instantaneous labor.

Let us begin with the writing. The pen draws calligraphic let-ters, tracing out both proper and common nouns. The quill pen is a small bit of bird's flesh. Dante, who never forgets the origin of things, remembers this, of course. His technique of writing with broad strokes and curves is transmuted into the figured flight of a flock of birds.

> E come augelli surti di rivera
> > Quasi congratulando a lor pasture,
> > Fanno di sè or tonda or altra schiera
> Sì dentro ai lumi sante crëature
> > Volitando cantavano, e faciensi
> > Or D, or I, or L, in sue figure.
> >   (*Par.* 18.73–78)

Just as the letters emanating from the hand of a scribe who is obedient to the dictation and who stands outside literature as a finished product, chase after the bait of meaning, as after sweet fodder, so precisely do birds, magnetized by green grass—some-times separately, sometimes together—peck at what befalls them, sometimes coming together in a circle, sometimes stretching out into a line . . .

Writing and speech are incommensurate. Letters correspond to intervals. The grammar of Old Italian exactly like our new Rus-sian grammar partakes of the same fluttering flock of birds, the same motley Tuscan *schiera*, that is, the Florentine mob which changes laws like gloves, and forgets by evening those laws pro-mulgated the same morning for the general welfare.

There is no syntax—merely a magnetized impulse: a yearning for the stern of a ship, a yearning for worm's fodder, a yearning for an unpromulgated law, a yearning for Florence.

- X I -

Let us return once more to the question of Dante's colors.

The interior of mineral rock, the Aladdin-like space concealed within, the lantern-like, lamp-like, chandelier-like suspension of piscine rooms deposited within, is the best key to understanding the coloration of the *Commedia*.

The most beautiful organic commentary to Dante is provided by a minerological collection.

I permit myself a small autobiographical confession. Black Sea pebbles tossed up on shore by the rising tide helped me immensely when the conception of this conversation was taking shape. I openly consulted with chalcedony, cornelians, gypsum crystals, spar, quartz and so on. It was thus that I came to understand that mineral rock is something like a diary of the weather, like a meteorological blood clot. Rock is nothing more than weather itself, excluded from atmospheric space and banished to functional space. In order to understand this you must imagine that all geological changes and displacements can be completely decomposed into elements of weather. In this sense, meteorology is more fundamental than mineralogy, for it embraces it, washes over it, ages it and gives it meaning.

The fascinating pages which Novalis devotes to miners and mining make concrete the interconnection between mineral rock and culture. This interconnection is illuminated out of rock—weather in both the formation of culture and in the formation of mineral rock.

Mineral rock is an impressionistic diary of weather accumulated by millions of natural disasters; however, it is not only of the past, it is of the future: it contains periodicity. It is an Aladdin's lamp penetrating the geological twilight of future ages.

Having combined the uncombinable, Dante altered the structure of time or, perhaps, to the contrary, he was forced to a glossolalia of facts, to a synchronism of events, names and traditions severed by centuries, precisely because he had heard the overtones of time.

Dante's method is anachronistic—and Homer, who emerges with his sword at his side in the company of Virgil, Horace and Lucan from the dim shadows of the Orphic choirs, where the four of them while away a tearless eternity together in literary discussion, is its best expression . . .

Indices of the standing still of time in Dante's work are not only the round astronomical bodies, but positively all things and all personalities. Everything mechanical is alien to him. He is disgusted by the idea of causality: such prophecies are suited only for bedding down swine.

Faccian le bestie Fiesolane strame
   Di lor medesme, e non tocchin la pianta,
   S'alcuna surge ancor nel lor letame . . .
                 (*Inf.* 15.73–75)

I would answer the direct question, "What is a Dantean metaphor?" saying, "I don't know," because a metaphor can be defined only metaphorically, and this can be substantiated scientifically. But it seems to me that Dante's metaphor designates the standing-still of time. Its roots are not to be found in the little word "how," but in the word "when." His *quando* sounds like *come*. Ovid's rumbling was far more congenial to him than Virgil's French elegance.

Again and again I find myself turning to the reader and begging him to "imagine" something; that is, I must invoke analogy, having in mind but a single goal: to fill in the deficiency of our system of definition.

Hence, just try to imagine that Patriarch Abraham and King David, the entire tribe of Israel including Isaac, Jacob, and all their kin, as well as Rachel, for whom Jacob endured so much, have entered a singing and roaring organ, as if it were a house with its door left ajar, and have concealed themselves within.

And, imagine that even earlier, our forefather Adam with his son Abel, old Noah, and Moses, the lawgiver and the law-abiding, had also entered . . .

> Trasseci l'ombra del primo parente,
>   D'Abèl suo figlio, e quella di Noè,
>   Di Moisè legista e ubbidente;
> Abraàm patriarca, e Davìd re,
>   Israèl con lo padre e co' suoi nati,
>   E con Rachele, per cui tanto fe' . . .
>   (*Inf.* 4.55–60)

Following this, the organ acquires the capacity to move—all its pipes and bellows become extraordinarily agitated, when suddenly, in a frenzied rage, it begins to move backwards.

If the halls of the Hermitage were suddenly to go mad, if the paintings of all the schools and great masters were suddenly to break loose from their nails, and merge with one another, intermingle and fill the air of the rooms with a Futurist roar and an agitated frenzy of color, we would then have something resembling Dante's *Commedia*.

To wrest Dante from the grip of schoolroom rhetoric would be to render a major service to the history of European culture. I hope that centuries of labor will not be required for this, but only joint international endeavors which will succeed in creating an original anti-commentary to the work of generations of scholastics, creeping philologists and pseudo-biographers. Insufficient respect for the poetic material which can be grasped only through performance, only through the flight of the conductor's baton—this was the reason for the universal blindness to Dante, to the greatest master and manager of this material, to the greatest conductor of European art, who forestalled for many centuries the formation of an orchestra adequate (to what?)—to the integral of the conductor's baton . . .

The calligraphic composition realized through means of improvisation—such, approximately, is the formula of a Dantean impulse, taken simultaneously as flight and as something finished. His similes are articulated impulses.

The most complex structural passages of the poem are performed on the fife, like a bird's mating call. The fife is nearly always sent forth to scout ahead.

Here I have in mind Dante's introductions, released by him as if at random, as if they were trial balloons.

> Quando si parte il gioco della zara,
>   Colui che perde si riman dolente,
>   Ripetendo le volte, e tristo impara;
> Con l'altro se ne va tutta la gente:
>   Qual vi dinanzi, e qual di retro il prende,
>   E qual da lato gli si reca a mente.
> Ei non s'arresta, e questo e quello intende;
>   A cui porge la man più non fa pressa;
>   E così dalla calca si difende.
>
> (*Purg.* 6.1–9)

When the dice game is ended, the loser in cheerless solitude replays the game, despondently throwing the dice. The whole group tags along after the lucky gambler; one runs up ahead, one pulls at him from behind, one curries favor at his side, reminding him of himself. But fortune's favor-

ite walks right on, listening to all alike, and with a hand-
shake for each, he frees himself from his importunate
followers . . .

And there goes the "street" song of the *Purgatorio* (with its
throngs of importunate Florentine souls demanding above all, gossip, secondly, protection, and thirdly, gossip again), enticed by the
call of the genre, resounding on the typical Flemish fife which,
only three hundred years hence, would become wall paintings.

Another curious consideration arises. The commentary (explanatory) is integral to the very structure of the *Commedia.* The
miracle-ship left the shipyard with barnacles adhering to its hull.
The commentary derives from street talk, from rumor, from
Florentine slander passing from mouth to mouth. The commentary is inevitable like the halcyon circling about Batyushkov's ship.

> . . . There now, look: it's old Marzzuco . . .
> How well he held up at his son's
> funeral! A remarkably staunch old man . . .
> But have you heard, Pietro de la
> Borgia's head was cut off for no
> reason whatsoever—he was as clean
> as a piece of glass . . .
> Some woman's evil hand was
> involved here . . . O yes, by the way,
> there he goes himself—let's go
> up and ask him . . .

Poetic material does not have a voice. It does not paint with
bright colors, nor does it explain itself in words. It is devoid of
form just as it is devoid of content for the simple reason that it exists only in performance. The finished poem is no more than a calligraphic product, the inevitable result of the impulse to perform.

If a pen is dipped in an inkwell, then the resultant thing is no more than a set of letters fully commensurate with the inkwell.

In talking about Dante it is more appropriate to bear in mind the creation of impulses than the creation of forms: impulses pertaining to textiles, sailing, scholasticism, meteorology, engineering, municipal concerns, handicrafts and industry, as well as other things; the list could be extended to infinity.

In other words, syntax confuses us. All nominative cases must be replaced by the case indicating direction, by the dative. This is the law of transmutable and convertible poetic material existing only in the impulse to perform.

. . . Here everything is turned inside out: the noun appears as the predicate and not the subject of the sentence. I should hope that in the future Dante scholarship will study the coordination of the impulse and the text.

(1933)

(Translated by Jane Gary Harris and Constance Link)

Eugenio Montale

Dante, Yesterday and Today

In a celebration like this one, to which illustrious individuals have contributed the weight or grace of their authority, he who is called to speak at the close is always received by the master of ceremonies with the ritual and consoling "last but not least." Which may be entirely justified in other circumstances; but for me, today, I don't feel it is necessary to gild the pill, for here before you I truly feel myself to be "last *and* least," last without extenuating circumstances.

And yet I am here, I have agreed to speak on this occasion, though I lacked the time and perhaps even the capacity to find something in myself which, in relating it to my own particular experience of Dante, could amount to something more than personal and therefore worthy of being reported and discussed here. It seemed to me, once my first bewilderment was over, that if Dante is a universal patrimony (beyond a certain level of necessary study)—and such he has become, even if he remarked more than once that he was speaking to few who were worthy of hearing him—then his voice can be heard today by everyone as it never was in other ages and as may never again be possible in the future, so that his message can reach the layman no less than the initiate, and in a way that is probably entirely new. After he was crowned with glory in his own lifetime, Dante's readership gradually declined up until the seventeenth century (his dark age), to dawn again with the advent of Romanticism and the simultaneous flowering of an entirely worldly philosophy which sees man as the master and even the creator of himself.

I am not unaware of the differences between these two movements, though I note their convergence. Romanticism looks to the ancient world for inspiration, not because it has renewed and emphasized its myths, but because it is dissatisfied with its own rationalist, enlightened age, and therefore it resolves into a poetic art. Materialism, which appears on the heels of Romanticism, not only accepts its own era but believes that it represents the highest phase in the total evolution of reason. The Gods are dead, even if they had to slake their thirst with human blood in the process, and the divine has come down to earth. Though they differ and are even opposed, these two movements both deserve to be called "modern," and for different reasons both look to Dante. For the first, Dante is a distant precursor of Romanticism and as such deserves to be rediscovered; for the second, his work is a miraculous product of poetic imagination, but this imagination is not Dante's wisdom, it is only one step and not the last, the *som de l'escalina*, of a Spirit which has not yet become conscious of itself.

Poetry, they have told us, is not reason and only reason can understand it and do it justice, but in the way the strongest does justice to the weakest. It would be unjust to reduce the eighteenth- and nineteenth-century understanding of Dante to this dichotomy. In fact, the nineteenth century saw the birth and early growth—not without some antecedents in the mid-1800s—of research by those who hope to raise the veil which obscures Dante's great creation and fully penetrate the mysteries of his allegory. In the nineteenth century the esoteric Dante is born or reborn, the Dante who even as an historical person (the most absurd hypotheses come to mind) was supposed to have had two faces, one of which remained virtually unknown: the Dante who was a Knight Templar or who enrolled as a Franciscan but then left the order before taking his vows, and above all the Dante who was supposed to have spoken a sectarian tongue that is only decipherable today, and only to the slightest extent, by those who have exhausted themselves in long and deep study. It is easy to criticize this particular aspect of modern Dantology (which in fact has been contested and rejected by a more modern philological and historical approach), but one must admit that apart from its pathological aspects it has the merit at least of having affirmed one great truth: that Dante is *not* a modern poet (a fact also recognized by modern critics and philosophers), and that the instruments of modern culture are not ideally suited to understanding him (a fact denied by the modern philosophers who believe themselves specially authorized to raise the veil). And how? By the extension of modern reasoning.

My conviction, however—and I state it for what it is worth—is that Dante is not a modern in any of these respects: which does not prevent us from understanding him at least partially, nor from feeling that he is strangely close to us. But for this to happen we must also come to another conclusion: that we no longer live in a modern era, but in a new Middle Ages whose characteristics we cannot yet make out. Since this is a personal conviction of mine, I shall refrain from discussing the reasons for it here, where it serves only as an hypothesis. The era which lies before us does not allow for short-term predictions, and to speak of a new Middle Ages is to speak equivocally at best. If the future sees the ultimate triumph of technico-scientific reason, even accompanied by the weak correctives which sociology can devise, the new Middle Ages will be nothing but a new barbarousness. But in such a case it would be wrong to speak of them as "medieval," for the Middle Ages were not merely barbarous, nor were they bereft of science or devoid of art. To speak of a new Middle Ages, then, could seem a far from pessimistic hypothesis to the man who does not believe that the thread of reason can unwind *ad infinitum*; and yet an entirely new barbarousness is possible, a stifling and distortion of the very idea of civilization and culture.

But I see that I must return to my argument and ask myself who was Dante, and what he can represent (and this is my theme) for a writer today: I don't say for a poet today, for compared with Dante there are no poets. The literary historians have asked themselves who Dante was and they have succeeded in sketching the outlines—though with many lacunae—of his existence on earth. Shakespeare, more fortunate than he, has so far covered his tracks. It is well known that Sidney Lee, after demonstrating that many of the themes and subjects of Shakespeare's sonnets belong to the *topoi* or commonplaces of the Renaissance sonnet, reached the conclusion that in the sonnets Shakespeare did not "unlock his heart" as Wordsworth believed but rather disclosed something very different. According to Lee, the only biographical inference which is deducible from them would be "that at one time in his career Shakespeare . . . disdained few weapons of flattery in an endeavour to monopolise the bountiful patronage of a young man of rank": the famous "onlie begetter" whose identity is disputed.[1]

Whether or not such a conclusion is just, it certainly fails to reveal the great poet of the tragedies. Not that unanswered questions do not hang over his life and part of his work; but modern criticism has managed to set them aside. Only his poetry exists. These are the conclusions of the new "close reading" which approaches poetry in a totally ahistorical manner. Dante's case is very different; his life and works are so closely associated that we shall never lose interest in the poet's biography. And there are many obscure points in Dante's life and work. The dates of his *rime estravaganti* [miscellaneous poems] have only been partially established; and not only poems, but also letters and until recently a treatise are disputed. Conversely, it may possibly be shown that he wrote the *Fiore*,[2] which until now has been attributed to Ser Durante. We do not know the year in which the first *cantica* of the *Commedia* was begun, nor do we know (apart from its uncertain beginning) when the poet started the actual drafting of the *Inferno* and the *Purgatorio*. We know only that for something like twenty years (some say fifteen) he dedicated himself, while also writing other works, to the composition of the *poema sacro*. There is also the question whether the *Vita Nuova* is known to us in a later version, which was necessary in order to connect that book to the poem, passing over the compromising second treatise of the *Convivio*. And certainly the questions do not end here. All this demonstrates that a reading of the poem, and naturally of the *rime*, which entirely neglects Dante's life, his background and education cannot take one very far. And yet an attempt to read him as one reads a modern poet, selecting the most vivid parts and leaving aside the rest—which is judged extraneous to the poetry—has given rise to strange complaints. De Sanctis seems to deplore the fact that too many medieval superstitions overshadowed the poet, impeding him from giving free rein to his characters. The conclusion of his analysis of the *Inferno* in his *History of Italian Literature* is well known: "these great figures, there on their pedestals, rigid and epic like statues, await the artist who will take them by the hand and toss them into the tumult of life and make them dramatic beings. And that artist was not an Italian: he was Shakespeare."

Dante, then, is more poet than artist. De Sanctis was very careful to distinguish between poetry and art, but he was never very sure of his distinction. This gave rise to misunderstandings which have lasted up until today. The truth is that if there was ever an artist in the fullest sense of the word, that artist is certainly Dante. But what was art for this Dante about whom we know so little, the first Dante? It was an art of convention, of tradition, the *ars dictandi* common to him and to those whom we can consider as his correspondents (the *stilnovisti* were not a *tertulia* [conversation club] and their precursor Guinizelli[3] died when Dante was ten). Within the limits of the school, the problem was not originality, but fidelity to one's Dictator. It was an accepted convention inherited from the Provençal troubadours that the poet was dictated to. But the poets of the *Dolce Stil Nuovo* adhere more closely to the Provençal theme and enclose it in a more perfect canon. Their language is the vulgate, but purified and therefore sweet. Guittone[4] can no longer serve as a model, he is considered rough and coarse. Dante starts from Guinizelli but simplifies and strengthens his style; he takes even more from the second Guido [Cavalcanti],[5] and the *Vita Nuova* cannot be understood at all if one does not recognize the presence within it of themes, contrasts, and "disruptions" from the poetry of his closest friend.

Nevertheless, there is also a new "style" in Dante, and consciously so. This should not surprise us. Always, at all times, poets have spoken to poets, entering into a real or imaginary correspondence with them. The poets of the new school pose problems, raise questions, expect answers in their poems. Contini has said that "the *Dolce Stile* is the school which with the greatest consciousness and good grace contains the idea of collaboration in a work of objective poetry"; and after analyzing the sonnet "Guido i' vorrei" in which he notes the theme of the flight to an unreal world, he adds: "The absolute separation from the real which is converted into friendship, this is the definitive emotional element in the *stil nuovo.*" The *donna salutifera*, the lady who heals and redeems, which is the most evident theme of the entire school, is lost in a chorus of friends, and the poet, insofar as he is an empirical individual, recedes. Naturally, the collection of *rime estravaganti* cannot be read as a *canzoniere* [a collection of thematically and/or stylistically related poems], nor as a collection of lyrics in the modern sense of the term. Although there is a great variety of tone in the so-called *canzoniere* and there are signs of an even greater technical restlessness, the fact remains that we cannot read this collection without recognizing it as the first step in a great poetic undertaking which will become conscious of itself in the *Vita Nuova* and which will continue through the doctrinal works to the three *cantiche* which posterity called divine and which Dante defined at two points in the *Inferno* as the *Commedia*.

Beatrice makes her first appearance in the *rime*, and some of the most famous *canzoni* and sonnets are dedicated to her; but it is also possible that the *donna gentile* whom we shall meet again in the *Vita Nuova* and in the *Convivio* and who has given Dante's hagiographers so much yarn to spin, appears along with her, in a group of poems composed between 1291 and 1293. And there are other ladies, other names which may be *senhals*:[6] the *pargoletta* [little girl] whom several readers identify with the *donna pietra* [lady of stone] and who in this group seems to have been the most dangerous for the poet, and later Fioretta, Violetta, Lisetta, Guido's lady, and still others, and finally the two *donne-schermo* [ladies who stand in for or screen us from Beatrice] whom we shall encounter in the *Vita Nuova*. And since the corpus of the *rime estravaganti* also included the poems inspired by the *donna pietra*, which are almost certainly later than the *Vita Nuova* and which indicate a familiarity with the *miglior fabbro*, Arnaut Daniel,[7] thus we see that the poems which will be fundamental in studying Dante's stylistic development and which will also influence Petrarch, as Ferdinando Neri has exhaustively shown, appear together in a rather unconvincing miscellany. It has been the fate of the *rime pietrose* to have been the source for "black" nineteenth-century Pre-Raphaelitism, which goes as far as Gustave Moreau in France; along with an entire school of English painting, the "white" variety includes considerable poetry, most notably "The Blessed Damozel" of Rossetti—a poet whom Eliot attacked. Perhaps *donna pietra* really did exist; insofar as she is a stylistic experiment, however, she will never coincide with a real lady. But if Dante had a precocious intuition of Beatrice's ultimate significance (and the *Vita Nuova* leaves little doubt of it), I would say that both *donna pietra* and the *donna gentile* would have had to be invented out of thin air if they did not exist; for it is impossible to imagine a process of salvation without the counterpart of error and sin.

After the research of Isidoro Del Lungo, which aroused great interest in 1891, one can no longer doubt the historic existence of a Bice or Beatrice whom Dante could certainly have known and loved, even without her having been aware of it. But what significance can this discovery have? There are two hypotheses: either the meaning which Dante attributed to her has no relation whatsoever to her actual existence; or one can believe, as Pietrobono came to, that the miraculous lady not only lived but was an actual miracle. For those who believe as I do that the miraculous may always be lying in wait at our doorstep, and that our very existence is a miracle, Pietrobono's thesis cannot be refuted by rational argument.

Dante's last years in Florence before his exile saw the composition of the *Vita Nuova*, which narrates in prose and verse the history of his love for Beatrice. We know about her that her short life and her death, as well as her apparition to the poet, took place under the sign of the number nine, and her own name appears nine times in the book. Fate has protected this mysterious girl and prevented many facts of her life from coming down to us: thus she can remain as the image of absolute perfection and the necessary intermediary in Dante's ascent to God. For a modern reader, the realization that the poet has mounted the tiger and can no longer get down begins with the *Vita Nuova*. At this point his destiny is definitively marked. One cannot speak of the *Vita Nuova* without forgetting that it would occupy an intermediate position in the *rime* if it were possible to place the poems in chronological order. Apart from the *rime pietrose*, the *estravaganti* include *canzoni* and *rime* in various forms which were written after the *Vita Nuova* and certainly after the period of inner darkness and distraction which Dante suffered following the death of Beatrice—a period of thirty months during which the poet immersed himself in the study of Boethius and Cicero and completed his reading of the classics (the *litterati poete*, i.e., the great Latin poets) and of Thomist philosophy.

The *Vita Nuova* thus comes at the time of an extraordinarily receptive and digressive poetic experience and gives a preliminary shape, already complete in itself, to what will become Beatrice's process of transhumanization. It does so in a form that would be called narrative today, if the term were appropriate, in which verse compositions alternate with others in prose, according to a scheme that Dante did not invent, narrating from beginning to end the history of Dante's love for the *donna salutifera*. The story, which is better called a vision, also dwells on details which seem realistic today but are included to give form to the conflict between human spirits and transcendent vocation that is defined here as never before in Dante. We shall never know whether the poet, who begins here to reveal himself as protagonist-author (which is apparent from the choice of poems included and even more from the prose commentary), also wished simultaneously both to hide and reveal the names of two ladies well known to his circle of friends in the episodes of the two *donne-schermo*. The problem is to know how deeply the playful spirit of mystification insinuated itself into the texture of his serious poetry. An analogous problem arises with the apparition of the *donna gentile*, who will be a rival here, if such she can be called, of Beatrice, and whom we shall later find transfigured as Philosophy in the *Convivio*, with no apparent reference to the significance which Beatrice assumed in the *Vita Nuova* and which she will take on again in the *poema sacro*. I shall pass over other episodes where the book steps out of its frame of mystical-intellectual adventure and becomes the material for a secular story. Perhaps this great technician of poetry invented these episodes to give greater emphasis to the last pages, with their blood-red color, which will become the color of the entire book in our memories. Certainly one does not err in seeing a distant prefiguration of the *Commedia* in the *Vita Nuova*, which is also indicated by the poet's desire to speak of her—of Beatrice—elsewhere. And the fact that the little book was composed with a great deal of rigor, excluding poems that would have been repetitious and others that would have been extraneous to its general design, only confirms one's sense of the work: that its structure is already determined, but is still in a certain sense preliminary. Perhaps readers who do not see a mystical experience in the *Vita Nuova* are correct. In it worldly experience is recreated as Christian experience; but it is not structured in steps as an ascent, but in a story set entirely within the worldly sphere (as D. De Robertis puts it).

But we have now arrived at the period of the poet's exile, which coincides with the beginning of the two treatises, the serving up of the high rhetoric of the *Convivio* and the *De vulgari eloquentia*, both of them left unfinished; and a similar parallelism will prevent us from creating a sort of psychological itinerary as we follow Dante. It was the opinion of Ferretti, confirmed by numerous internal and external indications, that the first seven *canti* of the *Inferno* were written before Dante's exile, hidden by the poet, and sent to him "four and more years later," according to events referred to by Boccaccio.[8] If Parodi is correct in his conjecture identifying Henry of Luxembourg as the 515 [DVX] (in which number the Jesuits saw Luther and the Reformation), it seems possible to claim that the composition of the *Inferno* and the *Purgatorio* should be placed between 1307 and 1312: while it is almost certain that the *Paradiso* occupied the poet's last years. Several scholars assign the commencement of the poem to 1313. Others (including Barbi) propose intermediate dates. The question of dating, however, is not merely academic, as is the problem of the *donne* to which I have alluded above. It involves affirming or denying the possibility that Dante submitted his work to revision and to later re-elaboration. Modern readers are undecided on this issue. On the one hand, we have the impression that many episodes in the *Commedia* were written at a single sitting, with little reworking, thus giving rise to the great prose that is hidden in the texture of the rhythm and rhyme, which, if it had been understood and brought to fulfillment, would have spared us centuries of curial, ceremonious prose. (An impossible hypothesis because the involuntary lofty prose of the poem did not prevent Dante from writing prose in Latin, which was also remarkable.) On the other hand, if we consider all the contributions which the rhetorical, philosophical, and theological culture of the Latin Middle Ages made to the poem and which make it virtually impossible to read its immense theophany in an ingenuous, virginal manner, we are stunned by Dante's encyclopedism and constrained to doubt our initial impression that he could have written at a gallop. That Dante knew and practiced the *labor limae*,[9] as Foscolo believed, seems undeniable to those who know the *rime pietrose*, the doctrinal *canzoni*, and the passages in the *Commedia* where he returns to the play of harsh and difficult rhymes. And yet there is no doubt that the conception of his poem, its very structure, had not been predetermined from its first line, but rather modified and enriched itself as it developed, though at the cost of evident contradictions in the course of its elaboration and of its hypothetical revision. Along with Dante the scholar, the learned poet, whom after the studies of Curtius and Auerbach we can no longer ignore, there is Dante the man of letters discovering and exploiting the possibilities of his new language, the man who turns inward and enriches his thought, the exile who hopes to be allowed back into his own country and who later, disillusioned, intensifies the expression of his rancor. Because of this, internal proofs and references are not always decisive in aligning the life and the poetry. The *Convivio*, the treatise which was supposed to have fifteen parts, only four of which were completed, is the work of a theoretician who wants to demonstrate to himself and to his patrons what he had learned in his study of grammar and to derive as far as possible from it the limits of a poetry written in the vernacular. It includes commentaries on three doctrinal *canzoni*, and there are indications that lead us to conjecture which two or three additional *canzoni* would have gone along with the others to make up the fifteen parts the poet planned. His use of the vernacular, on the other hand, is illustrated in the *De vulgari eloquentia*, a treatise planned as a sort of encyclopedia of linguistic science. The *De vulgari* is written in Latin because Dante believed that only Latin, the universal and eternal language, could master an argument which involves the developments of human language up to the "three-forked tongue" after the fall of man (the tower of Babel) had forever confused and corrupted the primitive language of men.

But my chosen subject, Dante's poetry for a writer of our time, forces me to leave behind his doctrinal works, the two I have mentioned, the *Monarchia*, which should be assigned a later date, and the *Quaestio de aqua e terra*, which is extraneous to my subject. Let me simply say that in respect to *gramatica* [Latin], to the *litterati poete*, Dante always had what today would be called an inferiority complex. He defended his choice to the last, but he made use of Latin as if to underline the exceptional nature of his undertaking; and if after him the vernacular won the field in the areas in which the *sermone umile* was called for, no other great early poet made use of it in approaching the subject matter of the sublime style, the epic.

And now I find myself face to face with the *Commedia*, which in certain respects could be considered an epic poem, but differs substantially in others. Indeed, the *Commedia* does have an heroic protagonist, and sings his adventures, not without the aid and presence of the Muses and the Sacred Scriptures; but to do this Dante employs a style which is not always tragic but is in fact an extraordinary mixture of styles and manners which certainly do not conform to the dignity and uniformity of the epic style. In the dedicatory epistle of the *Paradiso* addressed to Can Grande della Scala, the Poet explains that his method is poetic, fictive, descriptive, digressive, transumptive, and at the same time definitive, divisive, probative, reprobative, and exemplative. (We can imagine Can Grande's surprise if Dante wished, as we assume, to overwhelm him.)

Furthermore, here too, as previously in the *Vita Nuova*, but with many further complications (and these are poetically the richest of all), the protagonist-hero, protagonist of an undertaking which had up to now been reserved for Aeneas and St. Paul, is the writer himself, the Poet, accompanied of course by Virgil. Hence the poem's continual countersong, the possibility of reading it as a narrative which unfolds on only one level, and the temptation—even the necessity—to see it in filigree—not forgetting the significance of the journey beyond the tomb and into the nine heavens, or the reactions of the man either, his feelings and resentments, and the paradox of a double vision which on one side gives on the landscape of eternity and on the other describes earthly events which occupy a few years' time and one fixed place: the life of the city of Florence and what transpired there during the years of the poet's tenure of public office, and the part which the character Dante played in those events. And the fact that the journey into the beyond takes up at most seven days, though the canvas of the poem must extend to 100 cantos (the perfect number), is the reason for the extraordinary diversity of the figures who appear in the three *cantiche* and for the stroke of genius (as Curtius says) of introducing persons still living at the time of Dante's journey, friends and enemies of the poet, next to heroes or villains out of myth or ancient history or the history of the Church, with its blessed, its saints and angels (who are certainly not the last in the exalted hierarchies of the heavens and the general structure of the poem). What unifies material of this sort? First of all, the allegorical sense of the poem, which is extremely clear in its general outlines but vague in many particulars and thus not dense enough to hold together all the episodes of the narrative, in which the allegorical veil is often dropped and only the symbols are allowed to emerge, not all of them transparent. Here our insufficient familiarity with Dante the man and with his ideal library creates obstacles which would seem insurmountable. That Dante was at once a profound theologian and a particularly learned philosopher is not an opinion with which everyone will concur. That he was a mystic—

he who was so rational and so taken with the events and concerns of life on earth—has itself been disputed. A great reader and a great observer, he is supposed to have derived his theological ideas not only from St. Thomas but from other sources which he often misinterpreted. He even made use of the heretic Siger de Brabant and then reserved a place for him in Paradise. But even if this were true (and I am not competent to decide it), how useful to us can his allegory be? Yet there is a primary unity to the poem—which is sufficient because it has created countless readers of Dante all over the world who are happy with his literal meaning and pass over or are in fact ignorant of the allegorical and anagogical significance of various episodes—an undeniable unity afforded by the concreteness of Dante's images and similes and by the poet's capacity to make the abstract sensible, to make even the immaterial corporeal. It is a quality we encounter also in the English metaphysical poets of the seventeenth century, including mystics who did not read Dante or could not read him in his own language. So that one is permitted to question the opinion that questions the poet's mysticism.

But let us return for a moment to the possibility of sticking close to Dante's merely literal meaning and of reading him in the light of a poetic art that was not his. When I was young and had just begun my reading of Dante, a great Italian philosopher[10] admonished me to be attentive to the letter alone, and to ignore every obscure gloss. In Dante's poem, the philosopher said, there is a structure, a framework, which does not belong to the world of his poetry but has a practical function of its own. This framework is constructed with the materials which Dante found in his time and which permitted prefabricated structures: theological, physical, astronomical, prophetical, legendary materials which no longer resonate for us. These show us the medieval man in Dante, the man ensnared in prejudices which were not always different from the knowledge of his day, but which are certainly toneless, devoid of meaning for modern man. But over the inert scaffolding trails an efflorescence of bluebells or other vegetation which is Dante's poetry, poetry outside time as all true poetry is, and such that it makes us welcome Dante into the pantheon of the greatest poets if not precisely into the heaven of the great seers. This is a view which has found wide acceptance in Italy and will do so in the future as well: but it leaves unexplained the fact that the poem contains an enormous number of correspondences, of references which the literal arouses, while sending us back to its echoes, its mirror-games, its refractions; and that there is hardly a place in the poem—not one episode or line—which is not part of some web, which does not make its presence felt even when its totality appears to us to be more of an attempt at emulating divine wisdom than a universe in which we can dwell without asking for anything else. No poem was ever so crowded with figures, in the literal sense and in the sense of prefiguration or prophecy; in no other poem have actual history and the a-temporal history of myth or theology been so closely fused. Dante is really the end of the world or its anticipation: in historical terms, his prophecy is not of this world, and the symbols of the Cross and Eagle had already fallen into disuse before the *Commedia* was completed. But Dante was summing up, he was bringing an epoch to a close, and he needed many different threads.

Auerbach has shown us that the multiplicity of created things was necessary to Dante because no one of them *in una species* can achieve a total resemblance to God; adding that such multiplicity does not conflict with perfection and is not immobility but movement. He has also asked whether we can read Dante and accept forms and premises which are unrelated to us, as one submits to the rules of a game, and if perhaps there is the possibility in the *Commedia* of metamorphosis without loss of character. "It seems to me," Auerbach concluded, that the limit of the poem's power of transformation "has almost been attained when philosophical commentators begin to praise its so-called poetic beauties as a value in themselves and reject the system, the doctrine, and indeed the entire subject matter as irrelevancies which if anything call for a certain indulgence."[11] Certainly the limit is reached by philosophical commentators (though not by all of them, thank heaven), but it has proved unreachable for those endowed with a different sort of competence. In fact, anyone who has a feeling for poetry soon realizes that Dante never loses his concreteness even where his structure is least clothed by his so-called efflorescence. Thus one could say that his technical virtuosity reaches the height of its possibilities when plastic, visual representation is no longer sufficient. Look for example at the canto of Folchetto da Marsiglia (*Par.* 9) in which the musical theme of the characters is anticipated by a return of rough, difficult rhymes, which remain constant throughout the canto. There is nothing in effects like these to make us think of a formal game, of the skill of a Parnassian of the period. And here only a deaf man could try to distinguish between art and poetry. Dante doesn't write poems to make an impression according to the rules of a literary genre or school. The school is partly our invention, even if the poets of the *Dolce Stile* did in fact belong to an ideal community. Bonagiunta[12] can reprove the first Guido [Guinizelli] for having departed from the style of his predecessors, but Dante's verse would have been little different even if he had had other masters. His voice is entirely his own from the outset, even if he vulgarizes it in a noted *tenzone* or amuses himself in marginal exercises or agrees to write a few poems "on commission," thus giving future scholiasts something to write about; and there is no doubt that after the allegorical *canzoni* of the *Convivio* the poet's life has been well documented, and it is not the life of a man who aims at rhapsodic lyrical splendors. And if not everyone will accept the hypothesis that the poem's possibilities of transformation (or rather our capacity of understanding it) are virtually exhausted, it will be necessary to see what other literary hypotheses can give us a satisfactory reading.

While the allegorists have kept on desperately marking time—though not in every case—a method of reading which is still acceptable is that suggested by a modern poet, T. S. Eliot, in his essay of 1929. The poet hardly knew our language when he started reading the *Commedia*. And he found it an easy introduction. He thought that Dante's vernacular was still closely related to medieval Latin and that therefore a reading of the poem aided by a good literal version provided a first and sufficient approach. Further, in his view the allegorical process creates the necessary condition for the growth of that sensuous, bodily imagination which is peculiar to Dante. In short, the metaphorical meanings demand an extremely concrete literal meaning. Thus, from the still-massive figures of the *Inferno* (those figures which to the reluctant Goethe seemed to reek of the stable) to the more modeled figures of the *Purgatorio*, to the luminous, immaterial apparitions of the *Paradiso*, the evidence of the images may change in its colors and forms but remains forever accessible to our senses. The complexity of the embroidery never changes. Words like "carpet" and "tapestry" reoccur in this brief essay. In the *Paradiso* even abstraction is visible, and the most abstruse concept is inseparable from its form. And if in the carpet of the third *cantica* the plastic relief is less pronounced, this does not signify a lesser concreteness of imagination, but merely reveals the inexhaustible complexity of the meanings, and at the same time their ineffability. Our world no longer experiences visions, but Dante's world is still that of a visionary. Dante creates objects by naming them, and his syntheses are flashes of lightning. This is the source of his peculiar classicism, which is linked to a creationist and finalist philosophy. Through the narrow channel of the sensible, through the exaltation of forms, Dante negotiates the straits of scholastic thought; but let the experts discuss that. Eliot, however, doesn't mention it; instead he discusses the religious thought, or rather the faith, which the allegory supports. Is it necessary for the reader to share the "Belief," the faith of the poet? For Eliot it is only necessary for belief to be understood as a function of the poetry which it explains. This is a suspension of judgment which belongs to aesthetic experience, and it is the

typical mode of certain Anglo-Saxon culture to grant a certain
autonomy to art while denying the distinctions between the aesthetic and the conceptual proposed by idealistic philosophy. No
less interesting in Eliot is his rejection of that late falsification
of the stilnovistic world which we have already mentioned: Pre-
Raphaelitism. Yet even he, as we shall see before we finish, has felt
the stilnovistic temptation from time to time.

   I am not familiar with all the attempts which undoubtedly
have been made to supersede Eliot's theory of Dante's sensible
imagination. Setting aside the security that one who can explicate
the allegory in its entirety must feel, the most interesting inter-
preters are those who see the *Commedia* as an immense web of
correspondences and who try to follow every strand—or rather
certain strands—back to its center. The undertaking cannot be accomplished without an analysis of Dante's metaphors and an examination of the consistency of the situations and characters with
the particular psychological-moral and even topical states or levels
through which the poet must pass. And, as metaphors are not as
frequent in Dante as Eliot would have us believe, and in fact become increasingly rare as the poem progresses, we thus reach a
limit or an insufficiency in Eliot's proposed reading of the *Commedia*. Irma Brandeis has devoted herself to an analytic study in the
sense I have indicated—though certainly not an exhaustive one,
for that would require the labors of a generation of scholars—in
her book *The Ladder of Vision* (1961),[13] which is the most suggestive study I have read on the theme of the stairway which leads to
God, and which is entrusted for good reason to the patronage of
St. Bonaventura. "Since, then, one must climb Jacob's ladder before
descending it, let us place the first step of the ascent far down,
putting the whole of this sensible world before us as if it were a
mirror through which we may pass to reach God." Ladder or mirror, or mirrored ladder? I confess I don't know, for I have never
read St. Bonaventura, who sooner or later was certainly part of
Dante's library. What is clear is that for this new interpreter Dante

is an apprentice who must "undergo an immense schooling," i.e., complete his initiation into an immense patrimony of universal culture. And the entire poem is didactic, in a certain sense, because his instruction—which was equated with philosophy—was considered an integral part of the poetic work. In this way alone shall we be able to understand passages in Dante like Statius's discourse on the generations of men (*Purg.* 25.29–108), for Dante's point of view cannot coincide with the reader's, or rather the reader cannot expect that the poet is going another way, by other means.

And I would say that in general, once he has passed the stage where he is content with an ingenuous reading, the reader's interest grows rather than diminishes as the tangle of symbols becomes more problematic. This does not mean that one should ignore the literal meaning, which is primary in Dante. Precisely by basing her case on the literal, Miss Brandeis makes us feel how vivid and concrete the presence of Beatrice is throughout the poem and how the passages from the *Song of Songs*, St. Matthew, and the sixth book of the *Aeneid* are structurally necessary in order to make possible—and, I would add, credible—the apparition of the lady dressed in the three colors of faith, hope, and charity who can arouse the poet who has not forgotten his earthly love, and make him say to Virgil: "Men che dramma / dì sangue me'è rimaso che non tremi: / conosco i segni dell 'antica fiamma" (*Purg.* 30.46–48).[14]

It is late, and it is time now for me to ask, not of my audience but above all of myself: what does the work of Dante mean for a poet today? Is there a lesson, an inheritance which we can take from him? If we consider the *Commedia* as a *summa* and an encyclopedia of wisdom, the temptation to repeat and emulate the prodigy will always be irresistible; but the conditions for success no longer exist.

Dante brought the Middle Ages to a close; after him—once the *Monarchia* was burned in 1329 at Bologna and the wind had changed—the Frezzis and Palmieris[15] will certainly not win our attention. The chivalric poems of the sixteenth century are great works of art, but their encyclopedism does not engage man's deepest thinking. I can also pass over Milton, who is already neoclassic. In the one poem Byron left us which we can still read, his *Don Juan*, the irony and the sense of pastiche produce octaves of a vaguely "Italian" inspiration. I haven't forgotten *Faust*; but the Enlightenment esoterism that pervades it (to what extent I don't know) makes its protagonist and his pact with the Devil a story of greater interest to the anthropologist and the mythologist than the habitué of Dante's Middle Ages. Shelley and Novalis[16] were certainly among the Romantics who knew Dante, but were more musicians than architects. In our time, I would not think of Daübler's[17] *Das Nordlicht*, which is written in *terza rima* but brings down the light from the North; nor of *Ulysses*, which borrows themes from the *Odyssey* against the background of an infernal, almost symbolic Ireland. But Joyce doesn't look to Dante, nor does he have his monumental formal simplicity: reading him demands philological erudition, but the writer does not create language, he destroys it. On the other hand, the hundred and more *Cantos* of Ezra Pound give evidence of an attempt to "put one's hand" to a total poem of man's historical experience—but Pound did not try to imitate the symmetry and the rigorous structure of the *Commedia*. The *Cantos* contain all that can be known about a disintegrating world, and in them the sense of the "carpet" dominates that of a structure, of moving toward a center. (Though if it were true that the ultimate message of Dante's poem was the so-called donation of Constantine, then perhaps we could find a parallel in Pound's usury theme.) To sum up, it does not seem possible, in a world where encyclopedism can no longer create a universe but only an immense amassing of notions of a provisional character, to repeat Dante's itinerary in a highly structured form and with an inexhaustible wealth of both obvious and occult meanings. Even the illusion that a sensual imagination can give life in an acceptable manner to a Pre-Raphaelite tapestry is to be accepted with reservations. To convince ourselves of this, let us reread a few lines from Eliot's *Ash-Wednesday*:

> Lady, three white leopards sat under a juniper-tree
> In the cool of the day, having fed to satiety
> On my legs my heart my liver and that which had been
>   contained
> In the hollow round of my skull. And God said
> Shall these bones live? shall these
> Bones live? and that which had been contained
> In the bones (which were already dry) said chirping:
> Because of the goodness of this Lady
> And because of her loveliness, and because
> She honours the Virgin in meditation,
> We shine with brightness.

At moments like these we find ourselves face to face with the work of a poet, a great poet of our times: though if we had to choose, we should prefer the highly concentrated post-symbolist and quasicubist Inferno of *The Waste Land*. But it's useless to search for other examples: Dante cannot be repeated. He was considered practically incomprehensible and semi-barbarous a few decades after his death, when the rhetorical and religious invention of a poetry dictated by love had been forgotten. The greatest exemplar of poetic objectivism and rationalism, he remains foreign to our times, to a subjective and fundamentally irrational culture, which bases its meanings on facts and not on ideas. And it is precisely the reason for facts which eludes us today. A concentric poet, Dante cannot furnish models for a world which is progressively distancing itself from the center, and declares itself in perpetual expansion. For this reason the *Commedia* is and will remain the last miracle of world poetry. It was such because it was still possible then for an inspired man, or rather for a particular conjunction of stars in the sky of poetry, or must we consider it a miraculous event, beyond the humanly possible? Around Dante every opinion, indeed every suspicion, revolves. In opposition to those who claim that he really saw the *visibilia* in his poems (and they are few) are others who emphasize the mystificatory nature of his genius. To them, Dante would have been a man who invented himself as *poeta sacro* and at a certain moment, with the help of forces greater than himself, saw his invention become reality. That he was not a true mystic and that he lacked the total absorption in the divine which is characteristic of true mystics is suggested by the fact that the *Commedia* is not the last thing he wrote and that once he had finished the third *cantica*, he was obliged to come out of his labyrinth and rejoin his fellow men. But not for long; and an aging Dante present at the creation of his controversial legend is unimaginable for us. Still, I can consider Singleton's affirmation that the *poema sacro* was dictated by God and that the poet was only his scribe with equanimity. But I can only cite secondhand and I wonder whether that eminent Dantist meant his judgment literally, or whether here one should recall the inspired and thus received character of all great poetry. But even in the first case I would not object, and I would have no evidence to contest the miraculous nature of the poem, just as I was not frightened by the miraculous character attributed to the historical Beatrice we had thought we could do without.

But I will stop here. That true poetry is always in the nature of a gift, and that it therefore presupposes the dignity of its recipient, is perhaps the greatest lesson Dante has left us. He is not the only one to have taught us this, but he is certainly the greatest of all. And if it is true that he wanted to be a poet and only a poet, the fact remains, almost inexplicable to our modern blindness, that the more distant from us his world becomes, the greater grows our desire to know him and to make him known to those who are blinder than ourselves.

(1965)
(Translated by Jonathan Galassi)

Notes

1. Sidney Lee, *A Life of William Shakespeare*, revised edition (London: Smith, Elder & Co., 1915), p. 230.

2. An allegorical poem of 232 sonnets written between 1280 and 1310 in imitation of the *Romance of the Rose*. Ser Durante is the possibly symbolic name (*durante* = persevering, constant) of the author of the *Fiore*. The poem has been attributed to Dante da Maiano, an imitator of the Provençal poets and poetic correspondent of Dante's, and also to Dante Alighieri himself.

3. Guido Guinizelli (1230/40–1276). Bolognese Ghibelline poet and forerunner of Dante, originator of the *Dolce Stil Nuovo* [sweet new style]. Originally a follower of Guittone d'Arezzo (see below).

4. Guittone d'Arezzo (1220–94). Leading poet of the generation preceding Dante's, he wrote in the Provençal-influenced style of the Sicilian school.

5. (1255–1300). Florentine Guelph poet, leader of the *Stilnovisti*, friend of Dante.

6. *Senhal*: Provençal term related to the Italian word *segnale* [signal] to refer to the fictitious name designating the person to whom the troubadour addressed his poem.

7. (1150–?). Provençal troubadour, inventor of the sestina and leading practitioner of the *trobar ric*, or rich style, which advocated intense condensation of style.

8. Giovanni Boccaccio (1313–75). The great writer's works included the first biography of Dante, as well as a commentary on the *Inferno*, based on the lectures on Dante he began giving in Florence in 1373.

9. "Revision." See Horace, *Ars poetica*, line 291.

10. Croce.

11. Erich Auerbach, *Dante, Poet of the Secular World* [1929], tr. Ralph Manheim (Chicago: University of Chicago Press, 1961). The quotation on transformation appears on p. 159 of Auerbach's text.

12. Bonagiunta Orbicciani, also di Lucca. Thirteenth-century notary, leader of a school of poets influenced by the Sicilian school and Guittone d'Arezzo. Dante criticizes him in the *De vulgari eloquentia*, and he appears in *Purgatorio* 24.

13. Brandeis, *The Ladder of Vision: A Study of Dante's Comedy* (Garden City, N.Y.: Doubleday and Co., 1961).

14. Less than a drop / of my blood remains which does not tremble: / I know the signs of the ancient flame.

15. Federico Frezzi (1346–1416?). Poet from Foligno, author of the allegorical poem *Il Quadriregio*, written in imitation of the *Divine Comedy*. Matteo

Palmieri (1406–75): Florentine politician and writer, author of *La città divina* (1461–65), poem in tercets imitative of Dante.

16. Pen name of Friedrich Leopold von Hardenberg (1772–1801), great German romantic poet.

17. Theodor Daübler (1876–1934). Expressionist German poet born in Trieste and educated in Italy. His *Das Nordlicht* (1910) is a long religious allegory, showing the author's progress from agnosticism to mystical religion.

Jorge Luis Borges

The Divine Comedy

Paul Claudel has written—in a page unworthy of Paul Claudel—that the spectacles awaiting us after death will no doubt little resemble those that Dante showed us in the *Inferno*, the *Purgatorio*, and the *Paradiso*.

This curious remark is a proof of the intensity of Dante's text: the fact that while reading the poem, or remembering it later, we tend to believe that Dante imagined the other world exactly as he presented it. We inevitably assume that Dante believed that after death he would encounter the inverted mountain of Hell or the terraces of Purgatory or the concentric heavens of Paradise. Moreover, he would speak with shades—shades of classical Antiquity—and some of them would reply in Italian tercets.

This is, of course, absurd. Claudel's observation corresponds not to reason—for to rationalize it is to realize it's absurd—but rather to a sentiment, and one which could isolate us from the pleasure, the intense pleasure, of reading the work.

There is a great deal of evidence that refutes this. One is a statement attributed to Dante's son. He said that his father had proposed to show the life of sinners through the image of Hell, the life of penitents through the image of Purgatory, and the life of the just through the image of Paradise. He did not read it in a literal way. We have, moreover, Dante's own testimony, in the epistle to Can Grande della Scala.

The epistle has been considered apocryphal, but it could not have been written much later than Dante. Whoever wrote it, it is believable as a product of its time. In it, the author affirms that the *Commedia* may be read four ways: literal, moral, anagogical, and allegorical. Dante, then, would be the symbol of man, Beatrice of faith, and Virgil of reason.

The idea of a text capable of multiple readings is characteristic of the Middle Ages, those maligned and complex Middle Ages that gave us Gothic architecture, the Icelandic sagas, and the Scholastic philosophy in which everything was discussed. That gave us, above all, the *Commedia*, which we continue to read, and which continues to astonish us; which will last beyond our lives, far beyond our waking lives, and will be enriched by each generation of readers.

Dante never presumed that what he was showing us corresponded to a real image of the world of death. Nothing of the kind. Dante could not possibly have thought that.

I believe, nevertheless, in the usefulness of that ingenious concept: the idea that what we are reading is a true story. It serves to carry us away. Personally, I am a hedonistic reader; I have never read a book merely because it was ancient. I read books for the aesthetic emotions they offer me, and I ignore the commentaries and criticism. When I first read the *Commedia*, I was carried away. I read it as I had read other, less famous works. I would like to tell you—since we are among friends, and since I am talking not to all of you, but rather with each one of you—the story of my personal involvement with the *Commedia*.

It all began shortly before the dictatorship. I was employed in a library in the Almagro section of Buenos Aires. I lived at Las Heras and Pueyrredón, and I had to travel by slow and solitary streetcars all the way from the north side of town to Almagro South, to the library at Avenida La Plata and Carlos Calvo. Chance—except that there is no chance; what we call chance is our ignorance of the complex machinery of causality—led me to discover three small volumes in the Mitchell Bookstore (now gone—it brings back many memories). Those three volumes—I should have brought one with me, as a talisman—were the *Inferno*, the *Purgatorio*, and the *Paradiso*, in the English version by Carlyle (not Thomas Carlyle). They were very handy books, published by Dent. They fit into my pocket. On the left was the Italian text, and on the right a literal translation. I devised this modus operandi: I first read a verse, a tercet, in the English prose; then I read the verse in Italian; and so on through to the end of the canto. Then I read the whole canto in English, and finally in Italian. With that first reading I realized that the translations were no substitute for the original text. The translation could be, at best, a means and a stimulus for the reader to approach the original. This was especially true for a Spanish reader. I think that Cervantes, somewhere in *Don Quixote*, says that with two cents of the Tuscan language one can understand Ariosto.

Well, those two cents were given to me by the semantic brotherhood of Spanish and Italian. I observed at the time that poetry, above all the great poetry of Dante, is much more than what it says. Poetry is, among so many other things, an intonation, an accentuation that is often untranslatable. I saw this from the beginning. When I reached the peak of Purgatory, when I reached the deserted Paradise, there, at that moment in which Dante is abandoned by Virgil and he finds himself alone and calls out to him, at that moment I felt I could read the Italian text directly, only occasionally looking at the English. So I read the three volumes on those slow streetcar rides. Later I read other editions.

I have read the *Commedia* many times. The truth is that I don't know Italian. I only know the Italian Dante taught me, and later Ariosto, when I read *Orlando Furioso*. And then the simpler parts of Croce. I have read almost all of Croce, and though I am not always in agreement with him, I am enchanted by him. Enchantment, as

Stevenson said, is one of the special qualities a writer must have. Without enchantment, the rest is useless.

I have read the *Commedia* many times, in all of the editions I could find, and I have been distracted by the different commentaries, the varied interpretations of that multifaceted work. (Of all the editions, three in particular are noteworthy: those by Attilio Momigliano, Carlo Grabher, and Hugo Steiner.) I have found that in the oldest editions theological commentary predominates; in the nineteenth century, historical; and currently, aesthetic, which directs us toward the accentuation of each line, one of the great virtues of Dante.

I have compared Dante to Milton, but Milton has only one music: what they call in English a "sublime style." That music is always the same, regardless of the emotions of the characters. In Dante, however, as in Shakespeare, the music corresponds to the emotions. Intonation and accentuation are foremost; each phrase must be read aloud.

Truly fine poetry must be read aloud. A good poem does not allow itself to be read in a low voice or silently. If we can read it silently, it is not a valid poem: a poem demands pronunciation. Poetry always remembers that it was an oral art before it was a written art. It remembers that it was first song.

There are two lines which confirm this. One is in Homer—or the Greeks whom we call Homer—where he says, in the *Odyssey*, "The gods weave misfortunes for men, so that the generations to come will have something to sing about." The other, much later, is from Mallarmé, who repeats, less beautifully, what Homer said: "tout aboutit en un livre," everything ends up in a book. The Greeks speak of generations that will sing; Mallarmé speaks of an object, of a thing among things, a book. But the idea is the same: the idea that we are made for art, we are made for memory, we are made for poetry, or perhaps we are made for oblivion. But something remains, and that something is history or poetry, which are not essentially different.

Carlyle and other critics have observed that the most notable characteristic of Dante is intensity. If we think of the hundred cantos of the poem, it seems a miracle that that intensity never lets up, except in a few places in the *Paradiso* which for the poet were light and for us are shadow. I can't think of another example, except perhaps *Macbeth*, which begins with the three witches and continues to the death of the hero without a weak moment.

I would like to mention another aspect: the gentleness of Dante. We always think of the somber and sententious Florentine poem, and we forget that the work is full of delights, of pleasures, of tenderness. That tenderness is part of the structure of the work. For example, Dante must have read somewhere that the cube is the most solid of volumes. It was a current, unpoetical observation, and yet Dante used it as a metaphor for man, who must support misfortune: "ben tetragono ai colpi di fortuna," man is a good tetragon, a cube. That is truly rare.

I'd also like to recall the curious metaphor of the arrow. Dante wants to make us feel the speed of the arrow as it leaves the bow and hits the target. He tells us that it is fixed in the target, that it shoots from the bow, and leaves the string. He inverts the beginning and end to show how quickly this has occurred.

There is a verse that is always in my memory. It is the one in the first canto of the *Purgatorio* where he refers to that morning, that incredible morning on the mountain of Purgatory, at the South Pole. Dante, who has left the filth, the sadness, and the horror of Hell, says, "dolce color d'oriental zaffiro." The lines impose that slowness on the voice:

Dolce color d'oriental zaffiro
    che s'accoglieva nel sereno aspetto
    del mezzo puro infino al primo giro.

I would like to linger over the curious mechanism of this verse—but the word *mechanism* is too harsh for what I want to say.

Dante describes the Eastern sky, describes the dawn, and compares the color of the dawn to a sapphire. He compares it to a sapphire called *Oriental sapphire*, a sapphire of the East. The line is a game of mirrors, since the Orient is the color of the sapphire and the sapphire is an Oriental sapphire. That is to say, the sapphire is weighted with the riches of the word *Oriental*. It is full of *The Thousand and One Nights*, which Dante did not know, but which nevertheless is there.

I will also recall the famous last line of the fifth canto of the *Inferno*: "e caddi come corpo morto cade." The fall resounds through the repetition of the word *fall*.

The *Commedia* is full of felicities of this kind. But what sustains the poem is that it is a narrative. When I was young, narrative was scorned. It was considered to be nothing more than anecdote. It was forgotten that poetry began by being narrative, that the roots of poetry are the epic, that the epic is the first poetic genre. In the epic there is time: a before, during, and after. All of that is in poetry.

I would advise the reader to ignore the feud between the Guelphs and Ghibellines, Scholastic philosophy, the mythological allusions, and the lines of Virgil which Dante repeats, sometimes improving them, as excellent as they are in the original Latin. It is better, at least in the beginning, merely to follow the story. I don't think anyone can keep from doing so.

We enter, then, into a story, and we enter in a way that is almost magical. Normally, when dealing with the supernatural, one has an unbelieving writer guiding unbelieving readers, and he must prepare them for what is to come. Dante does not need this: "Nel mezzo del cammin di nostra vita / mi ritrovai per una selva oscura." That is, at thirty-five I found myself in a dark forest. It may be allegorical, but we physically believe it. Thirty-five is halfway through life because the Bible prescribes a life of seventy years for the prudent man. It is assumed that everything after seventy is *bleak*, as the English say; everything is sadness and anxiety.

So when Dante writes, "nel mezzo del cammin di nostra vita," he is not exercising a vague rhetoric. He is telling us exactly the date of his vision.

I don't think that Dante was a visionary. A vision is brief. A vision as large as the *Commedia* is impossible. His vision was voluntary: we may abandon ourselves to it and read it with poetic faith. Coleridge said that poetic faith is the willing suspension of disbelief. If we attend the theater, we know that, amid the scenery, there are costumed people speaking the words of Shakespeare or Ibsen or Pirandello which have been put in their mouths. But we accept that these people are not costumed, that the man in the antechamber slowly talking to himself of vengeance really is Hamlet, Prince of Denmark. We lose ourselves. Films are even stranger, for what we are seeing are not disguised people but photographs of disguised people, and yet we believe them while the film is being shown.

In the case of Dante, everything is so vivid that we begin to imagine that he believed in his other world, in the same way that he believed in a geocentric astronomy and not in other astronomies.

We believe Dante so profoundly for a reason that was pointed out by Paul Groussac: because the *Commedia* is written in the first person. It is not a mere grammatical artifice; it does not mean saying *I saw* for *they saw* or *it was*. It means something more. It means that Dante is one of the characters of the *Commedia*. According to Groussac, this was a new development. Before Dante, St. Augustine had written his *Confessions*. But those confessions, because of their splendid rhetoric, are not as close to us as Dante is; the rhetoric interposes itself between what he wants to say and what we hear.

Rhetoric must be a bridge, a road; too often it is a wall, an obstacle. We see it in writers as diverse as Seneca, Quevedo, Milton, and Lugones. In all of them the words come between them and us.

We know Dante more intimately than his contemporaries. One might say that we know him as he knew Virgil, who was a dream of his. We certainly know him better than we know Beatrice Portinari, better than anyone. He has placed himself in the center of the action. Everything is not only seen by him, but he is also an active participant. But his role is not always in accord with what he is describing.

We see Dante terrified by Hell. He must be terrified, not because he is a coward but rather so that we will believe in Hell. Dante is terrified, he is afraid, he comments on this and that. We know his opinions not by what he says but by the poetics, the intonation, the accentuation of his language.

There is another character. (In fact, there are three, but I will now speak of the second.) And that is Virgil. Dante has succeeded in giving us a second image of Virgil. The first is the image left us by the *Aeneid* or the *Georgics*. The second, the more intimate image, has been given to us by poetry, by Dante's pious poetry.

One of the subjects of literature—as it is of life—is friendship. I would say that friendship is the Argentine passion. There are many friendships in literature, which is a web of friendship: Quixote and Sancho; Fierro and Cruz, our two gauchos lost in the frontier; the old soldier and Fabio Cáceres; Kim and the lama. Friendship is a common theme, but in general writers tend to emphasize the contrast between the two friends.

In the case of Dante, the matter is more delicate. It is not exactly a contrast, although there is a filial relationship. Dante comes to be the son of Virgil, yet at the same time he is superior to Virgil for he believes he will be saved, since he has been given the vision. But he knows, from the beginning, that Virgil is a lost soul, a reprobate. When Virgil tells him that he cannot accompany him beyond Purgatory, he knows that the Latin poet will always inhabit the terrible *nobile castello* with the great shades of Antiquity, those who never heard the word of Christ. At that moment, Dante hails him with magnificent words: "Tu, duca; tu, signore; tu, maestro . . ." He speaks of the great labor and of the great love with which his work has been studied, and this relation is always maintained between the two. But Virgil is essentially a sad figure who knows he is forever condemned to that castle filled with the absence of God. Dante, however, will be permitted to see God; he will be permitted to understand the universe.

We have, first, two characters. And then there are the thousands, hundreds, a multitude of characters of whom it has been said that they are episodic. I would call them eternal.

A contemporary novel requires five or six hundred pages to make us know somebody, if it ever does. For Dante a single moment is enough. In that moment a person is defined forever. Dante unconsciously sought that central moment. I have wanted to do the same in many stories, and I have been admired for a discovery which actually belongs to Dante in the Middle Ages: that of presenting a moment as a cipher of a life. In Dante we have characters whose lives may consist of only a few tercets, and yet their lives are eternal. They live in a word, in a gesture; they need do nothing more. They are merely part of a canto, but that part is eternal. They keep living and renewing themselves in the memory and in the imagination of men.

Carlyle said that there are two characteristics of Dante. Of course there are others, but two are essential: tenderness and rigor, which do not contradict one another. On the one hand, there is his human tenderness, what Shakespeare called "the milk of human kindness." On the other, there is the knowledge that we are inhabitants of a rigorous world, that there is an order to it. That order corresponds to the Other, the third speaker.

Let us recall two examples. First, the best-known episode of the *Inferno*, the story of Paolo and Francesca in the fifth canto. I would not presume to summarize what Dante has said—it would be irreverent for me to say in other words what Dante has said for always in his Italian—but I'd like simply to recall the circumstances.

Dante and Virgil arrive at the second circle. There they see the whirlwind of souls and smell the stench of sin, the stench of punishment. There is Minos, twining his tail around himself to indicate to which circle the condemned must descend. It is physically disagreeable, deliberately ugly, because it is understood that in Hell nothing can be beautiful.

In that circle where the lustful are punished there are great, illustrious names. I say "great names" because Dante, when he began the canto, had not yet reached the perfection of his art, the point where the characters became something more than their names. But halfway through the canto, Dante makes his great discovery: the possibility of a dialogue between the souls of the dead and Dante himself, who will respond and judge in his fashion. No, he will not judge them. He knows that he is not the Judge, that the Judge is the Other, the third speaker, the Divinity.

Well then: there are Helen, Achilles, Paris, Tristan, and other luminaries. But Dante sees two whom he does not know, less illustrious, and who belong to the contemporary world: Paolo and Francesca. He knows that they have both died as adulterers. He calls to them and they come, "quali colombe dal disio chiamate." Here we have two sinners, and Dante compares them to two doves called by desire, because sensuality must also be the essence of the scene. They draw near, and Francesca, who is the only one to speak—Paolo cannot thanks him for calling them and speaks these pathetic words: "Se fosse amico il Re dell'universo / noi pregheremmo lui de la tua pace," if we were friends of the King of the universe—she cannot say God, because that name is forbidden in Hell and Purgatory—we would pray for your peace, since you have taken pity on our misfortune.

Francesca tells her story, and she tells it twice. The first time she tells it in a reserved fashion, but she insists that she is still in love with Paolo. Repentance is forbidden in Hell. She knows she has sinned and must continue to be faithful to her sin, which gives her a heroic grandeur. It would be terrible if she repented, if she denied what happened. Francesca knows the punishment is just; she accepts it, and continues to love Paolo.

Dante is curious about one thing, "Amor condusse noi ad una

morte": Paolo and Francesca were executed together. Dante is not interested in adultery, nor in the way they were discovered and brought to justice. What interests him is something more intimate, and that is how they knew they were in love, how they fell in love, how they reached the time of the sweet sighs. He asks them.

To digress for a moment, I would like to recall a stanza, perhaps the finest, of Leopoldo Lugones, who was no doubt inspired by the fifth canto of the *Inferno*. It is the first quatrain of his "Alma venturoso" ("Fortunate soul"), one of the sonnets of *Las horas doradas* (*The golden hours*) of 1922:

Al promediar la tarde de aquel día,
Cuando iba mi habitual adiós a darte,
Fue una vaga congoja de dejarte
Lo que me hizo saber que te quería.

Halfway through the afternoon that day,
As I bid you my habitual goodbye,
A vague dismay at leaving
Made me know that I loved you.

An inferior poet would have said that a man feels great sadness on leaving his woman, and he would have said that they see each other rarely. In contrast, "As I bid you my habitual goodbye" may be a slow and heavy line, but it expresses that they see each other frequently. And then: "A vague dismay at leaving / Made me know that I loved you."

The theme is essentially the same in the fifth canto: two people who discover that they are in love and didn't know it. This is what Dante wants to know; he wants them to tell him how it happened. She tells how, to entertain themselves one day, they were reading about Lancelot and how he complained of love. They were alone and suspected nothing. They did not suspect they were in love. And they were reading a story from the *Matière de Bretagne*, one of those books conceived by the British in France after the Saxon invasion—one of those books that fed the madness of Alonso Quijano and revealed their guilty love to Paolo and Francesca. Well: Francesca states that at times they blushed. Then, "quando leggemmo il disiato riso," when we read how the longed-for smile was kissed by such a lover, this one, who will never be separated from me, kissed my mouth, *tutto tremante*.

There is something that Dante does not say, but which one feels at a distance from the episode and perhaps gives it its virtue. Dante relates the fate of the two lovers with an infinite pity, and we sense that he envies their fate. Paolo and Francesca are in Hell and he will be saved, but they have loved and he never won the love of the woman he loved, Beatrice. There is a certain injustice to this, and Dante must feel it as something terrible, now that he is separated from her. In contrast, these two sinners are together. They cannot speak to each other, they turn in the black whirlwind without hope, yet they are together. When she speaks, she says "we," speaking for the two of them, another form of being together. They are together for eternity; they share Hell—and that, for Dante, must have been a kind of Paradise.

We know that he is quite moved. He then collapses as though he were dead.

Everyone is defined forever in a single instant of their lives, a moment in which a man encounters his self for always. It has been said that Dante is cruel toward Francesca, by condemning her. But that is to ignore the Third Character. The judgment of God does not always coincide with the feelings of Dante. Those who do not understand the *Commedia* say that Dante wrote it to take revenge on his enemies and to reward his friends. There is nothing more false. Nietzsche said, slanderously, that Dante is a hyena making verses among the tombs. A versifying hyena is a contradiction; moreover, Dante does not enjoy suffering. He knows that there are unpardonable, capital sins. For each he selects a person who has committed that sin. But in each there may be something admirable or worthy. Francesca and Paolo are not merely voluptuaries. They have committed no other sin, but one is enough to condemn them.

The idea of God as indecipherable is a concept we find in another of the essential books of mankind, the *Book of Job*. You will recall how Job condemns God, how his friends defend Him, and how at the end God speaks from the whirlwind and rebukes equally those who accuse or defend Him. God is beyond all human justice, as He Himself declares in the *Book of Job*. And the men humble themselves before God, because they have dared to judge Him, to defend Him. It is unnecessary. God, as Nietzsche would say, is beyond good and evil. He is another category.

If Dante had always agreed with the God he imagines, it would have meant that his was a false god, merely a replica of Dante himself. However, Dante must accept his God, as he must accept that Beatrice never loved him, that Florence is vile, as he will have to accept his exile and his death in Ravenna. He must accept the evil of the world, and at the same time, he must worship a God he does not understand.

There is a character missing in the *Commedia*, one who could not be there because he had become too human. That character is Jesus. He does not appear in the *Commedia* as he appears in the Gospels; the human Jesus of the Gospels could not be the Second Person of the Trinity that the *Commedia* requires.

I would like to turn to the second example, which for me is the high point of the *Commedia*. It occurs in the twenty-sixth canto, and it is the episode of Ulysses. (I once wrote an article titled "The Enigma of Ulysses." I published it, but later lost it, and I'd like to try to reconstruct it now.) I think that it is the most enigmatic of the episodes of the *Commedia*, and perhaps the most intense. But it is very difficult, when dealing with peaks, to know which is the highest—and the *Commedia* is made of peaks.

I have chosen the *Commedia* for this first talk because I am a man of letters and I believe that the apex of literature, of all literature, is the *Commedia*. This does not imply that I agree with its theology, or with its mythology, which is a combination of Christian and pagan myth. What it means is that no book has given me such intense aesthetic emotions. And, I repeat, I am a hedonistic reader; I look for emotion in books.

The *Commedia* is a book that everyone ought to read. Not to do so is to deprive oneself of the greatest gift that literature can give us; it is to submit to a strange asceticism. Why should we deny ourselves the joy of reading the *Commedia*? Besides, it is not difficult to read. What is difficult is outside of the reading: the opinions, the discussions. But the book itself is crystalline. And there is the central character, Dante, who is perhaps the most vivid character in literature, not to mention the other characters. But I will return to the episode of Ulysses.

They reach a ditch, I think it is the eighth, the one of swindlers. There is, in the beginning, an apostrophe against Florence, where he says that it beats its wings over heaven and earth and its name is spread through Hell. Then he sees above him countless flames, and inside the flames are the dark souls of the swindlers, dark because they continue to hide themselves. The flames move, and Dante almost falls. Virgil holds him back—the words of Virgil. He speaks of those who are inside the flames, and Virgil mentions two great names, Ulysses and Diomedes. They are there because together they plotted the strategy of the Trojan horse, which allowed the Greeks to enter the besieged city.

There are Ulysses and Diomedes, and Dante wants to meet them. He tells Virgil his desire to speak with these illustrious ancient shades, these celebrated and great ancient heroes. Virgil approves, but asks him to leave the talking to him, since we are dealing with two proud Greeks—it is better if Dante does not speak. This has been explained in various ways. Torquato Tasso believed that Virgil wanted to surpass Homer. That suspicion is totally absurd, for Virgil sang of Ulysses and Diomedes, and if Dante knows them it was because Virgil made them known. We may ignore the hypothesis that Dante was scorned because he was a descendant of Aeneas, a barbarian, worthless to the Greeks. Virgil, like Diomedes and Ulysses, is a dream of Dante's. Dante is dreaming them, but he dreams them with such intensity, in a way that is so vivid, that he can believe that those dreams—which have no other voice than that which he gives them, no other form than that which he lends them—may scorn him, he who is nobody, who hasn't even written his *Commedia*.

Dante has entered the game, as we enter it: Dante too is swindled by the *Commedia*. He thinks: they are celebrated heroes of Antiquity, and I am nobody, a poor man. Why should they take notice of what I say to them? Then Virgil asks them to tell how they died, and the voice of the invisible Ulysses speaks. Ulysses has no face; he is within the flame.

Here we come to what is wonderful, a legend created by Dante, a legend superior to many in the *Odyssey* or the *Aeneid*, or those that will be included in that other book in which Ulysses appears, as Sinbad of the Sea (Sinbad the Sailor), *The Thousand and One Nights*.

The legend was suggested to Dante by various things; above all, the belief that the city of Lisbon was founded by Ulysses and the stories of the Fortunate Isles in the Atlantic. The Celts were thought to have populated the Atlantic coast from those fantastic lands: an island with a river that rises up and crosses the sky and is full of boats and fish that do not fall back to earth; a revolving island of fire; an island where bronze greyhounds chase silver deer. Some of this must have been known to Dante; what is important is what he made of these legends. He originated something that is essentially noble.

Ulysses leaves Penelope. He calls together his companions and reminds them that, although they are now old and married men, they have crossed thousands of dangers with him. He proposes a noble enterprise: to pass through the Pillars of Hercules and cross the sea, to explore the Southern Hemisphere, which, it was then believed, was a hemisphere of water—it was not known if anyone was there. He tells them that they are men, not beasts; they have been born for courage, for knowledge; they have been born to know and to understand.

They follow him and "make wings of their oars." (It is curious that this metaphor is also found in the *Odyssey*, which Dante could not have known.) They sail and leave behind Ceuta and Seville, enter the open sea, and turn toward the left. (Toward the left, or on the left, means evil in the *Commedia*. To climb to Purgatory one goes to the right; to descend to Hell, to the left. That is to say, the "sinister" side has a double meaning.)

They sail for five months and then, at last, see land. What they see is a brown mountain in the distance, a mountain taller than any they have ever seen. Ulysses says that their joy was soon turned to grief, for a whirlwind blew from the land and the ship was lost. That mountain is Purgatory, as we will learn in another canto. Dante believes that Purgatory—he pretends to believe in poetic justice—is antipodal to the city of Jerusalem.

Well, we reach that terrible moment, and we wonder why Ulysses has been punished. Evidently it was not for the ruse of the Trojan horse, since the culminating moment of his life, the one told to Dante and to us, is another; it is that generous, bold enterprise of wanting to know the forbidden, the impossible. We ask ourselves why this canto has such force. Before answering I would like to mention something which has never been said before, as far as I know.

It is that other great book, a great poem of our times, *Moby-Dick* by Herman Melville, who certainly knew Dante in the Longfellow translation. We have the mad enterprise of the crippled Captain Ahab, who wants to revenge himself on the white whale. At the end they find the whale, who sinks the ship, and the great novel ends exactly as Dante's canto ends: the sea closes over them. Melville must have remembered the *Commedia* at that point, though I prefer to think that he had read it and absorbed it in such a way he could literally forget it; that the *Commedia* had become part of him, and that he could rediscover what he had read years before. But the story is the same, except that Ahab is not moved by a noble aim but rather by a desire for vengeance. Ulysses, in contrast, acts as the greatest of men. Moreover, he invokes a just reason, one related to intelligence, and he is punished.

To what do we owe the tragic weight of this episode? I think there is an explanation, the only valid one, and that is that Dante felt, in some way, that he was Ulysses. I don't know if he felt it in a conscious way—it doesn't matter. In some tercet of the *Commedia* he says that no one is permitted to know the judgments of Providence. We cannot anticipate them; no one can know who will be saved and who condemned. But Dante has dared, through poetry, to do precisely that. He shows us the condemned and the chosen. He must have known that doing so courted danger. He could not ignore that he was anticipating the indecipherable providence of God.

For this reason the character of Ulysses has such force, because Ulysses is a mirror of Dante, because Dante felt that perhaps he too deserved this punishment. Writing the poem, whether for good or ill, he was infringing on the mysterious laws of the night, of God, of Divinity.

I have reached the end, and again I would like to insist that no one has the right to deprive himself of this pleasure—the *Commedia*—of reading it in an open way. Later come the commentaries, the desire to know what each mythological allusion means, to see how Dante took a great line of Virgil and perhaps improved it by translating it. In the beginning we must read the book with the faith of a child, abandoning ourselves to it; then it will accompany us to the end. It has accompanied me for so many years, and I know that as soon as I open it tomorrow I will discover things I did not see before. I know that this book will go on, beyond my waking life, and beyond ours.

(1980)

(Translated by Elliot Weinberger)

W. H. Auden

from *The Vision of Eros*

Half the literature, highbrow and popular, produced in the West during the past four hundred years has been based on the false assumption that what is an exceptional experience is or ought to be a universal one. Under its influence so many millions of persons have persuaded themselves they were "in love" when their experience could be fully and accurately described by the more brutal four-letter words, that one is sometimes tempted to doubt if the experience is ever genuine, even when, or especially when, it seems to have happened to oneself. However, it is impossible to read some of the documents, *La Vita Nuova*, for example, many of Shakespeare's sonnets or the *Symposium* and dismiss them as fakes. All accounts of the experience agree on essentials. Like the Vision of Dame Kind, the Vision of Eros is a revelation of creaturely glory, but whereas in the former it is the glory of a multiplicity of non-human creatures which is revealed, in the latter it is the glory of a single human being. Again, while in the vision of Nature, conscious sexuality is never present, in the erotic vision it always is—it cannot be experienced by eunuchs (though it may occur before puberty) and no one ever fell in love with someone they found sexually unattractive—but physical desire is always, and without any effort of will, subordinate to the feeling of awe and reverence in the presence of a sacred being: however great his desire, the lover feels unworthy of the beloved's notice. It is impossible to take such accounts as a fancy poetization of any of the three kinds of unmystical erotic experiences with which we are all familiar. It is not simple lust, the detached recognition of another as a desirable sexual object, for in relation to anything one regards as an object one feels superior, and the lover feels inferior to the beloved. Nor is it sexual infatuation, the experience of *Vénus toute entière à sa proie attachée*, in which desire has invaded and possessed the whole self until what it craves is not sexual satisfaction only but a total absorption of the other self, body and soul, into itself; in this condition the dominant feeling is not of unworthiness but of anguish, rage and despair at not being able to get what one craves. Nor, again, is it that healthy mixture of mutual physical desire and *philia*, a mutual personal liking based on common interests and values, which is the securest foundation for a happy marriage for, in this state, the dominant feeling is of mutual respect between equals.

Moreover, all the accounts agree that the Vision of Eros cannot long survive if the parties enter into an actual sexual relation. It was not merely the social conditions of an age in which marriages were arranged by the parents which made the Provençal poets declare that married couples could not be in love. This does not mean that one must under no circumstances marry the person whose glory has been revealed to one, but the risk in doing so is proportionate to the intensity of the vision. It is difficult to live day after day, year after year, with an ordinary human being, neither much better nor much worse than oneself, after one has seen her or him transfigured, without feeling that the fading of the vision is the other's fault. The Vision of Eros seems to be much more influenced by social conditions than any of the others. Some degree of leisure and freedom from financial anxiety seems to be essential; a man who must labor ten hours a day in order not to starve has other matters to attend to: he is too occupied by practical necessities to think of more than his sexual need for a woman and his economic need for a good housekeeper and mother. And it would seem that the beloved must belong to a class of persons whom the lover has been brought up to regard as his social equals or superiors. One cannot, it seems, fall in love with someone whom one has been trained to think of as being less of a person, more of a thing than oneself. Thus Plato, though he came in later life to disapprove of homosexuality, can only conceive of the beloved as a male in his adolescence or early manhood because, in the Athens of his time, women were regarded as essentially inferior creatures.

The effect of the vision on the lover's conduct is not confined to his behavior towards his beloved. Even in his relations to others, conduct which before he fell in love seemed natural and proper, judged by his new standard of what he feels it should be to be worthy of her, now seems base and ignoble. Further, in most cases, the experience does not lead, as one might expect, to a sort of erotic quietism, a rapt contemplation of the beloved to the exclusion of others and the world. On the contrary, it usually releases a flood of psychic energy for actions which are not directly concerned with the beloved at all. When in love, the soldier fights more bravely, the thinker thinks more clearly, the carpenter fashions with greater skill.

The Church, whose institutional and intellectual concern in sexual matters is, and must be, primarily with marriage and the family, has always, very understandably, regarded the Vision of Eros with the utmost suspicion. Either she has dismissed it as moonshine, or condemned it offhand, without trying first to understand it, as idolatry of the creature and a blasphemous parody of the Christian love of God. Knowing that marriage and the vision are not compatible, she has feared that it will be, as it very often is, used as an excuse for adultery. Condemnation without understanding, however, is seldom effective. If the lover idolizes the beloved, it is not what we ordinarily mean by idolization, in which the worshipper makes his idol responsible for his existence. This kind of idolization can certainly occur in the relation between the sexes. Cases of men and women who shoot themselves and each other because the object of their affection does not return it, or loves somebody else, may be read of almost every day in the newspapers, but one knows at once that they cannot have been truly in love. The true lover would naturally rather his beloved returned his love than refused it, he would rather she were alive and visible than dead and invisible, but if she cannot return his love, he does not try to compel her by force or emotional blackmail, and if she dies, he does not commit suicide but continues to love her.

The two most serious attempts to analyze the Vision of Eros and give it a theological significance are Plato's and Dante's. Both agree on three points: (a) the experience is a genuine revelation, not a delusion; (b) the erotic mode of the vision prefigures a kind of love in which the sexual element is transformed and transcended; (c) he who has once seen the glory of the Uncreated revealed indirectly in the glory of a creature can henceforth never be fully satisfied with anything less than a direct encounter with the former. About everything else they disagree radically. One of the most important differences between them is obscured by the inadequacy of our vocabulary. When I say, "X has a beautiful profile," and when I say, "Elizabeth has a beautiful face," or "the expression on Mary's face was beautiful," I have to use the same adjective, though I mean two totally different things. Beauty in the first statement is a given public quality of an object; I am talking about a quality the object *has*, not about what it *is*. If (but only if) a number of objects belong to the same class, I can compare them and arrange them in order according to the degree of beauty they possess, from the most beautiful to the least. That is why, even among human beings, it is possible to hold beauty contests to elect Miss America, and possible for an experienced sculptor to state in mathematical terms the proportions of the ideal male or female figure. Beauty in this sense is a gift of Nature or of Chance, and can be withdrawn. To become Miss America, a girl must have in-

herited a certain combination of genes and have managed to escape any disfiguring diseases or crippling accident, and, diet as she
may, she cannot hope to remain Miss America forever. The emotion aroused by this kind of beauty is impersonal admiration; in
the case of a human being, it may also be impersonal sexual desire.
I may want to sleep with Miss America, but I have no wish to hear
her talk about herself and her family.

When I say, "Elizabeth has a beautiful face," I mean something
quite different. I am still referring to something physical—I could
not make the statement if I were blind—but this physical quality is
not a gift from Nature, but a personal creation for which I hold
Elizabeth to be responsible. The physical beauty seems to me a
revelation of something immaterial, the person whom I cannot
see. Beauty in this sense is unique in every case: I cannot compare
Elizabeth and Mary and say which has the more beautiful face.
The emotion aroused by it is personal love, and, again, this is
unique in every case. To the degree that I love both Elizabeth and
Mary, I cannot say which I love more. Finally, to say that someone
is beautiful in this sense is never simply a favorable aesthetic judgment; it is always a favorable moral judgment as well. I can say "X
has a beautiful profile but is a monster," I cannot say, "Elizabeth has
a beautiful face but is a monster."

As creatures, human beings have a double nature. As members
of a mammalian species which reproduces itself sexually, each of us
is born either male or female and endowed with an impersonal
need to mate with a member of the opposite sex; any member
will do so long as he or she is not immature or senile. As unique
persons we are capable of, but not compelled to, enter voluntarily
into unique relations of love with other persons. The Vision of
Eros is, therefore, double too. The beloved always possesses some
degree of that beauty which is Nature's gift. A girl who weighs
two hundred pounds and a woman of eighty may both have beautiful faces in the personal sense, but men do not fall in love with

them. The lover is, of course, aware of this, but what seems to him infinitely more important is his awareness of the beloved as a person. Or so, at least, Dante says. What is so puzzling about Plato's description is that he seems unaware of what we mean by a person. By beauty, he always seems to mean impersonal beauty and by love impersonal admiration.

> [The lover] should begin by loving earthly things for the sake of the absolute loveliness, ascending to that as it were by degrees or steps, from the first to the second, and thence to all fair forms; and from fair forms to fair conduct, and from fair conduct to fair principles, until from fair principles he finally arrive at the ultimate principle of all, and learn what absolutely Beauty is.

The more I study this passage, the more bewildered I become, and I find myself talking to Plato's ghost and saying:

"(1) As regards earthly things, I agree that I can compare two horses, or two men, or two proofs of the same mathematical theorem, and say which is the more beautiful, but will you please tell me how I am to compare a horse, a man and a mathematical proof and say which is the most beautiful?

"(2) If, as you say, there are degrees of beauty and that the more beautiful should be loved more, then, at the human level, it must be the moral duty of all of us to fall in love with the most beautiful human being known to us. Surely, it is very fortunate for all concerned that we fail to do our duty.

"(3) It is quite true, as you say, that a fair principle does not get bald and fat or run away with somebody else. On the other hand, a fair principle cannot give me a smile of welcome when I come into the room. Love of a human being may be, as you say, a lower form of love than love for a principle, but you must admit it is a damn sight more interesting."

How different, and much more comprehensible, is Dante's account. He sees Beatrice, and a voice says, "Now you have seen your beatitude." Dante certainly thinks that Beatrice is beautiful in the public sense that any stranger would call her beautiful, but it would never enter his head to ask if she were more or less beautiful than other Florentine girls of her age. She is Beatrice and that is that. And what is the essential thing about her is that she is, he is absolutely certain, a "graced" person, so that after her death, he is convinced, as a believing Christian, her soul is among the redeemed in Paradise, not among the lost in Hell. He does not tell us exactly what the sins and errors were which had brought him near to perdition nor, when they meet again, does Beatrice, but both speak of them as acts of infidelity to her, that is to say, if he had remained faithful to his vision of one human creature, Beatrice, he would not have committed offenses against their common Creator. Though unfaithful to her image, he has, however, never completely forgotten it (the Platonic ladder makes the forgetting of an image on a lower rung a moral duty), and it is this memory, the fact that he has never completely ceased to love her, which makes it possible for Beatrice to intervene from Heaven to save his soul. When, at last, they meet again in the earthly paradise, he re-experiences, though infinitely more intensely, the vision he had when they first met on earth, and she remains with him until the very last moment when he turns towards "the eternal fountain" and, even then, he knows that her eyes are turned in the same direction. The Vision of Eros is not, according to Dante, the first rung of a long ladder: there is only one step to take, from the personal creature who can love and be loved to the personal Creator who is Love. And in this final vision, Eros is transfigured but not annihilated. On earth we rank "love" higher than either sexual desire or sexless friendship because it involves the whole of our being, not, like them, only a part of it. Whatever else is asserted by the doctrine of the resurrection of the body, it asserts the sacred importance of the body. As Silesius says, we have one advantage over the angels: only we can each become the bride of God. And Juliana of Norwich: "In the self-same point that our Soul is made sensual, in the self-same point is the City of God ordained to him from without beginning."

(1964)

Robert Fitzgerald

Mirroring the Commedia:
An Appreciation of Laurence Binyon's Version

- I -

One brilliant episode of "the Pound era" has fallen into such obscurity as to remain unregistered in Hugh Kenner's book of that title, marvel of registration though the book is. In telling of Ezra Pound's life in London between 1908 and 1920, Kenner refers once or twice to his friendship with Laurence Binyon, poet and Deputy Keeper of Prints and Drawings in the British Museum. But he says nothing of Pound's interest, years later, in Binyon's translation of *The Divine Comedy*. Now, from early in 1934 to late in 1939, this interest animated a great deal of correspondence between the two men and ended with quite remarkable enthusiasm on the part of Pound. In fact, he all but took a hand in the translation. It would be fair to say that he gave as much time and attention to Binyon's work as he had in other years—in another way—to that of James Joyce, and for the same reason: that he thought the work supremely good. Pound could be wildly wrong about some things but not, I think, about a rendering of Dante in English verse. If anyone's ear and judgment had authority in such matters, his did.

Not only has this whole episode been lost to view, but the translation itself is generally and peculiarly disregarded. Teachers of Dante appear to be only dimly aware of it. And yet the rendering of the *Commedia* that most nearly reproduces the total quality of

the original poem is surely Laurence Binyon's. Why is it not likely
to be supplied to the student, or the serious reader of English, either at the University or elsewhere? After puzzling over this state
of affairs for some time, I have learned enough to realize that it,
too—this relative neglect—is a masterpiece in its way, a *capolavoro*
composed by the sheer accidents of history, the fortunes of war
and peace.

Here, then, is a story.

- I I -

At Oxford in 1890, Laurence Binyon won the Newdigate Prize
with a poem entitled "Persephone." The year and the title combine to bring us the essential fragrance of a period and to suggest
the poetic and scholarly tradition that Binyon inherited. Confining to the sensibility though it had certainly become, that tradition
had its points, as Binyon's life would demonstrate. He was a stu-
dious poet and a sober man. After Oxford he went to work in the
print division of the British Museum, where he was to become a
pioneer interpreter of the art of the East to the West, author of
Painting in the Far East (1908) and later a friend of Charles Freer
and Langdon Warner. In 1913 Binyon became Deputy Keeper of
Prints and Drawings at the Museum. He and young Ezra Pound
met one another from time to time and were notably unaffected
by each other's work. Binyon's poems, after all, were in the tradition that Pound proposed to shake. One of them became extremely well known: "To the Fallen," first printed in the London
Times in September, 1914. This turned out to be so memorable in
the English-speaking world that after 1918 many war memorials
throughout Britain and the Commonwealth bore a Simonidean
stanza from it, cut in stone: "They shall not grow old, as we who
are left grow old, etc."

It is worth remembering that in the Print Division Binyon's

eye received an education from the masters of line in East and
West. He did a great deal of work on Blake. To an eye so educated,
no poetry, probably, could match Dante's in visual fascination.
Binyon was not an Italian scholar, but as an amateur, early in the
'20s, with the advice and encouragement of his friend Mario Praz,
he began translating *The Divine Comedy*. In 1933 *Inferno* was ready,
and late in the year Macmillan published it in one volume with
the Italian text on facing pages. The book was dedicated to Praz
and carried a brief preface.

The modesty of Binyon's prefatory remarks may have veiled
the special nature and ambition of this poem. He had tried, he
said, to communicate not only the sense of the words but something of Dante's tone and of the rhythm through which that tone
was conveyed. This was not merely a matter of matching, with
"triple rhyme," Dante's *terza rima*. It involved a more intimate
correspondence. So far as English would permit, and in the decasyllabic line native to English, he had imitated the Dantean
hendecasyllable, scanning by syllables rather than feet, but through
systematic elisions achieving flexibility in syllable count. The result was a regular but very subtle refreshment and quickening of
rhythm, e.g., in *Inferno* 4.49–50:

> "Did ever any of those herein immured
>   By his own or other's merit to bliss get free?"

But this was not all, either. By using fine distributions of weight
and accent, he had contrived to avoid the beat of pentameters and
to even out his stresses on the Italian model. For one conspicuous
instance of this he prepared the reader, noting how he had occasionally rhymed on an unaccented syllable (*Inf.* 1.2, "That I had
strayed into a dark forest," rhyming with "oppressed")—not in-
tending an abnormal pronunciation, but as "the placing of a heavy
or emphatic syllable before the final word seems to have the effect
of mitigating the accent on that word, so that it is rather balanced

between the two syllables than placed with all its weight on one. Such elasticity of stress seems congenial to Dante's verse . . ." No doubt Binyon learned the possibility of this, and the advantage of it, from Dante Gabriel Rossetti, who had resorted to it here and there in his translations of Dante's sonnets and *canzoni* in the *Vita Nuova*.

But Binyon went far beyond Rossetti, as he had to, in working out a style adequate to the *Commedia*—a style versatile but consistent, firm, but well-wrought, and swift. Drawing on the English of earlier centuries, he would admit old forms and words, but with a selective and measuring ear, so that his archaicisms generally gave body and life to his verses, not quaintness. The diction, thus slightly expanded and elevated, was an accomplishment in itself. It stood, in fact, to twentieth century English very much as Dante's living Tuscan does to twentieth century Italian. One brief example may suffice (*Inf.* 25.64–66):

> As runneth up before the burning flame
>   On paper, a brown colour, not yet black,
>   And the white dieth, such their hues became . . .

Binyon's *Inferno* was published, as I have said, late in 1933. The editor of *The Criterion* in London, at Ezra Pound's request, sent this book to Pound for review. Pound was then living in Rapallo; he had left London thirteen years before, and he had not spent the interval extolling the English literary establishment, to which Binyon in a quiet way belonged. But a foolish note on Binyon's translation had fallen under his eye and aroused his curiosity. The editor of *The Criterion* must have awaited Pound's review with several kinds of interest. The review appeared in April 1934.

> I state, [wrote Pound], that I have read the work, that for thirty years it never would have occurred to me that it would be possible to read a translation of the *Inferno* from

cover to cover, and that this translation has therefore one DEMONSTRATED dimension . . . The venerable Binyon has, I am glad to say, produced the most interesting English version of Dante that I have seen or expect to see . . .

The younger generation may have forgotten Binyon's sad youth, poisoned in the cradle by the abominable dog-biscuit of Milton's rhetoric . . . At any rate, Dante has cured him. If ever demonstration be needed of the virtues of having a good model instead of a rhetorical bustuous rumpus, the life in Binyon's translation can prove it to next century's schoolboys . . . He has carefully preserved all the faults of his original. This in the circumstances is the most useful thing he could have done.

What these faults were, the reviewer did not expressly say, but it became clear that he meant inversions of word order. Unspeakable syntax had been a *bête noire* to Pound since the days of Imagism, and he now found himself irritated by "Binyon's writing his lines hind side before." But on reflection he had come round to seeing that some of this was appropriate.

The devil of translating medieval poetry into English is that it is very hard to decide HOW you are to render work done with one set of criteria in a language NOW subject to different criteria . . . The concept of word order in uninflected or very little inflected language had not developed to anything like twentieth century straightness.

When the reviewer got down to cases, his technical observations were as acute as might have been expected.

Working on a decent basis, Binyon has got rid of magniloquence, of puffed words, I don't remember a single decorative or rhetorical word in his first ten cantos. There are vast numbers of monosyllables, little words. Here a hint from the *De Eloquio* may have put him on the trail. In the matter of rhyme, nearly everyone knows that Dante's rhymes are "feminine," i.e. accent on the penultimate, *crucciata, aguzza, volge, maligno.* There are feminine rhymes in English, there are ENOUGH, possibly, to fill the needs of an almost literal version of the *Divina Commedia,* but they are of the wrong quality; *bloweth, knowing, wasteth.* Binyon has very intelligently avoided a mere pseudo or obvious similarity, in favour of a fundamental, namely the sharp clear quality of the original SOUND as a whole. His *past, admits, checked, kings,* [are] all masculine endings, but all having a residue of vowel sound in state of potential, or latent, as considered by Dante himself in his remarks on troubadour verse.

The fact that this idiom, which was never spoken on sea or land, is NOT fit for use in the new poetry of 1933–34 does not mean that it is unfit for use in a translation of a poem produced in 1321 . . . Coming back to the rhyming, not only are we without strict English equivalents for terminal sounds like *ferrigno, rintoppa, argento, tronca, stagna, feruto,* but any attempt at ornamental rhyme à la Hudibras, or slick epigrammatic rhyme à la Pope or trick rhyme à la Hood, or in fact any kind of rhyming excrescence or ornament would be out of place in the *Commedia* . . .

One ends with gratitude for [the] demonstration that forty years' honest work do, after all, count for something; that some qualities of writing cannot be attained simply by clever faking, young muscles or a desire to get somewhere in a hurry. The lines move to their end, that is, draw along the eye of the reader, instead of cradling him in a hammock. The main import is not sacrificed to detail. Simple as this appears in bald statement it takes time to learn how to achieve it.[1]

These remarks seem to be valuable above all in that they cast a shrewd—and unique—craftsman's light on the art of *The Divine Comedy* and the task of translating it. Pound obviously felt enticed by the challenge that Binyon had taken up—so much so that he could not stay on the sidelines. In the course of preparing his review, he wrote to Binyon on January 21st, 1934.

My dear Laurence Binyon, [he said], "If any residuum of annoyance remain in yr. mind because of the extremely active nature of the undersigned (it is very difficult for a man to believe anything hard enough for it to matter a damn *what* he believes, without causing annoyance to others)— anyhow . . . I hope you will forget it long enough to permit me to express my very solid appreciation of yr. translation of the *Inferno. Criterion* has asked me for a thousand words by the end of next week, but I am holding out for more space [he got six thousand] which will probably delay publication for heaven knows how long. When and if the review appears and if it strikes you as sufficiently intelligent, I shd. be glad thereafter to send you the rest of the notes I have made. Minutiae, too trifling to print. But at any rate I have gone through the book, I shd. think, syllable by syllable. And as Bridges and Leaf are no longer on the scene, the number of readers possessed of any criteria (however heretical) for the writing of English verse and at the same time knowing the difference between Dante and Dunhill is limited . . . I was irritated by the inversions during the first 8 to 10 cantos, but having finished the book, I think you have in every (almost every) case chosen the lesser evil in dilemma. For 40 pages I wanted you to revise, after that I wanted you to go on with the Purgatorio and Paradiso before turning back to the black air. And I hope you will. I hope you are surviving the New England winter . . .[2]

Binyon was surviving it very well. At sixty-five he had retired from his job at the British Museum and had gone to Cambridge, Massachusetts, for the academic year to give the Norton Lectures—he followed Eliot in that chair—lecturing not on poetry but on Oriental art. He replied from the Commander Hotel on February 18th:

> My dear Ezra Pound, I was very glad to hear from you, and to learn that you had read my Inferno version with so much interest. The difficulties are so immense—often I was in absolute despair—that after surmounting them in a way that didn't seem too bad one was inclined to rate the feat too highly: now, when I turn the pages again a lot of it seems terribly inadequate. (Of course *all of it* is inadequate; that goes without saying; but some passages read well, I think, at any rate apart from the Italian.) When you say "inversions," do you mean grammatical inversions or inversions of accent? I shall see when your review appears, if it does appear, as I hope. I shall certainly be very glad of your notes, as I know one can go on improving forever in the matter of details. Shall I go on with the Purgatory and Paradise? I don't know. It takes a devilish amount of time and hard work, but I have done I think 8 cantos of Purgatory so hope to finish that some day. We are having the severest winter on record in the States, but are surviving without any frostbitten members so far. The bright sun is welcome after grey London, which I have now left for good . . .[3]

So ran the first exchange—friendly if a trifle wary on the part of both men (I hear a reticent gesture of *rapprochement* in Binyon's last remark about London). This led to four or five other exchanges in the course of 1934. Pound's letters were copious and high-spirited, Binyon's briefer and plainer; every now and then he would patiently maintain a point. He enjoyed the *Criterion* review which he found waiting for him in June on his return to England and to his retired farmhouse in Berkshire. He wrote to say that he felt encouraged and grateful, and venerable though he might be he had lots of energy left and hoped to go on. Pound reported in June: "Yeats rumbled in last week / also agreed that you had done a damn good job (my phrase, not his) . . . he assented with noble dignity."[4] As he had promised, Pound sent Binyon his review copy of the book with marginal notations, which Binyon recorded gratefully before returning the book in July. "Of course," he wrote, "in many places you pounce on [things] I should vastly have preferred to be quite plain and direct, but it is devilish hard to get the rhyme, at the same time—as you know. In fact, sometimes impossible. However, you have noted a number of lines wh. I shall try to improve."

In August Binyon wrote to thank Pound for sending him a copy of the Cavalcanti *Rime* in Pound's edition. He said: "I quite see that the having music in view was a gain to the lyric of Campion, etc., necessitating clearness, lightness, a clear contour. But it seems to me that you couldn't go on forever within those limits: and I don't see that the alternative is necessarily rhetorical declamation. Poetry to me is a kind of heavenly speech . . ." As though by tacit agreement, neither man ever mentioned what each knew the other had in mind: the poetry of Milton. In November Binyon sent Pound versions of the first cantos of the *Purgatorio*. At the end of January, 1935, he added a few more and said that at Eliot's request he had sent the Sordello canto (5) to *The Criterion*. Then he went off to Egypt to lecture. Pound continued to think the work over. On the 29th of April he concluded a letter (the last in this series):

When you get the *Paradiso* done the edition shd. go into use in all university Dante study; at least in America. I don't know WHAT study is committed in England . . . possibly Dante is still considered an exotic. Temple edtn/ was used in my undergrad/ time, but yours sheds so infinitely much more light . . . And as translation, I don't mean merely of Dante, but in proportion to any translation I can think of, I don't know of any that is more transparent in sense that reader sees the original through it. A translation that really has a critical value, i.e. enlightens one as to the nature of the original. That is rarissima. I don't think my own DO. I have emphasized or dragged into light certain things that matter (to me at any rate) but it is not the same thing . . . I shall probably do a note on the Purg in Broletto [a new monthly magazine published at Como].[5]

After this there was a long hiatus in correspondence. It was nearly 3 years later, February 25th, 1938, when Binyon wrote again. "I imagine you will be thinking me extinct," he said. "I have at last finished the Purgatorio, and it has gone to the printer. I didn't want to bother you with bits at casual intervals but I wonder if you would care to look through proofs of the whole?" Pound agreed at once. Late in April the proofs were sent. Pound's letters with detailed comments now came thick and fast, more than half a dozen long letters on batches of cantos between April 22nd and May 12th.

Binyon had cautioned him: "But don't take *too* much trouble *now*; because, as my Inferno was a complete failure from the sales point of view and Macmillan lost over 200 over it, I can't expect them to pay for a heavy lot of corrections, nor can I afford to pay myself." This had not the slightest effect on Pound. Typical of Poundian comments gratefully received and acted on were his remarks on 11.86–87, *gran disio del eccellenza* as to which he wrote: " 'desire of excelling or beating someone else' is the meaning, not the 'desire of perfection,' Our 'excellence' is almost a synonym with 'goodness.' As the whole poem is one of fine moral distinctions, this dissociation is worth making."[6]

Wrote Binyon on April 27th: "What I have aimed at above all

is getting something like Dante's 'tone of voice,' and my Italian
critics and Italian friends all think this is the chief merit of my version. It is the first thing they say. (The English ones say terza rima
is un-English, etc.)" Pound's enthusiasm mounted as he read. After
canto 17 he wrote: "MAGNIFICENT FINISH! Utterly confounds the apes who told you terza rima isn't English . . . The
beauty here would *only* have been got by using terza rima. Lascia
dir gli stolti who don't see it and who have been for two centuries
content that *technique* went out of English *metric* with Campion
and Waller . . ." At canto 21 he exclaimed, "Banzai, my dear Bin
Bin . . ." and at 28, "Bravo, Bravo, Bravo . . ."

We might listen to a passage from that canto 28: the narrator's
account of his meeting with Matilda in the *paradiso terrestre*:

> Already my slow steps had borne me on
>   So far within that immemorial wood
>   That I could no more see whence I had gone;
> And lo! a stream that stopped me where I stood;
>   And at the left the ripple in its train
>   Moved on the bank the grasses where it flowed.
> All waters here that are most pure from stain
>   Would qualified with some immixture seem
>   Compared with this, which veils not the least grain,
> Altho' so dark, dark goes the gliding stream
>   Under the eternal shadow, that hides fast
>   Forever there the sun's and the moon's beam.
> With my feet halting, with my eyes I passed
>   That brook, for the regaling of my sight
>   With the fresh blossoms in their full contrast,
> And then appeared (as in a sudden light
>   Something appears which from astonishment
>   Puts suddenly all other thoughts to flight)
> A lady who all alone and singing went,
>   And as she sang plucked flowers that numberless

All round about her path their colours blent.
"I pray thee, O lovely Lady, if, as I guess,
    Thou warm'st thee at the radiance of Love's fire,—
    For looks are wont to be the heart's witness,—
I pray thee toward this water to draw near
    So far," said I to her, "while thou dost sing,
    That with my understanding I may hear.
Thou puttest me in remembrance of what thing
    Proserpine was, and where, when by mischance
    Her mother lost her, and she lost the spring."

The reader of severe contemporary taste and habituated to
contemporary style may find this idiom—one, as Pound put it,
"never spoken on sea or land"—at first glance an exercise in the
antiquarian. But he will be aware of its clearness and fluency, and
as he reads on he will, I believe, begin to feel, as Pound did, the
distinction of its fashioning as a medium for the great medieval
poem. This cumulative effect cannot be conveyed by quotation,
but from the quoted passage the reader may gain an inkling of the
means employed. One may notice, for example, in the third tercet
the limpid monosyllables of the enclosing lines and the cunning
"immixture" of polysyllables in the line enclosed. The fourth tercet is a good one in which to sense the evenness that Binyon
achieved in weight of syllables, like musical notes, an effect
twice assisted on this page by a flattening-out of the rhyme-
word ("contrast" and "witness"). In the final tercet one may hear-
ken not only to subdued alliteration ("puttest," "Proserpine,"
"mischance," "mother") but to covert internal rhyming ("hear,"
"where," "her"). Every one of these refinements is a resemblance to the Italian. So controlled and sustained is Binyon's artifice, and so free of any kind of flashiness, that it acquires a life of
its own, and this life in the end seems very nearly the life of the
original.

In canto 32 Pound came upon what he called "the *only* line of really *bad* poetry I have found . . . 'But when she rolled on me her lustful eye' might be Gilbert and Sullivan. Positively the only line that is out of the sober idiom of the whole of your translation. Like Omerus he SLEPT. Moderate verb and adjective wanted." (Binyon toned it down.) At the end Pound wrote: "Once again my thanks for the translation. And there are damned few pieces of writing that I am thankful for . . . Nobody has had such a good time of this kind since Landor did his notes on Catullus . . . And now, Boss, you get RIGHT ALONG with that Paradiso as soon as you've stacked up the dinner dishes . . ."

Binyon's *Purgatorio* was published in September, with an acknowledgment of Pound's assistance. As he had promised to do three years before, Pound wrote a notice of the book in Italian for *Broletto*. It appeared in Number 34, for October, 1938. This article has to my knowledge never been translated and has remained forgotten or unknown. Yet it expressed a serious and long meditated judgment, without reserve. It was headed: "BINYON: we greet a most valuable translation of the Divine Comedy," and it proceeded (my translation):

I can repeat all the praises published in *The Criterion* when the translation of the *Inferno* appeared; but I must add still others. Constantly developing his technique, Binyon in his description of the Terrestrial Paradise reaches a true splendor and clarity never achieved before. It seems to me that this can be said not only in comparison with the other translations of Dante, but perhaps also in comparison with the whole body of translations into English of any author whatever . . .

What about Golding's Ovid and Douglas's *Aeneid*, old favorites of Pound? These were, he observed, works of poetry that had no need of the originals and served not as interpretations of the originals but as "comment" of a special kind.

Binyon [he said], triumphs in another way, he triumphs through an honesty that from time to time amounts to genius. His version of Dante gives me a clearer sense of the original. It is like a window with glass so polished that one is not aware of it, one has the impression of the open air . . .

My generation in America suffered from the assumption that to understand Dante it was necessary to suffocate in a pile of commentary. I, at least, at seventeen was distracted by the abundance of comments and notes and sometimes lost the continuity of the poem. With a prose "argument" of half a page or less for each canto, Binyon has very clearly shown the falsity of this assumption . . .

As for *terza rima*, Binyon achieves beauties that he could never have attained except by making the effort to employ this form, in which he gets a very English flavor with words like *coppices*, or *highlander* for *montanaro* . . .

The defects of his version are superficial. I see none except in little inversions, which could easily disappear in a revision which the translator already intends to make as soon as he has finished the whole version of the poem. Some defects have already disappeared between the first proofs and those passed for the printer . . .

But undoubtedly Binyon has already made us a triple gift. First true poetry, in his most felicitous pages. Second: a sense of the continuity and comprehensibility of the poem. Third: an assistance to students . . . every class for the study of Italian poetry in any foreign university ought to make use of this version to facilitate the comprehension of the *Commedia*.

A decadence begins when attention turns to the ornamental element and is detached little by little from the meaning. In Dante (and in Guido) the meaning is extremely precise; if you doubt it, look at canto 18 of the *Pur-*

gatorio. The idiom of Binyon's version is the idiom suitable for translating a poet to whom meaning was far more important than ornament. The defects are like nutshells on the table after a magnificent meal.[7]

- I I I -

I digress from my story a little, but I'll return to it. The grace of God came to Dante in many forms but in none happier for his poem than the *terza rima*. It was a miraculous formal invention or *trouvaille*. As the formulaic hexameter buoyed and carried the Homeric singer, so the *terza rima* collaborated (it is not too much to say) in the making of the *Commedia*. It gave Dante what he needed for his narrative, a flexible unit beyond the line, capacious enough for description and figure, argument and speech, capable of endless varieties of internal organization, and yet so compact as to make for the famous concision; above all, through the ever-developing rhyme scheme, it gave him continuous movement forward. *Terza rima* is a formal paradigm of Aristotelian Becoming—the latent or "virtual" thing constantly coming into actuality, as each new tercet fulfils with enclosing rhyme the rhyme enclosed in the preceding one. The lyric tercet, moreover, conduced to the design of the poem in cantos or songs of lyric length (the average length in fact nearly conforms to Poe's limit for lyric, reckoned five hundred years after Dante). For these reasons and others, the life of the *Commedia* is inseparable from its form, and a prose rendering alters the nature of the animal even more drastically than usual. Implicit acknowledgment of this is made in the Temple Classics version where the Carlyle-Okey-Wicksteed prose is printed in units or versicles corresponding to Dante's tercets.

The "transparency" valued by Pound in Binyon's version was therefore a formal achievement: Binyon had emulated and matched in English the labor of the original poet in Italian, so that

the reader could see through the movement of the English poem
the movement of the original composer's invention, working in
verse and in verse of just this kind. Of just this kind? Yes, insofar as
the Italian hendecasyllable can be matched by decasyllabic lines in
English. And in fact the one is closer to the other than may superficially appear. It is close historically, because Chaucer wrote his
heroic line with continental syllabic verse, in particular Dante's
Italian, in his ear (he was Dante's first translator), and easily every
third line in Chaucer is hendecasyllabic because of the nature of
Middle English. It is close rhythmically, by virtue of the phenomenon noted by Pound: that in many a "masculine" ending in English the terminal consonant will carry a latent following vowel
sound similar at least to the semi-syllable of "e muet" if not to the
Italian full vowel. The poet and scholar, F. T. Prince, has been able
to argue that it was from the Italian hendecasyllable that Milton
derived his line in *Paradise Lost*,[8] and Binyon in turn derived his
system of elision from Milton as analysed by Robert Bridges. By
the device he pointed out in his Preface and by other subtle
means, he gave his lines the metrical character of the lightly running Italian.

   Now twenty years of work on Binyon's part and nearly six
years of attentive participation by Erza Pound led up to nothing
less than the miseries and oblivions of the Second Great War. After
sending drafts of the first *Paradiso* cantos to Pound and writing to
him on December 29th, 1939, Laurence Binyon never heard again
from his friend in Rapallo. The correspondence they had already
had remained in their respective files. No English translation of
Pound's *Broletto* article appeared, or was to appear until this writing. Binyon kept his pad on his knee in the wartime evenings;
he finished his *Paradiso*. Macmillan published it in 1943. On
March 10th of that year Laurence Binyon died in a nursing home
in Reading, and his obituary appeared next day in the London
Times. Along with it appeared news of the Russian armies defend-
ing Kharkov and the latest R.A.F. raid on Germany—five hundred

tons on Munich. It was not a good year for Italian studies. If Macmillan had lost money on Binyon's *Inferno*, it certainly did not make any on his *Purgatorio* and *Paradiso*. In the event, indeed, all three volumes were allowed to go out of print for long periods and have almost never been in print at the same time.

So matters stood when the war ended in 1945. What trouble had come upon Ezra Pound it is hardly necessary to recall; few people knew or would know for years of his admiration for Binyon's Dante or the reason for it. Some Dantisti remained aware of the Binyon translation. When Paolo Milano edited a *Portable Dante* for Viking in 1947, Macmillan, for a "courtesy fee," allowed him to include Binyon's entire *Divine Comedy*. "Binyon," wrote Milano, "never distorts the original style; he never takes us beyond the range of Dante's own voice." But Binyon's preface, with its clues as to how this great virtue had been worked for, did not appear, nor was it quoted, in the Viking Portable.

W. H. Auden reviewed this book briefly but appreciatively in *The New York Times*; so did Louise Bogan in *The New Yorker*. In the United States the portable sold moderately for a while (bringing nothing, courtesy of Macmillan, to the Binyon heirs), and moderately, again, in a paperback edition (1955), but there was no counterpart in England during the '40s. In those years, however, Penguin Books began to bring out, as "Penguin Classics" under the general editorship of E. V. Rieu, paperback translations, like Rieu's *Odyssey*, priced within range of the railway bookstall trade. For the Penguin Dante, the translator selected was Dorothy Leigh Sayers, and her *Hell* was published in 1949.

It was a formidable work. She, too, had done the poem in English *terza rima*. She quoted Binyon's friend Maurice Hewlett as saying that for the translator of Dante it was "*terza rima* or nothing." With Anglo-Catholic ardor and intellectual bounce, the author of *Gaudy Night* and *The Nine Tailors* provided a long introduction, extremely full notes, and a glossary. In her time Dorothy

Sayers had won a first in medieval literature at Somerville College, Oxford, and she wrote with professional skill. Her *Hell* caught on and has been reprinted practically every year. She followed it with a Penguin *Purgatory* in 1955, and after her death in 1957 her friend Barbara Reynolds, General Editor of the *Cambridge Italian Dictionary*, added the concluding dozen or so cantos of *Paradise* for publication in 1962. *Purgatory* and *Paradise* have been reprinted many times. All are to be found in university book stores in the United States.

One result of these estimable works, however, was not fortunate. If Macmillan had ever intended in the fullness of time to venture a new printing of Binyon's *Divine Comedy*, in the edition with Italian and English on facing pages, the currency of the Sayers version in inexpensive Penguins must have made such a venture seem quixotic. In 1965, in fact, when the question arose, Macmillan pondered a new printing and decided against it. One further development has probably ruled out the possibility forever. In 1972, Chatto and Windus brought out the Viking *Portable Dante* in England, re-titled *Dante: The Selected Works*. Remarkably enough, Binyon's name appears neither on the cover nor on the title page of this book, but his version of the *Divine Comedy* is now in print in this form (again minus the preface) in the United Kingdom. Neither there nor in the United States can you buy the bilingual edition that Pound thought should supplant the Temple Classics edition for the undergraduate study of Dante, and the chances are heavily against undergraduates or anyone else ever having it.

This being the case, and admitting the seriousness and utility of Dorothy Sayers' presentation, the quality of her translation, which has already represented the poetry of Dante to several generations of students, invites a little study. When she undertook her work, she was apparently unaware of Pound's *Criterion* review of Binyon's *Inferno*, nor could she have known of the Pound-Binyon correspondence, since none of it appeared in print until eight of Pound's letters were published by D. D. Paige in *The Letters of Ezra Pound* in 1950. If thereafter she became aware of this material, she gave no indication of it in her *Purgatory* or *Paradise*. This may or may not have been to her advantage. Consider the question of feminine rhyming in imitation of the Italian hendecasyllabic line.

"I have used a liberal admixture of feminine rhyme," she wrote in her first introduction. "This is the usual English custom, and I do not know why Dante's translators for the most part fight shy of it." It was perhaps an understandable perplexity, but it had already been resolved by Binyon and Pound. Even without benefit of that solution, the translator might have reflected that a *liberal* admixture of lines that differ in termination from the norm is not like Dante's practice. His *versi tronchi* (accent on the ultima) and *versi sdruccioli* (accent on the antepenult) are rare and exceptional. But once her decision was taken, Sayers went vigorously ahead and allowed herself a good deal of the rhyming "excrescence" that Pound thought out of place in the *Commedia*. At the opening of *Inferno* 22, for example, she composed four successive tercets with nothing but feminine rhymes and in the fifth added a flourish of the *sdrucciolo* type. It is true that in the Italian of this passage there are subtle irregularities of accent, but the effect of the Sayers English is to carry these to the point of burlesque—and what is true of this passage is true of all too many others.

One might argue that variety of this kind, not only in meter and rhyming but in diction as well (she did the Provençal of Arnaut in *Purgatorio* 26 in Border Scots) make the Sayers translation more readable and save it from monotony. That may be true in this sense: clearheaded and ingenious as she was, but endowed with limited gifts as an English poet or stylist, Dorothy Sayers did well to conceive her work in a way that would utilize her strengths. Her translation is not often dull and is almost always clear—at times clearer than Binyon's. Let one example suffice, *Paradiso* 8.49–51:

Così fatta, mi disse: "Il modo m'ebbe
     giù poco tempo; e se più fosse stato,
     molto sarà di mal, che non sarebbe . . ."

BINYON: Transfigured thus, it spoke: "The world below
          Held me not long; and much would not have happed,
          Had it been longer, that now comes in woe . . ."

SAYERS: And shining thus he said: "The earthly scene
          Held me not long: had more time been allowed
          Much ill that now shall happen had not been . . ."

With her command of workmanlike English and her chosen latitude in rendering, she managed often enough, as in this case, to
avoid the "faults of the original"—and of Binyon—in the matter
of inverted word order. Without reference to the Italian, as an extended work converting Dante tercet by tercet into English verse,
her *Comedy* is a considerable achievement.

   Binyon's is simply an achievement of a higher order. His taste is
finer. He does not indulge those bright ideas that confuse everything. His style is distinguished and steady, as for all its resources of
idiom and invention one feels Dante's style to be. He had indeed
caught Dante's "tone of voice." His or any English must be more
humid than the dry burning Italian, more muted in sonority, less
Latinate and closely-knit. But line by line he represents his original with that honesty amounting to genius that Pound remarked.
In order fairly to support this judgment, let me examine in both
versions a passage of some length, at a point in the poem where
each translator after much practice may be supposed capable of his
best—the opening of the *Paradiso*.

          La gloria di colui che tutto move
             per l'universo penetra e risplende
             in una parte più e meno altrove.

SAYERS: The glory of Him who moves all things soe'er
        Impenetrates the universe, and bright
        The splendour burns, more here and lesser there.

Occurring at the end of the first line, "soe'er" could not be a more
noticeable archaism. It is also an addition to what the Italian says,
and it concludes the line with a double sibilance following the
plural "things." No less conspicuous in another way is "impene-
trates" in line 2, an uncommon word that seems tautological
rather than intensive; in fact, as it adds nothing to the idea of penetration, it seems forced. In line 3, the verb "burns" goes beyond
the Italian, and does so emphatically through the position of the
verb at the point of caesura.

BINYON: The glory of Him who moveth all that is
        Pervades the universe, and glows more bright
        In the one region, and in another less.

Here there is archaism in the old form, "moveth," but the word
occurs midline and is compact, not fluttery. It serves to avoid sibilance, and it reproduces the dissyllabic Italian *move*. "All that is"
preserves the singular of the Italian *tutto*. In line 2, "pervades" is
the right word to render penetration by light, and the three syllables of "glows more bright," follow the contour of *risplende*. Getting in the comparative in this line not only accords with English
idiom but makes it easy for the next line to retain the chiastic order of the Italian, "more . . . in the one region . . . in another . . .
less." Moreover, the word *parte* is translated here, as it is not by
Sayers.

      Nel ciel che più della sua luce prende
        fu'io, e vidi cose che ridire
        ne sa ne può chi di la su discende;

SAYERS: Within that heav'n which most receives His light
       Was I, and saw such things as man nor knows
       Nor skills to tell, returning from that height:

    "Most" in line 1 is adverbial with "receives" and barely suggests the partitive genitive of *più della sua luce.* The verb "receives" connotes more passivity than *prende.* In line 2, "was I" closely renders the past definite *fu'io,* as "saw" does *vidi,* but vagueness begins with "as man nor knows / nor skills to tell." First of all, this adds a good deal to the Italian by making the subject generic. The implication that this is an experience of mankind in general befogs the precision of the singular (though indefinite) subject understood and the singular pronoun of the Italian. Secondly, by pressure of English idiom (we cannot say that one "knows to tell"), as by the line division here, the alternatives suggested are knowing on the one hand and having skill to tell on the other, which misrepresents the original.

BINYON: In that heaven which partakes most of His light
       I have been, and have beheld such things as who
       Comes down thence has no wit nor power to write;

    "Partakes most of His light" renders the active force of the Italian verb and partitive expression. "I have been," the English perfect, though a looser rendering of *fu'io,* is not only allowable but suitable to the tone of the passage as expressing a more contemplative and less purely narrative time sense. There is concision in "comes down thence," and "has no wit nor power" not only renders the alternatives correctly but unfolds what is latent in the two Italian verbs.

       perché appressando sé al suo disire,
         nostro intelletto si profonda tanto,
         che dietro la memoria non può ire.

SAYERS: For when our intellect is drawing close
                To its desire, its paths are so profound
                That memory cannot follow where it goes.

The first line and a half closely render the Italian, but the next clause expands the metaphor with an image, "paths," that raises two questions: first, why the plural? and second, why such a degree of concreteness as to make that question arise? In line 3, *dietro ire* is presumed to mean "follow," implying a relationship between intellect and memory that is only superficially plausible.

BINYON: Such depth our understanding deepens to
                When it draws near unto its longing's home
                That memory cannot backward with it go.

Here line 1 subtly embodies equivalences to the quality of the Italian: a four-syllable word, "understanding," to match and even chime with the participle *appressando*, and alliteration of four "ds" to match the "s's" and "ds" of the original. In line 3 the Italian is interpreted more precisely than in the Sayers version; here it is not that memory cannot "follow" the intellect but that it cannot return with it, taking *dietro* to mean "back," or indeed "back again," rather than "behind."

   Are such points as these mere niggling? Before us on the open page is the philosophical poem of Christendom. It was written, as Ezra Pound once said, to make people think. In every line it exemplifies that activity. The translator's first job is to render Dante's meaning exactly and with delicacy. His second but no less crucial job is to render what he can—and again, with delicacy—of the verbal and metrical form in which the poet did his thinking. It sees that in both respects, again and again, one translation surpasses the other—not a bad one, either—bearing out what Pound said in *Broletto* about Binyon's idiom. But let us continue.

> Veramente quant'io del regno santo
> nella mia mente potei far tesoro,
> sarà ora materia del mio canto.

SAYERS: Yet now, of the blest realm whate'er is found
Here in my mind still treasured and possessed
Must set the strain for all my song to sound.

"Whate'er" in line 1 rarefies the solid *quanto.* The agent *io* and the past action of treasuring up are transposed to a present passive construction. In the monosyllabic line 3, there is insensitive alliteration of four "s's," and the businesslike *sarà ora materia* becomes a tired poeticality, "must set the strain."

BINYON: Nevertheless what of the blest kingdom
Could in my memory, for its treasure, stay
Shall now the matter of my song become.

The echo of the Latin *verumtamen* in *Veramente* has been perceived and carried into the rendering. *Quanto* is, curtly, "what," and is first the subject of a past action as in the Italian it was the object of one, then the subject of a future statement exactly, and in exactly the same terms, as in the Italian.

> O buono Apollo, all' ultimo lavoro
> fammi del tuo valor sì fatto vaso,
> come dimandi a dar l'amato alloro.

SAYERS: Gracious Apollo! in this crowning test
Make me the conduit that thy power runs through!
Fit me to wear those bays thou lovest best!

Here several displacements have occurred, from *buono* to "gracious" for Apollo, from *ultimo lavoro* to something quite different, a "crowning test," and most interesting of all, from *vaso* to a "conduit" through which the god's power is conceived to run. For the covert and intricate alliterative pattern of the third Italian line (*me . . . man . . . ma . . .* and *di . . . di . . . da*) we have "bays . . . best." In this final phrase a small ambiguity appears: do we understand that bays in general are what the god loves best, or that there are certain ("those") bays that among all bays he loves best?

BINYON: For the last labour, good Apollo, I pray,
    Make me so apt a vessel of thy power
    As is required for gift of thy loved bay.

Here lines 1 and 2, without obscurity or difficulty, adhere to the vocabulary of the Italian including "vessel" for *vaso*, not less felicitous for not narrowing the conception to an open channel or pipe. The last line lacks any such obvious alliteration as that of the Sayers version, but the closing consonants of "gift" are quietly echoed by those of "loved," and the vowel sound of "required" is echoed by "thy."

- I V -

Though Binyon finished his *Paradiso* without benefit of Pound's criticism, he undoubtedly brought to bear on it what he had absorbed from Pound's notes on the other two *cantiche*. As to the *Inferno*, in recording Pound's marginal notations in 1934 he said he intended some-day to bring out a revised edition, and this in fact became a serious undertaking. Using an extra set of clean page proofs of the poem, he went through it canto by canto, making in pen revisions of lines or passages that either he or Pound had found improvable. It is uncertain when most of this work was done; whether he did indeed wait until he had finished the *Paradiso* before returning to the "black air," as Pound suggested, or whether he began at once in 1934 and gave occasional hours to revision over the next eight or nine years. When he died he left among his papers a full set of page proofs of all thirty-four cantos, each bearing a number of revisions, in all more than 500, in almost all cases clear improvements.

The value of this concluding labor was clear to Binyon's widow, who typed out all the revisions and intended to have them incorporated in a new Macmillan printing. This has never taken place. The revisions remained among Binyon's papers until the late '60s when Binyon's daughter, Nicolete (Mrs. Basil Gray), contrived to get them incorporated in the *Viking Portable* text, in a new edition dated 1969. The very first of these revisions may stand as representative of them all. Canto 1, line 1 of the *Inferno* in 1934:

> Midway the journey of this life I was 'ware . . .

In the new edition:

> Midway life's journey I was made aware . . .

The first version announced to the ear at once Binyon's system of elisions (journey of) and his deliberate allowance of a quota of archaism in style ('ware). Evidently to his later judgment, certainly influenced by Pound, these features were not enough to justify such a finicky line. He replaced it with what Pound called "straightness."

(1981)

Notes

1. Ezra Pound, "Hell," *Literary Essays of Ezra Pound*, ed. with an introduction by T. S. Eliot (London, 1954), p. 201.

2. Ezra Pound, *The Letters of Ezra Pound*, ed. D. D. Paige (New York, 1950), p. 251.

3. This and other letters of Laurence Binyon are quoted by kind permission of Nicolete Gray and The British Society of Authors. I am very grateful to Mrs. Gray for her consideration in placing these and other papers of her father at my disposal.

4. Quoted from letters in the possession of Nicolete Gray. For permission to use these letters I am grateful to the Literary Executors of Ezra Pound.

5. From a letter in the possession of Nicolete Gray.

6. Ezra Pound, *The Letters of Ezra Pound*, p. 310.

7. Ezra Pound, "Binyon," *Broletto, Periodico della Città di Como*, 3 (October, 1938), p. 14. For the opportunity of consulting this periodical and copying portions of Pound's article, I am indebted to the kindness of Professor Louis Martz, in 1975 Director of the Beinecke Rare Book Library of Yale University.

8. F. T. Prince, *The Italian Element in Milton's Verse* (Oxford, 1954), rev. 1962.

Robert Lowell

Dante's Actuality and Fecundity in the Anglo-Saxon World

I have been asked to bear witness, and to bear witness briefly, to Dante's *actuality* and *fecundity* in the Anglo Saxon world. Forgive me for repeating this mischievously over-literal translation of my assignment. The other day, I ran into a perfect example of Dante's infecundity. A few blocks from our apartment, in New York, rise the huge, unadorned, perpendicular white slabs of the new Philharmonic Hall, Opera House, and Theatres of the civic art center. Infinitely below them and overshadowed by them, lies a little triangle, or sliver, of park space, on which someone has set a large, lumpish bad statue of Dante. Misbegotten, misplaced and gilded, the statue vibrates in the heavy traffic, and will soon be pulled down and junked to improve the vista. Even now, in its glory, it looks like a cheap paper weight, and has little authority and relation to Dante.

I do not want to offer Dante another gilded statue, so I hurry away from the intangible sublimities of his public esteem in America. Dante's influence on English writers is luckily something much more limited, precise and provable. One is tempted, perhaps, to make it too precise and limited. Shortly before his death, T. S. Eliot wrote that "our important debt to Dante does not lie in borrowings, or adaptations, passages in which one has taken him as a model, or to which the critic can point the finger and say that this and this wouldn't have been written if the writer hadn't had Dante in mind." Eliot then describes the three most important things that he himself has learned from Dante. The first is that Dante among the great poets is the most painstaking and conscious practitioner of the craft of poetry; above all in his language, he teaches that the great master of language is the great servant of it. The second thing to be learned is that Dante is able to see, hear and put into words, thoughts, perceptions and emotions that are beyond the range of ordinary men; and, last of all, Dante is the most universally European of all the great European writers. I would agree with Eliot that Dante's most important influence is something along these lines, and only add that this sort of influence is almost impossible to prove without going into the autobiographies of English writers and making wild, though perhaps genuine, claims.

Dante's definite influence is a simple matter. Down to the nineteenth century, he had none at all. The *Commedia* took the techniques and fashions of its time to places where no one else dreamed of going, or dared to. It had no imitators, and hence no influence. Why this was, I am unsure. Probably it was simply the change in literary styles; typical new Renaissance methods were rapidly developing and Dante was soon forgotten even as a forerunner. Something too in his character must have awed and scared men off by its arrogance, he was too mystical for other men of letters, too worldly for other mystics, too embroiled in the *ephemera* of his times, too Italian, too much the eternal judge.

Anyway, English poetry came too late to be influenced by Dante. Chaucer, writing fifty years after his death, read him, revered him, and found him dated. Here a problem arises which will arise again and which I cannot answer. Boccaccio, a close student of Dante, perhaps couldn't have written without his example. Chaucer, whose most ambitious poem is a translation and enlargement of Boccaccio, of course needed Boccaccio. Did he need Dante? I cannot say anything except that I can find no important direct trace. Among Chaucer's contemporaries, and immediate successors, the more secular were out of sympathy with Dante's whole character, the more religious were too narrow or provincial to use him, or probably even to know him. The English sixteenth century, the great Renaissance century, could honor and imitate almost any classical Greek or Roman, or modern Frenchman or Italian. Dante must have influenced writers who influenced Englishmen of this time, but he himself leaves no discernible mark on these writers and was unknown to them. To the metaphysical and baroque poets of the earlier seventeenth century, and to the neo-classical of the late seventeenth and entire eighteenth, Dante was increasingly remote. No new writers were added to the Renaissance canon of classics, and some were dropped. In all this time, Milton is the only writer, perhaps, who really read Dante and honored him as a pioneer "Protestant" and humanist. He may even have felt obscurely influenced by this other poet-prophet and politician that is Dante, but though Milton could use such dissimilar poets as Euripides, the author of Job, Virgil and Tasso, Dante must have seemed fantastic to him as an example and technician, a Goth knotted up in the barbarities of Rhyme and many worse superstitions.

In the nineteenth century, Dante suddenly changed from an *unread* name to one of the three or four great poets of the world. Coleridge wrote acute comparisons of Dante and Milton, Shelley wrote two of his greatest poems in *terza rima* and was clearly inspired by Dante, and Keats read Cary's translation, and made remarkable Dantesque revision in his *Hyperion*. *Terza rima*, by the way, poses a problem. It is such a difficult meter to even make sense with in English, that one is tempted to imagine that no one undazzled by the glory of Dante would have the folly to try it. Dante is the source of Allen Tate's *terza rima*, possibly also of one of Robert Frost's best sonnets, but certainly not of Sir Thomas Wyatt, who introduced this meter in English, and had a later Italian poet in mind. The rest of Dante's influence on later English writers is quickly told. Dante began the last century by being compared with Milton, later Matthew Arnold used quotations from Dante to show up the limitations of even the greatest English poets, and still later few questioned that Shakespeare was the only English poet who could be placed beside him. In poetic practice a minor English literary revolution was accomplished, when Dante Gabriel Rossetti and the other Pre-Raphaelites imitated and translated the minor poems of Dante and his contemporaries into fine and still more minor English poems. Dante is closer, I think, to Americans than to the British. He fits in with the dark, allegorical geniuses of Hawthorne and Melville, pleases our reckless Protestant earnestness and wish to be free of the English past. In the writings of Santayana and the later Henry Adams, Dante is carefully studied and proposed as a moral and aesthetic cause. Today Dante, though not perhaps popular or of a major influence, is surely at the height of esteem. One serious book of poems out of ten will echo or use him in some way.

I want to end my paper on his reality and influence by looking at Browning, Pound and T. S. Eliot. Browning seldom if ever shows a definite debt to Dante, and yet I think he must always have had Dante in his mind. Browning keeps his Victorian distance, yet he shows this nearness by many troubadour and Pre-Raphaelite enthusiasms, by constantly turning to the Italian past and present for material, and by cramming his poems like Dante with the prose of speculation, fact and people. In Pound, whose *Cantos* take off from Browning, and make perhaps our one serious modern stab at an epic, the connection with Dante is closer. Pound praises Dante and his Italian and Provençal predecessors often in his prose, fills his lines with quotations and paraphrases from Dante, and seems to be consciously trying to emulate Dante in his use of politics and the classics and history. In their development, the *Cantos* seem to move from the world of crime and history to an earthly paradise, and flashing images of spiritual light.

The poet, however, who is much the most intimately close to

Dante is T. S. Eliot. He goes farther than any other literary critic to describe and praise Dante. I've never felt sure whether Eliot preferred Dante to Shakespeare and didn't wish to say so, or merely wished he could prefer Dante. He speaks of Dante going higher and deeper, of his having the advantage of being backed by a profound system of thought and of his being a safer model than Shakespeare for contemporary poets. Eliot's religion sometimes seems like Dante's religion, only more so, with politicians, worldly love and the classics left out. His first important poem, *Prufrock*, is prefaced by lines spoken by Guido of Montefeltro in the *Inferno*; his *Waste Land*, as a visit to hell and modern Europe, is dotted with Dante's quotes that almost enframe it; his lyrical sequence, *Ash-Wednesday*, is modelled on the last cantos of the *Purgatorio*; and his last great poem, *Four Quartets*, concludes with a passage imitated from the Brunetto canto. This is the supreme example of a passage inspired by Dante in English. By magical, tactful and intuitive touches, Eliot has made Dante charming, by innovations, he has made him contemporary, and by a lifetime of dedication, he has made his own collected poems one single long poem, a journey through Hell and Purgatory to the *flickering* of Paradise. The two poets seem libered together. In the end, after seven hundred years, Dante's astonishing presence in the poetry of T. S. Eliot and Ezra Pound shows his vitality in the way most gratifying to a poet—in the works of his fellow poets who write long after, in other styles and other languages.

(1965)

Robert Lowell

Epics

"Poetry makes nothing happen," Auden said; but the great epics, like our own classics, must mean something, not by didactic pedagogy, propaganda, or edification—but by their action, a murky metaphysical historic significance, a sober intuition into the character of a nation—profundities imagined, as if in a dream, by authors who knew what they had written. Even to the Philistine *podestà*, Dante was the soul of Italy.

Homer—hexameters must have slid from his tongue, as easily and artfully as Shakespeare's last blank verse. He had no necessity or license to vary meter, and had less anxiety than even Walt Whitman for the triumphs of overcurious craft. This and narrative genius were his simplicities to celebrate the cycle of Greek radiance, barbarism, and doom with the terrible clairvoyance of a prophet.

The *Iliad* is the epic of Greece, written when Greece was still half Asiatic and tossing in the womb of her brilliance. Here, already foreshadowed, are deviously debating fractious Greek leaders, kings of petty city-states; the bisexual warrior, heroic comradeship, the lonely man of Excellence, unreliable, indispensable, ostracized at the height of his fortune—here, too, the theme of Greek pathos, the young men carved on the stele for Marathon, the victory's *gloria mundi* killed in full flower.

The *Iliad*, unlike other world epics, is dialectical: thesis, antithesis—the synthesis is wearisome to work and transitory . . . fury, then contrition—insensate rage of Achilles forced to relinquish his concubine, Briseis, to Agamemnon, then his recoiling on himself after the death of Patroclus to rejoin the Greek fighting—then his rabid butchery of the Trojans, then gently relenting to return Hector's body to Priam, the helpless father . . . what no other Greek would dare to do. Achilles is the most mercurial and psychic mind in epic narrative—if mind may be defined as wavering, irresistible force, a great scythe of hubris, lethal to itself, enemies, and the slaves—animator of the actual.

Alexander carried the *Iliad* with other Greek classics on his own Asian invasion, and mysteriously relived with greater intelligence, though a Macedonian alcoholic, the impulsive brutality and forgiveness of Achilles. General Fuller writes: "He was both mystical and practical . . . It was in his outlook upon women—in nearly all ages considered the legitimate spoil of the soldier—that Alexander stood in a totally different moral world compared with the one inhabited by his contemporaries . . . Yet, in spite of this extraordinary respect for womanhood, his highest moral virtue is to be discovered in one of the final remarks Arrian makes in *The Anabasis*[:] 'But I do know that to Alexander alone of the kings of old did repentance for his faults come by reason of his noble nature.' " It's the same Achilles, imitated by a long line of Plutarchan Greeks, from Themistocles and Socrates of Athens down to Philopemon of Megalopolis. What can Homer teach . . . the generosity in cruelty?

Milton's run-on blank verse is very baroque, but strangely unlike other ornate verse, it is hard and idiomatic. I believe him when he boasts that with time his numbers became easy and unpremeditated, an inspired, various instrument whenever his plot condescended to him.

"Milton wrote in fetters when he wrote of Angels & God, and

at liberty when of Devils & Hell." Thus Blake, of course, in the most famous comment on *Paradise Lost*. Blake based a whole heretical theology on it, many revolutionary *Songs of Experience* . . . and much distrait sprawling. Blake was right. One can prove this by running through *Paradise Lost* and marking the good lines or groups of lines. The only celestial angels are fallen.

I do not understand Milton's intention. Who or what is Satan? He is not ultimate evil, though in Milton's myth the origin of human ill. He lacks many of the common vices of tragedy: disloyalty to friends, cowardice, and stupidity. By title the Father of Lies, he is not provably a liar. What he says to the rebel angels, Eve, and even Christ might well seem true to the sage and unorthodox Milton. He is no devil but a cosmic rebellious Earl of Northumberland, Harry Hotspur, with an intelligence and iron restraint. He is almost early American, the cruel, unconquerable spirit of freedom.

He has great moments—rousing his followers prostrate in the infernal bog, his great oratory to them, the Cromwellian drill and parade of his defeated armies. One feels Milton knew more of military tactics than Shakespeare, whose battles are charade. This can't be simply the limitations of the Elizabethan stage. Yet Shakespeare understood most realistically the evil and pestilence of civil war. In Book Two's great parliamentary speeches, the devils organize their words like old parliamentarians, less dishonest, and more concise. Satan defying the sun at the beginning of Book Four might be Milton addressing his blindness, his head only ringing now with ideal upheaval. Satan even animates Eve, though Adam has never been able to, nor she him. He brings out all the good in her, then her ruin. We can't deprive Satan of his power to destroy—". . . yet all his good proved ill in me . . . evil be thou my good." In *Paradise Regained*, a diminished Satan, maybe himself in disguise, makes all the brilliant speeches. Christ is only a rocky, immobile Puritan breakwater—the voice of denial? Which voice rings true? Are both schizoid anti-selves of one person?

Paradise Lost is alone among epics in being without human beings, except perhaps Eve and Adam. Satan is the engineer of ruin.

> His troubled thoughts . . . stir
> The Hell within him, for within him Hell
> He brings, and round about him, nor from Hell
> One step no more than from himself can fly.

After twenty centuries of Christianity, we see our ruin is irrepara-
ble. Satan cannot be discovered by faith or science. Could he have
been plausible to Milton in the 1660s? *Paradise Lost* is one of the
world's great poems; I do not see the author's intention. Is Satan
the hermetic God . . . *Christus Liberator?*

Dante was virtually a Ghibelline, a fanatical one. His *Commedia* is
a Ghibelline epic. The Ghibellines looked for a German Emperor,
their shadowy hope, who would unify, but not annex, Italy. They
loathed popes as principals of disharmony and internecine murder. They had leanings toward heresy. They led lives, as did the
Pope's adherents, the Guelphs, that sinned in a hundred common
ways: adultery, sodomy, murder, treason, intrigue. In the *Commedia*,
they are tortured for these misdeeds—but who is ever hurt in a
poem? Almost all Dante's poetically inspired or humanly attractive
characters are Ghibelline—if they are not, like Francesca and
Ulysses, they seem the Ghibelline underground. There's one ar-
guable exception, Beatrice, but I will come to her in time. The
great sinners are imagined with such sympathy that Erich Auerbach believed that they almost crack Dante's theological system.

With saints, Dante is apathetic. They are written with a dry
pen, and parsimonious vision. St. Francis, St. Dominic, St.
Bonaventure, Cato, etc., seem almost like primitive lives of the

saints read in the silence of a Trappist dinner. They are *nature morte*, and hardly nature, though girded in cunning coils of scholastic philosophy.

Dante's unique genius as a writer of epic—I even include Melville's prose—is that his chief characters are not heroically enlarged, but life-size. Masaccio, alone among the old Italian painters, had this wish for human proportion, lost by the grandeur and embellishment of his greater successors. It's in Farinata's "But who are your ancestors?" Or, holding himself upright in his fiery tomb "as if he held the Inferno in disdain." Ugolino's eating his own starving children, who willingly sacrifice themselves to save their father from starvation. Or Manfredi in the *Purgatorio*, a type of the liberator German Emperor and solider than Othello, "Biondo era e bello," etc., down to his burial, *a lume spento*, without the rites of the Church. He is the bastard son of Federico Secondo, the *stupor mundi*, and the greatest Ghibelline, who, though only listed in the *Inferno* among those damned for heresy, somehow overshadows the whole *Commedia* with a revered spirit; just as Pope Boniface VIII is its devil, though paradoxically consigned to Purgatory, not Hell [*sic*]. I am suggesting that the *Commedia*, like *Paradise Lost*, is in part hermetic, and means at times the opposite of what it asserts.

I find it hard to consider Dante as entirely orthodox. Much in his political preference and poetic training, in the *dolce stil nuovo* derived from the Provençals, points toward heresy. But Christian Faith is alive in him, not cold as in Milton. The Church gave his writing a dialectical confusion and intensity. Two forces, not one. His dogs of the Church, Hell's torturers, are real dogs. The *Commedia* is not just a political epic but also, perhaps with less ebullience, a religious epic. *Pilgrim's Progress*. In canto 100 of the *Paradiso*, by far Dante's greatest purely sacred poem, dogma changes miraculously to mystical contemplation, the most magnificent in Christian literature.

Beatrice? Saving Grace? She was born in Provence, in the heretical Toulouse of the troubadours—the lady, not one's wife, but the one the troubadour truly loves—chastely by necessity with Dante, but not always in the tradition. Where, where, in the whole *Commedia*, are Mrs. Dante and the Dante children? Dante's meeting with Beatrice in the *Purgatorio* burns with a fiercer love than Francesca's for Paolo. Without Beatrice, Dante's *Comedy* wouldn't exist but, as Pound said, would be "a ladder leading to a balloon."

Unlike other epics, *Moby-Dick*, though an allegory, is also an exact whaling voyage. It is not hermetic; things are what they are, and do not opaquely suggest the opposite. The plot is as uncompli-cated and straight as its harpoons. Ahab, of course, is other things than a veteran Nantucket whaling captain. In "the Guinea-coast slavery of his solitary command," he suggests Melville's copy-clerk, Bartleby, and Pierre crazed on his withdrawal to write—three cut off from society by the wreck of seclusion. Ahab's perverted reli-gious hunt to kill the White Whale is monomaniacal. He is apoc-alyptic, with a rage that drowns ship, shipmates, and himself. His destiny is analogous to heroes in Norse Saga, Wagner's *Götterdäm-merung*, and, in real life, Adolf Hitler. " 'The first thing that but of-fers to jump from this boat, I stand in, that thing I harpoon' . . . all directed to that fatal goal which Ahab their one lord and keel did point to . . . how they still strove through the infinite blueness to seek the thing that might destroy them." There's no doubt of Ahab's courage and ability—in action he is more subtly alert and correct than his subordinates.

Moby Dick, the Whale, is more ambiguous. Contradictory scholars label and symbolize him as both evil and its opposite, na-ture. Let him be nature, a Leviathan with the dolphin's uncanny psychic brain—superior, his enthusiasts would claim, to man, whom he never fought except to save his life. His evil is strength to kill the killer whalemen. Indestructible by Ahab, he is not immortal, and is often permanently wounded.

Homer is blinding Greek sunlight; Virgil is dark, narrow, morbid, mysterious, and artistic. He fades in translation, unlike Homer, who barely survives. By combining the plots of the *Iliad* and the *Odyssey*, Virgil has seemed a plagiarist, attempting an epic as a task for rhetoric. He is as original as Milton. Dryden and the Restoration critics were wrong in thinking the *Aeneid* something like their regilding of Jacobean tragedy . . . giving alloy and polish to old gold.

One cannot doubt that Virgil sincerely and deeply admired the Emperor Augustus, not only for personal patronage but for the peace he brought Italy after her ulcerous, unceasing civil wars, from Marius and Sulla, Caesar and Pompey, Marcus Antonius and Brutus, to Marcus Antonius and Octavian . . . to Augustus. Aeneas is a peace-bringer, a bringer of peace through carnage. I feel Virgil, like a more ambivalent and furtive Milton, was also on the devil's side.

The *Aeneid* is the song of Rome's annals in prophecy and hindsight. Aeneas, unlike Achilles and Odysseus, is darkened by destiny—his actions do not emanate in the present, or from impulsive passions. He exemplifies the grit, torture, and sacrifice that made Rome's unification of the Mediterranean possible. One's heart goes to the defeated. How could Virgil, an outlander, sympathize with Rome's bloody, centralizing conquest of Italy? Why does he make us weep for the deaths of Camilla, Mezentius, and Turnus, outlanders like himself? It's interesting how instinctively and without justifying himself, Virgil chose archaic heroes of his country from both Trojan and Italian.

MEZENTIUS:

"nunc vivo neque adhuc homines lucemque relinquo sed
linquam."

(10.855–56)

CAMILLA:

"hactenus, Acca soror, potui; nunc volnus acerbum conficit et
tenebris nigrescunt omnia circum . . ."

vitaque cum gemitu fugit indignata sub umbras.

(11.823–24, 831)

Aeneas puzzles, a force more than a person—nothing here of
Achilles' dialectic, or the crafty, resourceful companionship of
Odysseus. He lumbers through his irresistible march in the last
books, less a living man than a Patroclus, hit on the head and
stunned by Apollo—or Sintram, paranoid, brave, riding half para-
lyzed by his costly armor through the bedeviled wood of Dürer.
He thinks little, thinks up little, though subject to heartfelt depression. Whatever his author was, he is not an *anima naturaliter Chris-
tiana.*

Aeneas has a moment or two of imagination and clairvoyance—his hallucinated and almost surrealist narrative of the fall of
Troy in Book Two—dust, smoke, butchery, deceit, terror, the anni-
hilation of his home and city. Some authentic murmur in Aeneas'
voice makes us unwilling to believe this book was ghostwritten by
Virgil. With Dido too, he is alive. Dido is hell, Phèdre, Madame
Bovary, talkative, repetitive—her few words symbolize thousands.
Yet our love goes with her, her beauty, her bravery, her misfortune;
and Aeneas, her deserter, seems no man. After her suicide, Aeneas
must descend to the underworld, a Roman cemetery with shades
like statues: the Illustrious, his dead comrades and unborn descen-
dants. Dido alone is alive, when she turns her back and says nothing to Aeneas' false, forced appeals.

Aeneas is sometimes swollen and Rubenesque, as if painted for
the peaceful triumphs of Marie de' Medici—I wish he were
greater and had more charm. Yet Virgil, like Frankenstein, put a
heart and mind, his own, into his Colossus, the triumphant Roman general, the soul of his great epic, if not of Rome. He bears
all, he suffers all, a man of sorrows, if human . . . He mislays his
wife, while himself escaping the ruin of Troy. He ungrapples
mighty Dido, though almost as unfitted for this struggle as
Prufrock. Don't doubt him; his soldiers move forward undeflected.
They do not fight helter-skelter like Greeks, but rather as legion-
naires drilled by Marius or Caesar to slaughter the barbarian. All
Italy is turned on its head by Aeneas for him to marry Lavinia—
she must have loved his victim, Turnus, whose plea for life is refused by Aeneas with stoical severity. Turnus' last action is the final
line of the *Aeneid*:

vitaque cum gemitu fugit indignata sub umbras.
(12.952)

Forever, indignation—too many beautiful things were crushed by
the conquest. Too much attrition for the slavery to be immortal
for the Romans hard as nails. Virgil may have understood his epic,
its prophecy that the Empire of the Divine Augustus was inevitably eroding.

Moby-Dick, like most of our nineteenth-century masterpieces, was
published stillborn, and sold so little it soon snuffed out Melville's
popular reputation. It's our epic, a New England epic; unless we
feel the enchanted discontinuity of Pound's *Cantos* qualifies. *Moby-
Dick* is also our one epic in prose. Are there epics in prose? I know
one, Carlyle's *French Revolution*, also stylized as poetic extrava-
gance. The modern British historian Taylor wrote: " . . . more than
five hundred errors, some of them by no means minor. But what

does it matter? When you read Carlyle's *Revolution*, you are there."
Epics as verifiable history have too many pitfalls, too many to
tempt a rival.

Moby-Dick is fiction, not history—beside James or Dickens,
how thin and few its characters, how heroic and barbarous its adventure. As a librettist once said to me, "Not the faintest whisper
of a female voice." Often magnificent rhythms and a larger vocabulary make it equal to the great metrical poems. Parts, of course,
are not even prose, but collages of encyclopedic clippings on ce-
tology. It is our best book. It tells us not to break our necks on a
brick wall. Yet what sticks in mind is the Homeric prowess of the
extinct whaleman, gone before his prey.

Melville had much experience, if sailing on whalers brings
more than working like Hawthorne in a Customs House . . . as
Melville himself did for the remainder of his life . . . twenty unfathomable years of marriage, parenthood, customs, whatever—
then thinking of the oceans, and possibly allegorizing himself a
little, Melville wrote his final and imperfect masterpiece, *Billy
Budd*, the blond, innocent young seaman, hanged from the
yardarm by naval law.

(1977)

Robert Duncan

The Sweetness and Greatness of
Dante's Divine Comedy

We meet tonight to honor Dante in the seven hundredth year [1965] of his birth. The very name *Dante*, the poet Saint-John Perse said in his lecture on Dante in Florence in April of this year, "the very name, a word of power, retains today the most exalted resonance even to the depths of the poetic cave." In the constellations of Poetry there are thousands of distant stars and more immediate planets, lighting the night sky of those who delight in that art with a plenitude of brilliancies, and in time each new poet in his vocation comes to realize that he has a kind of horoscope or constellation of his own in which particular poets in the past appear as influencing spirits in his shaping of his poetic destiny. But two poets—Dante and Shakespeare—are surely so immediate and so radiant that they stand not like stars but like two suns in our poetic world in whose presence there is day and in whose absence there is night, two suns to whom we must turn for the main stream of that fire of poetic creation to awaken fully in us and for that illumination that will open our eyes to what is going on in this art to which we have been called to reveal the objects of our world in its poetic light.

Dante undertook to make Italian the vehicle of his highest thought and in so doing forged the soul of a people. But we, who are not Italian nor who have any fluency of that tongue, meet here

tonight to do him honor which is also dues or duty, for Dante undertook at the same time to make Poetry the vehicle of man's
highest thought, and in so doing he forged the very soul of man
and of Poetry anew. He so exalted speech within the given grace
of his tongue—by the sweetness of his language so entered into
the evocation of the supreme sweetness he knew to be the order
of all orders in his universe—that every intuition and yearning we
have to be brought into the orders of a great music must be
haunted by the thought of the poetic vision of his *Commedia*; just
as every reflection we would make upon the meaning and revelation—upon the trials and dangers—of romantic love—I mean
here the love that is known in the spirit of romance in poetry—
every study we would make of the nature of love must return to
those entities of Dante's poetic imagination, to the angel Amor
and to the transcendent Beatrice. Charles Williams, whose life was
devoted to the psychology, the philosophy and the theology of romantic love, has given us in his great work, *The Figure of Beatrice*, a
study of the *Commedia* worthy of its subject. It is a book which has
been a source again and again for my own approach to Dante. But
in my preparation over these past three months, returning to the
Purgatorio and reading for the first time the *Convivio*, I found myself not only recognizing everywhere that spirit of romance that,
after the troubadours of Provence and of the court of Sicily, Dante
brought to its first fullness, but also following another aspect of
Dante's vision in which the persons and scenes of the *Commedia*
hid in their fiction certain truths of what his art was. The operations and mysteries of Poetry itself as Dante reveals them are as
subtle, and central to his vision of the Real as the operations and
mysteries of Love are. They are not separate, for their reality is one;
they have their source in the same literal ground of the poem. Poetry as well as Love is revealed in terms of that four-fold understanding that Dante would have us have. "The sense of this work is
not simple," he writes in the letter in which he dedicates the *Commedia* to his patron, Can Grande: "but on the contrary, it may be

called *polysemous*, that is to say, 'of more senses than one.' " In the
literal sense, Dante tells Can Grande, the *Commedia* presents the
state of souls after death—Hell, Purgatory, Heaven. Here I would
turn to the Second Treatise of the *Convivio* where Dante first expounds this concept of reading the poem:

> The literal sense should always come first as the one in the
> meaning whereof the others are included, and without
> which it were impossible and irrational to attend to the
> others.

This doctrine of the literal, the immediate and embodied
sense, as the foundation of all others, is striking to the modern
poet, for it very much is the meaning of the insistence of the
Imagists upon the image in its direct presentation, from which all
meanings may flow, as the primary in poetry, and of their abhor-
rence of all abstractions if they be divorced from the primal reality
of incarnation. Not only in Theology but in Poetry too, something
goes awry if in our adoration of the Logos we lose sense of or
would cut loose from the living body and passion of Man in the
actual universe. Words can float away in a light of their own, taking the light *for* their own, as if the universe of actual things, that
we rightly call Creation, were, as the gnostics believed, a material
antagonistic to meanings. Dante's insistence upon the literal, the
actual, the human experience is pervasive. For him, as for Plato, an
idea is a thing seen. And he is careful and concerned always to portray for us the terms of the experience. A thing may be presented
not only in its immediacy, but in dream, in ecstatic trance, in work
of art, even in word of mouth—as in canto 18, where a voice
shouts "Mary ran with haste to the hill country," reminding us of
Our Lady.

> Wherefore inasmuch as the literal meaning is always the
> subject and material of the others, especially the allegorical,

it is impossible to come at the knowledge of the others before coming at the knowledge of it.

In this poetics, the actual world and man are not weavings of a
beautiful illusion, as in the Buddhist doctrine of Maia, nor are they
in their matter bonds of evil and darkness to meaning, as in the
gnostic vision, but the universe and our experience in it is a text
that we must learn to read if we are to come to the truth of it and
of ourselves. Dante, I think, incorporates the actualities of history,
of his own life and of the history of man, as essential to his poem,
because it is essential in his religion that God was actually and historically incarnate. Poetics as well as Theology is involved in the
conflicting doctrines of the transubstantiation in the Mass, where
men have their controversy as to whether the Presence is literal,
actual, or whether It is symbolic; whether, as for those who would
abstract Christ as a mere idea, it is sentimental, or, as for the positive logicians, a psychotic fancy without intelligible meaning. The
declaration in the opening passages of William Carlos Williams's
Paterson that has been one of the axioms of a new poetry—"no
ideas but in things"—is catholic and in the spirit of Dante.
    The second sense in which we are to take what we experience
is called the allegorical, and this, Dante tells us, "is the one that
hides itself under the mantle of these tales, and is a truth hidden
under beauteous fiction." Dante is careful to remind us in the
Convivio that the theologians take this sense otherwise than the
poets do. "But since it is my purpose here to follow the method of
the poets," he continues, "I shall take the allegorical sense after the
use of the poets."
    I was not wrong then perhaps when I was led to read Dante's
meaning in the *Commedia* in search of an allegory of his poetics.
And here I would give some account of the way I interpret
Dante's allegorical or fictional sense in its relation to his literal
sense, for I return to read Dante with a concept of fictions that, if
it be in part derived from earlier readings of Dante, is derived from

many other sources in the course of my own life and thought in poetry. With Dante, I take the literal, the actual, as the primary ground. We ourselves are literal, actual beings. This is the hardest ground for us to know, for we are *of* it—not outside, observing, but inside, experiencing. It is, finally, I believe, the only ground for us to know; for it is Creation, it is the Divine Presentation, it is the language of experience whose words are immediate to our senses; from which our own creative life takes fire, *within which* our own creative life takes fire. This creative life is a drive towards the reality of Creation, producing an inner world, an emotional and intellectual fiction, in answer to our awareness of the creative reality of the whole. If the world does not speak to us, we cannot speak with it. If we view the literal as a matter of mere fact, as the positivist does, it is mute. But once we apprehend the literal as a language, once things about us reveal depths and heights of meaning, we are involved in the sense of Creation ourselves, and in our human terms, this is Poetry, Making, the inner Fiction of Consciousness. If the actual world be denied as the primary ground and source, that inner fiction can become a fiction of the Unreal, in which not Truth but Wish hides. The allegorical or mystic sense, Dante says in his letter to Can Grande, is the sense which we get through the thing the letter signifies. It is our imagination of what the universe means, and it has its origin in the universe. To put it another way, it is by the faculty of imagination that we come to the significance of the world and of man, imagining what is in order to involve ourselves more deeply in what is.

So, in turn, Dante's remaining senses in which we are to read— the moral and the anagogical (in which all things "signify some portion of the supernal things of eternal glory")—take their life in the fictional and ultimately and primarily in the literal, and are each clarifications of the intent of the whole, as they are deepenings of our personal, psychological and spiritual involvement—of *our* intent then—in the destiny of the universe and of man.

Having raised this Duncanian heresy in which the literal is so identified with the actual, and the linguistic with the universal, I would return now, as I prepare to consider the themes of greatness and sweetness in Dante's *Purgatorio*, to remind us all—as Dante is conscientious to do in the *Convivio*—that he presents the use of the poets not that of the theologians or philosophers. And the immediate actual world of the poem is a world of language. Its factors are already fictions or signs. Yes, but then one of the secrets of Poetry, as I have been meaning to suggest, is that for the poet the actual experience of his life and the literal body of his work are not to be abstracted as if one stood for the other. The reality of the world is immediate to his writing as the poet works.

In the opening canto of the *Purgatorio*, emerging from Hell's depths, Dante's rising spirit calls upon the spirit of poetry that had been mortified in Hell to rise. "Ma qui la morta pocsì risurga," he sings, where "risurga" rimes with the "purga" of "dove l'umano spirito si purga" in the preceding tercet—"where the human spirit is purged"—"e di salire al ciel diventa degno"—"and becomes worthy to ascend to Heaven"—so that in the rime we may feel how the purgation is a sweetening, and the sweetness of song seems linked throughout the *Purgatorio* with the choruses and colors of Heaven.

> Ma qui la morta poesì risurga,
>   O sante Muse, poiche vostro sono,
>   e qui Calliope alquanto surga
>
> But here let dead poetry rise up again,
>   O holy Muses, for I am yours,
>   and let Calliope—the voice of beauty—rise

Then Dante evokes sweetness in a sweetness of image and of language in which he must surely be supreme, a sweetness and an ardor all but heretical in the poetics of our own day:

Dolce color d'orïental zaffiro
　　che s'accoglieva nel sereno aspetto
　　dell' aer puro infino al primo giro

Sweet color of orient sapphire
　　that was gathering in the clear countenance of the sky
　　pure even to the first gyre

The vowel leadings of "dol" to "col" in "dolce color" and then of
"lor" to "dor" in "color d'oriental" sets up such a thrill—a sweetness—of riming in the ear that seems to gather in the ensuing
verses as the blue of the sapphire in Dante's image gathers in the
countenance of the sky, a sweetness of color.

With this "dolce color," the blue of dawn, or later in the *Purgatorio* another "dolce color," the green that means hope, we would
remember here a contrasting color where in the *Inferno* the words
that are written above the Gate of Hell are of a dim or dark or obscure color, "di colore oscuro," just as Dante's way when he was
lost had been "per una selva oscura," in a dark wood, that must
have for our English speaking ears a ghost of the word "self" in
"selva" and always comes to my mind with the echo in meaning
of "in a darkness of self."

We cannot work it out schematically that there will be no poetry in Hell, for in that area of Limbo where those sages who
knew not Christ and were not baptized are gathered, four great
poets—Homer, Horace, Ovid and Lucan—"those lords of highest
song, which, like an eagle, soars above the rest," Dante calls
them—with Dante's Master, Virgil, make Dante one of their number. It is in Hell, among these honored and noble souls who have
yet the eternal sadness of being without Christ, that Dante is given
the sign of the greatness of his mission in poetry: "so that I was a
sixth amid such intelligences."

Dante can have his moments of humility. In the *Convivio* he
tells us that every good workman should so ennoble and beautify

his work that it may leave his hands the more noted and the more precious. "And this it is my purpose to do," he says then: "not that I am a good workman, but that I aspire after such."

It may seem to us for whom the workmanship of Dante in language is surpassing that his humility here is posed. But the artist's sense of his failure may come from his sense, in the exaltation of his art, of what workmanship must mean. The poet Yeats in 1905, who at that time was already a master of prose as I understand such mastery, noted: "One casts something away every year, and I shall, I think, have to cast away the hope of ever having a prose style that amounts to anything." And I can imagine that even for Dante the potential beauty of the medium in which he works—the pure gold that the poet as alchemist would render free from the medium of words—must remain always a challenge before which the poet must ever labor towards a higher art. When Dante tells us he aspires to be a good workman, he tells us something of *his* vision, beyond our vision, of what art demands.

In this same treatise of the *Convivio* in which Dante discourses upon the nature of man's nobility, in the twenty-sixth chapter he writes that courage is one of four manly virtues, and he defines courage as "consciousness of greatness, which virtue shows us where to make a stand and fight." And this virtue is coupled with temperance, "which shows the limit up to which the pursuit is to be carried." These are virtues of a man's character and of his soul; but they are also the moral virtues of a man's art as a poet. For now I think we should see how Dante's courage in the *Divine Comedy* is his ever-present consciousness of the greatness demanded. His courage appears in the person of the poet Virgil. It is the amazing courage of Dante to be the follower of Virgil.

For Dante is abashed before Virgil as he tells us in the *Inferno*: "Art thou then that Virgil, and that fountain which pours abroad so rich a stream of speech?" he answers him. "With bashful countenance," Dante says—"con vergognosa fronte." And in the Fourth Treatise of the *Convivio*, Dante tells us that "vergogna" is one of three emotions contained in the abashment which is the most obvious token of nobleness in adolescence; and Dante defines "vergogna" then as "bewilderment of mind on seeing or hearing, or in any wise perceiving, great and wonderful things; for in so far as they appear great, they make him who perceives them reverent toward them, and in so far as they appear wonderful they make him who perceives them desirous to have knowledge of them."

"O degli altri poeti onore e lume!"

"O glory and light of other poets!"

Dante addresses Virgil.

May the long zeal avail me, and the great love
that made me search thy volume.

"Tu se' lo mio maestro, e 'l mio autore;"

"Thou art my master and my author;
thou alone art he from whom I took
the good style—"

(or is it "the beautiful style," for the French *beau, belle* echoes in the Italian to my ear)

lo bello stilo, that hath done me honor.

Calling here upon the courage—the good style—of Virgil, Dante calls upon his greatness.

In the *Purgatorio* the poet Sordello is so amazed and in all his pride so abashed as he realizes that it is Virgil with whom he speaks. "As one who seeth suddenly a thing before him whereat he marvels, who believes, and believes not, saying: 'It is, it is not';

such seemed he, and forthwith bent his brow, and humbly turned back towards my Leader." Sordello falls at Virgil's feet to embrace his knees. "Oh glory of the Latins," he cries, "by whom our tongue showed forth all its power . . ."

So a fellow poet addresses Dante's Master in the very poem in which Dante's art shows forth *their* vernacular, Italian the successor to Latin, in all *its* power. Even as Dante, at the age of twenty-four, took his *Vita Nuova* in the common language, in his mother tongue—the vernacular, he tells us in *De vulgari eloquentia*, is the speech of our nurses—and even as Dante in his mission of greatness, the *Commedia*, gave new life in greatness to the language in which he wrote, so ennobling Italian that it stands as the first language in modern poetry—Dante, the first of modern poets!—even as Dante showed forth the new Italian in all its power, he needed the courage that is greatness to so do as Virgil had done before him. So that we today would need great courage in poetry to address Dante as he addressed *his* Master: "Thou art my master and my author."

The greatness extends throughout the concept of the poem, it is this courage, this consciousness of greatness demanded that is the source of the ordered severity of the *Inferno*. "Here must all distrust be left," Virgil warns Dante. He must trust indeed in his mission and in the consciousness of greatness that must attend him. "All cowardice must here be dead. We are come to the place where I told thee thou shouldst see the wretched people, who have lost the good of the intellect." And in the opening of this third canto of the *Inferno*, we have learned that it is the good of the intellect that has the courage to discriminate Hell. "Justice moved my High Maker," the inscription upon Hell Gate reads: "Divine Power made me, Wisdom Supreme, and Primal Love."

But these powers that appear in the poem as referring to God's eternal will in Creation are also the powers of Dante's *poetic* will, the eternal will of the *Commedia*. Behind the poet's evocation of God's orders, we are aware that the *Inferno* presents also the orderly requirements of the poem itself, and that Dante's poetic will is moved by definitions of justice, power, wisdom and love, that are, within the poem, divine, supreme and primal.

The greatness, the courage, of Dante's creative task is evident in the *Inferno* and impersonated in Virgil. Now with the *Purgatorio* we are immediately aware of the second virtue of Dante's poetry—its sweetness. The souls in Purgatory rejoice in their pains, for these are not the pains of Hell but the pains-taking of a labor towards Heaven. They suffer the flames of the moral virtues in which they must be fired if their souls are to be liberated from the bonds of pride, envy, wrath, sloth, avarice, gluttony, lust and sweetened in the practice of humility, charity, meekness, zeal, liberality, temperance and chastity—each sin conquered in the sweetness of the beatitude it had excluded. The moral virtues appear then in the day sky of Purgatory as four stars that in their burning preside over the work to be done. "The heavens seemed to rejoice in their flames," Dante says.

The sweetness of song, the sweetness of the laboring pains in Purgatory and the sweetness of the blue of the dawn of a new life or of the green of the hope for heaven—these are one in their source that has something to do with the intercession of the Lady in High Heaven whose messengers are Lucia and Beatrice. But mistaken, misunderstood, the sweetness appears as an alluring and side-tracking beauty, where Dante is tempted to linger in the sweetness of sound or image, as in another place he is tempted to linger in the wonder of great men, and to forget himself, to forget the ascent he must make, in it. This is the great temptation of all true poets to be so enraptured by the beauty of the language in love of which they have been called to their life work, so taken in by the loveliness of words or by the wonder of images and persons that the art projects, that they lose the intent of the whole, the working of the poem towards the fullness in meaning of its form. As the song rises in the *Purgatorio*, Dante must be awakened again and again by Virgil to his grave task or by messengers of the Lady to his high inspiration. The intent of the poet that must govern the man—the demand of the poem to come into its proper form—is analogous here to the intent and demand of God that must fire souls to make the ascent towards the *Paradiso*. The trial of Purgatory in its poetic meaning is the trial which the writing of the *Commedia*, demanding years of work and constancy in poetic inspiration and craft, demanding arduous study and ardent thought, represents to the poet himself.

In the beginning cantos of the *Purgatorio*, we are presented with an Ante-purgatory, a realm in which souls must serve time before being admitted into the torments that give blessing above, and we are reminded here of how souls too can delay even in the very pleasures which are intimations of the heights towards which they should be on their way.

A host of souls arrives upon the shores of the Ante-purgatory, and Dante recognizes among them Casella, a musician who had set Dante's verses to be sung. "Casella mio," Dante addresses him and embraces him, and later Dante asks Casella, if he still have memory and skill of the amorous song, would he sing:

> If a new law take not from thee
> > memory or use of that amorous song
> > which was wont to quiet my every desire
> may it please thee therewith to console awhile
> > my soul, that, with its mortal form
> > journeying here, is sore distressed.

Here again, in the lines "memoria o uso al' amoroso canto" and "l'anima mia, che, con la sua persona," in the following tercet, it seems to me that Dante calls upon a special sweetness to haunt the passage with its suggestion. Our sense of this sweetness excited, so that we are moved ourselves to be enraptured with the imagination of his singing, Casella begins with Dante's "Amor che nella mente mi ragiona"—"Love that in my mind discourseth to me"—Casella in our minds singing to us. He begins, Dante says, "so sweetly / that the sweetness yet within me sounds"—"si dolcemente / che la dolcezza ancor dentro mi suona." So, I have suggested, the melodic key of a poem may lie in a single passage—this is the economy of high art—that in its penetrating sweetness seems to sound within all other passages of the poem.

This beauty of sound is, for Dante, first and last, the essence of his art. We are to have our beginning in understanding there. Falling in love with the sound we revere the literal, and search out the excellence of the word as we would search out a beloved. And if at last we have come to no further understanding, we have still the beauty of that sound. In the ode *Voi che intendendo il terzo ciel movete*, Dante addresses the ode itself in the *tornata*:

> Ode! I believe that they shall be but rare who
> shall rightly understand thy meaning,
>   so intricate and knotty is thy utterance of it;
>   Wherefore if perchance it come about
> that thou take thy way among such men as seem not
>   rightly to perceive it;
>   Then I pray thee to take heart again,
> And say to them, O beloved:
>   "Give heed at least how beautiful I am."

The sound, mother to the word, is so pure a thing of poetry that even in languages we do not understand we recognize when we hear the presence of poetic grace and are sure then of the poet's art and vocation. So, in the first treatise of the *Convivio*, Dante argues against translations of poetry, saying that his odes themselves do not will "that their meaning should be expounded where they themselves could not carry it together with their beauty." "And therefore let everyone know that nothing which hath the harmony of musical connection can be transferred from its own tongue into another without shattering all its sweetness and harmony."

Now the whole company listening to Casella—not only Dante, but Virgil too—seemed so glad, Dante tells us, as if none gave heed to any other thing. "We were all so fixed and intent upon his notes." At this point the venerable Cato breaks their rapture: "What is this, you laggard spirits! What negligence, what tarrying is this? Haste to the mount and strip you of the sloth, that lets not God be manifest to you!"

Virgil himself, being a poet, had been taken in—in the beauty of Casella's voice—and now, it seems to Dante that Virgil is gnawed by self-reproach. "O noble conscience and clear," Dante exclaims, "how sharp a sting is a little fault in thee!"—where there may be a tenderness it seems to me in the word "little," because in itself this delight in song in this scene is so innocent in its rapture. Except—except— In the terms of our sense of an allegory here of poetic experience, the loveliness of Dante's "Amor che nella mente mi ragiona," that came for the poet as an inspiration or a surpassing grace in his work, belongs to the period before the work of the *Commedia*, belongs to the Ante-purgatory then, and is true, but here as everywhere one is not to be lost in truth. For the poet who must be engaged with the task of the *Commedia*, it is another thing; to languish now in the beauty or the good or the truth of what he has done in the past or to lose his way as he works in rehearsing old inspirations of his art is to chew grace like a cud. Later, in the circle of the slothful, in the travail of Purgatory itself, Dante is to have a terrible vision of such a chewed-over once-was sweetness that would stand in the place of the sweetness of new life or new song.

But in this scene of Casella's singing we know the song to be truly sweet, the more truly sweet since conscience, the good Cato,

arouses us on our way. He is the very person of the four moral
virtues that in the sky of Purgatory are stars watching over the
struggling souls.

Now I would move on to a second scene of loveliness that I think
later to relate to the exploration of the ideas of greatness and
sweetness in poetry. In this second scene, as night comes on,
Sordello leads Virgil and Dante to a refuge where a bosom—
"grembo" Dante's word is—has been made in the mountain-side
of Purgatory—"dove la costa face di sé grembo." And indeed this
valley seems like the bosom of a lady's dress, so that it is as if the
poet's soul were taken in from its day-time of trials and manhood
where it had been guided by the strictures of the moral stars, and
each evening were given rest, watched over by the three stars of
the theological virtues that preside in the night sky, given rest like
a child once more upon a mother's lap:

> "There," said the shade, "we will go where the
>   mountain-side makes of itself a bosom, and
>   there will await the new day."
> Neither steep nor level was a winding path that
>   led us to the side of that hollow, there where
>   the valley's edge more than half dies away.
> Gold and fine silver, cramoisy and white, Indian
>   wood bright and clear, fresh emerald at the
>   moment it is split,
> would each be surpassed in color by the grass and
>   by the flowers placed within that fold, as the
>   less is surpassed by the greater.
> Not only had Nature painted there, but of the
>   sweetness of a thousand secrets made there one,
>   unknown and indefinable.

> There, seated on the grass and on the flowers,
>   singing *Salve Regina*, saw I souls who because
>   of the valley were not seen from without.
> "Ere the little sun now sinks to his nest,"
>   began the Mantuan who had led us aside,
>   "desire not that I guide you among them."

In our language *il poco sole*, "the little sun," has immediately another meaning in its homonym, "son," so that we see the little son return to his nest at evening in his mother's lap. But this is truly an appearance of such grace that we do not do wrongly to suspect that the will of a Lady is projected. Throughout the ages of Christendom, this Lady and Her Son have been portrayed.

> 'Twas now the hour that turns back the desire of
>   those who sail the seas and melts their heart,
>   that day when they have said to their sweet friends adieu,
> and that pierces the new pilgrim with love, if
>   from afar he hears the chimes which seem to
>   mourn for the dying day . . .

Again there is the announcing sweetness of "che paia il giorno pianger che si more"—"which seems to mourn for the dying day"; and the company gathered in this retreat sing now the *Te lucis ante* so devoutly and "con sì dolce note"—"with such sweet tone," that again Dante tells us that he was rapt from his very sense of self. But here there is a permission. Not only does this nest have a supernal grace, but the song is not an *amoroso canto*, soothing troubled desires in the music of desire, nor is it, moreover, a song now of long ago, beguiling the soul in the sloth of a nostalgia; but this song is a hymn, a song reaching towards eternal things, and its sweetness turns the soul towards its source:

And the others then sweetly and devoutly accompanied it through the entire hymn, having their
   eyes fixed on the supernal wheels.
Reader, here sharpen well thine eyes to the truth,
   for the veil now is indeed so thin, that of a
   surety to pass within is easy.
I saw that noble army thereafter silently gaze
   upward, as if in expectancy, pale and lowly;
   and I saw two angels come forth from on high . . .
Green, as tender leaves just born, was their rai-
   ment, which they trailed behind, fanned and
   smitten by green wings.

In Dante's picture of the two angels who arrive I would call our attention first to the reappearance of the "dolce color" of the little valley, the fresh-emerald-at-the-moment-it-is-split green of life in its leaves and grasses which appears again in the robes of these guardians and even in the green of their wings, for this color of hope belongs as does the sweetness of song to the grace of a higher power:

"Both come from Mary's bosom"
—"del grembo di Maria"—
said Sordello, "as guard of this vale, because
of the serpent that straightway will come."

As if to warn us again that in the midst of all our too human delight in whatever partakes of heavenly beauty there is danger if we take no thought of God and our eternal life, the adversary or a token of the adversary, a reminder of evil, arrives in the form of a snake that glides through the brocade of grasses and flowers, turning round upon itself lasciviously to lick its scales as it goes, like a beast sleeking its fur. And as if to demonstrate that beauty is the property of Heaven, the two angels swoop like falcons to drive the serpent away.

We know that the Queen of Heaven Herself is concerned for Dante's progress in the *Commedia* and that it is by Her grace that his courage was awakened from the impediment of that dark wood to undertake his way. For in the opening cantos of the *Commedia*, before the descent into the *Inferno*, Virgil discloses how a Lady called him—"so fair and blessed that I prayed her to command"—and how this Lady Beatrice, "with angelic voice," told him that a noble Lady in High Heaven had such pity for Dante's distress that she had sent for Lucia, and through Lucia, for Beatrice to come to Dante's aid. Virgil then, greatness, is under the commission of these three. "What is it!" Virgil exclaims, upbraiding Dante in the *Inferno*: "Why, why haltest thou? Why does such a coward fear lodge in your heart? . . . When three such blessed ladies care for thee in the court of Heaven, and my words promise thee so much good?"

Thus, from the beginning, we have known that grace moved to stir greatness in Dante's heart. His courage opened in him, Dante says, like flowers open upon their stems in the sun.

And when in the thirteenth canto of the *Purgatorio* Virgil addresses a hymn to the sun, O *dolce lume!*, the sweetness of the light may tell us that it too appears in Purgatory as a presentation of Mary—"in whose trust I enter on the new way, do thou lead us," Virgil continues, "thy beams must ever be our guide."

Presentations of Mary appear in every circle of Purgatory and with them, circle by circle, the sequence of hymns and beatitudes. They stand over against presentations from Hell, so that the images of Heaven and the images of Hell are ever present to the choice of the purgatorial souls. In the circle of the proud, there is sculptured in the white marble of the mountain-side the scene of the Annunciation where She appears in Her humility "who turned the key to open the supreme love"; in the circle of the envious, a voice cries out her words at the marriage of Cana, "Vinum non habent," exemplifying charity and the sharing of goods that love wills; in the circle of the wrathful, Dante caught up in a dream of ecstasy sees a young mother who says tenderly, "My son, why hast thou thus dealt with us? Behold, thy father and I sought thee sorrowing," in which Mary, speaking to Jesus in the temple, exemplifies parental concern without anger; in the circle of the slothful, a shout goes up, "Mary ran with haste to the hill country." Then, as if spirits of the poem at the name of Mary cried out to the poet, voices exhort:

> "Haste! Haste! let no time be lost through
>   little love," cried the others afterwards, "that
>   striving to do well may renew grace."

Images and news of Our Lady reappear as a great rhyme of the quickening of love and the freeing of the will for love that are the works of Purgatory, accompanied by the rhyming of hymns and the recitation of beatitudes as the soul making its way upwards towards the completion of the work has its impediments removed. Think of the labor the poet has undertaken in the *Commedia* itself, the grace that must ever descend in the poem to inspire the rhyming tercets and to illuminate the thought of the poet in this high matter. How often Dante must have had to be aroused with the resolve that no time be lost through little love in order to carry on this vast work. The *Purgatorio* here presents the striving to do well; as the *Inferno* presents the depths of Dante's bitterness and fear from which, he tells us in the opening canto, he was called by Virgil to make the journey of this poem; as the *Paradiso* presents the glory and sweetness of the poem's inspiring form.

In the circle of the slothful, Dante falls into a sloth of thought, a confusion, so that from one thought to another and then to many he rambles, and he closes his eyes, he tells us, for very rambling. Here, in a hideous Nightmare, or rather, Day Fairy, of the

Siren, Dante looks upon the very Mistress of that Song chewed in the cud that I spoke of earlier in this lecture:

> there came to me in a dream, a stuttering woman,
>> with eyes asquint, and crooked on her feet,
>> with maimed hands, and of sallow hue.
> I gazed upon her; and, as the sun comforteth the
>> cold limbs which night weighs down, so my look
>> made ready
> her tongue, and then set her full straight in
>> short time, and her pallid face even as love wills
>> did color.
> When she had her tongue thus loosed, she began to
>> sing, so that with difficulty should I have turned
>> my attention from her.
> "I am," she sang, "I am the sweet Siren, who leads
>> mariners astray in mid-sea, so full am I of
>> pleasantness to hear.
> "I turned Ulysses from his wandering way with my
>> song, and whoso liveth with me rarely departs, so
>> wholly do I satisfy him."

Then there appears a lady in Dante's dream, "santa e presta," "holy and alert," who calls upon Virgil to expose to Dante the blasphemous and slothful nature of this apparition, as Beatrice called upon Virgil in the opening of the *Inferno* to set Dante upon the true path of the *Commedia*.

> "O Virgil, Virgil, who is this?" angrily she said:
>> and he came with eyes ever fixed on that honest
>> one.
> He seized the other, and rending her clothes, laid
>> her open in front and showed me her belly; that
>> awakened me with the stench which issued therefrom.

For Charles Williams, reading the *Commedia* as an allegory of true Romantic Love, the Siren is "the romantic Image in the pseudo-romantic mirage," "Ideal Gratification . . . vitalized within out of the night of Sloth by the mere attention of the soul." For us tonight, reading the *Purgatorio* as an allegory of Poetry, she is not only Anti-Love but Anti-Poetry. She is music played false.

For the Siren is an impersonation of that Wish that would seduce the poet in his fantasy and take the place of Truth in his poetic fiction. She is wishful thinking, feeding upon the poet's attention to take her voice and her color from what he wants her to be. In the realm of poetics, she is the false muse of the poet's vanity in which he no longer aspires to be a good workman but admires what he has done, no longer follows the inspiration of the Lady in High Heaven but is lost in the gratifications his own voice provides. "So wholly do I satisfy him," the Siren boasts. Where the Star of Our Lady protects and guides mariners at sea, the Siren leads them astray; where the Grace of Our Lady frees the will to make that ascent that leads to the fulfillment of its true nature, the Siren claims that "whoso liveth with me rarely departs."

In this figure of the Siren we see what poetry is in the absence of the moral and theological virtues, in the denial of the good of the intellect. This monster of a mereness of song in its seduction, so patently making its claim to be admired in itself—this art for art's sake—is prefigured in the opening lines of the *Purgatorio* where Dante refers to those daughters of Pierus who considered themselves superior to the Muses and, no longer acknowledging them as the source of music, challenged them to a contest and, in penalty for their presumption, were changed into magpies. "But here led dead poesy rise up again," Dante addresses the deities of song, "O holy Muses, since yours am I, / and here let Calliope rise somewhat"—

> accompanying my song with that strain
>   whose stroke the wretched Pies felt
>   so that they despaired of pardon.

In Ovid's story of the metamorphosis of the Pierides, Dante must have been struck the more with the contest of the true and false, for the Divine Muses themselves were Pierian—Pierides. Just as the daughters of Pierus in their conceit sing against the song of the Muses, so here is the very Pie herself who would sing and claim our admiration in ignorance and contempt of the divine inspiration of true music. She so lies and would take as her own property the properties that belong to supernal good that we hear the very word "dolce"—Our Lady's word—upon this Siren's lips so that it seems to stink. Now there are clearly two kinds of sweetness, the one proper, and the other sickening sweet. "Io son dolce Serena," she announces herself.

Who are then the true Muses for Dante? In the Second Treatise of the *Convivio*, speaking of Intelligences, "which are vulgarly called Angels," Dante relates them to the powers which Plato called Ideas. "The Gentiles called them gods and goddesses," he continues, "though they did not conceive them so philosophically as did Plato . . . The which opinion is manifested by the testimony of the poets, who from time to time outline the fashion of the Gentiles both in their sacrifices and in their faith." It is clear that Dante considers the Olympian gods to be such Intelligences, as they were conceived by men when "the truth was not yet perceived, and this both by defect of reason and by defect of instruction." "No one—" he continues: "neither philosopher, nor Gentile, nor Jew, nor Christian, nor any sect—doubts that either all of them, or the greater part, are full of all blessedness, or doubts that these blessed ones are in the most perfect state." So, in the circle of the proud in the *Purgatorio*, Dante sees represented the giants who fought against the Olympians and Niobe and Arachne who in their pride blasphemed Leto and Athena, as in the opening of the *Purgatorio* he announces the theme of the nature of sin in his reference to the blasphemy of the Pierides. Reason and instruction will bring us to understand the mythical identities of these divine powers of the pagan world in the light of Christian revelation towards the fullness of truth. "O holy Muses," Dante cries, evoking the Intelligence of Music in the terms of the mythical, and then, in the *Purgatorio*, we are to have revealed to us in their literal, their allegorical, moral, and anagogical meanings the identities of three Ladies who inspired the *Commedia* and fired Dante's courage and steadfastness to complete his work.

They are first, the Virgin Mary, Mother of God and second and third, her emissaries, Lucia and Beatrice, who give the two benefactions of language: Lucy, the eyes that see through words, the imagination; and Beatrice, the workings of wisdom that reveal meanings, the intellect. And, for a moment, suspended at the close of our homage to Dante and our thought upon the greatness and sweetness that inform his work, I would dare to leave the thought that Mary, mother of the Logos and of the Living Body of Man in One, may be sound, mother of the word in its letters, and light, mother of the appearance of all bodies.

Postscript

The three Heavenly Muses of Dante must stand in striking contrast to the three-fold or three-faced Muse proposed by Robert Graves in his historical grammar of poetic myth, *The White Goddess*. This internal Muse, the trinity of Hekate-Persephone-Kore of the witch cult, who, in Graves's dogma, is the true Queen of Poetry, is the very Siren of Dante's dream in the circle of Sloth, and Graves argues that the true poet seeks the bondage of her spell. "The function of poetry," he writes, "is religious invocation of the Muse, its use is the experience of mixed exaltation and horror that her presence excites." Though in *The White Goddess* Graves declares that "poets can be well judged by the accuracy of their portrayal of the White Goddess. Shakespeare knew and feared her," he makes no reference to the passage in which Dante portrays the Siren in all her conceit, surely a most telling vision of that would-be Mistress of poets. Graves does not dare to confront Dante directly it would seem, yet his argument appears so in antithesis to Dante's poetics that we may have the sense that he often forms his ideas in reaction to Dante. It is not surprising that Graves would persuade us that "true poets do not find it consistent with their integrity to follow Virgil's example," for it is Virgil in Dante's *Purgatorio* who—"like all intelligence and all great art," Charles Williams put it in *The Figure of Beatrice*—exposes the falseness of the White Goddess as the Anti-muse in the *Commedia*.

(1965)

Howard Nemerov

The Dream of Dante

The dream nowhere says it's about Dante, it doesn't even mention his name, nevertheless I woke up knowing it was. It came at a time when I was desperate over an essay about the *Comedy* that wasn't going at all well, and I was saying such things to myself as "If we go on like this right to the deadline we'll have a hundred and fifty single-spaced pages and no essay on Dante." It is true, however, that I go through these agonies with any and every piece of writing that cannot be completed in a day; so maybe this dream, which I apply to the piece on the *Comedy*, means to be paradigmatic about my troubles in this line generally.

We are having, it seems, an emergency, but one which ought to be handled with great ease, for we have a stretcher and ambulance (the scene is a garage), and the hospital itself is visible just across the street. (Who is the patient? That remains undisclosed.)

Instead of the obvious and easy solution, however, I find myself upstairs with two or three other people confronting a big, shabby truck, which, moreover, carries atop its cab a sort of thick rug or mattress about the size of a tennis court. We get this latter object down and folded, then it seems we have to strip the truck into parts small enough to carry downstairs so that we can assemble it again elsewhere. And this we do, under the supervision of a bald, squat German who is understood to be a professional mover. We have to pass through a second floor which is evidently the ware-house of a museum or antique shop, crowded with junk from the ages, chiefly furniture, pedestals for statues, and so on.

Outside at last, we are on a football field. More people keep arriving to help put the truck together, and when at last this is done everybody gets in and I am obscurely aware that now there will be no room for whoever the patient was, but this doesn't bother me much at all. What does bother me, though, and bothers everyone else, is that the radiator cap won't stay on. I fiddle with it and discover it is so dilapidated it has no thread on the screw. But I hold it precariously in place with my finger.

Dearly beloved, the patient who never appears and eventually gets forgotten altogether is Dante Alighieri, and I very much fear that the name of the German professional mover is Scholarship, while the truck, of course, is Scholarly Apparatus, a theme reiterated in the warehouse of museum or antique shop. The dream as a whole reflects my nervousness about tackling the great work head on—is that why a football field appears?—as well as, perhaps, a certain sense that the world does not stand in dire need of one more essay on the *Divine Comedy*. My defense, and this is not the first time the thing has happened, is to pretend earnestly to be a scholar, which I am not, and try to sound learned throughout perhaps a dozen false starts, before getting down to being my mere self again, and simply saying what I think. All that is figured by the business of taking apart the truck—and that damn mattress—carrying the pieces downstairs through a collection of antique dreck which perhaps stands for footnotes—there are four editions of the poem on my office desk and two more, different ones at home—and putting it all back together elsewhere, with the help of a growing throng of scholars; while the concluding image, of the damaged radiator cap which I hold down with my finger, merely shadows forth my sorry-cynical belief as to the probable result of all my efforts.

Even the assertion that "I go through these agonies with any

and every piece of writing that cannot be completed in a day,"
though appearing above, belongs to the dream-thoughts, for one
of the things which chiefly amazes me about Dante is his successful determination to complete a huge design, a true life task last-
ing many years,

> il poema sacro
> al quale ha posto mano e cielo e terra,
> sì che m' ha fatto per molti anni macro . . .
>
> (Par. 25.1–3)

as he says with a kind of divine chutzpah redeemed only by his
being quite right.

This is a power of poetry, a power of mind itself, far beyond
what I could have imagined without having the proof of the
poem to hand. As if he had said to the Muse—dared to say to
Polyhymnia, Muse of Sacred Song—"Lady, you show up at nine
every morning for a decade and more, and I'll let you know when
we're finished."

Struggling with the thoughts that were to make this essay,
which had been giving me a bad time for a couple of weeks, it
happened that I took the children to a night game. But Dante's
poem, for anyone working with it closely, has the power of infect-
ing a good many thoughts about things that would seem quite remote from it, so that when on some occasion of local triumph I
saw on the electric scoreboard a bright red cardinal swooping
madly up and down and across, I thought: O dear, that's the trouble, isn't it? I mean, that Cross in the heaven of Mars, the imperial
Eagle in the heaven of Jove, the ladder in the heaven of Saturn, all
made up of spirits who are lights (after you get up past Justinian in
canto 6 they no longer have human faces)—we can actually do, or
show, these things. That scoreboard could as readily flash out to us
glowing crosses and ladders and eagles as it can that cardinal or the
pitcher of pouring golden beer which will likely come next . . .

and what a vulgar reduction it is. Surely poesy rules in the realm of the impossible just because it *is* the impossible; realization is ruin.

But a few nights after, taking the children to the Fourth of July fireworks, and seeing those truly wonderful sprayings and flowerings, those glowing showers of embers slowly going out—they actually do make people say ooh! and ah!—I thought, with a kind of stupid relief, Ah, well, that's more like it, the spirits on cross and ladder come and go swiftly, like the fireworks, brilliant with heat as well as light, and with the continuousness of a musical phrase, *legato* . . . only they don't go out. And I felt better, heaven knows why. For both these comparisons, scoreboard and fireworks, had merely obtruded themselves on my vision of the poem because I saw them while preoccupied with the poem. The poem, however, is to be read with the mind's eye, not the body's eyes, which are the necessary but not sufficient receivers of its words or of its visions.

Still, the poem is near seven hundred years old, and if much has remained the same—including death, cruelty, stupidity, and smiles—ever so much has changed. And, still thinking on cross and eagle and Jacob's ladder, I remembered two quotations bearing on this matter, though written three centuries apart. I'd had them about for some years, and here seemed to be an occasion for putting them together.

What a beautiful hemisphere the stars would have made, if they had been placed in rank and order; if they had all been disposed of in regular figures . . . all finished, and made up into one fair piece, of great composition, according to the rules of art and symmetry.

That is Bishop Burnet, as it were introducing the eighteenth century. But here is how the same thought occurs to George Santayana, introducing the twentieth:

. . . imagine the stars, undiminished in number, without losing any of their astronomical significance and divine im-
mutability, marshalled in geometrical patterns; say in a Latin
cross, with the words *In hoc signo vinces* in a scroll around
them. The beauty of the illumination would be perhaps increased, and its import, practical, religious, cosmic, would
surely be a little plainer; but where would be the sublimity
of the spectacle? [And he answers] Irretrievably lost.

It's a matter of your—or your century's, perhaps—taste in universes. Dante's cosmology is as absurd to us as—well, as ours
would be to Dante. In effect, he might claim with reason, in spite
of all our chains of zeroes hiding behind the exponents, we don't
have a cosmology at all, any more than the ancient Maya, who
kept accurate calendars extending many thousands of years into a
future in which there would not happen to be ancient Maya,
could be said to have a cosmology.

Much has changed, yes. On this point, an anecdote.

A student came to his teacher just after commencement, and
paid him what at first looked to be, and certainly was intended to
be, a tremendous compliment, "Sir," he breathlessly said, "there was
one thing I learned in your course that is of greater significance
than anything else I have been taught in my four years at this university." Teacher, bridling prettily, inquired what this wonderful
one thing might be. "Why, that right during John Milton's lifetime
the sun stopped going around the earth, and"—he made a twisting motion with his arms—"the earth began going around the
sun!"

As a testimonial to effective teaching, that's as pathetic as it's
funny. But if that teacher had happened to take his motto from
Leibniz—"there's nothing so stupid I can't learn from it"—he
might have gone on to consider thus.

A silly error, yes. But also a convincingly surrealist metaphor
about how it might have felt mentally if not physically, that violent

wrenching of the frame of things begun by Copernicus and Kepler, Brahe and Galileo. And if you continue along the lines it indicates about the relations of mind and world, you might wonder at other of the great changes since Dante's time, changes having to do with the age of the universe, of the earth, of life, of human life; and changes having to do with the size of the universe, which has grown so exponentially from the little local affair it was to something of a size so unimaginable that it has to be expressed in light years—to give one figure only, our sun and its system lie on the rim of our galaxy 26,000 light years distant from the center, which is to say, being interpreted, the distance covered by light traveling 6,000 billion miles a year multiplied 26,000 times . . . Can you say with utter confidence whether changes of such quality and magnitude take place in the world or in the mind, whether Aristotle himself would be quite clear as to whether they are recognitions or reversals? So it might be with the Copernican Revolution just as that student said: the sun stopped going around the earth and the earth started going around the sun, with consequences, including the demythologizing of knowledge, the dissociation of cosmos and consciousness, physics and faith, which I am sure you are as much and as little familiar with as I. Much has changed.

But when I look up into the night sky—and no matter how much science insists that the direction of my gaze is out, not up, my neck tells me I am looking up—I see not Dante's neat Ptolemaic universe, nor the elegant Copernican universe that replaced it, still less the vast universe more recently offered us by Harlow Shapley and others; I see, as men always have seen, the appearances which were to be accounted for by these universes; indeed, I don't see very many of them, owing to the smog, which seems to be one of the conditions under which it becomes possible for men in windowless buildings watching television monitors to send travelers to the Moon and Mariners out past Mars. So that although the size of the Milky Way has increased to include an unimaginable and indeed incredible 200 billion stars, it is among the effects of the scientific and technological civilization which makes this and the like assertions that I was unable, at last look—Fourth of July again—to see any Milky Way at all. That's a bit more of the much that has changed.

So Dante's cosmos does indeed look silly, but only until I try to contemplate my own and learn that I don't effectively have one. Not only the smog that prevents me from seeing the stars, but the electric light so effective in demythologizing the world that it shields me from demon and angel alike, and insures that save for the Fourth of July I will not worry enough about the stars to go outdoors and see whether I can see them or not. And not only that, but this: Increased knowledge increases ignorance exponentially, and every triumphant advance in knowing means that millions of us won't know it.

That, perhaps, is poetically the point. Dante has a small universe, but a full one, and he knows it thoroughly. I have, if I can in any sensible way be said to have it, a vast universe, but it is empty and dark, and compared with what is to be known I do not know it at all.

Away from the *Comedy*, I may have my doubts. But while I am reading, the illusion of plenitude is complete; I am convinced. I don't know whether to be more amazed at his faith or at his knowledge, at his humility or at his pride, but when I read the poem I am kept constantly under an enchantment that says, "Everything you need to know is here." So much is this so, that when I hear at the opening of *Inferno* 21:

Così di ponte in ponte, altro parlando
    che la mia comedìa cantar non cura,
    venimmo . . .

So from bridge to bridge, talking of other things
    which my comedy cares not to sing,
    we went along . . .

I am amazed all over again to learn that Dante and Virgil said things to one another in Hell that we are never going to be told.

This must be, I think, the supreme illusion possible to poetry, perhaps to any power of the mind, and it makes me think of the *Comedy* as a kind of holography, in which everything is always present at every point. Or of Borges' Aleph; or of a famous remark of Whitehead's, that "In a certain sense, everything is everywhere at all times, for every location involves an aspect of itself in every other location. Thus every spatio-temporal standpoint mirrors the world." Or of this that happened between Juliana of Norwich and her Saviour: "He shewed me," she says, "a little thing, the quantity of an hazel-nut, in the palm of my hand; and it was round as a ball. I looked thereupon with the eye of my understanding, and thought: 'What may this be?' And it was generally answered thus: 'It is all that is made.' "

This illusion of plenitude has to do in the first place with an exact fit between inside and outside in the poet's arrangements. There are in the main two sorts of outside, the articulation of the poem and the articulation of the universe, and they too coincide to give the impression that everything is contained within them and that nothing remains outside them. But then there is the inside, the human action that expands so as to fit exactly with its ordained outward.

The briefest reminder of these articulations ought to do, as they are well known to every reader of the poem. First, the arithmetic, built chiefly upon three and ten. Three canticles of thirty-three cantos each, with one canto for general prologue to the whole, bringing the total to one hundred. The cantos are of varying lengths, but average out so as to make each canticle about the same number of lines, and the poet keeps a strict awareness that this is so, warning himself at the end of the *Purgatorio* that all the pages ordained are filled up, so that the curb of art allows him to go no further; and being similarly warned toward the end of the

Paradiso that it is time to stop, like the careful tailor who cuts the garment according to the cloth at hand, he stops.

To these purely arithmetical or numerological dispositions the physical and moral natures of the universe conform themselves. Corresponding to the three canticles, the three realms of Hell, Purgatory, Heaven. Each of these is again divided into three main stages of the moral life imaged forth in the architectural arrangements of circles, terraces, and spheres. In Hell these divisions descend in the order of incontinence, violence, and fraud; in Purgatory they ascend in the order of perverse, defective, and excessive love; in Heaven they are represented as raying outward according as the blessed were affected by worldliness (and are accordingly seen within the cone of the earth's shadow) or lived lives of action or of contemplation. Outside of these schemes is another realm of a different order, bringing the total in each canticle to ten: Limbo, the Antepurgatory, the Empyrean.

The marvelous thing, poetically, is that this scheme is not set forth complete but built up for us by stages of description and reminder until it stands forth in memory with its symmetries and balancings and intricate cross-relations, all deriving ultimately from the mind of God but all, the one and the many, experienced serially as an adventure of the pilgrim through the types of the adventures of mankind generally—*exemplorum positivus*, as he says elsewhere—driven home by examples. And in the mystery of the many examples we are gradually to perceive the mystery of the link between human freedom and the workings of divine necessity, the link between individual and type. It is as Blake described it in a famous passage of *Jerusalem*:

All things acted on Earth are seen in the bright Sculptures
of Los's Halls, & every Age renews its powers from these
Works With every pathetic story possible to happen from
Hate or Wayward Love; & every sorrow & distress is carved
here, Every affinity of Parents, Marriages & Friendships are

here In all their various combinations wrought with wondrous Art, All that can happen to Man in his pilgrimage of
seventy years.

Indeed, Blake, who illustrated the *Comedy*, may even have been
thinking of it in these lines, and perhaps especially of the marvelously carved illustrations on the cornices of Purgatory.

So, in a fanciful comparison, the poet is like Theseus, led by the
thread of love in such a way that in the journey to the Minotaur
he also learns the labyrinth as a whole.

So far we have stressed the architecture, in its correspondence
to the articulation of the divine plan, or Necessity. Through this
web of geometry, geography and cosmology, all the creatures
move, as Beatrice says, to diverse ports over the great sea of being.
But at the very fulcrum of the poem, the middle of the fiftieth
canto, Marco Lombardo makes it clear that human beings have
freedom from stellar or other necessity; they have minds, which
the heavens have not in their charge; hence their salvation or
damnation is not under the doom of Necessity, though it will indeed illustrate Necessity.

This is the mystery of individuality itself, and in it the problem
of universals is not so much solved as set forth and assumed poetically to be solved. Against the background of the circles of Hell,
the terraces of purgation, the starry wheels of Heaven—all that in-
sane arithmetical regularity as circular as a Kandinsky, which in my
moods of disaffection with the poem make me think of it as *The
Rube Goldberg Variations*—is placed the wild richness and unpredictable particularity of people on their ways through the dark
wood or their moving over the great sea of being.

Here perhaps is where the illusion of plenitude is most convincing, or is totally convincing. Dante knows so many people; he
knows so many stories! He seems never at a loss for a story striking in its individuation, epigrammatic in its allusive concision, and
pointed as to its illustrative quality with respect to salvation or

damnation and exact moral type. This quality chiefly is what led me to say that Dante's universe, though small in both space and time compared to ours, and more especially *closed* in both space and time, is a full universe, and one which he knows thoroughly, is utterly at home in—as one could be only in a universe which, at whatever size, is closed. The inside exactly fills up the outside. Hence my impression while reading the poem that everything is in it.

This impression is reinforced by the multitude of symbolic resonances and redundancies that echo through the work and are the other side of his striking power of individualizing his figures. Dante's habit of mind is deeply, almost involuntarily, typological, not only with respect to the correspondences between the Old and New Testaments but with respect also to the correspondences between scriptural history and pagan myth and history, and the continuity between both of these and the history of contemporary Europe. It is in this poetic power of com-position, literally of putting together, that he is supreme.

He is also the most learned of poets, or the one who, among the greatest poets, relies the most upon learning and allusion. Side by side with his magnificent attentiveness to the visual, the power of putting before us with the utmost plainness what he is seeing, so that we see it too, there is this other power of riddling diction that is constantly making us supply more information than the words themselves convey, and infer whole stories from an image or a line. Consider, in this light, such things as the sketches of the images of Pride carved on the pavement of Purgatory, where in thirty-odd lines of paralleled tercets he swiftly reviews a succession of paired examples from Scripture and Greek myth: Satan and Briareus, the Titans and Nimrod, Niobe and Saul, Arachne and Rehoboam, Alcmaeon and Sennacherib, Cyrus and Holofernes, finishing with the ruins of Troy. Or consider the arrogant virtuosity of Justinian's history of Rome under the figure of the imperial

Eagle, sweeping *cito et velociter* back and forth across Europe so as to summarize the span from Aeneas to Charlemagne, about a millennium and a half from the founding of the city, and on to the disputes of Ghibelline and Guelf of Dante's own time, all in eighty lines or less, only for the poet to balance all this gorgeous speed and strength against the story of the humble pilgrim Romeo, a spectacular contrast of pride, power, scope and speed with a quiet tale of a faithful servant misprized and exiled to beg his way through the world in poverty and age (in which respect he may be, as so many others are throughout the poem, a type of Dante himself). The passage about Rome is thick with famous names to which the reader's memory must supply the stories, and includes even the crucifixion and the destruction of the Temple under Titus, given in a sentence so riddling that its full elucidation by Beatrice takes up the whole of the next canto.

One last illustration of what I have been calling the illusion of plenitude returns us to that idea of the presence of everything in something, which is of the essence of the art of poetry and which is imaged forth in such stories as that of Juliana and the hazel-nut.

The scheme of the poem is in a certain sense anecdotal and picaresque. Our hero, alone alive among a host of the dead, alone moves on through all the three realms, and there is consequently a temptation to read each episode as entirely separate from all the others, if only because the persons in it will never reappear.

But there is, owing to Dante's power of composition, a further dimension, of resonance, of symbol, of mysteriously allusive interconnection, between this example and that, between the examples and Dante himself, and so on.

Dante sees his poem as a sea voyage, as is well known; the chief places are the beginning of the *Purgatorio*—

Per correr miglior acque alza le vele
  omai la navicella del mio ingegno

—and near the beginning of the *Paradiso*, with its ominous warning to the reader not to put forth on a sea never sailed before unless he is one of the few who have stretched forth their necks to the bread of angels, a passage followed by an odd comparison to Jason and the Argonauts.

Human life, too, is a sea voyage, says Beatrice, over the great sea of being.

Later on, Beatrice mentions, as a warning against believing one has seen deeply into the divine will, having seen a ship complete a long voyage only to be wrecked on coming into harbor; whereupon one can't help hearing a faint echo of the mad voyage of Ulysses, shipwrecked within uncomprehending sight of salvation, the mountain of Purgatory.

Now Ulysses' voyage, very likely invented by Dante, was characterized not only as the *folle volo*, the mad flight in pursuit of knowledge, but also as the *alto passo*, the deep passage, the high adventure, which is the term already applied by the poet to his own pilgrimage.

Such dark prophecy as Lewis Mumford has seen in the technological schemes of Leonardo, as Loren Eiseley in Bacon's summons to the study of nature, as Eiseley and Richard M. Weaver in the apparition of the witches to Macbeth, I seem to see in Dante's story of Ulysses: a story of heart-breaking brightness on the way to doom.

Ulysses wants knowledge, and for knowledge he will break his ties with Telemachus, Laertes, even Penelope, to sail westward through the Mediterranean after escaping the enchantments of Circe, who turns men into beasts. The object of this knowledge? It is at first to become expert in the world, learned in human vice and human worth; but this knowledge is dismissed in three lines of tourism: he and his men saw Spain, Africa, Morocco, Sardinia and some other islands; then, old and slow with age, they come to the straits of Gibraltar where Hercules had set down his pillars as signs to men of limits, that they should go no further. Here worldly knowledge can no longer be the goal, because there is nothing out there, nothing but water. Ulysses exhorts his fellows, in the name of the dangers they have shared in reaching the westernmost limit of the world, to continue in the name of knowledge (*esperienza*) even though, or just because, the knowledge is of nothing, of the unpeopled world behind the setting sun. As if the journey were to begin with what indeed it presently becomes, a journey into death. And again, as if remembering Circe, he concludes what he calls "this little speech" by reminding them that they were not made to live as beasts but to pursue *virtute e conoscenza*. One of my editors says tersely of *virtute* that it means *il bene*, but perhaps we may see in anticipation here the Baconian coupling of knowledge and power. What knowledge and power may be expected of the void, however, we are never told. Instead, Ulysses conveys rather backhandedly his opinion of his fellow men by saying that the "little speech" so fired them up that he could not have held them back from what he knows (now, or even at the time?; the text will tell us nothing on this point) to be "the mad flight."

So they turn the poop toward the rising sun—given the consistency of the symbolism of the sun throughout the poem, even this navigational detail is a telling one—and row out into vacancy, always bending leftward, to the sinister side; indeed, to the sinister, for this is forsaking the *via diritta* in its bodily form.

And out of all this, after five months, they do achieve a distant view of Purgatory mountain—dark with distance—and are peremptorily struck down by the whirlwind of the divine displeasure, though even now Ulysses knows the will behind the storm only as "what pleased Another."

That is the strange story told in dark Hell out of a tongue of fire, a story full of the freshness of sea, wind and sky, a story of courage, nobility, and strength, and, as it happens, madness. The voyage of Ulysses is a mad flight, yes, but it is also the *alto passo* (the deep passage? the high adventure?) which is the term the poet has already applied to his own journey proposed by Virgil

(*Inf.* 2.12). It is like a fleeting glimpse, from the closed and closing universe of the high Middle Ages, of the coming of the Voyages of Discovery, which themselves were associated in men's minds with the chance of finding the way back to the Earthly Paradise from which their first parents had, being driven out, driven out all.

But it is more than that. It is also, I think, an account of the *terribilità*, nobility and pathos of the drive toward knowledge that has with an increasing acceleration obsessed the world since Dante's time. Not, obviously, that the men of the Middle Ages were not themselves obsessed with knowledge; if we had Dante's poem for the only evidence of that, it would be enough. But this seems an intuition of the practical knowledge—*esperienza*, our poet calls it—that Bacon would associate with power: the knowledge that imposes upon the knower an ultimate compulsion to know, to experience, to find out, even if the object of the knowledge be nothingness, even if the result of the finding be death and hell.

And when, from high in heaven, the poet turns at Beatrice's command for one of his two marvelous looks back and down at the *aiuola che ci fa tanto feroci*, the little threshing-floor of earth that makes us so ferocious, he remembers just in passing that voyage of Ulysses—as though, one feels, it formed some sort of doomed counterpart to his own fortunate and blessed voyage.

Ulysses and the fall of man both relate to knowledge and lust. Whenever Ulysses turns up, three times in all, it is in the company of some sort of sexual enchantment. When he tells his story, he begins with leaving Circe, who had kept him for over a year, and his exhortation to his crew includes a denunciation of bestiality. In Purgatory, Dante dreams of a siren who mentions having enchanted Ulysses just before she is revealed by Virgil as a creature of falsehood and filth. The last memory of Ulysses and his *varco folle*, high in heaven, is companioned in the next line by a reminiscence of Europa's rape. So sexuality, bestiality, and the voyage are brought together in these fleeting and riddling allusions, which echo over great spaces of the poem. And, remembering these things well enough to put them together as a dream might do, we remember that Dante began his journey somewhat as Ulysses did—threatened by bestiality in the form of three beasts, previously guilty of allowing himself to be seduced by both sexuality and knowledge (in the form of philosophy, his own Circe), for which in the Earthly Paradise he will suffer the scornful rebuke of Beatrice—with the sole redeeming difference that Dante is under the protection of faith, the protection of a Lady who is not Circe or the Siren or Europa.

And the vision of the voyage returns once more, with all these various voyages, to form its overtones in a figure of the strangest harmony in all poetry:

> Un punto solo m'è maggior letargo
> che venticinque secoli alla 'mpresa,
> che fé Nettuno ammirar l'ombra d'Argo.
> (*Par.* 33. 94–96)

This one moment in the presence of God is both a moment, a timeless Now, and the moving Now of all of human time, and both are made equivalent. It is a greater *letargo*—the word includes both fatigue and oblivion—than all the five and twenty centuries since the enterprise that made Neptune marvel at the shadow of the Argo, the first ship, hence the beginning of the enterprise of history. In this strangely displaced figure the unitive experience of the divine compounds the consciousness of the long fatigue of history with unconsciousness itself, the moment as part of duration with the moment as timeless and already in eternity, and—poetically, at least—the Christian revelation and promise with the ancient pagan god of the sea and with Jason on another of those doomed and damned voyages like that of Ulysses . . . for one remembers already, long ago, having seen Jason, stalking so proudly through Hell that even Virgil admires his royal port; and to have heard of him once again, intruding figuratively into the warning to the reader near the beginning of the *Paradiso*, where the furrow ploughed by the poet's keel reminds him of Jason ploughing at Colchis in the presence of his marvelling crew.

Such resonances, whatever they mean—and of their nature, perhaps, our idea of their meaning will be flickering and mysterious as is the meaning of coincidence and relation in life itself— seem to touch upon an essence of the purest poetry in their strange power of balancing, blending, harmonizing many diversities across great and sounding distances, giving a riddling hint of a oneness in the world that for a moment shines through the manifold appearances—the moment, as it were, just before metaphor is born and explanations—such as these helpless ones of mine— begin.

(1974)

James Merrill

Divine Poem

Many readers will have encountered, as I did, their first Dante in the "Prufrock" epigraph. We learned to smile at the juxtaposition of ineffectual daydreamer and damned soul speaking from the fire. "For this is hell, nor are we out of it," we innocently marveled, peering forth from our own gemlike flames at worktable and bookshelf, sunset and dozing cat. Purgatory and paradise awaited us too, in the guise of the next love affair. In a single elegant stroke Eliot had shown us one way to approach *l'altissimo poeta*: Dante's passionate faith and our intrepid doubts could be reconciled by triangulation with the text itself.

To believe, however, that Dante had in any real sense seen God threatened both the poem and us. Who wanted song to curdle overnight into mere scripture, or himself to be trivialized in the glare of too much truth? Yet we must—or so I begin to think, decades later—allow that something distinct from mere "inspiration" came to Dante. It had come to others; he is not after all our only mystic, just more literary and more fortunate than many. In an age that discouraged the heretic, his vision reached him through the highest, most unexceptionable channels. Its cast included saints, philosophers, emperors, angels, monsters, Adam and Ulysses, Satan and God. To these he added a poet he revered, a woman he adored, plus a host of friends and enemies whose names we should otherwise never have heard; and garbed them in patterns of breathtakingly symmetrical lights-and-darks woven from a belief everybody shared. Even the pre-Christian souls in hell know pretty much what they are damned for not having known in time. No question ever of an arcane, Blakean anti-mythology, Dante's conceptual innovations—as when he lifts purgatory to the surface of the earth, or reveals his lady as an agent from highest heaven—refigure rather than refute the thought that preceded them. As for his verbal ones, he was in the historical position to consolidate, virtually to invent, for purposes beyond those of the lyric, a living Italian idiom. No poet could ask for more; yet more was given him.

Revelation can take many forms. St. Paul was "caught up into paradise, and heard unspeakable words"—a one-shot trip. Milton, on the other hand, dreamed each night the next day's installment of his poem. Blake kept open house, through much of his life, for spirits with whom he conversed wide awake. Yeats, married to a medium, took down the voices that spoke through her. A lay visionary—where poetry is at issue, someone whose powers of language and allusion aren't up to the demands made upon them—reports a complex, joyous wonder compressed into a few poor human moments and verging dangerously upon the unutterable. Much as it may change his life, the experience defeats his telling of it. Dante imagined this to be his case; it was not.

For he was already a poet. He had completed his apprenticeship in lyrics of high perfection. As for allusion, he had read widely and seriously if, to us, eccentrically. Homer lay beyond his ken, but he knew Paulus Orosius and the *Voyage of St. Brendan*, and may well have come across this sentence from the Sufi Ibn Arabi (found by me heading the chapter on Beatrice in Irma Brandeis' *The Ladder of Vision*): "When she kills with her glances, her speech restores to life as though she, in giving life, were thereby Jesus."

The *Comedy*'s energy and splendor suggest that Dante indeed

"saw the light" in a timeless moment. Its prophetic spleen and resonant particulars hint at something not quite the same, that like
Milton or Yeats he had mediumistic powers—a sustaining divina-
tory intelligence which spoke to him, if only (as Julian Jaynes
would have it) from that center of the brain's right hemisphere
which corresponds to Weinecke's area on the left. This much
granted, it would still remain to be amazed in the usual fashion
when faced by a masterpiece: How on earth was it brought safely
into being and onto the page?

Poets nowadays are praised for performing without a net. "These
poems take risks!" gloat the blurbs. Akhmatova saddles Dante with a
cold and implacable Muse. I wonder. One does not wince *for* him
the way one does for Rimbaud. He is spared even the mortification
of a system that dates. The electronic marvels of paradise—stars clus-
tering into eagles, and all that—have according to Beatrice been devised to suit the seer: a laser show of supreme illusion projected
through Dante's human senses and image banks. (Do hell and purgatory keep being modernized to extract the maximum pain and
penance from the new arrival? I suppose they do.) Page after page
the Powers overwhelm the pilgrim, while treating the poet—the
textures of his verse affirm it—with kid gloves.

A reader whose experience of *terza rima* is limited to Shelley
can but faintly imagine its force and variety in the hands of its inventor. At the humblest level it serves as a No Trespassing sign,
protecting the text. A copyist's pious interpolation or unthinking
lapse would at once set off the alarm. No verse form *moves* so
wonderfully. Each tercet's first and third line rhyme with the middle one of the preceding set and enclose the new rhyme-sound of
the next, the way a scull outstrips the twin, already dissolving oarstrokes that propel it. As rhymes interlock throughout a canto, so
do incidents and images throughout the poem. Thus any given
tercet reflects in microcosm the triple structures explored by the
whole, and the progress of the verse, which allows for closure only
when (and because) a canto ends, becomes a version "without

tears" of the pilgrim's own. Rendering here some lightning insight or action, there some laborious downward or upward clambering, the *terza rima* can as well sweeten the pill of dogmatic longueurs ("This keeps moving, it will therefore end") and frame with aching fleetness those glimpses of earth denied now to the damned and the blest alike.

We feel everywhere Dante's great concision. He has so *much* to tell. Self-limited to these bare hundred cantos averaging a scant 140 lines apiece, he can't afford to pad—he is likelier to break off, pleading no more room—let alone spell out connections for a torpid reader. This *we* must do, helped by centuries of commentary. And what a shock it is, opening the *Comedy*, to leave today's plush avant-garde screening room with its risk-laden images and scrambled sound track and use our muscles to actually get somewhere. For Dante's other great virtue is his matter-of-factness. Zodiacal signposts, "humble" similes, glosses from philosophy and myth— there is nothing he won't use to locate and focus his action as sharply as possible.

A random example. Sun is climbing toward noon above the Ganges as we enter a smoke "dark as night" on the slopes of purgatory; meanwhile, these moles that come and go in a passing phrase are kin, surely, to Miss Moore's real toads:

> Ricorditi, lettor, se mai ne l'alpe
> 　　ti colse nebbia per la qual vedesti
> 　　non altrimenti che per pelle talpe . . .

Singleton renders this: "Recall, reader, if ever in the mountains a mist has caught you, through which you could not see except as moles do through skin . . ." Helpful; but was the mole in Dante's day thought to see through its *skin*? A note explains what is made clear enough in Longfellow's version, where alliteration, moreover, brings a certain music to "pelle talpe," that tiny consonantal lozenge we have paused, I trust, to savor:

> Remember, Reader, if e'er in the Alps
> A mist o'ertook thee, through which thou couldst see
> Not otherwise than through its membrane mole . . .

It is the merest instance of that matter-of-fact concision I have in mind, and makes a small plea for translation into verse such as this which deftly evokes, as prose or indeed rhymed versions so rarely can, the diction and emphasis of the original. (Why, oh, why is the Longfellow *Comedy* not in print? Comparing it with the latest prose version, by Charles Singleton, and allowing for pains rightly taken by the latter to *sound* like prose, one is struck by how often he has had apparently no choice but to hit on that good gray poet's very phrase. There is also Longfellow's delectable nineteenth-century apparatus, including essays by Ruskin and Lamartine—"Dante a fait la gazette florentine de la postérité"; Boccaccio's account of the dead Dante guiding his son to the missing final cantos of the *Paradiso*; and James Russell Lowell on the poet's monument in Ravenna: "It is a little shrine covered with a dome, not unlike the tomb of a Mohammedan saint . . . The *valet de place* says that Dante is not buried under it, but beneath the pavement of the street in front of it, where also, he says, he saw my Lord Byron kneel and weep.")

Those moles, to resume, are just one filament in a web whose circumference is everywhere. They presently mesh with an apostrophe to the imagination, which also sees without using its eyes. A case made in passing for divine inspiration ("A light moves you which takes form in heaven, of itself . . .") gives way to three trance-like visions—Procne, Haman, Amata—appropriate to this level of the mountain Dante climbs. The center of the web is still far off, almost half the poem away, but we may as well glance at it now.

The passage in question, long a commentators' favorite, has lately begun to engage the scientists as well. Mark A. Peterson proposes

(*American Journal of Physics*, Dec. 1979) that Dante's universe "is not as simple geometrically as it at first appears, but actually seems to be a so-called 'closed' universe, the 3-sphere, a universe which also emerges as a cosmological solution of Einstein's equations in general relativity theory." Let who can, experience for themselves the full complexity and symmetry of the resulting figure. Roughly, two spheres are joined *at every point* through their "equator," itself a third sphere of sheer connectivity, and the whole suspended within a fourth dimension. The figure has finite volume but no boundary: "every point is interior."

On the threshold of the Empyrean, Dante is given his first glimpse of God, an infinitesimally small, intensely brilliant point reflected, before he turns to gaze at it directly, in Beatrice's eyes. Around it spin concentric rings or haloes gaining in brightness and speed in proportion to their closeness to it. These represent the angelic orders, from inmost seraphim to furthest messengers, and compose one of the two interconnected "semi-universes" of Peterson's figure. The other, also composed of nine rings, has at its center the little "threshing-floor" of earth far down at which Dante has just been peering, and extends through the geocentric levels to his present vantage in the Primum Mobile. What he is looking at *now*, explains Beatrice, is the "point" on which "the heavens and all nature are dependent." All nature: the mole and the mountain, the sinner and the sun.

That her words paraphrase Aquinas in a commentary on Aristotle cannot account for the hallucinatory wonder of this little point. We may picture it partly as a model of electrons whirling round the atomic nucleus—in our day, the point on which all nature and its destruction depend; partly as an abstracted solar system—only with the relative planetary speeds reversed, since these Intelligences turn physics inside out. According to Peterson, however, this is exactly what they do *not* do. For the fourth dimension here is speed of rotation, or in Dante's view the dimension of divine precedence. The inmost ring moves fastest, as does the Pri-

mum Mobile outermost among the other set, because both are
nearest to God. The two universes, heavenly and natural, are alike
governed by that tiny point. The vision as reported sets the mind
reeling. What must it have been to experience?

Here too we understand, not for the first time, how Dante is
helped by Beatrice. Seeing this light through her eyes will enable
him to put it into words, to translate into his poem's measures
those that depend upon this timeless and dimensionless point, to
receive what he may of the mystery and not be struck mad or
dumb by it. A further, more profound glimpse will indeed be
largely wiped from his mind by the uncanny image of the Argo's
shadow passing over amazed Neptune.

Concise and exact, Dante is naturally partial to points. We have
come across others before this one: the "point" in the tale at which
Paolo and Francesca read no further; the high "point" of the sun's
meridian over Jerusalem; the "point" where all times are present,
into which Cacciaguida gazes to read Dante's future. A children's
book comes to mind—"Adventures of a Hole" or whatever—
where the small round "hero" piercing the volume from front to
back serves as focus to the picture on every page. It would be in
some such fashion that each episode or passing image in Dante
connects with absolute Good—or Evil. For there is finally the
very terrible point in the last canto of the *Inferno*. At the moral and
physical universes' nether pole, it is the other center required by
Peterson's scheme.

Here also are angelic spheres, those of the fallen angels. Satan,
who as Lucifer belonged to that halo nearest the point of light,
now towers waist-deep in ice, "constrained by all the weights of
the universe," and at first glance oddly unthreatening. Nine rings
narrow downward to this figure of raging entropy. From one to
the next we have felt the movement decelerating. Wind-driven
souls (Francesca) give way to runners (Brunetto), to the painfully
walking hypocrites cloaked in gilded lead, to the frozen, impacted
souls of Cocytus. This is "natural" movement; unlike those angels

of the Empyrean, it obeys the second law of thermodynamics.
W. D. Snodgrass has traced (*In Radical Pursuit*) the pilgrim Dante's
regression, as he faces the murderers of parents and children,
through the traumatic phases of early childhood, infancy, and
birth. Last comes this nadir, this "point" he must pass in order to
be reborn. It lies at the exact center of earth, of gravity, of the entire Ptolemaic universe. As the pilgrims skirt it, everything
abruptly turns upside down, psychological time once again flows
forward, and their ascent begins toward the starlight of earth's further side.

To my knowledge no one appears to have defined this point
much beyond the account of it above. "Here all is dark and mysterious," says Singleton. Dante himself, as he clambers down between the deep floor of ice and Satan's shaggy thigh—there
"where the thigh curves out to form the haunches"—averts his
eyes and language: "Let gross minds conceive my trouble, who
cannot see the point I had passed." He means, as we know, earth's
center, but he would hardly be Dante to leave it at that. Hell, reads
the inscription on its gate, was made by "the divine Power, the
supreme Wisdom, and the primal Love"—the trinity in action. In
Satan's figure, to which we've been led by a parodied Latin hymn,
we see these reversed. Power becomes impotence; wisdom, a matter of mechanical gnawing and flapping; love, a congealing wind.
As counterpoise to that radiant, all-engendering point in heaven,
we may expect something more graphically awful than a fictive
locus. "The sacred number *three* is symbolic of the whole male
genitalia," writes Freud in the *Introductory Lectures*; it is the source
of endless jokes in Greece today. Satan, as an angel, would lack
genitals—a touch appropriate to the nullity Dante wishes to convey. For surely this point in hell is where they would have been
and are not: a frozen, ungenerative, nonexistent trinity. And it is
hardly from squeamishness or to spare his reader that Dante con-
trives to "miss the point" in hell. He has come a long way since
Virgil's own hands prevented a stolen glance at the Medusa. His

wiser reticence here implies a risk to the spirit, which might have vanished at a closer look, as into a black hole.

The point—my point and everyone's by now, not these of Dante—is that the *Comedy* throughout sustains the equilibrium we have been told to look for in a haiku by Basho. There is no rift, as in conventional allegory, between action and interpretation, physical and moral, "low" and "high." All is of a piece. It is a mystic's view of the world, if you like. It is also a scientist's. And to have it tally with Einstein? For the year 1300, that's seeing the light in spades.

What diction, then, is even faintly suited to divine grace when it illuminates all things great and small? The answer must lie in the entire range, from the courtly metaphysics of the love poems, on which Dante would draw for his highest flights in paradise, to the broad innuendo of those sonnets to Forese. These also served him, as a farting devil in the Malebolge reminds us. Like the Jongleur de Notre-Dame in the pureness of his heart doing *what he can*, Dante will run through his whole bag of tricks, and the performance will be rewarded by an extraordinary universal Smile.

This wealth of diction and detail gave the *Comedy* its long reputation for a grotesque farrago flawed by "the bad taste of the century." The mature Milton asked *his* Muse to help him soar "with no middle flight"—a costly decision. Whatever its glories, the diction of *Paradise Lost* labors under its moral regalia, its relentless pre-Augustan triumphs over precisely this eclectic middle style which allows Dante his touching, first-person particularity, moles and all. It also suggests why he is continually being rediscovered by poets—now by Hugo, now by Pound—and why translations, especially into verse, keep appearing.

(1980)

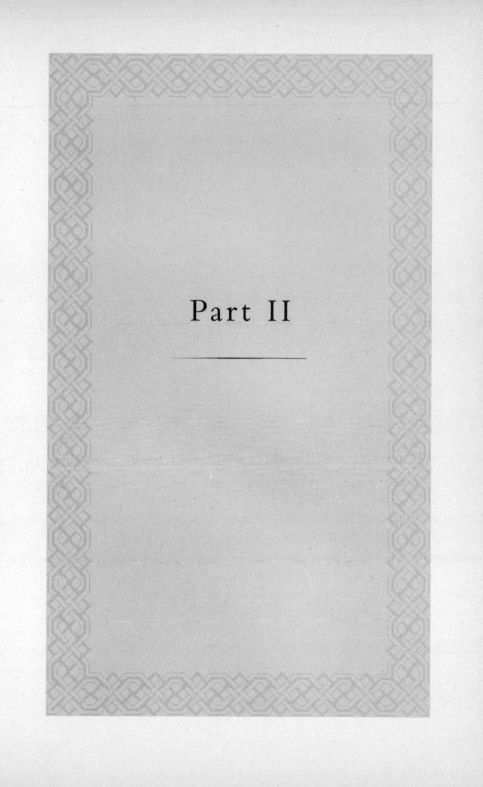

Part II

Seamus Heaney

Envies and Identifications: Dante and the Modern Poet

- I -

I think he fashioned from his opposite
An image that might have been a stony face
Staring upon a Bedouin's horse-hair roof
From doored and windowed cliff, or half upturned
Among the coarse grass and the camel-dung.
He set his chisel to the hardest stone.
Being mocked by Guido for his lecherous life,
Derided and deriding, driven out
To climb that stair and eat that bitter bread,
He found the unpersuadable justice, he found
The most exalted lady loved by a man.[1]

Yeats's lines about Dante come in his poem "Ego Dominus Tuus"—the title itself is a quotation from the *Vita Nuova*—and they were written when Yeats was beginning to set out in his verse certain laws which he assumed to be operative in the psychology of the artist and of human beings generally. Energy is discharged, reality is revealed and enforced when the artist strains to attain the mask of his opposite; in the act of summoning and achieving that image, he does his proper work and leaves us with the art itself, which is a kind of trace element of the inner struggle of opposites, a graph of the effort of transcendence.

It was obviously necessary for Yeats to test the truth of his insight against the case of Dante, "the chief imagination of Christendom," but typically, of course, what we get in the poem is not so much a questioning as an affirmation: it was Dante's rumoured lechery which drove him to create "the most exalted lady loved by a man." I quote these lines at the outset as a reminder that when poets turn to the great masters of the past, they turn to an image of their own creation, one which is likely to be a reflection of their own imaginative needs, their own artistic inclinations and procedures.

Geoffrey Hill, for example, a poet whose religious angst is as severe and penitential as it is unusual in contemporary England, condenses into the five lines of his poem "Florentines" an image of the world of the *Commedia* which is also an image of Hill the poet. It is a costumed image, perhaps, but one in which his sense of Dante and his own sense of the world coalesce within his stern and slightly punitive metres:

> Horses, black-lidded mouths peeled back
> to white: well-groomed these warriors ride,
> their feuds forgotten, remembered, forgotten . . .
> a cavalcade passing, night not far-off;
> the stricken faces damnable and serene.[2]

It is tempting just to keep quoting poems where Dante's informing presence has been given a deliberate place within the works of individual poets. There is, for example, Wilfred Owen's "Strange Meeting" in which Owen's mastery of half-rhyme combines with his memory of the fallen angels in Milton's *Paradise Lost* to present a typically Dantean encounter with the figure of his enemy, at once familiar and unexpected:

> It seemed that out of battle I escaped
> Down some profound dull tunnel, long since scooped
> Through granites which titanic wars had groined.

Yet also there encumbered sleepers groaned,
Too fast in thought or death to be bestirred.
Then, as I probed them one sprang up, and stared
With piteous recognition in fixed eyes,
Lifting distressful hands as if to bless.
And by his smile, I knew that sullen hall,
By his dead smile I knew we stood in Hell.[3]

Thomas Kinsella also has long been fascinated by the great dream journey to the underworld and the land of the dead. There is a whole study to be written about the way Kinsella's exploration of the individual's quest for coherence and integrity in a world of constant disintegration and slippage has been informed by the deep stream of Dantean example flowing at the back of his mind. The inner journeys adumbrated in poems like "One" and "Finistère" may have the *Book of Invasions* as their native source and Pound's early cantos as their immediate progenitor, but the *Commedia* has been part of this poet's mental furniture from early on, and his river journey poem, "Downstream," published more than twenty years ago, depends explicitly upon the *terza rima* stanza to link the boat trip downstream through the Irish midlands with the descent begun in the middle of the dark Tuscan wood. Here it is as much formal influence as mythic structure that we are witnessing, a case of identification between a twentieth-century maker and the medieval master; and, once again, the poem is a testimony to the generating power of the *Commedia*, its long reach into the first and deepest levels of the shaping spirit:

Again in the mirrored dusk the paddles sank.
    We thrust forward, swaying both as one.
    The ripples widened to the ghostly bank

Where willows, with their shadows half undone,
    Hung to the water, mowing like the blind.
    The current seized our skiff. We let it run

Grazing the reeds, and let the land unwind
  In stealth on either hand. Dark woods: a door
  Opened and shut. The clear sky fell behind.[4]

Beguiling as all these poems are, however, it is the critical writings of two other great modern poets which will most concern
me in this essay; and having looked at them, I shall add some brief
remarks about the influence which Dante has had upon work I
have been doing recently.

– I I –

T. S. Eliot's work is haunted by the shade of Dante, and nowhere
more tellingly than in the second section of "Little Gidding." This
part of *Four Quartets* is set in the dawn, in wartime London, a
modern dream vision, shimmering with the possibility of discovery and certitude, concerned to some extent with strictly literary
matters but ultimately involved with the universal sorrows and
penalties of living and aging. The poet exchanges intense but
oddly neutral words with "a familiar compound ghost" and the
section ends like this:

"From wrong to wrong the exasperated spirit
  Proceeds, unless restored by that refining fire
  Where you must move in measure, like a dancer."
The day was breaking. In the disfigured street
  He left me, with a kind of valediction,
  And faded on the blowing of the horn.[5]

The phrase "the blowing of the horn" operates in the same way
that the word "forlorn" operates in Keats's "Ode to a Nightingale."
It tolls us back to our sole selves. It is bleaker than Keats's word
because the world outside Eliot's poem is even bleaker than the

world outside Keats's "Ode." "The blowing of the horn" is, in fact, the sounding of the "all clear" at the end of an air-raid, and it recalls us to Eliot's historical situation when the poem was being composed and he was doing his duty as an air-raid warden during the London blitz. Indeed, the strange and suggestive lines at the beginning of the section about "the dark dove with the flickering tongue" which passes "below the horizon of his homing" and the image of "three districts whence the smoke arose" are also documentary of the historical moment, insofar as they suggest the bomber's withdrawal and the burning city after the raid. Yet to talk like this about blitz and bombers and air-raids and burning cities immediately does violence to the mood and intent of the poetry. That poetry, like the poetry of Keats's "Ode," escapes the local trappings of the historical moment and is suspended in the ether of a contemplative mind. The language conducts us away from what is contingent; it is not mimetic of the cold morning cityscape but of the calescent imagination. We can say, as a matter of literary fact, that the lines are more haunted by the squadrons of Dante's *terza rima* than by the squadrons of Hitler's *Luftwaffe*.

We can also say that the language of the lines is more affected by Eliot's idea of Dante's language than it is by the actual sounds and idioms of those Londoners among whom Eliot lived and over whom he was watching during his "dead patrol." The lines have something of the quality which Eliot ascribes to Dante in his 1929 essay on the poet:

> Dante's universality is not solely a personal matter. The Italian language, and especially the Italian language in Dante's age, gains much by being the product of universal Latin. There is something much more *local* about the languages in which Shakespeare and Racine had to express themselves . . . Medieval Latin tended to concentrate on what men of various races and lands could think together. Some of the character of this universal language seems to me to

inhere in Dante's Florentine speech; and the localization ("Florentine" speech) seems if anything to emphasize the universality, because it cuts across the modern division of nationality.[6]

In a similar way, the language of the "Little Gidding" passage seeks for things which "men of various races and lands could think together"; it tends to eschew the local, the intimate, the word which reeks of particular cultural attachments, and opts instead for words like "unappeased and peregrine," "impelled," "expiring," "conscious impotence," "laceration," "re-enactment," "exercise of virtue," "exasperated," "valediction." Indeed, at its most primitive and dialect moment, the moment in the animal heat of the byre at milking time, it interposes the smooth and decorous and monosyllabic noun, "pail," as if to distance us from the raucous and parochial energies of the usual "bucket."[7]

All this, of course, reinforces one of our perennial expectations from art, that it deliver what Sir Philip Sidney called a "golden world" to defy the "brazen world" of nature, that it offer us ideal melodies which transcend and to some extent rebuke the world of sensual music. It is a constant part of our desires, this hankering for an absolute and purely delineated world of wisdom and beauty, and it sometimes asks literature to climb the stair of transcendence and give us images free from the rag-and-bone-shop reek of time and place. Such a dream of perfection is best served by a language which gives the illusion of absolute authority, of a purity beyond dialect and tribe, an imperial lexicon, in fact, a Roman vocabulary which is socially and historically patrician. Eliot's achievement in his Dantean stanzas is to create just such an illusion of oracular authority by the hypnotic deployment of perfected latinate words.

The essay on Dante was written six years after the appearance of *The Waste Land*, a poem which arose from personal breakdown and a vision of decline and disintegration in the Europe that was once called Christendom. By the nineteen forties, however, Eliot was composing his soul rather than rendering images of its decomposition. His critical concerns were less with the strictly verbal and technical aspects of poetry, more with the philosophical and religious significances which could be drawn from and relied upon within a work of poetic art. The essay on Dante, in fact, ends up as an essay about conversion, and understandably so, since at the time the intellectual mysteryman from Missouri was mutating into the English vestryman. In the essay Eliot is concerned, among other things, with Dante's concentration upon states of purgation and beatitude, his allegorical method, his system of beliefs, even his love of pageantry (corresponding to "the serious pageants of royalty, of the Church, of military funerals")[8] and these concerns are symptomatic of his own concerns in 1929. He ends with an evocation of the world of the *Vita Nuova*, of the necessary attempt, "as difficult and hard as rebirth,"[9] to enter it, and bows out with the declaration that "there is almost a definite moment of acceptance when the New Life begins."

It is curious that this born-again Anglican and monarchist did not make more of the political Dante, the dreamer of a world obedient to the spiritual authority of a cleansed Papacy and under the sway of a just emperor, where, without bitterness or corruption, Christ and Caesar would be hand in glove. But perhaps we are meant to deduce this Dante from that praise of "universal language," the Tuscan speech which transcended its local habitation because of its roots in classical and ecclesiastical Latin. Eliot's joy in praising this lucid European instrument springs from his joy in a writer who speaks not just as himself but as "the whole mind of Europe." By contrast, poets of other European tongues, because they work farther from the pure Latin source, are condemned to a more opaque idiom and a less than central relevance.

To clinch this argument, Eliot takes those lines of Shakespeare's where Duncan is introduced to Macbeth's castle, lines full of air and light, and contrasts them with the opening lines of the *Commedia*. More is lost, he maintains, in translating Shakespeare than in translating Dante. "How can a foreigner find words to convey in his own language just that combination of intelligibility and remoteness that we get in many phrases of Shakespeare?"

> This guest of summer
> The temple-haunting martlet, does approve
> By his loved masonry that the heaven's breath
> Smells wooingly here: no jutty, frieze,
> Buttress, nor coign of vantage, but this bird
> Hath made his pendant bed and procreant cradle:
> Where they most breed and haunt, I have observed
> The air is delicate.[10]

Agreed. This English is erotic and feels for warmer and quicker nubs and joints of speech, and as it forages its voice cannot quite maintain its civil blandishment but relapses towards a muttering urgency in "jutty" and "buttress," rather like an excited Mellors slipping into dialect. The poetry, in other words, is to a large extent in the phonetics, in the genetic energies of English words discharging their load of association, the flitting of the swallow being airily present in phrases like "they most breed and haunt" and "the air is delicate," while the domineering presence of stone architecture is simultaneously conjured by the minatory solidity of terms like "masonry" and "buttress."

Yet if we look at the opening lines of Dante's poem again, we might ask ourselves if the Italian is so essentially different in its operation. Eliot would have us take this as a clean lexical exercise, devoid of any local self-consciousness, and indeed the ghosts of first declension Latin nouns stand in the open doors of the Italian vowels like sponsors of the much sought universality:

> Nel mezzo del cammin di nostra vita
>   mi ritrovai per una selva oscura
>   che la diritta via era smarrita

"Nostra vita," "una selva oscura," "la diritta via": we are in earshot not only of the Vatican but also of the Capitol; and out of that common murmur one voice begins to emerge, the voice of Virgil, a prophetic figure in the medieval mind, the pagan precursor of the Christian dispensation, the poet who had envisaged in an eclogue the world of allegory and encyclical in which Dante had his being. As the great poet of the Latin language, Virgil can walk naturally out of the roots of this Tuscan speech, a figure of completely exemplary force. Virgil comes to Dante, in fact, as Dante comes to Eliot, a master, a guide and authority, offering release from the toils and snares of the self, from the *diserta*, the waste land. Ladies and leopards begin to appear in Eliot's poems of the late nineteen twenties; the hushed and fragrant possibilities of a heavenly order which we hear in canto 2 of the *Inferno* are overheard in sections 2 and 4 of *Ash-Wednesday*; the soul's journey as outlined by Marco Lombardo in canto 16 of the *Purgatorio* is rehearsed in "Animula."

It is a moment of crisis, of turning towards and of turning away, when the converting Eliot begins to envy the coherence and certitude, the theological, philosophical, and linguistic harmonies available to his great predecessor. Shakespeare he admires, yes, but does not envy. Shakespeare's venturesome, humanist genius, his Elizabethan capacity for provisional and glamorous accommodations between faiths and doubts, his opportunistic dash through the high world of speculation and policy, still fresh from the folk-speech and hedge-school of the shires, all this disruptive, unaligned cognition and explorativeness is by now, for Eliot, suspect. It is the symptom of a breakdown which, during his own lifetime, had come out of potential and into the historical convulsion of the First World War and its disillusioned aftermath.

But when he makes Dante's confident and classically ratified language bear an almost allegorical force, he does less than justice to the untamed and thoroughly parochial elements which it possesses. To listen to Eliot, one would almost be led to forget that

Dante's great literary contribution was to write in the vernacular
and thereby to give the usual language its head:

> Nel mezzo del cammin di nostra vita
>   mi ritrovai per una selva oscura,
>   che la diritta via era smarrita.
> Ahi quanto a dir qual era è cosa dura
>   esta selva selvaggia e aspra e forte
>   che nel pensier rinova la paura!

"Smarrita." *The Concise Cambridge Italian Dictionary* gives "smar-
rire, to mislay; to lose; to mislead; to bewilder," yet each of these
English equivalents strikes me as less particular, less urgently local
than the Italian word, which has all the force of dirt hitting a
windscreen. Eliot underplays the swarming, mobbish element in
the Italian, which can be just as "selvaggia e aspra e forte" as the
dark wood itself. Say those first two adjectives aloud and then decide whether they call up the refined *urbs* or the rough-spoken
rus. "Selva selvaggia" is as barbarous as Hopkins, "aspra e forte" less
suggestive of the composure of the classics than of the struggle
with the undergrowth. Dante may be writing about a mid-life crisis within the terms of the allegory, but he is also writing about
panic, that terror we experience in the presence of the god Pan,
numen of the woods.

   Eliot was recreating Dante in his own image. He had always
taken what he needed from the work and at this stage what he
needed was a way of confirming himself as a poet ready to submit
his intelligence and sensibility to a framework of beliefs which
were inherited and communal. The poet of distress had come to
stress the need for acceptance. The poet who earlier in his career
could inhabit the phantasmagoria of canto 3 of the *Inferno*, that region populated by hollow men, flibbertigibbets blown about after
wheeling contradictory standards, whispering together in quiet
and meaningless voices, that poet would now be reborn as the

alien judging figure who walks among them, the thoroughly human presence who casts a shadow and displaces water when he
steps into Charon's boat.

It is instructive to compare Dante's influence upon *The Waste
Land* and upon the poem published nearly twenty years later. In
the earlier work, the *Commedia* provided Eliot with a theatre of
dreams and gave permission for the symbolist arbitrariness of
oneiric passages such as the famous ending of "The Burial of the
Dead," a scene which provides a striking contrast with the London
passage in "Little Gidding." The influence of the *Inferno* is found
not just in the famous echo of the line from canto 3 about the
great multitude of the dead, nor in the shocking confrontation
with Stetson, a revenant from the sinister past. It is also to be
found in the sense of bewilderment and somnambulism, of being
caught in a flow of energies that go their predestined and doomed
ways, of losing direction in a foggy populous drift:

> Unreal City,
> Under the brown fog of a winter dawn,
> A crowd flowed over London Bridge, so many,
> I had not thought death had undone so many.
> Sighs, short and infrequent, were exhaled,
> And each man fixed his eyes before his feet.
> Flowed up the hill and down King William Street,
> To where Saint Mary Woolnoth kept the hours
> With a dead sound on the final stroke of nine.
> There I saw one I knew, and stopped him, crying: "Stetson!
> You who were with me in the ships at Mylae!
> That corpse you planted last year in your garden,
> Has it begun to sprout?"[11]

Here Dante was actually giving Eliot the freedom to surrender to
the promptings of his own unconscious, and the language is more
allied to the Shakespearean-local-associative than to the latinate-

classical-canonical. For the moment, the imagination is in thrall to romantic expressionism, bewildered on the flood of its own inventiveness.

Twenty years later, things have changed. In the "Little Gidding" scene, the consecutive thought, the covenant between verse and argument, the tone of gravity and seniority all reflect a rebirth out of the romance of symbolism into the stricter disciplines of *philosophia* and religious orthodoxy. The definitive Dante of the 1929 essay and the definitive Eliot of *Four Quartets* have established a mutually fortifying alliance. The Dante whom Eliot now prefers and expounds walks in the aura of cultural history and representativeness. He is a figure in whom the commentaries on the *Commedia* are implicit; he stands for the thoroughly hierarchical world of scholastic thought, an imagined standard against which the relativity and agnosticism of the present can be judged. For all his talk about Dante's visual imagination—an imagination which sees visions—Eliot's ultimate attraction is to the way Dante could turn values and judgements into poetry, the way the figure of the poet as thinker and teacher merged into the figure of the poet as expresser of a universal myth that could unify the abundance of the inner world and the confusion of the outer. There is a stern and didactic profile to this Dante and as Eliot embraces a religious faith he turns towards that profile and would recreate it in his own work.

- I I I -

During the nineteen thirties, while Eliot was putting the finishing touches to his classical monument, an image of Dante as seer and repository of tradition, another poet was busy identifying Dante not with the inheritance of culture but with the processes of nature, making him a precursor of the experimental and unnerving poetry of Arthur Rimbaud rather than an heir to the Virgilian *gravitas*. Osip Mandelstam's Dante is the most eager, the most inspiring, the most delightfully approachable recreation we could hope for and what I want to do next is to indulge in what Mandelstam says Dante indulges in, "an orgy of quotations." These all come from his indispensable essay, "Conversation about Dante," never published in Russia in his lifetime but available in English translation in *The Complete Prose and Letters of Osip Mandelstam*.[12] The quotations are not in the order in which they appear in the essay, which is a tumultuous affair anyhow, but I have arranged them to give a contrast to Eliot and to suggest the unpredictable intuitive nature of Mandelstam's genius:

For how many centuries have people been talking and writing about Dante as if he had expressed his thoughts directly on official paper? . . . Dante is discussed as if he had the completed whole before his eyes even before he had begun work and as if he had utilized the technique of moulage, first casting in plaster, then in bronze.

The process of creating this poem's form transcends our conceptions of literary invention and composition. It would be more correct to recognize instinct as its guiding principle . . . Only through metaphor is it possible to find a concrete sign to represent the instinct for form creation by which Dante accumulated and poured forth his *terza rima*.

We must try to imagine, therefore, how bees might have worked at this thirteen-thousand-faceted form, bees endowed with the brilliant stereometric instinct, who attracted bees in greater and greater numbers as they were required. The work of these bees, constantly keeping their eye on the whole, is of varying difficulty at different stages of the process. Their cooperation expands and grows more complicated as they participate in the process of forming the combs, by means of which space virtually emerges out of itself.

When I began to study Italian and had barely familiarized myself with its phonetics and prosody, I suddenly understood that the center of gravity of my speech efforts had been moved closer to my lips, to the outer parts of my mouth. The tip of the tongue suddenly turned out to have the seat of honor. The sound rushed toward the locking of the teeth. And something else that struck me was the infantile aspect of Italian phonetics, its beautiful child-like quality, its closeness to infant babbling, to some kind of eternal dadaism.

It seems to me that Dante made a careful study of all speech defects, listening closely to stutterers and lispers, to nasal twangs and inarticulate pronunciations, and that he learned much from them.

I would very much like to speak about the auditory coloration of canto 32 of the *Inferno*.

A peculiar labial music: "abbo"—"gabbo"—"babbo"—"Tebe"—"plebe"—"zebba"—"converebbe." It's as if a nurse had participated in the creation of phonetics. Now the lips protrude in a childish manner, now they extend into a proboscis.

Precisely those who are furthest from Dante's method in European poetry and, bluntly speaking, in polar opposition to him, go by the name Parnassians: Heredia, Leconte de Lisle. Baudelaire is much closer. Verlaine is still closer, but the closest of all the French poets is Arthur Rimbaud. Dante is by his very nature one who shakes up meaning and destroys the integrity of the image. The composition of his cantos resembles an airline schedule or the indefatigable flights of carrier pigeons.

Mandelstam's Dante is more like Eliot's Shakespeare: he is not distinguished by his cultural representativeness, his conservative majesty or his intellectual orthodoxy. Rather, he is fastened upon and shaken into new and disconcerting life as an exemplar of the purely creative, intimate, and experimental act of writing itself. This Dante is essentially lyric; he is stripped of the robes of commentary in which he began to vest himself with his epistle to Can Grande, reclaimed from the realm of epic and allegory and made to live as the epitome of a poet's creative excitement. Which is not to say, of course, that Mandelstam is not alive to the historical and literary contexts in which Dante wrote, what he calls the great "keyboard of references"; but what Mandelstam emphasizes, and what is invaluable in his emphasis, is the thrilling fact that, in the words of W. H. Auden, poetic composition probably feels much the same in the twentieth century A.D. as it did in the twentieth century B.C.

Eliot and Pound envied Dante and to some extent imitated him in the forms and procedures of their poems. Pound's *Cantos* are the great epic homage in English in this century, too large a subject to address here, but they too sway to the authority of Dante the historian, Dante the encyclopaedic mind, the plunderer and harbourer of classical and medieval learning. The *Cantos* are intent upon repeating the *Commedia*'s synoptic feats of inclusion and correspondence; the gigantic is what both attracts and finally daunts Pound—and his reader as well, it could be said. The two Americans at once restored and removed Dante in the English speaking literary mind because they both suggested what Mandelstam was at pains to mock, that Dante's poem was written on official paper. They came to Dante early, as students; as young men, they studied him in an academic context; they wore his poem like a magic garment to protect themselves from the contagion of parochial English and American culture; and finally they canonized him as the aquiline patron of international modernism.

What Mandelstam does, on the other hand, is to bring him from the pantheon back to the palate; he makes our mouth water to read him. He possesses the poem as a musician possesses the score, both as a whole structure and as a sequence of delicious sounds. He transmits a fever of excitement in the actual phonetic reality of the work and shares with us the sensation of his poet's delight turning into a sort of giddy critical wisdom. And this personal neediness and rapture which we find in Mandelstam's responses has much to do with the fact that he came to Dante not as an undergraduate but as an exile in his thirties. In her memoir, *Hope Against Hope*, Nadezhda Mandelstam tells us that her husband had no copy of Dante until this late stage in his life but that it was one of the few books he took with him when he was banished from his beloved Petersburg to the dark earth of Voronezh. By the time he came to dwell with the *Commedia*, his powers as a lyric poet had been tested and fulfilled, and his destiny as a moral being, in the middle of the journey, was being tragically embraced.

Mandelstam's exile from Petersburg was the result of a poem he had written against Stalin, an uncharacteristically explicit and publicly directed poem which was reported to the Kremlin by an informer. But this poem had come at the end of four or five years of poetic silence, and the silence was the result of Mandelstam's attempt at connivance, compromise, acceptance—call it what you will; for a number of years he had been trying to make an accommodation with Soviet realities. He had been attempting to quell his essentially subjective, humanist vision of poetry as a kind of free love between the auditory imagination and the unharnessed intelligence, trying to submerge his quarrel with the idea of art as a service, a socialist realist cog in the revolutionary machine. He had worked as a translator, he had attempted to persuade himself that his pre-revolutionary espousal of poetry as a self-delighting, self-engendering, musical system based upon what he called "the steadfastness of speech articulation," was an expression of "inner freedom," and that this vision of art could be maintained and exercised within the Soviet dispensation where art, nevertheless, had to be, in Joyce's terms, kinetic, directed towards forwarding a cause, ready to forget its covenant with the literary past and the individual's inner sense of the truth. Yet Mandelstam's whole creative being strained against this attempt and, indeed, even when he was under the shadow of the death to which Stalin eventually hounded him, his creative being was helpless to change. He tried, a little shamefacedly in his own eyes and, to his credit, entirely unsuccessfully, to write a poem in praise of a hydro-electric dam, but he could manage nothing.

So in order to breathe freely, to allow his lips to move again with poems which were his breath of life, he had to come clean, spur his Pegasus out of the socialist realist morass, and thereby confront the danger of death and the immediate penalty of exile. And his essay on Dante was written in the aftermath of this tragic choice. It is no wonder therefore that Dante is not perceived as the mouthpiece of an orthodoxy but rather as the apotheosis of free, natural, biological process, as a hive of bees, a process of crystallization, a hurry of pigeon flights, a focus for all the impulsive, instinctive, non-utilitarian elements in the creative life. Mandelstam found a guide and authority for himself also, but a guide who wears no official badge, enforces no party line, does not write paraphrases of Aquinas or commentaries on the classical authors. His Dante is a voluble Shakespearean figure, a woodcutter singing at his work in the dark wood of the larynx.

- IV -

I hesitate, in this mighty context, to get personal. But perhaps I can exit from this consideration of Eliot and Mandelstam by reading a passage of my own which is mindful of "Little Gidding" in its form but is finally in debt to Mandelstam for what it says. It comes from a sequence of poems set on Station Island in Lough Derg, a *purgatorio* in itself, the site of a three-day pilgrimage involving a dark night and a bright morning, a departure from the world and a return to it. I would not have dared to go to Lough Derg for the poem's setting had I not become entranced a few years ago with the *Divine Comedy* in translation, to the extent that I was emboldened to make my own version of the Ugolino episode from the *Inferno* and to translate (though not to publish) the first four cantos. With Dante's example, however, I was encouraged to make an advantage of what could otherwise be regarded as a disadvantage, namely, that other writers had been to Lough Derg before me—William Carleton, Sean O'Faolain, Patrick Kavanagh, Denis Devlin, to mention only the English language forerunners. But then I thought that Carleton could be a sort of Tyrone Virgil and Kavanagh a latter-day County Monaghan Cavalcanti, and although that is not how the thing turned out, it gave me the impulse to get started.

What I first loved in the *Commedia* was the local intensity, the vehemence and fondness attaching to individual shades, the way personalities and values were emotionally soldered together, the strong strain of what has been called personal realism in the celebration of bonds of friendship and bonds of enmity. The way in which Dante could place himself in an historical world yet submit that world to scrutiny from a perspective beyond history, the way he could accommodate the political and the transcendent, this too encouraged my attempt at a sequence of poems which would explore the typical strains which the consciousness labours under in this country. The main tension is between two often contradictory commands: to be faithful to the collective historical experience and to be true to the recognitions of the emerging self. I hoped that I could dramatize these strains by meeting shades from my own dream-life who had also been inhabitants of the actual Irish world. They could perhaps voice the claims of orthodoxy and the necessity to refuse those claims. They could probe the validity of one's commitment.

Yet the choice of Lough Derg as a locus for the poem did, in fact, represent a solidarity with orthodox ways and obedient attitudes, and that very solidarity and obedience were what had to be challenged. And who better to offer the challenge than the shade of Joyce himself? He speaks here to the pilgrim as he leaves the island, in an encounter reminiscent of "Little Gidding" but with advice that Mandelstam might have given; yet the obvious shaping influence is the *Commedia*:

>   "Your obligation
> is not discharged by any common rite.
> What you must do must be done on your own
> so get back in harness. The main thing is to write
> for the joy of it. Cultivate a work-lust
> that imagines its haven like your hands at night
>
> dreaming the sun in the sunspot of a breast.
> You are fasted now, light-headed, dangerous.
> Take off from here. And don't be so earnest,
>
> let others wear the sackcloth and the ashes.
> Let go, let fly, forget.
> You've listened long enough. Now strike your note."

(1985)

Notes

1. *The Collected Poems of W. B. Yeats* (London: Macmillan, 1950, 1963), p. 181.
2. Geoffrey Hill, *Tenebrae* (London: André Deutsch, 1978), p. 40.
3. *The Collected Poems of Wilfred Owen*, ed. C. Day Lewis (London: Chatto & Windus, 1977), p. 35.

4. Thomas Kinsella, *Selected Poems 1956–1968* (Dublin: Dolmen Press, 1973), p. 56.

5. *The Complete Poems and Plays of T. S. Eliot* (London and Boston: Faber & Faber, 1969), p. 195.

6. T. S. Eliot, *Selected Essays* (London: Faber & Faber, 1951, 1976), p. 239.

7. Eliot, *Complete Poems and Plays*, p. 194: "And the fullfed beast shall kick the empty pail."

8. Eliot, *Selected Essays*, p. 262.

9. Ibid., p. 276.

10. Ibid., p. 241. The prose quotation immediately preceding this quotation is from the same page.

11. Eliot, *Complete Poems and Plays*, pp. 62–63.

12. *The Complete Prose and Letters of Osip Mandelstam* (Ann Arbor: Ardis Press, 1979), pp. 397–451.

Charles Wright

Dantino Mio

It's easier to talk about nothing than to talk about something. It's easier to concoct a design than to explain a design. Dante is the Great Design. Dante is the Great Something. He is difficult, as I say, to talk about. I came to him originally through Ezra Pound, as I came to many things: Provence, T'ang China, Modernism, Victorian/Edwardian London, Modern Italy, Renaissance Italy, and Social Credit. Italy, Dante, and the T'ang poets remain in their original delight. Other things less so. It seems to me that Pound has been the great proponent and privileger of Dante in English in this century. Or perhaps it was "Eliopound." It's the same thing. Ezra was always the squeaky wheel.

He said, from St. Elizabeth's, that the structure of the *Cantos* was:

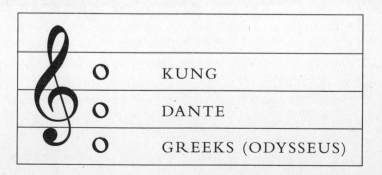

So I read a little Confucius (Pound was translating the *Odes* at the time—September 7, 1953, given to Donald Pearce—but Confucius had been a longtime doppelgänger), a bunch of Dante, and what Greeks who looked me in the mouth. But mostly Dante. And my sin has been to keep on nosing around, unlike Dante, in the unknown without a map (an Aquinas map, which Dante had and which Pound lacked, and which I lack), and without an entry point or exit, i.e., Dabblesville. But serious Dabblesville, hoping to catch the right train, hoping to find the right city. Doomed from the start.

Still, "the gods exist." States of mystical exaltation exist in nature. It is notoriously difficult to get these down in art. But Pound rises time after time to the challenge, given Dante's example and Dante's hyper-example. Saying the unsayable, trying to express the inexpressible. Following their lead, I've tried to raise myself from my own ground, into my own blue.

Provence was as key to Pound as it was to Dante—*la donna ideale* runs like a silk thread through the work of both, from Beatrice to *Beatrice intronizzata*, from Audiart to Dryad in the *Pisan Cantos* (Olga says it's she; Dorothy says it's she. Perhaps. And perhaps it's just the concept, *il concetto*, "the dynamic form . . ."). The *forma*, as Pound says, "the concept rises from death." Which is where *la donna ideale* comes from and goes to, from the banks of the Arno to the immaculate rose of Paradise, from the banks of the Schuylkill to the clouds above Monte Pisano (Taishan). Pound, in a way, never left Provence. Dante did. Therein probably lies the difference—or one of them—between periplum and paradise.

Still, as I say, Pound is the great highway into Città Dante in our time. Eliot used him, but Pound genuflected, lit the candles, and swung the censer. And never for a minute believed the pomp and circumstance, *tutta la ceremonia* (indeed, loathed it and its applications), but was wholly into the message, the journey, the sacred headland at voyage's end.

All of this is big medicine and hard to ignore or refuse to take.

And take it I did when young, and swallowed it whole. Over the years, it has dispersed and dissipated, and now it is a glittering sediment under everything I do. What we start with is what renews us and tends to redeem us at the end. Thus Dante and Pound. Thus Eliot, as he so famously said. Thus, I hope, myself and my triple trilogies, *Country Music, The World of the Ten Thousand Things*, and *Negative Blue*. By the Adige and Arno, the waters of A, I lay me down.

I first studied Dante in Rome with Maria Sampoli, an extraordinarily gifted scholar who taught the Fulbright literature students at the University of Rome. I owe her both Dante and Montale, really two of the three great poetic influences of my life. We read the *Inferno* in both Italian and English. That was in 1963. Fifteen years later, in 1978, I got the Singleton edition of the complete *Comedy* and began to read it more systematically. Each morning of the week, I'd sit on a large couch in the living room in my house in Laguna Beach, California, spread out both the commentary volume and the English-Italian text and go through a canto. One canto a day. I'd read the English trot first, then the Italian. That way I knew what the story was and could enjoy the miracle of the Italian text without stopping at every other word to look it up. Then I would read the commentary, go back, and read the Italian. So I knew the story line and I'd get the story again, plus the music, plus the language, plus the everything else. It was the most glorious three months of reading I've ever done. I didn't write a line of my own during that entire time, I was so completely filled and fulfilled. Nothing like that had ever affected me so before and I doubt anything ever will again. By the time I got to the great Rose of Paradise, I realized the *Inferno*, which I had loved so much, was merely gossip. Inspired, but gossip nonetheless. And since the *Comedy* is, I suppose, ultimately a diagram for the salvation of the soul, its seriousness is more than made manifest. Also, since it's a diagram and not a textbook, you can take from it various truths without having to be concerned that the pedagogic one has escaped. It is as diamond-hearted as the Book of Revelation, and as great-minded.

Structure is the thing to me that is endlessly discoverable—or at least so far it's been endlessly discoverable. Pound's attempt at form, the whole *Cantos*, for instance, was the search for a Final Form, an Ultimate Form. It's a failure, but what a great try! I believe it was found once, given the terms in which it was tried, and that was in the *Divine Comedy*, where the form, the structure, the story line, all the characters—the three Dantes—everything in there works. It really does come together, and people have been trying to imitate that for a long time. Dante had a great advantage in that the world was more circumscribed than it is now, as far as what was possible and what was not.

Dante remains the great Buddhistic center of absolute attention and regard, the true magnetic field of seriousness toward which all real poems gravitate. One is influenced by Dante only in ways that time tells and that one's poems continually aspire to. The river of light is not a tributary; the songs rise and the songs converge. All the great poets of light—Donne, Pound, Blake, Cavalcanti, Dickinson, etc.—can be said to be "going back." All of them have the small, indestructible diamond of Neoplatonism under their skins, or tucked in some loose fold of their centers, the ticket home.

Dante, to anyone who reads him seriously, should be a seminal force in his experience, either artistic or spiritual. One would hope both. He is surely the greatest poet (including Shakespeare; well, as has been said—one was deep, the other wide) we have had in two thousand years and surely the poet most spiritually affecting. His poetry is relevant to me, as I would hope to aspire to the condition his poetry lays down for us: spiritual quest and spiritual attainment. A very famous American critic once said to me that he didn't really like Dante—though he had only read the *Inferno*—because the narrative creaked. Perhaps so, but that's sweet music to my ears. After Dante finishes with the gossip and revenge in the

Inferno, the narrative starts to smooth out and eventually, as it rushes through the layers and heavens of Paradise, it flows as smoothly as the river of light he is after. Or the source of that river he is after. Dante makes you think seriously about your own life. He makes you want to *have* your own life, and to do the best you can with it. His poem is a great Platonic model of both art and life.

Reading the *Paradiso* is almost enough to convert you. And the concept of the *Paradiso*, the incredible concept of the entire project, is so overwhelming, and the language is so amazing, and the form of the poem, and the correspondences and the unbelievable glory of the fulfillment. What I took away from Dante is what one always takes away from great art, I suppose—wonder and immense thanks. When you see the best in your own line of work, all you can do is give thanks and say amen.

I remember writing once—regarding the hubris and arrogance of poets—that everyone is no one: we all huddle behind our tiny rocks when the shadow of Dante's great wings goes over us. I find, as it turns out, that I have little to add to that either. Though I will say that the poets I have loved first, Ezra Pound and Eugenio Montale, tried to write like Dante and knew they did. And both the poets I came to love best, Emily Dickinson and Gerard Manley Hopkins, tried to write like Dante and probably didn't know it. Everyone who has his eyes above the dirt—and those who don't—owe him either a debt or a tip of the hat. If you write poems about God or Man—and there are, I think, few other categories—his tracks precede you. There's nothing for it but to follow him.

I find, for me, it's hard to talk about Dante on a personal level. His work and vision remain a light source still after all these years, something I read by, and something I write under. I go to Dante as I go to a dictionary—to find out what something means. His influence is not systematic, but systemic. Thinking about him and his poem has made me medieval-minded aesthetically, and has made my own series of books, the three trilogies of poems, medieval-minded as well, in structure and formal aspirations. No matter how up-to-date and pluralistic their clothing—and I hope it is; I hope it's hip—their bones are old and single-minded and walk in their one direction: the walled city at the road's end, whose lights are the lights of stars.

And one last thing. A couple of days ago my brother sent me, from Savannah, Georgia, five photographic slides he had discovered in going through some stored-away family stuff. April, 1960. Ugolino Golf Club outside Florence, Italy. An American golf tournament. Five pictures of me playing, taken by him. I'm twenty-four, he's twenty-two, Tuscan spring, olive trees, and wildflowers. As Sam Snead would say, "some flippy-wrist, limber-back kid." Ugolino! My background was golf and fraternity parties, not literature. Count Ugolino, Archbishop Ruggieri, Cocytus, Ptolomea, and Antenora meant nothing to me yet. The tower of hunger, the mountain that keeps Pisa from seeing Lucca (Monte Pisano, Tai-shan), meant nothing to me. Later I read a little and learned a little, but the idea of playing golf on a course called Ugolino, in Tuscany among the olive rows and the wine rows, is still as amazing to me as it was then when the name meant nothing except a landscape that was to die for merely, and not yet to gnaw on.

Jacqueline Osherow

She's Come Undone: An American Jew Looks at Dante

The first time I ever read a line of Dante's, I thought I was reading T. S. Eliot. And I'm really not sure how long it was before I was disabused of this notion. The line of course was "I had not thought death had undone so many," quite a good translation of "non averei creduto / che morte tanta n'avesse disfatta . . ." and it appeared in the first section of *The Waste Land* with no quotation marks or attribution whatsoever. A glance at the footnotes would've set me straight, but then, I didn't glance at the footnotes. To Dante's credit, it was my favorite line in *The Waste Land*, which I now see as a sort of confirmation of Eliot's insistence that if you read Dante to primitives, they will recognize it as poetry. I was certainly primitive; it was certainly recognizable as superior poetry.

The second time I encountered him was when I raced through a fairly large chunk of the *Inferno* for a huge introductory lecture course in Western philosophy. I dropped the class after I was hit by a drunk driver on the sidewalk as I was leaving the Dante lecture. I wasn't badly hurt, but I figured it was a sign. The fact is, I would have dropped it anyway. Even the cursory glimpse I had given the *Inferno* between midnight and three a.m. the night before had made clear to me that I did not want to discuss it as philosophy. For one thing, the philosophy was utterly alien to me, belonging to that almost limitless category my grandparents would have dismissed with the word *goyish*. And, for another, I wasn't interested in extracting its ideas. I was interested—even in translation—in the way it worked as poetry. Now that I think of it, surely it was then that I discovered the origins of my favorite T. S. Eliot line. If I force myself, I can almost remember the instant of recognition and surprise . . .

For me, the thrill of Dante—that shock about what is actually possible in poetry—didn't begin to occur until it was inextricable from my whole new sense of what was possible in a city and in a country. For me, the poetry was—and actually remains—attached to the walls and buildings and streets that, despite their obvious splendor, seemed to feel the need to beautify themselves with lines from the *Divine Comedy*, carved on little plaques. After all, I come from a country whose greatest poet, by the end of her life, rarely left her room; she never published a book, barely published a poem, and died absolutely unheard of. Her experience was—and still is—my model of what a poet can expect from the world. I still figure that if I'm not sitting alone upstairs in a white dress, I'm light-years ahead of the game.

And here was a place where anyone who'd been to high school could, whether he wanted to or not, quote at least something from Dante: tenth grade, *Inferno*, eleventh grade, *Purgatorio*, twelfth grade, *Paradiso*. ("Would that he'd never lived," a guy hanging out in the Umbrian hill town of Spello once told me, "so he wouldn't have busted our balls for three years . . ." But he only said this after I'd exclaimed delightedly at his quoting—which passage was it?—from the *Inferno*.) Surely this entire nation of people who have spent—however—three years closely examining great poetry—must be different from those of us whose only shared national literary references were all originally written for TV (and most of those, for advertisements . . .).

I don't mean to suggest that American schools accomplish nothing, that our required *Julius Caesar* and *Romeo and Juliet* have no effect on our consciousnesses, but only that the poetry we Americans take in affects us individually, not in any wider, shared context. I might think of a certain poet as *mine*, but certainly not as *ours*, much less, as Florentines do Dante, as *one of us*. There isn't a single line of American poetry that one can assume every American citizen knows, much less a body of work. But even the English don't live with their Shakespeare as Italians seem to do with their Dante. Besides, I wouldn't be surprised if you'd find more of Shakespeare's own lines (albeit translated into Italian) on plaques in Italy than in Shakespeare's own homeland: I'd lay odds that, at least somewhere in Verona, you can read an Italian rendering of "fair Verona where we lay our scene," as you can read a choice bit of Elizabeth Barrett Browning every time you pass the Casa Guidi. And this is, to my mind, entirely Dante's doing. He made poetry a necessity.

Of course, being a Jew, I've always been perfectly well aware of the way an entire civilization can be centered on great poetry. Indeed, my Hebrew is decent, and I've spent a reasonable amount of time in synagogue. It was surely that experience—a language in itself regarded as holy, hundreds of bits of psalms and prophets known and sung by heart, handwritten scrolls you kissed as they were carried by—that opened me to poetry in the first place. But that poetry was part of the holy—not the daily—world. (I suppose if I'd grown up more religious, it would have been daily. But for us, prayer and psalm and Torah were reserved for Sabbath and holidays.) The idea of a poetry that one simply walked by every day was utterly new to me. But, perhaps more to the point, Hebrew poetry was pretty much all there was in the civilization—there was no great art, as there was in Italy, no great architecture—nothing material whatsoever, just rules, ceremonies, and the words out of which they had come.

What I loved about Dante was that his great poetry was incorporated both into dailiness and into a material world that was by no means otherwise bereft of inspiration. The Dante I began to read was not the major figure behind T. S. Eliot and Western philosophy, but the person whose words were plastered all over my new home's old walls, the person whom everybody I met on the streets had had to reckon with. The great thing about him was that he was, after all, a person. Inspiring as the Hebrew Bible was to me, its poetry didn't seem to emanate from a single human source; who can ever say where it came from? It certainly wasn't connected to anything I ever imagined I could do.

But here was poetry by a single person that had changed a world's perception of itself, had made an inaccessible landscape familiar. With Dante's descriptions as blueprints, infernos started popping up all over Florence's churches, complete with the requisite number of circles. I think Nardo di Cione did it first, in Santa Maria Novella, but I especially like Fra Angelico's version of about a hundred years later, in an altarpiece now in the Museum of San Marco; I usually can't take my eyes off the daintily bent elbows of his dancing angels, but if I chose to look across the great divide, I'd see devils pushing a, for the most part, exceedingly well-heeled crowd (including a cardinal or two and what appears to be a pope, as well as a monk who, I assume, belongs to a different order than Fra Angelico's own Dominicans) into a realm divided into those same identifiable circles. In truth, the circles are infinitely more frightening in language. The representations are sort of minimizing and maybe even a little silly to this particular non-Christian, who isn't especially worried about the torments of Dante's Hell. All I see in them is the amazing power of poetry: that it could capture the imagination of a world, that even Beato Angelico couldn't rise to its occasion.

And while a sensible person would find Dante's single-handed overturning of world vision thoroughly intimidating, I somehow took it another way. It's certainly not as if I ever expected my efforts at poetry to change the way the world imagines itself—but I liked thinking I was engaged in a pursuit that had actually been known to do that. And at the same time, perhaps because I've turned Dante into a sort of *lanzman*, I have a little trick of finding him *less* intimidating. After all, I know where he hung out. I know precisely which fireflies he means, when he says:

> Quante 'l villan ch'al poggio si riposa
>> nel tempo che colui che 'l mondo schiara
>> la faccia sua a noi tien meno ascosa,
> come la mosca cede a la zanzara,
>> vede lucciole giù per la vallea,
>> forse colà dor'e'vendemmia e ara:
>>> (*Inf.* 26.25–30)

(Charles Singleton translates: As many as the fireflies which the peasant, resting on the hill—in the season when he that lights the world least hides his face from us, and at the hour when the fly yields to the mosquito—sees down along the valley . . .) I know those Tuscan hills alive with fireflies (and mosquitoes) and remember any number of moonless nights when a person really could have mistaken the hillside below my terrace for the sky—except that the Milky Way didn't blink quite that much . . . Couldn't I write, if I wanted to, about the "lucciole giù per la vallea"? There's no difference between Dante and me. It's only that he got there first. It's not his genius anyway, it's the fireflies', I could tell myself; if I hang out here long enough, and keep my eyes open, maybe I'll be able to do it too . . .

Italy does have that effect on people. Call it dizzying expectations. I'll never forget my Florentine friend's disgust in a perfectly all right, if ordinary, Tuscan hill town, where we happened to stop for gas, "Why would anybody build a place so ugly?" Of course, I never really believed that beauty would get into my poems by osmosis. But there was something about the proximity of Dante, this sense of knowing his raw material, that made me believe in his poetry as something humanly possible. Of course, I knew that the fireflies—memorable as they were—had nothing to do with it, that he could have turned us all on our heads with anything at all; but that, in fact, was part and parcel of what became, for me, his most emboldening lesson. There's something about the intrinsic provincialism of Dante that I find profoundly encouraging. He talks about precisely what he wants to talk about. If he bears a grudge against someone, it's that person he displays to us in all his torments, burning forever in the inferno; if he cares for someone—like the teacher damned as a homosexual—he immortalizes the sadness of the man's eternal fate with "Siete voi qui, ser Brunetto?" And if he wants to end a canto with a fart, he ends a canto with a fart.

What a would-be poet learns from this is that poetry can do anything and be about anything; that a poet's job is to make poetry accommodate the very things he or she truly (and, with any luck, uniquely) has to say. This is not to say that poetry needn't have large aims; only that they can be carried out in the most surprising manner. Dante, after all, had an entire religious system to immortalize, a new vernacular to set in literary motion—he wasn't just getting even with old enemies and making fart jokes. But I'm always newly amazed by how very much of what simply couldn't have mattered to anybody but Dante becomes universal as it makes its way into his poem. If Dante wants us to care about something, we will. This is the power of poetry—its true magic: that it really is, if not *creatio ex nihilo*, then *creatio ex quodlibit*: creation out of whatever you like. It's a *pasticcio*, concocted with what happens to be at hand; it really can be made out of absolutely anything.

In his case, of course, it's made not only out of personal grudges and Christian devotion, but also out of the explosive potential of triple rhyme. I've heard all kinds of reasons expressed for the nature of *terza rima*, from a desire to pay poetic homage to the Trinity to a need to foil sloppy (or independent-minded) medieval copyists, with a rhyme scheme that was just too difficult to alter.

I'm quite sure that Dante wouldn't have wanted his words tampered with and have no doubts at all about his affection for the Trinity, but it seems to me that the way the form actually operates through the poem is surely what brought him to use it. Any nine lines or so from anywhere in the *Divine Comedy* demonstrate the amazing virtues of the form in Dante's hands. I don't know of another form that so propels a poem forward and I don't know another long poem that moves so swiftly. Those interlocking rhymes that just have to keep coming create an unstoppable poetic momentum; they also (perhaps surprisingly?) create astonishing room for diversity of tone, subject matter, and mode. Writing in *terza rima*, one gets to be discursive and lyric simultaneously; one gets to be both narrative and descriptive. At least in Dante's hands—and this is the form's great power—the reader gets, no matter how much description and thought and philosophy and digression he is faced with—to feel himself perpetually in motion.

There are none of the built-in pauses of a varied rhyme scheme—like the couplets in Spenserian stanzas or *ottava rima*— nothing of the quatrain's movement toward silence. Indeed, the only variations are the subtle differences between the first-, second-, and third-time incarnations of a given rhyme. The first is often pushed into the next line, as if bent not only on suggesting, but on moving in, a direction, the second usually accelerates the movement, and it's astonishing how often the third becomes an occasion for the sublime. I haven't made a thorough search—this is among the reasons a lover of poetry becomes a poet rather than a scholar; poets don't really have to be thorough—but my haphazard and eccentric investigation has convinced me that every one of Dante's undisputed great single lines—the memorable and excerptable lines—coincides with the third installment of the rhyme. I speak of lines that are almost household phrases even in English, like "lasciate ogne speranza, voi ch'intrate" (abandon every hope, you who enter; *Inf.* 3.9), "quel giorno più non vi leggemmo

avante" (that day we read no farther in it; *Inf.* 5.138), or exquisite
lines like "pur me, pur me, e 'l lume ch'era rotto" (at me alone, at
me alone, and the light that was broken; *Purg.* 5.9), and my personal favorite: "amor mi mosse, che mi fa parlare" (love moved me
and makes me speak; *Inf.* 2.72).

Of course every reader of poetry knows the miraculous experience of reading what seems utterly necessary or revelatory, or
simply, true, and spontaneously hearing its ideal musical fit—this
is, of course, the value of rhyme: the way it lifts what needs to be
said to an exalted realm, where it seems inevitable, perfect, even
divine. But the double sonic preparation afforded by the *terza rima*
makes that delivery even more resonant and long-lasting. Certainly "amor mi mosse, che mi fa parlare" is beautiful on its own.
Hell, it's even beautiful in a direct, no-nonsense translation into
English [love moved me and makes me speak] but it's indescrib-
ably exquisite coming to us as it does this way:

> Or movi, e con la tua parola ornata
>   e con ciò c'ha mestieri al suo campare,
>   l'aiuta sì ch'i'ne sio consolata.
> I' son Beatrice che ti faccio andare;
>   vegno del loco ove tornar disio;
>   amor mi mosse, che mi fa parlare . . .
>   (*Inf.* 2.67–77)

The best I can do in an English version that maintains the rhyme
scheme is:

> Now move, and with your poet's fluency
>   take whatever trouble it might take;
>   Deliver him and thereby comfort me.
> I, Beatrice, make you go; I would turn back
>   to the place I come from, where I long to be;
>   love moved me and makes me speak

(I needn't—perhaps shouldn't?—have rhymed the penultimate line of this passage with the first and third; I just thought it would help create, despite the slant rhymes I felt compelled to use, some inkling of the culminating power of the six lines in Italian.)

Not only is this exquisite line the third appearance of the rhyme, it's also the third-hand echo of its own utterance—Dante is quoting Virgil quoting Beatrice. And surely every poet has been moved to speak by love and has wanted to say so—but what a great thing to say it in someone else's voice quoting someone else . . . It's almost as if that three-fold return of sound is always functioning, at least in part, as a divine echo. Who knows? Maybe it is the Father, Son, and Holy Ghost after all.

But it's also Florence and the olive groves and my former neighbor, a seamstress addicted to telenovellas, transported by Vittorio Gassman reading passages of the *Divine Comedy* on Rai 3. It's every fourth Bacio Perugino, whose wax-paper wrapper says "amor, ch'a nullo amato amar perdona." It's also—and this is the peculiar sweetness of acquiring a language through its literature— the way the entire Italian world can seem to be composed of bits of cantos. One's own native tongue predates poetry; its words are the originary vocabulary out of which everything has been made; rarely does an ordinary word call to mind a line of poetry. But, in Italy, for me, there are so many words that spring directly from— and point directly to—the places where, in my limited acquaintance, only Dante ever used them. So in Pisa's Galileo Galilei Airport, five months pregnant, with a two-year-old I couldn't carry and a stroller that had been lost by British Airways, I was not even remotely annoyed or angry, but, instead, transported, when I had to enter an office signposted, Bagagli Smarriti. The only other thing I had ever experienced as *smarrita* (the word I always used in conversation was *persa*) was Dante's "diritta via." There I was, in Dante's own dark wood, in the absolute thick of absolute poetry, masquerading as a lost-luggage office in the Pisa International Airport. What can I say? I was ecstatic.

But, of course, in the case of Dante's own language, this is especially true. Italy really is composed out of Dante's poetry—he took Tuscan dialect and made it the Italian language. Imagine it— this man needed to write poetry himself in order to experience poetry in his native tongue. Maybe it's his own language—as yet unproven poetically—that was his dark wood; hence he needed Virgil (and Latin poetry) to get him out of it . . . It would be an interesting approach, wouldn't it, to insist that every poem feel like a first-time appearance of an individual language?

And that language would have to be made up of other languages—the languages in which poetry has previously revealed itself—like the Latin hovering in Dante's wings. And not just Virgil's Latin. Recently, opening the *Purgatorio*, I was amazed to find the opening line of Psalm 114, translated, of course, into Latin, in the mouths of spirits being transported by "l'angel di Dio." I don't know how I never noticed it before, but there they were: singing what I've sung on every Jewish festival of my life, or, rather, every Jewish festival on which I'd made it to synagogue early enough— one of the few parts no one leaves out of the seder. Somehow, it made Dante into another kind of *lanzman*. He didn't feel up to the task of writing lyrics for those beings transported by God's angel . . . For all his bravado (imagine anyone announcing that Virgil, Homer, Horace, Ovid, and Lucan had included him among their company!) he, too, felt serious limitations.

Indeed, he makes a point of the spirits singing the entire psalm, precisely as it is written:

> "In exitu Isräel de Aegypto"
>   cantavan tutti insieme ad una voce
>   con quanto di quel salmo è poscia scripto
>   (*Purg.* 2.46–48)

(Singleton translates: "*In exitu Isräel de Aegypto*" all of them were singing together with one voice, with the rest of that psalm as it is written.) It's so moving to me that Dante, as much as he insists upon the presence of the psalm in its precise entirety in his poem, dare not quote the whole psalm, as if it might overwhelm his non-sacred vernacular. It's as if he, too, must both call upon and keep his human distance from an eternal, holy language.

Of course, there is probably no Western poet who was not at least in part inspired by the Psalms—as no one after Dante wasn't at least in part inspired by Dante. But still, the fact that Dante could find nothing else for his spirits to sing but what I'd sung all my life as "Bitzet Yisrael Mimitzraim" is exquisitely dear to me. It's too bad I didn't come upon T. S. Eliot long after I did. I would have loved him, I suppose, for needing *my* Dante.

Dante would probably have shuddered at *my* Dante, would have thought it unthinkable that anyone could be moved at all by his poem and remain non-Christian. And probably these Dantes we poets create for ourselves, these poor, pathetic shadows of the great Dante, are, more than anything else, self-delusions to enable us to write our own little poems. Calling him *my* Dante is surely an insult, a proof of my inferior reading skills, my self-centeredness, my faulty ear. If I really knew how to read him, I wouldn't write another word.

Dante wouldn't want to be my *lanzman* either, despite our shared affection for Psalms and fireflies. And I'm not sure he would like my crediting him for my treasured experience at my favorite *merceria* (why not give them a plug? Quercioli e Lucherini on the Via Calimala) where I went on my last visit to buy the best underwear in the world (I'll plug them too: Oscalito—not only is it luxuriously comfortable, it lasts forever; what I bought nearly twenty years ago is in excellent shape, despite its forbidden knowledge of the tumble dryer). There I was, about to spend ridiculous amounts of money on perfectly simple white cotton underwear, and what should appear on the cellophane wrapping, but "Estraneo a la bellezza, non può essere nessuno"—Emily Dickinson. (Estranged from beauty—none can be, the first line of poem 1474.

I told this to a colleague who thought they'd missed an opportunity; they should have used: "There is a certain slant of light.") Surely, only in the country Dante's language helped create would anyone feel a need for my (I suppose I'm insulting her too, but I do claim her), *my* Emily Dickinson to sell their already flawless, already far-too-good-for-the-likes-of-me underwear. I bought even more than I'd intended and a camisole for my mother. And I saw this as yet another of Dante's coups. It was his hand, the necessity that he'd turned poetry into, that had liberated Dickinson from that little room and brought her into the very material world. Good for him. Good for her. Good for Oscalito. What Dante achieved was to create a civilization in which it is genuinely difficult for anyone to be estranged from poetry's beauty. And as for me, I'm still not over it. I'd never dreamed that poetry could have undone so many . . .

J. D. McClatchy

His Enamel

The Dante my parents owned was the Cary translation, in three volumes, each with marbled covers and a gold-stamped, faded leather spine the color of—now I notice—my liver spots. In a fifteen-year-old's hands, those books were a dream—not the poem, but the engravings by Doré. They thrilled me. I would study them by the hour, their spaniel and scholar: how the black stony backdrops of Hell gradually gave way to a pencilly purgatorial grizzle that finally brightened and whorled into the heavenly host's white rose. The illustrations had both the immediacy and the distance of, say, the stereopticon or marble low relief, of the parish church's gallery of exalted tortures or the confessional's accusatory dark. And Doré's own fantasies—everywhere fleshed out with over-muscled men and women—corresponded uncannily to the seductions and anxieties that violent sex inspired in my adolescent imagination.

Like most readers, Doré was drawn downward. He made eighteen engravings to illustrate the *Paradiso*, itself an illustration of the fact that, once past the melodrama of damnation or atonement, Heaven is merely a difficult idea. There are forty-two illustrations for the *Purgatorio*, most of them less cinematic than tapestried. But Doré made seventy-five for the *Inferno*—and they were the stations of my teenaged cross. Their sheer theatricality seems now a magnification of Dante's own—from his sudden fainting to those paradisal pageants, to say nothing of his Puccini-like instinct for exciting entrances and exits. But decades ago, no tercet could transfix me the way the picture of Farinata rising from his tomb did—the riven rock, the luminous veins bulging on his arms, the noble face standing against his own obelisk of shadow, the glare of condemned pride outlining the two poets' profiles and their flame-shaped laurels. It wasn't Bertran de Born holding his own severed head like a lantern in the darkness of his haphazard treachery—the troubadour clutching his own lyric voice—but lower down in the picture, the arm torn from a body and grabbing at the hem of Dante's cloak, as if to draw the poet unconsciously into the scheme . . . that bloody arm transfixed me, in retrospect because it's an image of what I am writing this sentence with.

Like Dante, my father was in advertising. In the old days, advertising agencies were often attached to lithography companies, which actually produced and distributed the ads. So while my father dreamed up plots and slogans for Seagram, say, or Black & Decker, down the hall were giant printing presses that produced what he'd concocted. As a boy, I loved to visit the pressroom. The smell of the inked rollers, the astonishing mechanized intricacy of the press, its polished steel, its brass cogs, the embossed label of its Italian manufacturer—it all corresponded to my sense of the imagination. The muse of that machine was an old black man named Virgil who smoked thin White Owl cigars, with their tiny plastic mouthpieces, and loved—between his coughs and spitting into a coffee can—to explain the workings of things.

By the time I was in eighth grade at Waldron Academy, and we had to write class reports, I'd decided to ask Virgil for his help. In the fall, I wrote about Theodore Roosevelt. In the spring, I wrote about Dante. In retrospect, it does not seem an accidental pairing: both used the bully pulpit. But at thirteen, I saw the two of them as thundering adventurers, and made little distinction between them, as if Teddy were charging up San Juan hill in a robe and laurel crown and Dante were exploring Hell with a pith helmet and rifle. I knew that Virgil was an amateur draughtsman, and asked if he would design covers for my reports. I'd bring him my assiduously typed reports in thick plastic binders, and he would glue his design onto the front cover. For Teddy Roosevelt, my now forgotten title was lettered over a drawing of the Mount Rushmore image with its marvelously opaque stone monocle. After it was returned to me by the teacher, I sent the report on to Roosevelt's grandson, whom I had discovered lived nearby. He wrote back graciously and said he'd add it to his library. Even then I was uncertain whether or not to believe him.

In the spring, I asked Virgil to outdo himself. This time his cover was black-green and of an enameled luster. My title now was in Gothic lettering, mannered with knurls and spires. And inset in the center was a white three-inch courtyard where he'd sketched the familiar portrait of Dante. It was a line drawing of intense severity. The prominent nose, the beetling brow and shaggy eyebrows . . . everything was in place. But instead of the anticipated profile, Virgil had turned the figure slightly. One eye now stared out at the reader—or no, just beyond him, over his shoulder as if back toward something the reader had already missed. That eye, at once dreamy and accusatory, haunted me. It glistened, the more so the longer I stared into it. It was as if—how did Virgil know?—the eye were the center of the poem.

I sent that report on too. I sent it on to the reader I would become.

It was Henry Francis Cary who, in 1814, ushered Dante into English entire. The *Divine Comedy* was thereby a Romantic poem. One thinks of Shelley's *terza rima*, or remembers Byron. In Ravenna, it is said that Dante's body was not buried in his marble tomb—which looks more like a *hammam* than a mausoleum—but was actually interred in a plot that is now under the pavement of the street in front of the shrine. It was on that pavement that Byron knelt and wept. It was Doré's illustrations—of Paolo and Francesca, of Ugolino—that made my first impression of Dante over into a swirling, sulfuric, heart-stricken Byronic epic. Undoubtedly too, Cary's stout Miltonic pentameters fired the imaginations of a Shelley or a Keats, and later readers—myself among them—first read Dante as less a Milton (though Milton is our truest English equivalent to Dante) than a more softly refulgent Romantic epigone:

> The hour was morning's prime, and on his way
> Aloft the sun ascended, with those stars
> That with him rose when Love Divine first moved
> Those its fair works . . .
>
> (*Inf.* 1.37–40)

Only twice during the course of the entire epic does Doré depart from Dante's setting and illustrate the story a character is telling. In canto 5, he takes us into Francesca's ornate chamber, and then in canto 33, into Ugolino's cell, both scenes from some unwritten Romantic closet drama. As an impressionable young reader, I shared Doré's impatience with Dante's narrative method. The symbolic couldn't hold a shivering candle to the psychological. It took only seconds to read Dante's reticent version of the story of Paolo and Francesca. But Tchaikovsky's tone poem—which in those perfervid years I'd listen to enthralled and which clocks in at a swaggering twenty minutes—conjures the passionate details it then slavers over. Later, once I'd heard Sergei Rachmaninoff's torrid tableaux, I understood what I'd been missing. And that was as nothing when later still, as a college student summering in Italy, I happened upon a performance of Riccardo Zandonai's opera *Francesca da Rimini*, based on Gabriele D'Annunzio's

play, which the poet himself called his "epic of blood and lust."
Hours in a gold-and-velvet *fauteuil* spent watching adultery, blackmail, murder: here was the heart's own *verismo* melodrama, which
one pants to prolong. Never before had Dante's poem seemed
more like the cathedral, each martyr's or doctor's story confined to
a single niche, a certain stone attitude, everything a broken wheel
or lion could suggest but never dramatize.

For the Ugolino story, Doré outdoes himself, his fascination
fixated on the horror. "My father, why dost thou not help me?"
the languid hermaphroditic Gaddo implores. It was Dante as
Dickens. "Then hunger did what sorrow could not do." Curiously,
the very next illustration is of Satan, his mouths full of traitors.
Cannibalism—the gruesome crux of the Christian belief, after
all—is central to these cantos, and it is important to recall that it
figures in Dante's first vision of Beatrice in the *Vita Nuova*. As he
tells it there, it is an eerie anticipation of both *Inferno* stories:
Ugolino's cell is here the dream-state, and Paolo and Francesca's
first smitten meeting is here an encounter first ecstatic, then
grotesque, until they are swept back up into the wheeling current
of sinners. Dante is as passive as the reader while he watches his
beloved eat his own inflamed heart.

> She turned her eyes to where I was standing faint-hearted
> and, with that indescribable graciousness for which today
> she is rewarded in the eternal life, she greeted me so mirac-
> ulously that I seemed at that moment to behold the entire
> range of possible bliss. It was precisely the ninth hour of
> that day, three o'clock in the afternoon, when her sweet
> greeting came to me. Since this was the first time her words
> had ever been directed to me, I became so ecstatic that, like
> a drunken man, I turned away from everyone and I sought
> the loneliness of my room, where I began thinking of this
> most gracious lady and, thinking of her, I fell into a sweet
> sleep, and a marvelous vision appeared to me. I seemed to

see a cloud the color of fire and, in that cloud, a lordly
man, frightening to behold, yet he seemed also to be won-
drously filled with joy. He spoke and said many things, of
which I understood only a few; one was *Ego dominus tuus* [I
am your master]. I seemed to see in his arms a sleeping figure, naked but lightly wrapped in a crimson cloth; looking
intently at this figure, I recognized the lady of the greeting,
the lady who earlier in the day had deigned to greet me. In
one hand he seemed to be holding something that was all
in flames, and it seemed to me that he said these words:
Vide cor tuum [Behold your heart]. And after some time had
passed, he seemed to awaken the one who slept, and he
forced her cunningly to eat of that burning object in his
hand; she ate of it timidly. A short time after this, his happiness gave way to bitterest weeping, and weeping he folded
his arms around this lady, and together they seemed to ascend toward the heavens. (*Vita Nuova* 3)

So much of the commentary about the *Comedy*—which has,
almost from the start, overshadowed the poem and for many
pedants seems to have replaced it—portrays Dante's cosmology as
a machine: whirring gears, flywheels and differentials, pistons and
pumps, grim economies and golden chimes. Once again, it was
Doré's fluid forms, the contortions of flesh in agony, burning lakes
and crags, that forestalled my having any more rigid sense of
things. The hourglass rather than the clock told the time. And my
first taste of Hell was as one long, twisting digestive tract. The icy
anus where it concludes is at once a dramatic anticlimax and a
cosmological puzzle. Logic presides over drama. Satan's three faces,
each engorged with a traitor, is made to resemble a mock Golgo-
tha, Judas replacing Jesus as if in some black mass. But as T. S. Eliot
sensed, Milton's sweeping rhetoric is wanted to bring Dante's dark
fresco to pulsing life:

So stretched out huge in length the Arch-fiend lay
Chained on the burning lake . . .
. . . .
                He, above the rest
In shape and gesture proudly eminent,
Stood like a tower: his form had yet not lost
All her original brightness, nor appeared
Less than archangel ruined, and the excess
Of glory obscured.
                (*Paradise Lost* 1.209–10, 589–94)

What has always fascinated me about Dante's Satan is not his theological posture in Judecca, or the symbolic division of his face, but his body hair. That may be in part because when I first read the poem I was searching, under the sheets at night with a flashlight, for any sign of my own sprouting. Dante and Virgil approach Satan's shaggy thigh and find enough room between his hide and the ice for them to climb down . . . a hairway to Heaven! "We were come," in Longfellow's rendering, "to where the thigh revolves / Exactly on the thickness of the haunch," and then they turn themselves upside down, as if in a birth canal, still holding fast to the stiff hairs.

I lifted up mine eyes and thought to see
    Lucifer in the same way I had left him;
    And I beheld him upward hold his legs.
And if I then became disquieted,
    Let stolid people think who do not see
    What the point is beyond which I had passed.
                (*Inf.* 34.88–93)

This vertiginous moment—too much perhaps even for Doré who neglects to illustrate it—when a monstrous, ice-bound gravity is set reeling, with the reader trapped inside Dante's confused perspectives, is all the more extraordinary because, while commentators knowingly insist that "quel punto" here is the earth's exact center, any reader with the body's topography in mind realizes that the poets are passing Satan's sphincter. That the path to paradise should begin here! It is at such moments when Dante's invention—his immediate, tactile handling of things—surpasses his scheme, and astounds us.

Henry Wadsworth Longfellow, at the time the most famous and acclaimed American poet, published his translation of the *Divine Comedy* in 1865, to coincide with the six-hundredth anniversary of Dante's birth. Longfellow's was the first American translation of the complete poem. He had begun it early in his career, but for a quarter-century, it languished in his desk drawer. Only when his beloved second wife died did he return to Dante as a sort of consolation. The *Inferno* was the last to be completed—an eerie consolation considering that Longfellow's wife was burned to death in a freak accident. It was an influential translation, helping to popularize Dante in this country. But Longfellow's work was not universally hailed. His friend James Russell Lowell complained that Dante had been translated not into the English language, but into the English dictionary. And to present-day ears, the Longfellow translation will often seem awkward and fussy. Its devout literalism—the English word placement, for instance, had to mirror the Italian exactly, whatever the cost to sense—brings to mind Nabokov's ill-fated translation of Pushkin's *Eugene Onegin*.

Longfellow also wrote six sonnets about the *Comedy*, a pair of which prefaced each canticle of the translation. On August 25, 1842, while on a trip to Germany three years after he had begun work on his Dante and after many years of studying the poem, he wrote another sonnet, which takes the most familiar Dantean motif and offers what might be construed as a radical reading of the poem. Its title is "Mezzo Cammin."

Half of my life is gone, and I have let
   The years slip from me and have not fulfilled
   The aspiration of my youth, to build
   Some tower of song with lofty parapet.
Not indolence, nor pleasure, nor the fret
   Of restless passions that would not be stilled,
   But sorrow, and a care that almost killed,
   Kept me from what I may accomplish yet;
Though, half-way up the hill, I see the Past
   Lying beneath me with its sounds and sights,—
   A city in the twilight dim and vast,
With smoking roofs, soft bells, and gleaming lights,—
   And hear above me on the autumnal blast
   The cataract of Death far thundering from the heights.

What if the vision granted to (or, more likely, contrived by) Longfellow here were a map of Dante's poem? What if we read his city of Dis as the world of the *Inferno*, the world of the Past? That would make the ascent through the *Purgatorio* and the *Paradiso's* celestial visit a version of Death itself—Death the negative sublime, the twin eternity, the black rose, the new life.

Like most visionary poets, Dante is obsessed with death, if only by so often denying its force or finality. The pilgrim guide is Virgil, the poet of memory. I watch the *Aeneid*—voyage or contest or battle, camp or palace—through a scrim, the *sfumato* effect of sadness. The sadness is neither grief nor weariness. It is psychological perspective and moral tone. Virgil wrote the consummate elegy of aftermath. And like Proust's novel, the *Aeneid* is a poem about memory, its intolerable system of weights and releases, the screech owl beating against the shield. Memory is fury and muse, and drives the poem's plot and characters. The poet's use of prophecy—"hindsight as foresight" in Auden's scolding phrase—is his shuttle. No earlier poem, and few later, pleated time so seamlessly. The past can force a civilization, or turn a heart inside out.

In either case, only suffering is finally of use. Like his master Lu-
cretius, Virgil saw love and war—Venus the mother of Aeneas, and
Mars the father of Romulus—as the ancestors of Rome, as they
are of memory itself, which both restores and festers.

But a visionary poet is something altogether other. At one
point in his own visionary epic, *The Changing Light at Sandover*,
James Merrill remarks that Dante's vision of Heaven was real
enough, but that he made up the rest of the poem:

> The resulting masterpiece takes years to write;
> More, since the dogma of its day
> Calls for a Purgatory, for a Hell,
> Both of which Dante thereupon, from footage
> Too dim or private to expose, invents.
> His Heaven, though, as one cannot but sense,
> Tercet by tercet, is pure Show and Tell.

That seems entirely credible. History's deck of cards, dealt out one
at a time onto the table by the bitter exile: this is clear-eyed ac-
counting. And in any case, the elaborate map of the pilgrim's voyages out and back have all the ruler marks and compass-needle
pricks, the erasures and creases, even the ornamental detail of the
master craftsman. But the closing pages of the poem are different.
At various times in the *Paradiso*, the celestial sphere is called "la
dolce sinfonia di paradiso" (21.59), or "un riso / de l'universo"
(27.5), even "alta fantasia" (33.142). But by the end, both memory
and metaphor are effaced. Language and the poem itself are
threatened.

> How all speech is feeble and falls short
>   Of my conceit, and this to what I saw
>   Is such, 'tis not enough to call it little.
>   (*Par.* 33.121–23)

The triune circles of light shimmer from rainbow to flame. The final lightning bolt of grace grants him both vision and comprehension.

> But my own wings were not enough for this,
>   Had it not been that then my mind there smote
>   A flash of lightning, wherein came its wish.
> Here vigor failed the lofty fantasy:
>   But now was turning my desire and will,
>   Even as a wheel that equally is moved,
> The Love which moves the sun and the other stars.
> (Par. 33.139–45)

Nothing is described, everything is felt. Yet behind it all, one senses the darker vision of loss. Even while addressing the glorious Christ at the end, the redemptive figure is made almost to resemble someone else. Again, Longfellow's mellifluous, fuzzy rendering catches the ambivalence:

> That circulation, which being thus conceived
>   Appeared in thee as a reflected light,
>   When somewhat contemplated by mine eyes,
> Within itself, of its own very color
>   Seemed to me painted with our effigy,
>   Wherefore my sight was all absorbed therein.
> (Par. 33.127–32)

That painted effigy I read—I want to read—not as the Son of Man's, but as the dead beloved's, a double portrait of the impossible.

> From the first day that I beheld her face
>   In this life, to the moment of this look,
>   The sequence of my song has ne'er been severed.
> (Par. 30.28–30)

"The cataract of Death far thundering from the heights" in Longfellow's sonnet is the same river of light Dante sees. "There is in God," wrote Henry Vaughan, "a deep, but dazzling darkness." Mightn't the last vision be identical to the first? Mightn't the whirling point of light be the dark pupil of Beatrice's eye when she first looked at the poet—and after which he had his first dream-vision of her devouring him? Black pupil and convex lens so sheer as to be luminous and reflective, the poet's own ecstatic passion and longing for the dead girl shining back at him. Hasn't he converted his unbearable loss of the beloved into a vision of Love that is seen by and redeems no one but Dante himself? Blasphemous? No more than any Ovidian tale. No more than the compensatory visions of other mystics. A deep but dazzling darkness, reverse of the black hole of Hell's center and yet somehow its mirror image, a vision both forbidden and redemptive, death as emblem of infinity, the blazing core of the beloved's heart, *das Ewig-Weibliche zieht uns hinan.*

In *Modern Painters*, John Ruskin marvels at Dante's precision of detail—how, for instance, the river Phlegethon is described as "paved with stone at the bottom, and at the sides, *and over the edges of the sides*," just like the baths of Bulicame or the embankments at Bruges—and reluctantly he wags his finger at Milton:

> For it does not follow, because Milton did not map out his Inferno as Dante did, that he *could* not have done so if he had chosen; only it was the easier and less imaginative process to leave it vague than to define it. Imagination is always the seeing and asserting faculty; that which obscures or conceals may be judgement, or feeling, but not invention. The invention, whether good or bad, is in the accurate engineering, not in the fog and uncertainty.

Limbo is, by definition, the realm of vagueness. Canto 4 of the *Inferno* plunges into a hotly contested area of claims and counterclaims, not a factor in the scene itself, but in the cloud of theological argument that had for centuries settled over the matter of which innocents should be condemned, long since an image problem for the Merciful God. When Dante presents in this canto his crowd of Greek and Roman worthies—whom he worships but must abandon, even including his master Virgil—the drama is as much internal as external. Dante is, for the first and last time— at least until that final hesitant moment before the ultimate vision—, questioning his own imagination. He is confronted here by a choice between love and duty, between everything that has made him a poet and all that makes him a believer. It is a choice made without any doubt but not without some hesitation. (Myself, I am not religious, but, of course, I believe there are things more important than my art—no, more than art itself—though belief is not one of them.)

In the Elysian half-light, Dante is introduced by Virgil to "four mighty shades": Homer (whom Dante knew of only by reputation), Horace, Ovid, and Lucan.

> When they together had discoursed somewhat,
>   They turned to me with signs of salutation,
>   And on beholding this, my Master smiled;
> And more of honor still, much more, they did me,
>   In that they made me one of their own band;
>   So that the sixth was I, 'mid so much wit.
> Thus we went on as far as to the light,
>   Things saying 'tis becoming to keep silent,
>   As was the saying of them where I was.
>   (*Inf.* 4.97–102)

The arrogance here is positively Whitmanian! He is voted into the literary elect, and then pushes us out of hearing. No writer ever had more pride than Dante, but here even an admirer may snicker. Still, in the same way that in this limbo Virgil dwells with his own character Aeneas, so may Dante be making a character of his own ambition. "Without hope we live on in desire" (*Inf.* 4.42) is how Virgil has explained his own fate and that of his peers. A modest reading of this scene would ascribe a similar motive to Dante's self-portrait.

As if entering into the pantheon, Dante has his little cenacle advance next to a moated, seven-walled castle—surely one of the stranger moments in the entire poem. Whether this "nobile castello" is, as some suggest, the castle of learning surrounded by the trivium and quadrivium, or the castle of fame defended by the seven liberal arts, it is a shrine to the intellectual life, to the ennobled life, to the glory that, in Dante's increasingly narcissistic fable, poets, philosophers, and statesmen share. Once inside the castle gates, they are paradoxically in the midst of a meadow—a sequence that should alert one to a dream-state, or better, to a dream-within-a-dream, a literary swoon. An element of enchantment or even delirium prevails. But things get eerier still. The Group of Six moves to higher ground, from which they can survey the scene, figures afar quietly conversing. What they see next are "the mighty spirits," the ancient world's philosophers, scientists, poets, gods, and heroes. But the meadow on which they've all been standing has changed, once Dante is at a remove from it, and all of them are "upon the green enamel." Ruskin comments:

> The first instance I know of its right use, though very probably it had been so employed before, is in Dante. The righteous spirits of the pre-Christian ages are seen by him, though in the Inferno, yet in a place open, luminous and high, walking upon the "green enamel."
>
> I am very sure that Dante did not use this phrase as we use it. He knew well what enamel was; and his readers, in order to understand him thoroughly, must remember what

it is,—a vitreous paste, dissolved in water, mixed with metallic oxides, to give it the opacity and colour required, spread in a moist state on metal, and afterwards hardened by fire, so as never to change. And Dante means, in using this metaphor of the grass of the Inferno, to mark that it is laid as a tempering and cooling substance over the dark, metallic, gloomy ground; but yet so hardened by the fire, that it is not any more fresh or living grass, but a smooth, silent, lifeless bed of eternal green. And we know how *hard* Dante's idea of it was; because afterwards, in what is perhaps the most awful passage of the whole Inferno, when the three furies rise at the top of the burning tower, and, catching sight of Dante, and not being able to get at him, shriek wildly for the Gorgon to come up, too, that they may turn him into stone, the word *stone* is not hard enough for them. Stone might crumble away after it was made, or something with life might grow upon it; no, it shall not be stone; they will make enamel of him; nothing can grow out of that; it is dead for ever.

Again, eternity is equated with death. And death with art. This first circle of Hell, luminous limbo, is the dim foreshadowing of the final celestial circle of divine love, a memory of the absent beloved's eye. In her eye, he can see himself. And her eye is a construct of all he has read and dreamt, admired and idealized. The project of Dante's poem has been to *fix* his feelings, as an eye will; to stare down his losses; to see his fresh and living grass become hard, timeless enamel.

W. S. Merwin

Poetry Rising from the Dead

If a poem is not forgotten as soon as the circumstances of its origin, it begins at once to evolve an existence of its own, in minds and lives, and then even in words, that its singular maker could never have imagined. The poem that survives the receding particulars of a given age and place soon becomes a shifting kaleidoscope of perceptions, each of them in turn provisional and subject to time and change, and increasingly foreign to those horizons of human history that fostered the original images and references.

Over the years of trying to approach Dante through the words he left and some of those written about him, I have come to wonder what his very name means now, and to whom. Toward the end of the *Purgatorio*, in which the journey repeatedly brings the pilgrim to reunions with poets, memories and projections of poets, and the recurring names of poets, Beatrice, at a moment of unfathomable loss and exposure, calls the poem's narrator and protagonist by name—"Dante"—and the utterance of it is unaccountably startling and humbling. Even though it is spoken by that same Beatrice who has been the sense and magnet of the whole poem and, as he has come to imagine it, of his life, and though it is heard at the top of the mountain of Purgatory, with the terrible journey done and the prospect of eternal joy ahead, the sound of his name at that moment is not at all reassuring. Would it ever be? And who would it reassure? There was, and there is, first of all, Dante the narrator. And there was Dante, the man living and suffering in time, and at once we can see that there is a distinction, a division, between them. And then there was, and there is, Dante the representation of Everyman, of a brief period in the history of Italy and of Florence, of a philosophical position, a political allegiance—the list is indeterminate. Sometimes he seems to be all of them at once, and sometimes particular aspects occupy the foreground.

The commentaries date back to his own lifetime—indeed, he begins them himself, with the *Vita Nuova*—and the exegetes recognized from the beginning the importance of the *Comedy*, the work, the vision, as they tried to arrive at some fixed significance in those words, in a later time when the words themselves were not quite the same. Any reader of Dante now is in debt to generations of scholars working for centuries to illuminate the unknown by means of the known.

Any translator shares that enormous debt. A translation, on the other hand, is seldom likely to be of much interest to scholars, who presumably sustain themselves directly upon the inexhaustible original. A translation is made for the general reader of its own time and language, a person who, it is presumed, cannot read, or is certainly not on familiar terms with the original, and may scarcely know it except by reputation.

It is hazardous to generalize even about the ordinary reader, who is nobody in particular and is encountered only as an exception. But my impression is that most readers at present whose first language is English probably think of Dante as the author of one work, the *Divine Comedy*, of a date vaguely medieval, whose subject is a journey through Hell. The whole poem, for many, has come to be known by the *Inferno* alone, the first of the three utterly distinct sections of the work, the first of the three states of the psyche that Dante set himself to explore and portray.

There are surely many reasons for this predilection for the *Inferno*. Some of them must come from the human sensibility's immediate recognition of perennial aspects of its own nature. In the language of modern psychology, the *Inferno* portrays the locked, unalterable ego, form after form of it, the self and its despair forever inseparable. The terrors and pain, the absence of any hope, are the ground of the drama of the *Inferno*, its nightmare grip upon the reader, its awful authority, and the feeling, even among the secular, that it is depicting something in the human makeup that cannot, with real assurance, be denied. That authority, with the assistance of a succession of haunting illustrations of the *Inferno*, has made moments and elements of that part of the journey familiar and disturbing, images which remain current even in our scattered and evanescent culture.

The literary presence of the *Inferno* in English has been renewed in recent years. In 1991, Daniel Halpern asked a number of contemporary poets to provide translations of cantos of the *Inferno*, which would eventually comprise a complete translation of the first part of the *Comedy*. Seamus Heaney had already published fine versions from several of the cantos, including part of canto 3 in *Seeing Things* (1991), and ended up doing the opening of the canticle. When Halpern asked me to contribute to the project, I replied chiefly with misgivings. I had been trying to read Dante, and reading about him, since I was a student, carrying one volume or another of the bilingual Temple Classics edition—pocket-sized books—with me wherever I went. I had read parts, at least, of the best-known translations of the *Comedy*: Cary's, because it came with the Doré illustrations and was in the house when I was a child, Longfellow's, through a late-adolescent resistance to nineteenth-century poetic conventions, Binyon's, at the recommendation of Pound (although he seemed to me terribly tangled), and Ciardi's, with which I found other faults. The closer I got to feeling that I was beginning to "know" a line or a passage (having the words by memory, repeating some stumbling approximations of the sounds and cadence, pondering what I had been able to glimpse of the rings of sense), the more certain I became that— beyond the ordinary and obvious impossibility of translating poetry or anything else—any translation of Dante had a dimension of impossibility. I myself had even lectured on the poet and demonstrated the impossibility of translating him, taking a single line from the introductory first canto, and examining it word by word:

Tant' è amara che poco è più morte
                    (*Inf.* 1.7)

I indicated the sounds of the words, their primary meanings, implications in the context of the poem and in the circumstances and life of the narrator, the sound of the line insofar as I could simulate it and those present could repeat it aloud and begin to hear its disturbing mantric tone. How could all that, then, *really* be translated? It could not, of course. It could not be anything other than what Dante had written in his vernacular. It could not be the original, in other words, when brought into another language. I presented the classical objection to translation with multiplied emphasis.

But if the translation of poetry is an enterprise that is always in certain respects impossible, it has on occasion produced something new, something else, of value. Sometimes, on the other side of a sea change, it has brought up poetry again.

Daniel Halpern did not dispute my objections but told me which poets he was asking to contribute something to the project. He asked me which cantos I would like to do if I decided to try any. I thought, in spite of what I had said, of the passage at the end of the twenty-sixth canto where Ulysses, adrift in a two-pointed flame in the abyss of Hell, tells Virgil "where he went to die" after his return to Ithaca. Ulysses recounts his own speech to "that small company by whom I had not been deserted," exhorting them to sail with him past the horizons of the known world to the unpeopled side of the earth, in order not to live "like brutes, but in pursuit of virtue and knowledge," and of their sailing, finally, so far that they saw the summit of Mount Purgatory rising from the sea before a wave came out from its shore and overwhelmed them. It was the passage of the *Comedy* that had first caught me by the hair when I was a student, and it had gone on ringing in my head as I read commentaries and essays about it, and about Dante's reworking of this ancient figure.

Ulysses says to Virgil,

> Io e' compagni eravam vecchi e tardi
> (*Inf.* 26.106)

In the Temple Classics edition, where I first read it, or first remember reading it, the translation by John Aitken Carlyle, originally published in 1849, reads

> I and my companions were old and tardy

It was the word "tardy" that seemed to me not quite right from the start. While I was still a student, I read the John Sinclair translation originally published in 1939, where the words read

> I and my companions were old and slow

"Slow," I realized, must have been part of the original meaning, the intent of the phrase, but I could not believe that it was the sense that had determined its being there.

The Charles Singleton translation, published in 1970 in Princeton's Bollingen series (in thick volumes so flimsily made that mine have long since collapsed into bundles of pages held together with rubber bands and patience) is a masterful piece of scholarly summary. Once again, it says

I and my companions were old and slow

This translation has considerable authority, and it was, after all, technically correct, the dictionary meaning; the companions surely must have been slowed down by age when Ulysses spoke to them. But I kept the original in my mind: "tardi," the principal sense of which, in that passage, I thought, had not been conveyed in English.

When I told Daniel Halpern that I would see whether I could provide anything of use to him, I thought of that word "tardi." It had never occurred to me to try to translate it myself, and I suppose I believed that right there I would have all my reservations about translating Dante confirmed beyond further discussion. As I considered the word in that speech, it seemed to me that the most important meaning of "tardi" was not "tardy," although it had taken them all many years to sail from Troy. And not "slow," despite the fact that the quickness of youth must have been diminished in them. Nor "late," which I had seen in other versions, and certainly not "late" in the sense of being late for dinner. I thought the point was that they were late in the sense that an hour of the day may be late, or a day of a season or a year or a destiny. "Late" meaning not having much time left. And I considered

I and my companions were old and near the end

and thought about how that went with what we knew of those lines, how it bore upon the lines that followed. Without realizing it, I was already caught by a task I once thought should not be undertaken.

Inferno 26 had always been for me one of the most magnetic sections of the first canticle, and among the reasons this is so has to do with the fact that the figure of Dante's Ulysses, the voice in the flame, is very far from Homer's hero (whom Dante knew only at second hand, from Virgil and other Latin classics and translations). Apparently, the final voyage of Ulysses we read about in *Inferno* 26 is largely Dante's invention—one which allows him to construct in some sense a "modern" figure who pursues knowledge for its own sake. This Ulysses strikes close to home: in Dante's own eagerness to learn about the flames floating like fireflies in the abyss, he risks falling into the dark chasm himself.

The story of Ulysses' final voyage is one of the links, within the ultimate metaphor of the poem, between the closed, immutable world of *Inferno* and the open, transformational realm of Mount Purgatory. It represents Ulysses' attempt to break out of the limitations of his own time and place by the exercise of intelligence and audacity alone. In the poem, Mount Purgatory had been formed out of the abyss of Hell when the fall of Lucifer hollowed out the center of the earth and the displaced earth erupted on the other side of the globe to become the great mountain at the antipodes. *Inferno* 26, moreover, bears several suggestive parallels to the canto of the same number in the *Purgatorio*. In the latter, once again, there is fire, a ring of it encircling the mountain, as well as spirits hidden within the flames. On this occasion, some of the spirits whom Dante meets are poets. They refer to each other in sequence with an unqualified generosity born of love of each other's talents and accomplishments (this is where the phrase "il miglior fabbro" comes from, as one of Dante's predecessors refers to another). Their fault is "unmeasured" love, presumably worldly love. The end of that canto is one of Dante's many moving tributes to other poets and their work. When at last he addresses the great Provençal troubadour Arnaut Daniel, the latter generously refers to Dante's question as "courteous"—a word which, within decades of the great days of the troubadours and the courts of love, and then the vicious devastation of the Albigensian Crusade, evokes an entire code of behavior and view of the world. In Dante's poem, Daniel's reply, eight lines that are among the most beautiful in the *Comedy*, is written in Provençal and echoes one of Daniel's own most personal and compelling poems. The effect is intimate, affectionate, eloquent, and reminiscent of the string quartets Mozart dedicated to Haydn.

The *Comedy* must be one of the most carefully planned poems ever written. Everything seems to have been thought out beforehand and yet such is the integrity of Dante's gift that the intricate consistency of the design is finally inseparable from the passion of the narrative and the power of the poetry. The poet's interest in numerology, as in virtually every other field of thought or speculation in his time, was clearly part of the design at every other point, and the burning in the two cantos numbered twenty-six is unlikely to have come about without numerological consideration. His evident attraction to the conditions of the souls, to their "faults," is a further connection between the cantos. Indeed, the link between the Ulysses passage and Mount Purgatory was one of the things that impelled me to go on trying to translate *Inferno* 26 for Daniel Halpern's project.

In my years of reading Dante, after the first overwhelming, reverberating spell of the *Inferno*, which I think never leaves one afterward, it was the *Purgatorio* that I had found myself returning to with a different, deepening attachment, until I reached a point when it was never far from me; I always had a copy within reach, and often seemed to be trying to recall part of a line, as if it were some half-remembered song. One of the wonders of the *Comedy* is that, within its single coherent vision, each of the three sections is distinct, even to the sensibility, the tone, the feeling of existence. The difference begins at once in the *Purgatorio*, after the opening lines of invocation where Dante addresses the holy muses (associated with their own Mount Helicon) to ask that poetry rise from the dead—literally "dead poetry" ("la morta poesì") "rise up

again." Suddenly there is the word "dolce"—sweet, tender, or all
that is to be desired in that word in Italian and Provençal and
French—and then "color." There has been nothing like that before. Where are we?

We—the reader on this pilgrimage, with the narrator and his
guide, Virgil—have crawled upside down in the dark frozen depths
of Hell through the bowels of the Evil One, at the center of the
earth, and have made our way through the tunnel of another birth
to arrive utterly undone at the sight of the stars again. We are
standing on a shore seeing the first light before dawn seep into the
sky, and the morning star, "lo bel pianeta che d'amar conforta,"
the beautiful planet that to love inclines us (*Purg.* 1.19), with all
the suggestions of consolation after the horrors of the infernal
world. We are seeing the sky, our sky, the sky to which we wake in
our days. There is no sky in Hell. There are no stars there, no hours
of daylight, no colors of sky and sea. One of the first vast differences between Hell, the region of immutable despair, and Purgatory, is that the latter place, when we step out on it, is earth again,
the ground of our waking lives. We are standing on the earth under the sky, and *Purgatorio* begins with a great welling of recognition and relief.

Of the three sections of the poem, only *Purgatorio* happens *on*
the earth, with our feet on the ground, crossing a beach, climbing
a mountain. All three parts of the poem are images of our lives, of
our life, but there is an intimacy peculiar to the *Purgatorio*. Here
the times of day recur with all the sensations and associations that
the hours bring with them, the hours of the world we are living in
as we read the poem. Tenderness, affection, poignancy, the enchantment of music, the feeling of the evanescence of the moment
in a context beyond time, all occur in the *Purgatorio*, as they do in
few other places in the poem, and hope, as it is experienced
nowhere else in the poem, for there is none in Hell, and Paradise
is fulfillment itself. Hope is central to the *Purgatorio* and is there
from the moment we stand on the shore at the foot of the moun-

tain, before the stars fade. To the very top of the mountain, hope is mixed with pain, which brings it still closer to the living present.

When I had sent the two cantos of the *Inferno* to Daniel Halpern, I was curious to see what I could make of the twenty-sixth canto of the *Purgatorio*, which had captivated me for so long, and also of the lovely poem of Arnaut Daniel's which Dante echoed in that canto, and of at least one of the poems of Guido Guinizelli, to whom he spoke with such reverence, as to a forebear.

Then I turned to other moments in the *Purgatorio* that had held me repeatedly. Almost thirty years earlier, on the tube in London, I had been reading the fifth canto, which was already familiar ground. It was like listening to a much-loved piece of music, hearing a whole current in it that had never before seemed so clear. I rode three stops past my destination and had to get off and go back and be late. Here once again, trying vainly to find equivalents for words and phrases, I was in the grip of the *Purgatorio*. After the twenty-sixth canto, I went back to the beginning.

The opening cantos that comprise the section known as the Ante-Purgatory are among the most beautiful in the whole poem. I thought of trying to make something in English just of those, the first six in particular. I turned them over slowly, line by line, lingering over treasures such as La Pia's few lines at the end of the fifth canto, hoping that I was not betraying them by suggesting any other words for them (though Clarence Brown once said to me, to reassure me about another translation of mine, "Don't worry, no translation ever harmed the original") or at any rate betraying my relation to them. They were lines that had run in my head for years, their beauty inexhaustible. The morning of the first day, looking out to sea, in canto 1

> L'alba vinceva l'ora mattutina
>   che fuggia innanzi sì che di lontano
>   conobbi il tremolar del la marina.
>   (*Purg.* 1. 115–17)

What could anyone do? My attempt ran:

> The dawn was overcoming the pallor of daybreak
>   which fled before it, so that I could see
>   off in the distance the trembling of the sea.

It was, I kept saying, *some* indication of what was there, what was at least worth trying to suggest in English. I wanted to keep whatever I made by way of translation as close to the meaning of the Italian words as I could, taking no liberties, so that someone without any Italian would not be misled. I hoped to make the translation a poem in English, for if it were not that, it would have failed to indicate what gave the original its memorable power.

The *Purgatorio* is the section of the poem in which poets, poetry, and music recur with fond vividness and intimacy. The meetings between poets—Virgil's with his fellow Mantuan, Sordello, over twelve hundred years after Virgil's own life on earth; Virgil's meeting with the Roman poet Statius, Dante's with Guido Guinizelli and with Arnaut Daniel and the singer Casella—all are cherished, moving moments.

It is worth noting something about the current of poetic tradition that Dante had come to in his youth. The subject of love, including aspects of it that were being purged in the twenty-sixth canto of the *Purgatorio*, was the central theme of the great flowering of troubadour poetry in the twelfth and thirteenth centuries. In that surge of new poetry and feeling, the forms of love ranged from the openly sensual to the unattainably ethereal, and from such familiar treatment as may have verged upon folk poetry of the time (and is still to be found in the popular culture of our own time) to courtly, allusive, highly stylized poetry that seemed to treat love on many planes at once.

In its rapid development, the tradition of troubadour poetry evolved the convention of a beloved to whom, and about whom, the poems were written. Of course, love poetry, both erotic and idealized in one way or another, had existed and had been important in other ages and in many—perhaps in most—cultures. The figure of the beloved who is the subject of the poems and to whom they are addressed had often been there, whether idealized or not. But the theme and elevation of a beloved emerged with particular intensity in the tenth-century Arabic poetry of the Omayed Moorish kingdoms of southern Spain. In the highly cultivated poetry and culture that had evolved there, a code of attitudes, behavior, and gestures developed, a stylized choreography that was clearly the matured result of an ancient tradition.

The rhymed and highly stylized poetry of the troubadours, with its allegiance to music, the codes of the courts of love, and the Hispano-Arabic assimilation of the philosophy of classical Greece, were essentials of the great Provençal civilization of the twelfth and early thirteenth centuries. The secular splendor of that culture and its relative indifference to the tedious *imperium* of the church were, at the opening of the thirteenth century, barbarously and viciously ruined by the wave of political ruthlessness and deadly self-righteousness known as the Albigensian Crusade, one of the great atrocities of European history. (It was a bishop, Arnaud de Cîteaux, who gave the order, at the sack of Béziers, "Kill them all. God will know His own." And they did.) Both that rich, generous, brilliant tradition and the devastation that had been visited upon it were part of Dante's heritage. The latter had taken place less than half a century before he was born; the Mantuan poet Sordello, for one, had spent a major part of his life at the court of Toulouse. The legacy of the troubadours survived even beyond Dante. Petrarch is sometimes described as the last of the troubadours. The attention given to the manners, the psychic states, the perspectives, the ultimate power of love, the exalted beloved, the forms of verse including rhyme—all come from the culture of Provence either directly or via the court of Frederick II of Sicily.

However, Dante's beloved, Beatrice, did have an earthly original in his own life and youth. From what can be known at present she was named Bice, daughter of Folco Portinari. Dante describes his first sight of her, in 1274, when he was nine. She eventually married, and then died in 1290, when he was twenty-five, ten years before the ideal date of the *Comedy*. In the *Vita Nuova*, finished in the years just after her death, Dante vows to leave her literary monument "in rhyme" such as no woman had ever had. So she led him, he tells us, to the journey that becomes the *Comedy* and his own salvation.

We know as much as we ever will about what Dante looked like from a description by Boccaccio. A long face, aquiline nose, large jaw, protruding lower lip, large eyes, dark curly hair (and beard), and a melancholy, thoughtful appearance. None of the surviving portraits is entirely trustworthy, though two have become famous and are commonly accepted.

· Since adolescence, I have felt what I can only describe as reverence for Dante, a feeling that seems a bit odd in our age. It is there, of course, because of his poetry, and because of some authority of the imagination in the poetry, some wisdom quite distinct from doctrine, though his creed and his reason directed its form. I am as remote from his theological convictions, probably, as he was from the religion of Virgil, but the respect and awed affection he expresses for his guide sound familiar to me.

I have read, more or less at random and over a long period, in the vast literature of Dante studies. Not much, to be sure, in view of how much of it there is. I am particularly grateful for works I have read at one time or another by Erich Auerbach, Irma Brandeis, Charles S. Singleton, Allan Gilbert, Thomas G. Bergin, Helmut Hatzfeld, Charles Speroni, Frances Fergusson, Robert Briffault, Philippe Guiberteau. Yet there has been no consistent method in my reading of studies about Dante. I have come upon what seemed to me individual illuminations of his work partly by chance, over a period of time, forgetting as I went, naturally. The one unfaltering presence has always been a love of the poem that has been with me ever since my first inchmeal reading. Despite the translation I have undertaken, I am as conscious as ever of the impossibility of putting the original into any words but its own.

Robert Pinsky

The Pageant of Unbeing

Frances Fergusson, one of the few truly great American literary critics of the twentieth century, suggests that we speak not of a work's meaning but of its action.

What is the action of the *Inferno*? To go through this entire world, all the way through into Hell at the world's core, and on through all of Hell to come out on the other side of the world. This physical action, *to go into it in order to come out of it*, embodies a moral action as well: to penetrate the world's ways and behold the realm of pain; to go through all the infernal spectacle of sin and suffering, and to emerge from that spectacle newly situated, on a terrain opposite from the beginning.

That moral action, in other words, is to go into the world of evil and through its core, to experience the nature of sin in order to come out of it, in some spiritual sense newly situated. To penetrate the dark in order to emerge in brightness on the other side.

This "movement of the soul," in Ferguson's paraphrase of Aristotle, characterizes the action not only of Dante and Virgil, but of many of the souls they encounter, who frequently go back into their sins by narrating them or reliving them. Their action recalls the English phrase for vocal immersion in some experience or topic: "Shall I go into it?" Even souls who initially resist speech or self-revelation sometimes end by going into it, helplessly compelled by the overall action of the *Inferno*—bound by the nature of the *Inferno* as a locale and as a work of art. Moreover, because the souls who address Dante often hope that he will carry their stories into the bright world above, they, in some sense, mean to complete the action of emerging into light, if only by proxy. In that sense, they, too, go into it in order to come through it into light.

Going into the state of sinfulness, witnessing it in detail in order to come through it on the other side: why is this spiritual action so significant? The completion of its physical counterpart occurs in the final canto of the *Inferno*. Virgil and Dante climb out of Hell by grasping the shaggy, ice-matted hair of the Devil and clambering, hand over hand, with Dante clinging to his guide— their faces all but pressed against the furry pelt—until at the midpoint of the Devil's body, the umbilicus or anus or genitals, they pass through the center of gravity and ascend toward the light. They pass that central point and by continuing they begin to emerge, having gone as far down as possible. The reversal or flipping of gravity confuses Dante and introduces the cosmological explanation that to some readers has seemed a tremendous anticlimax or delay, a pedantic misstep by the poet. What is the moral action that underlies that cosmological reversal and makes Virgil's explanation of it, in his climactic speech of the *Inferno*, meaningful?

The answer lies in the nature of sin. As I understand the Thomist or Augustinian notion, evil is not a positive force but an absence, a nonbeing, as cold is the absence of heat energy or dark is the absence of light energy. In this theological idea of privation, a particular sin or evil is a place where the moral energy of God's creation is withdrawn, or shriveled away, or destroyed. The sin is a dead place in the soul, a hole or area of absolute zero, just as Hell is a place of dark and cold.

The sin is a wound that hurts, and it is, moreover, a selfinflicted wound. The idea of privation, with its corollary that sin is a place where the soul has torn part of itself away, reminds me of a

saying I have heard quoted from the Talmud, to the effect that the
evils others do to us are as nothing compared to the evils we do to
ourselves. The remarkable fact is that for most people (excepting,
for example, victims of oppression, torture, famine, disease), this is
true. We wound ourselves, and that fact is one of the great moral
mysteries. As Dante says in canto 7:

> Justice of God! Who is it that heaps together
>   So much peculiar torture and travail?
>   How is it that we choose to sin and wither?[1]
>   (*Inf.* 1. 19–21)

In summary, the sin is a self-inflicted absence, a hole or dead place
that the soul tears into itself. In the *contrapasso* or fittingness of this
definition, the punishment does not merely fit the crime; in some
sense, it *is* the crime. Hell, as the realm of unbeing, corresponds
precisely to the painful or destructive deprivation of being in the
hurt soul. Christ's very presence harrowed Hell, when he descended there, making it feel its nonexistence. In a parallel way, the
very notion of being, perfection (the entirely created), makes the
soul feel pain in its places of deadness or absolute zero. The *Inferno*,
for the pilgrim and for the reader, presents a parade or pageant
variously illustrating that process.

As a non-Christian, I first encountered the theological notion
of sin as privation in English poetry of the sixteenth and seventeenth centuries. The idea of evil as negative, as a form of nonbeing, an idea that is potentially arid and theoretical, was made
pressing and real for me by the writing of John Donne, George
Herbert, Ben Jonson, William Shakespeare, and others. It was not
merely the eloquence of this poetry that energized the concept. It
was a specific application of the concept by such poets to their
own, actual situations. It was the idea of sin as a self-inflicted
wound that had power for me, and particularly the specific sin that
seemed to preoccupy these poets.

In this English poetry, I encountered the idea of wanhope or despair: the fatal sin that keeps the soul from praying sincerely for grace. Though mercy is infinite, the soul succumbs to fear: it believes it is too fallen or corrupted to be saved. This sin is the one Donne reserves for the climax of his "Hymn to God the Father": "I have a sin of fear," he writes, reserving fear for the final position, as the greatest obstacle to redemption. Despair or wanhope deprives the soul of grace, and ultimately of being. God's very perfection, contrasted with the soul's imperfections, can throw us into despair. Thus, Jonson begins his poem "To Heaven" with the pertinent question,

> Good and great God, can I not think of Thee,
> But it must, straight, my melancholy be?

This problem—that perfection can increase the soul's despair, so that it deprives itself of being, shrinking away—is strikingly addressed by poem ninety-nine in Fulke Greville's sequence *Caelica*. I will inspect this poem in some detail, because I think it illustrates the power of the Thomist notion of sin as absence, and because I think it illuminates Dante's action in the *Inferno*. In poem ninety-nine, the poet beholds himself in God as in the polished, flawless surface of a mirror:

> Down in the depth of mine iniquity,
> That ugly center of infernal spirits,
> Where each sin feels her own deformity
> In these peculiar torments she inherits—
> > Deprived of human graces and divine,
> > Even there appears this saving God of mine.

> And in this fatal mirror of transgression
> Shows man as fruit of his degeneration
> The error's ugly infinite impression,

Which bears the faithless down to desperation.
    Deprived of human graces and divine,
    Even there appears this saving God of mine.

In power and truth, almighty and eternal,
Which on the sin reflects strange desolation,
With glory scourging all the spirits infernal,
And uncreated hell with unprivation—
    Deprived of human graces, not divine,
    Even there appears this saving God of mine.

For on this spiritual cross condemnëd lying
To pains infernal by eternal doom,
I see my Saviour for the same sins dying,
And from that hell I feared, to free me, come.
    Deprived of human graces, not divine,
    Even there appears this saving God of mine.

The bad place in the "center" of the poet's soul corresponds precisely to "that hell I feared": it is an "ugly, infinite impression" visible in the perfect mirror of being. The language of negatives, notable in "deprived," at the beginning of the refrains, begins with the negative prefix of "iniquity" and "infinite," redoubled by the playful redundancy of "bears the faithless down to desperation"—"faith" and Latin *spes* being almost synonyms—and the paradoxical phrase "fruit of his degeneration."

These phrases only initiate the poem's language of nonbeing, which becomes more explicit and more strenuously folded with Christ's harrowing of the infernal spirits, scourging "uncreated Hell with unprivation." Hell, in the Augustinian system, is a center of nonbeing; that is why Jesus Christ's very presence there caused harrowing pain and disruption to Hell: being hurts and destroys nonbeing. Divine being extends itself even into the cold, dark center of nothingness. In the traditional parallel, Christ in his infinite mercy enters even the soul that is in despair at its own corruption, even the conscience that feels hopeless.

The change in Greville's refrain, from:

Deprived of human graces and divine,
Even there appears this saving God of mine

to:

Deprived of human graces, not divine,
Even there appears this saving God of mine

registers the poem's action, a reversal from despair to hope, inspired by the notion of Jesus Christ suffering on the same spiritual cross—of despair, along with other human sins—as the sinner who feels "desperation." The multiple meanings of this refrain invite contemplation of the last words on the cross, and the question of Christ feeling despair itself, the ultimate failing, in order to take on all sin: an interesting direction for thought which is not germane to my present discussion of the *Inferno* and its action.

Greville's poem illuminates, for me, certain elements of that action: the centrality of despair as a sin in the Christian system; the absence of hope as an example of the negative, privational nature of sin; and the soul curing or freeing itself from despair by going down into the Hell of it, to experience wanhope's nature until, in a binary reversal, hope is restored. The *Inferno* is the greatest work ever written about the moral state that in our time's jargon we call "depression."

If Dante's own sin is despair, a spiritual fearfulness that threatens his survival, the opening lines of his poem demonstrate the beginning of his action into and through Hell, as a journey of spiritual and intellectual work:

Midway on our life's journey, I found myself
  In dark woods, the right road lost. To tell
  About those woods is hard—so tangled and rough
And savage that thinking of it now, I feel
  The old fear stirring: death is hardly more bitter.
  And yet, to treat the good I found there as well
I'll tell what I saw, though how I came to enter
  I cannot well say, being so full of sleep
  Whatever moment it was I began to blunder
Off the true path. But when I came to stop
  Below a hill that marked one end of the valley
  That had pierced my heart with terror, I looked up
Toward the crest and saw its shoulders already
  Mantled in rays of that bright planet that shows
  The road to everyone, whatever our journey.
Then I could feel the terror begin to ease
  That churned in my heart's lake all through the night.
  As one still panting, ashore from dangerous seas,
Looks back at the deep he has escaped, my thought
  Returned, still fleeing, to regard that grim defile
  That never left any alive who stayed in it.

(*Inf.* 1.1–21)

"The old fear" never dies completely; this is consistent with doc-trine. The passage is, among other things, a demonstration of the glorious power of light penetrating even the darkest, wildest, most savage places. It is the last image quoted that presents an epitome of the *Inferno's* overall action.

The survivor looks back at the deep he has escaped. Dante, in his thoughts, returns to the place where he found good as well as the spectacle of evil. Indeed, telling of that good is his explicit mo-tivation here at the outset of the *Comedy*. The image is of one who, while running away from the scene of terror and near-destruction, looks back, as over a shoulder, to inspect that which he has escaped. This particle of action, looking back at the fearsome deep, embodies the first phase of a larger action of inspecting, interrogating, and penetrating the realm of dread.

The passage embodies the first steps of a great three-part journey and work. As the first of one hundred cantos, canto 1 is a prelude to the entire *Comedy*, a fact emphasized by the closing lines of canto 1, in which Dante agrees to undertake a journey through Hell and Purgatory with Virgil as his guide and through Paradise with a superior guide.

The *Inferno*, then, begins its action twice: first, at the opening of canto 1, with Dante lost in the dark woods and with the image of looking backward to regard the danger, and then again, at the beginning of canto 2, which is, in a sense, the beginning of the *Inferno* proper. So, having agreed at the end of canto 1 to embark on his arduous three-part journey, with what action does Dante begin canto 2?

The answer, consistent with the idea of wanhope or despair, is that he gets cold feet. Fear threatens to overcome him. Canto 2 begins with a passage that moves from something like military duty, through complaint about the solitary mission, then into a request for appraisal, which devolves into damaging comparisons leading to self-deprecation, fear of ridicule, and finally a loss of resolve:

> Day was departing, and the darkening air
> Called all earth's creatures to their evening quiet
> While I alone was preparing as though for war
> To struggle with my journey and with the spirit
> Of pity, which flawless memory will redraw:
> O Muses, O genius of art, O memory whose merit
> Has inscribed inwardly those things I saw —
> Help me fulfill the perfection of your nature.
> I commenced: "Poet, take my measure now:
> Appraise my powers before you trust me to venture

Through that deep passage where you would be my guide.
   You write of the journey Silvius's father
Made to immortal realms although he stayed
   A mortal witness, in his corruptible body.
   That the Opponent of all evil bestowed
Such favor on him befits him, chosen for glory
   By highest heaven to be the father of Rome
   And of Rome's empire—later established Holy,
Seat of great Peter's heir. You say he came
   To that immortal world, and things he learned
   There led to the papal mantle—and triumph for him.
Later, the Chosen Vessel too went and returned,
   Carrying confirmation of that faith
   Which opens the way with salvation at its end.
But I—what cause, whose favor, could send me forth
   On such a voyage? I am no Aeneas or Paul:
   Not I nor others think me of such worth,
And therefore I have my fears of playing the fool
   To embark on such a venture. You are wise:
   You know my meaning better than I can tell."
And then, like one who unchooses his own choice
   And thinking again undoes what he has started,
   So I became: a nullifying unease
Overcame my soul on that dark slope and voided
   The undertaking I had so quickly embraced.

                                        (*Inf.* 2.1–42)

Aeneas and St. Paul, like Christ himself, descended into the Underworld and returned. Dante makes this comparison in order to
say that neither he nor others would place him in such heroic
company—rhetorically, a way of making the comparison he refuses, as well as a way to explain his nullifying dismantling—the
"uncreation," to borrow Greville's term—of his own choice.

When Dante says he fears playing the fool, I believe that the min-
gled diffidence and confidence are those not only of the pilgrim
who fears the ambitious journey he has undertaken, but also those
of the author, who fears the ambitious poem he has undertaken,
and the prospect of ridicule as pretentious or grandiose. Despair is
the enemy, and the deep internal failing, of both pilgrim and poet.

Virgil's response provides both diagnosis and cure:

> "If I understand," the generous shade retorted,
> "Cowardice grips your spirit—which can twist
>   A man away from the noblest enterprise
>   As a trick of vision startles a shying beast.
> To ease your burden of fear, I will disclose
>   Why I came here, and what I heard that compelled
>   Me first to feel compassion for you: it was
> A lady's voice that called me where I dwelled.
>
> (Inf. 2.43–54)

Virgil here states in the second person Donne's first-person "I
have a sin of fear." Dante's self-belittling request to be judged, his
comparison of himself to saint and hero, embodies the sin of weak
faith—not Christian humility, but wanhope as the form of pride
which declines the opportunity to imitate Christ. It is the sin that
underlies all others, the sin of giving up on one's soul.

The cure for this sin of despair, the way out of it, is for Dante
to witness all the pageant of unbeing, to experience all the ways
that souls hurt or destroy themselves. The compulsive reenact-
ments or retellings of the shades he encounters lead him both into
pity, anger, identification, and out on the other side. Implicitly,
even revenge is entered into, identified as a form of despair, and
gone beyond in the climactic scene of Ugolino's endless unsatis-
fied gnawing at the skull of Ruggieri. This climax in the pageant
of unbeing too must be witnessed and recognized without flinch-

ing, its fearsome quality overcome. As Virgil says, interpreting the inscription on the gate in canto 3, "All fear must be left here, and cowardice die."

The cosmological passage in canto 34, which can seem a pedantic anticlimax, in fact presents an allegory of the process or action of the whole, a use of all that is fearsome to climb up out of despair. Virgil grips the shaggy flanks of the Devil, explaining to Dante that this horrible body is the stairway which they must climb. Where the haunch is at its thickest, Virgil turns around, confusing Dante as they pass through that center of gravity—the point, in effect, at which Greville's refrain reverses its polarity: "Deprived of human graces, not divine."

In the *Inferno*'s final exchange between the pilgrim and Virgil, the physical explanation precisely parallels the moral process of immersion, penetration, and reversal, the action that reverses the despair or depression:

> "Before I free myself from the abyss,
>   My master," I said when I was on my feet,
>   "Speak, and dispel my error: where is the ice?
> And how can he be fixed head-down like that?
>   And in so short a time, how can it be
>   Possible for the sun to make its transit
> From evening to morning?"
>
>   (*Inf.* 34.100–6)

The reversal, by which the descent eventually becomes an ascent, seems to transform night to day. Comprehension of that reversal or flipping, the result of Dante's spiraling down through the pageant of nonbeing, far from being a cosmological digression, is the final requisite before turning toward the *Purgatorio*. Virgil's answer figuratively summarizes the first third of Dante's journey, recapitulated by their climbing the Devil's body:

He answered me,
  "You imagine you are still on the other side,
  Across the center of the earth, where I
Grappled the hair on the evil serpent's hide
  Who pierces the world. And all through my descent,
  You were on that side; when I turned my head
And legs about, you passed the central point
  To which is drawn, from every side, all weight.
  Now you are on the opposite continent
Beneath the opposite hemisphere to that
  Which canopies the great dry land therein:
  Under the zenith of that one is the site
Whereon the Man was slain who without sin
  Was born and lived; your feet this minute press
  Upon a little sphere whose rounded skin
Forms the Judecca's other, outward face.
  Here it is morning when it is evening there;
  The one whose hair was like a ladder for us
Is still positioned as he was before.
  On this side he fell down from Heaven; the earth,
  Which till then stood out here, impelled by fear
Veiled itself in the sea and issued forth
  In our own hemisphere.

                            (*Inf.* 34. 106–24)

Significantly, the force that distorted the earth, creating the mountain where Dante's struggle begins, is identified as fear. Fear in this passage, like Love earlier, is treated as an awesome physical force of tremendous magnitude. A geological force that shaped the world, inward fear distorted and menaced the exile's soul, nearly to the utter surrender of despair, absolute unbeing, the profound absence of Hell. By a bewildering yet natural process, the downward immersion into the manifold instances and detailed forms of that absence, darker and darker, has led eventually into the startling presence of light.

Note

1. All translations are from Robert Pinsky, *The Inferno of Dante: A New Verse Translation* (New York: Farrar, Straus and Giroux, 1994).

Geoffrey Hill

Between Politics and Eternity

The editorial brief for contributions to *The Poets' Dante* invites a response to several questions which presuppose—if I understand them—some degree of significant prior involvement with Dante's life and writings: significant to the contributor, that is. While not wishing to tap into the confessional mode, I have to say that my own (insignificant) involvement with Dante began no earlier than mid-summer 1999 when I belatedly agreed to write a piece for this collection. If for nothing else, I decided, the necessary labor would serve as a challenge to my own ignorance. I foresaw a certain austere *volupté* in working myself into the subject, rather as Henry Adams, though no economist, had relished working up a magisterial paper on the New York Gold Conspiracy. My academic essays are usually undertaken in an endeavor to clear my own meanings in relation to a given or elected topic. "Clear my own meanings" is a suggestive phrase, appropriated forty years ago from a review by A. Alvarez, which until now has probably influenced my approach to scholarly and critical method more than anything else that I have read. I was about to say "poetry is another matter entirely," but I cannot rest assured any longer that this is the case.

As will be evident from my opening gambit, these introductory paragraphs have been written last. I had to know where I had got to, before I could give any indication as to where I think I am bound. Having now completed the essay I can say that the *Monarchia* is crucial to my present understanding of authorial purpose in life and art. In the pages that follow, I shall attempt to indicate, or adumbrate, the significance of the *Monarchia* in its historical contexture. If it cannot be shown to possess such significance, its importance to me is scarcely relevant. There would be little value in its being prized as a collector's item.

Significance is given to a work by its own "presence," as I choose to call it; my sense approximates to Ruskin's use of the term "intrinsic value." Such a presence does not require celebrity or even notoriety. Early in its life, the *Monarchia* was condemned by the papal legate and narrowly escaped burning. It was placed on the Index in 1564, almost two and a half centuries after the author's death. A scandal to the political church of Pope John XXII, and designed to be so, it was not otherwise widely noticed.[1] So, what is this "presence," this intrinsic value? I will answer by analogy. Antonio Gramsci's "Il canto decimo dell' *Inferno*," written between 1929 and 1932, one of the many prison writings which Gramsci regarded as notes to himself, does have this presence. Eliot's *Dante*, published in 1929 as one of a series of Faber monographs, The Poets on the Poets, does not. I cannot finally determine why that should be so; or rather, I *can* determine it but cannot bring it to irrefutable demonstration. "Irrefutable" is not hubris: I am not making any special claim for my own powers.

It may be that the difference between having and not having such "presence" relates to, or results from, a difference in degrees of attention. The Faber monographs were designed as antepasts to enjoyment and the refining of taste. There are values and virtues more significant than enjoyment, which shares with other taste-derived qualities an air of condescension, of the proprietorial. Enjoyment of this kind is closely related to apathy. Eliot's *Dante*, preceded in the series by V. Sackville-West's *Marvell*, was itself followed by Lascelles Abercrombie's *Wordsworth*, Humbert Wolfe's

Tennyson and Edmund Blunden's *Coleridge*. It is a gesture of apathy rather than a sign of elective affinity that Marvell should be supposed in need of V. Sackville-West's sponsorship or that Tennyson might be thought more accessible after an introduction from Humbert Wolfe.

When on the other hand I read Gramsci's notes on canto 10 of the *Inferno*, I am attending to someone who is caught up into "the great canzone of inner debate." Robert Durling's phrase, used by him of a particular poem—no. 264 of Petrarch's *Rime Sparse*—I here apply to an entire order of reciprocity (it can embrace doubt and dissension) between poet, poem, and reader. Such reciprocity is a matter of sustained accurate attention, both to the texture of a piece of writing and to the contextures of circumstance in which it was first set down and received; together with a sense of urgency not to be confused with the importunity of the press release, the opportunism of the lobbyist. The difference between urgency and mere importunity may be understood in the same mode as the platonic distinction noted by Stanley Rosen between "knowledge that resides in what genuinely is" and the "meal of opinion."[2]

In his surviving notes on canto 10 of the *Inferno*, Gramsci is able to reveal the "presence" of the work by presenting his own mind to the particularities of Dante's grammar. Benedetto Croce, in *La Poesia di Dante*, had insisted on the inferiority of "struttura" to a nebulously superior quality "poesia." Dante's "struttura" was, according to Croce, the arid doctrinal argument, to be ploughed through and forgotten, the "poesia" was an essence uncontaminated by coarse mundanities. First published in 1921, Croce's was a view of the Dantean genius widely disseminated and influential throughout the 1920s. Gramsci declares his opposition to Crocean aesthetics by insisting that the beauty of Dante is delineated in his structure (e.g., grammar) and not in the nebulosities of sentimental empathy: "The crucial word in the line 'Forse cui Guido vostro ebbe a disdegno' is not 'cui' or 'disdegno,' but only '*ebbe.*' The 'aesthetic' and 'dramatic' accent on the line falls on '*ebbe.*' " When

Gramsci writes that Dante "volò con le ali che aveva" (flew with the wings he had), he does not mean that Dante somehow "made do" with whatever material was immediately to hand. Dante's wings were suffering, study, and constant application (as were Gramsci's); and in canto 10 of the *Inferno*, it is the precise placing of "ebbe," "il verbo al passato," that empowers the tragedy: the pilgrim's use of the passato remoto ("ebbe a disdegno") to describe Guido Cavalcanti is misinterpreted by Cavalcanti's father to mean that his son is dead. "The structural passage is not only structure, then, it is also poetry, also a necessary element of the drama that has taken place." Gramsci's phrase ("il brano strutturale non è solo struttura; dunque, è anche poesia") is both a rebuttal of Croce and a revelation of the way in which Dante is able to make the most literal elements of grammar the agents of ethical and psychological perception or apprehension; at once precise and resonant.[3]

It is with this proposition in mind that I bring myself to consider the recalcitrant texture of the *Monarchia*. The treatise is now generally accepted as being a late work and shows Dante reverting to the use of Latin for international discourse at a time when he was already well advanced in the composition of his *Comedy* in Tuscan. It is, of course, true that, having by this time advanced the poem as far as—perhaps—the *Paradiso*, he had himself made Latin redundant as an instrument of the creative Imagination, but it is also evident that in writing the *Monarchia*, his mind was on things other than his own creative grandeur. Dante believed that he had a good case and a grand cause; public resistance to the encroachments of the political Ecclesia upon the domain of secular Sovereignty. His argument here is of a piece with that of *Epistles* 5–7 and passages throughout the *Comedy*:

> Questo si vuole e questo già si cerca
>   e tosto verrà fatto a chi ciò pensa
>   là dove Cristo tutto dì si merca . . .
>   (*Par.* 17.49–51)

So it is willed, so already plotted, and
so shall be accomplished soon by him
who ponders upon it in the place where
every day Christ is bought and sold.

But "secular" here is not the secular politics of nineteenth-century European radicals and liberals. As Passerin d'Entrèves has observed, "Dante's wholehearted allegiance [was] to the Aristotelian and Thomist notion of the State." Although such a commitment is—to say the least—debatable, the least sustainable objection is to the archaic irrelevance of Dante's political theology: to require the *Comedy* to float free of its sunken encumbrances is to move to abolish its foundations. The Marxist Gramsci, as much as the Catholic Etienne Gilson, gives us grounds for refusing the concession ("non è solo struttura, dunque, è anche poesia"). A further objection may be more sustainable; namely, that Dante's excoriation of the pope's fullness of power (*plenitudo potestatis*) as being indistinguishable from lust for domination, *libido dominandi*, might have been directed with equal or greater force against the secular *imperium* to which he gave allegiance. But there is no reason to suppose Dante ignorant of such self-implicating consequences of the Fall.[4]

My essay's title, taken from Michael Oakeshott's introduction to Thomas Hobbes's *Leviathan*, requires explanation. "To establish the connections in principle and in detail, directly or mediately, between politics and eternity is a project that has never been without its followers." Our contemporary demand for relevance (making the past relevant to *us*) is in need of redirection (making *us* relevant to the past). Dante's *Monarchia* requires of us such a chastened understanding of relevance. The choice—to return to, and upon, Latin—I see as essential to Dante's own inner debate on matters of issue and relationship. From first to last, I would say, Dante's works interpret cultural personality and civic politics *sub specie aeternitatis*, not in order to diffuse and dissipate worldly significance but rather to precipitate and crystallize the nature of its being and the quality of our understanding—or, as Dante writes, paraphrasing Aristotle: "Consequently the first point to bear in mind is that God and nature do nothing in vain" ("propter quod sciendum primo quod Deus et natura nil otiosum facit," *Monarchia* 1.3). Dante is not idly sheltering here beneath the aegis of a Scholastic commonplace. As Kay observes, Aristotle's "nihil frustra" has become Dante's "nil otiosum," while an original plural verb "faciunt" has become the singular "facit," "thus stressing that God is the ultimate cause of everything that is done by nature." Such evidence raises questions that relate to a process I here term *analytical recreation*: the mind that is attentive (a) to the grounding necessity of Aristotle's dictum and (b) to the need for an immediate rectifying of its doctrinal irregularity is at the same time a mind well able to attend to the problem in the instant. Grammar is not so much mediating as immediate. It is also tenacious. Dante is now conflating phrases from Aristotle, phrases which are themselves adaptations of pre-Aristotelian maxims.[5]

What I call "tenacity" works in more than one dimension. Dante is in the first instance tenacious of his own extreme prejudice against papal interference in the running of the Empire. As E. H. Kantorowicz writes, "To the third book of the *Monarchy* Dante assigned the task of proving that the emperor derived his power from God directly, and not through papal mediation, and even less so from the pope as the ultimate source of imperial power." And, as has been shown, Dante is prepared in this business to make even Aristotle malleable to his will. It is to him, in a literal sense, his business. I draw this conclusion from that word change already referred to: from Aristotle's "nihil frustra faciunt" to "nil otiosum facit." Dante cannot but be aware of the classical status of "otium," defined by the *Oxford Classical Dictionary* as "time available for leisure, politics, education, and culture" and of the derivation of "negotium" (business) from "nec-otium," i.e., insufficient time for leisure. The implied loss of status from "otium" to "otiosum" ("having no practical use or purpose, ineffectual, useless") is evidence that the public and private sectors of civic and political life interact in the minute particulars as well as in the generalities and broad commitments. From whatever point of view one sees it, the *Monarchia* is an exercise in *negotium*: it is engaged in a difficult business. It has nothing in common, so far as I can see, with the political writings of key figures of our own time—Yeats, Pound, Eliot, MacDiarmid—all of whom, in one way or another, aestheticize politics.[6]

It is in this connection that I wish both to accept and to question Etienne Gilson's Thomist observation in *Dante et Beatrice*, that whereas in the Holy Scriptures the literal sense is true, in the genre of poetry the opposite is the case: "There, it is the allegorical sense that is true, and its truth alone justifies the literal sense, whose only purpose is to signify it." Gilson accurately records Aquinas's sharp distinction; a distinction moreover which Dante himself appears to uphold when, in the *Vita Nuova* 30, he explains that his abrupt excursus from Tuscan into Vulgate Latin—"Quomodo sedet sola civitas"(How solitary lies the city!)—is in fact like building a gateway ("quasi come entrata") to "the new matter that cometh after" (della nuova materia che appresso viene). Jeremiah's words for the destruction of Jerusalem are the "literal" from which Dante is to venture into allegorical depiction of the destructiveness of carnal grief—truly destructive even when the carnality has been spiritualized.

It is in keeping with Aquinas's sense of the secondary status of (secular) Imagination that he should attribute the presence of metaphor in poetry simply to the pleasure principle, "hence representation is naturally delightful to men" (representatio enim naturaliter homini delectabilis est). Gilson rightly detects the insufficiency of this; nonetheless, his response also relies on the pleasure principle, albeit with suggestions of enriched significance gleaned from reading Dante's *Convivio* 2.11.8–10: "And it is all this—truth, goodness, beauty—which is the literal sense of the song." This is a crucial reading, in that it affirms the significance of

the literal as an element indivisible from symbolic understanding;
it is also noteworthy for its sense of the place the *Monarchia* must
be given in any just estimation of the intelligence that created the
Comedy. Finally, however, Gilson remains within the Beauty-Truth
axis which is—notoriously—self-stultifying.[7]

If we diminish the literal integrity of the *Monarchia* by claiming
that its significance is somehow subsumed into the ineffable significance of the *Comedy*—burned off, like the alcohol from a hot
wine sauce or other trimming accompanying the main roast—we
diminish the significance of the *Comedy* itself. I would argue for
the acknowledgment, both explicit and tacit, of the irreducibility
of the *letter*, as a defining quality of Dante's genius. This requires
me to return to the question of metaphor and the adequacy or inadequacy of Aquinas's description. I would agree that Aristotle, in
the *Poetics*, presents a far more radical description of this rhetorical
figure. His key is "ἀλλότριον," variously translated as "alien
name" (T. K. Butcher) or "strange term" (H. Rockham):
"Metaphor is the application of a strange term." In the *Vita Nuova*,
as already indicated, Dante erects a metaphor to stand for the use
of metaphor: metaphor is the entrance ("entrata"), the passage
through to "the new matter that cometh after." Metaphor is a
means of moving forward. And yet, in the great exemplar which
gives Dante his cue—"Quomodo sedet sola civitas"—the movement of Dante's mind is rather that of an electric charge leaping
across a gap: from literal (the death of Beatrice) to literal (the desolation of Jerusalem) rather than from trope to gloss. The Scholastic drive, powerfully present in Dante's own intellect, is towards
the further elaboration and refinement of a syllogism; the poetic
intelligence of Dante is a radical energy which cannot be described in conventional terms, whether of medieval Scholasticism
or of Enlightenment commonplace. The closest I can come to its
delineation is by taking out of context Dante's own affirmation

that "the work proper to the human race . . . is always to actualize the full power of the possible intellect [est actuare semper totam potentiam intellectus possibilis], primarily for contemplating and . . . secondarily for operating through its extension" (*Mon.* 1.4). It is of course true that Dante's own affirmation, as I call it, is closely derived from Averroes's interpretation of an Aristotelian concept and, as such, verges on the heretical: it is another instance of the mind's leap—lateral rather than ongoing. It is this "leap"—out of and into strangeness—which I here understand as a major qualifier of the conventional term "ad speculandum," the term employed by Dante himself.

As already indicated, the context from which I removed this quotation is that of the *Monarchia*. It does not altogether surprise me that it is from this work, more than from the *Vita Nuova* or the *Convivio*, that I draw a sense of the immediacy of Dante's poetic intelligence *in potentia*. Aristotle asserts in the *Poetics* 22.7–10 that "the right use of metaphor" is a sign of genius: a sense of striking resemblance is not to be disassociated from an awareness of strangeness; from the recognition of the abyss of proximity between, let us say, politics and eternity. In such minute particularization of judgment and alienation, Dante anticipates Shakespeare's Troilus as he struggles to comprehend the extraordinariness of the commonplace betrayal that has been inflicted upon him:

> This is, and is not *Cressid*.
> And yet the spacious breadth of this division,
> Admits no orifex for a point as subtle
> As *Ariachne*'s broken woof to enter.

Whether or not Eliot's claim in *Dante* that European "disintegration . . . began soon enough after Dante's time" can resist scrutiny, I would describe the *Divine Comedy* as the last great European work of the imagination to fully understand itself in relation to Aristotelian polity. In book 7.4.7 of the *Politics*, Aristotle recommends that "in order to decide questions of justice and in order to distribute the offices according to merit it is necessary for the citizens to know each other's personal characters, . . . haphazard decision is unjust in both matters, and this must obviously prevail in an excessively numerous community." The city-state of Florence during Dante's lifetime, together with numerous other such centres which feature in his biography and in Petrarch's, may have provided a political and civic ambiance more closely approximating than any other constitution to Aristotle's projected ideal. Throughout the *Inferno* the prescriptions of *Politics* 7.4.7 strike me as being enforced with a coherent, albeit inverted, sense and with an inexhaustible malign gusto. In the *Purgatorio*, also designed in accordance with Aristotelian rules of proximity, the encounters are exemplary and intimate. In both canticles, Dante either knows beforehand, or is quickly made privy to, the personal characters of those citizens of filth or flame whom—either damned or penitent—he encounters.

In his monograph, Eliot rightly emphasizes that, throughout the *Inferno*, it is the character presentations that strike us first, a suggestion which may have focused Warman Welliver's more recent references to the characteristic succession of "angry deceitful autobiographers" intermingled with Dante's own "anger and vindictiveness and despair." Here also we detect what I have likened to an electric charge leaping across a gap: from literal to literal. I also recall here Gramsci's observations on canto 10 of the *Inferno*: "The 'aesthetic' and 'dramatic' accent on the line falls on 'ebbe' ('il verbo al passato')." Eliot is again both accurate and suggestive when he observes that the Dantean hell is "not a place but a state." In this respect—and I understand it to be a preeminent quality of the Dantean imagination—I can draw no distinction between the mode in which Dante's intelligence realizes itself in the *Inferno* and the mode in which it attends to its business in the *Monarchia*. In such arduous, illuminating congruities wrought from incongruity can be found the essential paradigm for writers of our own epoch.[8]

To apply—albeit anachronistically—two Kantian terms, I suggest that *Gegenstand*, taken by Rosen to mean "an object of public perception," applies to Dante's estranged literalness in moral and political argument and that *Objekt*, understood as a "quasi-object of private perception or sensation," is applicable to the aestheticized politics of a number of major writers in our century including Yeats and Pound and not excluding Brecht. As an instance of Eliot's aestheticized—and aestheticizing—politics, consider the epigraph to his *Dante*, a sentence taken from *Le Conseil de Dante*, a (then) recently published book by Charles Maurras, the founder of *Action Française*, to whom Eliot's monograph is dedicated: "La sensibilité, sauvée d'elle-même et conduite dans l'ordre, est devenue un principe de perfection" (Sensibility, redeemed from itself and reduced to order, became a basis of perfection). These words assist our understanding of Eliot's *Ash-Wednesday*, but they do nothing to strengthen our grasp of the *Comedy*.[9]

The proposition that poets in general are vocationally privileged, gifted with a particular insight into the workings of poetry that sets them apart from commentators who are merely scholars, is one that should not pass unchallenged. Only in exceptional cases, such as that of Mandelstam on Dante, could it be confidently asserted that there exists a unique intensity of acumen and illumination which only the practice of poetry to a high level of achievement can bestow upon the critical process.

The suggestion has more than once been made that the *terza rima*, employed by the Earl of Surrey and by Sir Thomas Wyatt in both satire and verses of penitence, derived from Dante by way of Petrarch and Alamanni. Provided that no claim for *direct* influence is insinuated, the connection seems to me irrefutable. I would add that Surrey and Wyatt, even though not directly influenced by Dante, are more truly Dantean than is Eliot. If Surrey and Wyatt are of Dante's lineage, it is because they recognize their poetry as existing on the same plane, and subject to the same conditions, as the conduct (and indeed misconduct) of their daily existence; a life which, in their closely related cases, had repeatedly to be fought for—on more than one occasion literally—as an object of public perception. Dante anticipates also the life and work of Milton; in his generosity of imagination—many times at odds with anger and vindictiveness, many times transfiguring his own inequities; in the relation of verse to prose—compare the role of the *Monarchia* with that of *The Tenure of Kings and Magistrates*, or *A Treatise of Civil Power in Ecclesiastical Causes*; in the sense of the inescapable body of politics where individual involvement takes on some of the formal characteristics of the *agon*.

Dante's *Monarchia* is profoundly unaesthetic. The relationship, in our own time, between poetics and politics (a connection vital to both orders, and to be insisted on even at the cost of inordinate misunderstanding) would have been stronger if the brute power of the literal had been recognized as plainly as Dante recognizes it here: "It was necessary to establish such a principle, as was said before, as a benchmark by which whatever is to be proved may be measured as if by the most evident truth" (Kay, *Mon.* 1.4). Kay's "benchmark," for "signum prefixum," where other translators have "predetermined concept," "agreed point of reference," "point of departure," "common ground," is well judged even if anachronistic. Such a mark is cut "into durable material" and Dante's own hardness and durability is based on, and levelled with, the Law and the Prophets. In *Monarchia* 2.5, he cites with marked assent a phrase from St. Martin of Braga, believing it to be by Seneca: "legem vinculum humane societatis" (law is the bond of human society). We are bound by the letter of the law: if not by that, then by the force-field of Death and Chaos. St. Martin's axiom, understood in the way that I believe Dante—or indeed any of his contemporaries—would read it, is given its own bearings from two widely separated passages in the Vulgate Bible: Genesis 42.16 and the Epistle of Jude, 6. These are two scriptural instances in which "vincula," rather than "catenae" or "in manicis ferreis," is used of the chains which bind slaves or felons. First: "Send one of you, and let him fetch your brother, and ye shall be kept in prison [in vinculis], that your words may be proved, whether there be any truth in you: or else by the life of Pharaoh surely ye are spies." Secondly: "And the Angels which kept not their first estate, but left their own habitation, he hath reserved in everlasting chains (*vinculis aeternis*) under darkness, unto the judgment of the great day." The letters of the law are the benchmarks by which the builders of civil society keep level with the durable material of the world's foundation: the fact of Original Sin and the fact of Redemption. Between politics and eternity, aesthetic considerations, as, for instance, "taste" and "enjoyment," are quite simply irrelevant; alien to the purpose and quality of the *Monarchia* as they are to the work of Antonio Gramsci who dismissed Croce's aesthetics and would have rejected Eliot's had he known of them. As an Anglo-Catholic conservative, I arrive at this conclusion reluctantly but hardly with surprise.

Notes

1. "Certainly [the *Monarchia*] exerted little influence on late medieval political thought. Instead it was a curiosity, known to a few and more esteemed for its links to Dante and classical humanism than for its theses." Richard Kay, ed., *Dante's* Monarchia (Toronto: Pontifical Institute of Medieval Studies, 1998), p. xxxv. I have used Kay's translation throughout.

2. Stanley Rosen, *Metaphysics in Ordinary Language* (New Haven: Yale University Press, 1999), p. 49.

3. Antonio Gramsci, *Selections from Cultural Writings* (Cambridge, Mass.: Harvard University Press, 1985), pp. 156, 152–53. Quotations in Italian are from Gramsci, *Opere*, vol. 6 (Turin: Einaudi, 1950), pp. 36–37.

4. Passerin d'Entrèves, *Dante as a Political Thinker* (Oxford: Clarendon Press, 1952), pp. 18, 21–25.

5. Except where noted, all translations of Aristotle are from the Loeb Classical Library editions (Cambridge, Mass.: Harvard University Press).

6. E. H. Kantorowicz, *The King's Two Bodies* (Princeton: Princeton University Press, 1957), p. 456.

7. Etienne Gilson, *Dante et Beatrice* (Paris: J.Vrin, 1974), pp. 94, 91.

8. T. S. Eliot, *Dante* (London: Faber & Faber, 1929), pp. 19–28; Warman Welliver, *Dante in Hell* (Ravenna: Longo, 1981), pp. 18, 25.

9. Rosen, *Ordinary Language*, p. 146.

Rosanna Warren

Words and Blood

Readers of the *Divine Comedy* find there a vastly complex medieval theology penetrating all order—doctrinal, moral, aesthetic, political, and scientific—along with a lifetime's reading list of sources and corollary texts. This is not the hunger I first brought to the poem. What struck me, when I blundered into its precinct as a teenager, was its dramatic spiritual psychology in a poetry embodied in sounds, objects, and action. I can still hardly write about it, because I absorbed the poem first in the almost pre-articulate fervor of late adolescence. This was poetry to be tasted, gnawed, turned on the tongue.

I was eighteen, living alone in Rome, wandering through a canto or two a day in my grandmother's shabbily elegant calfskin edition before wandering later each day through the hallucinatory city. These grandeurs seemed mystifying, urgent. Like the city, the poem appealed to the sensory intellect, drawing its sense from the senses. I felt then, I still feel, that we can recognize our own desires and deformations in Dante's cast of characters, as we recognize our physical world in his, boiling pitch, fireflies, mirrors, candles, shadows, and all. Such a poetry is incarnational in a lowercase, secular sense. But its majesty, strain, and challenge arise from its profane communions being set always in the light of a specific religious communion, its human words in the light of a sacred Word. Into that gulf between word and Word, the poem radiates its illusion and its promise.

As Virgil describes the journey to be taken through Hell, he promises the wayward pilgrim an experience as powerfully auditory as it will be visual:

> ove udirai le disperate strida,
>   vedrai li antichi spiriti dolenti,
>   ch'a la seconda morte ciascun grida.
>   (*Inf.* 1.115–17)

> where you shall hear the despairing shrieks and see the ancient tormented spirits who all bewail the second death. (All translations are by Charles Singleton.)

Before Dante even enters the gates of Hell, it is the infernal cacophony that strikes his imagination. Light is mute here, but sighs, groans, cries, keening, and curses resound in every language of the earth. The deeper he descends, the greater the range of utterances of grief and fury he will hear. There is political rhetoric, obscenity, slang, nonsense (the quasi-significant gibberish of Pluto and Nimrod) and, almost at the bottom, the heartbreaking echo of the sacred in Ugolino's tale of his dying son Gaddo: "Padre mio, che non m'aiuti?" (Father, why do you not help me? *Inf.* 33.69), the "Eli, eli, lama sabacthani" still misunderstood, misheard, by Ugolino, who seems impervious to the model of sacramental sacrifice his son has offered him. Hell is the grimly familiar landscape of most human desire and action, and its sounds, too, are familiar. This is our language. This is what we have made of the Word that was in the beginning, and was with God, and was God. Dante the pilgrim has traveled as if with a tape recorder, preserving our distortions; Dante the poet plays them across the potentially redemptive grid of *terza rima*, so that they may take on meaning beyond our meanness.

If the poet can do this, it is because the Bible has already schooled him in the drama of the Word's falling and rising, its corruption and regeneration. Language falls throughout the Hebrew Bible, even before Babel, in the seductions of Eden, in Cain's insolent "Am I my brother's keeper?" and in the whole sordid unwinding of vice and stupidity we call history. It is saved in the declaration and redeclaration of the Covenant, and in each self-positioning by those who have heard the Lord's voice ("Here I am"); it is saved and codified in the Law, in prophecy, and most intimately in the Psalms. Throughout the Hebrew Bible, human language, in a world created initially by God's speech, struggles back toward sacred sense. In the Gospels, that sense is understood, quite physically and even primitively, as the Word made flesh. If Christ's injured flesh can redeem the lost likeness of the Divine Image in our ruined faces, so His flesh as Word can be felt—is felt, I think, by Dante—to heal our mangled speech. But the poetic word is not a sacred word, as the poem warns us over and over in its images of literary pride and delusion: Arachne, the magpies, the Siren, Marsyas. The poem not only depicts the language of its characters as deformed and reforming, but works itself within the medium of deformation. No telepathies or instant fixes here. The poet slogs through the mire of fallen language, and it is a long haul through narration, dialogue, meditation, exposition, and prayer, all organized by *terza rima*. Even the visions and voices of Paradise, increasingly transmitted as brain waves though they seem to be, have to be represented, if at all, as traces in human language moving through the ordered time of verse.

It is the "morta poesia" of *Inferno* that I most recognize. Facing again in memory the frozen lake of traitors in *Inferno* 32, the poet laments not having rhymes sufficiently harsh and grating to "press out the juice of his conception." But the Muses, whose help he implores, have already given him a transfusion of bubbling, gurgling, hissing syllables, doubled glottals, grating vowels; in vocabulary, the poet has felt free not merely to use the vernacular, but to ransack it, serving up tar, shit, farts, and assholes along with Francesca's romantic and courtly self-justifications and Farinata's eloquence.

In *Purgatorio*, the canticle of redemptive imagination, Hell's physical and literal imagery gives way to a dazzling series of moving pictures and speaking bas-reliefs, a compendium of ways in which an art of hyperrealism instructs the mind. In kindred spirit, poetry in *Purgatorio* meditates on the conditions of its own making and higher purposes, as individual poets, ancient and modern, find their verses trained upon the larger trellis of collective and sacred words: Psalms, scriptural quotation, prayer. Before we experience poetry's reintegration, however—before Dante, Virgil, and the questing souls are scolded for dallying, listening to Casella sing one of Dante's own earlier love poems; before Arnaut speaks in Provençal out of the refining fire; before Virgil's own verses for Marcellus and Dido are recycled in a context of new loss and new love—in Hell, we chew and gag on the raw material of language. Our language. For we are made by language, as Genesis 1 teaches: God creates by speaking. If Dante the pilgrim has any hope, it is a grace that comes to him, not *from* language—his love for Beatrice must have been, originally, a shock beyond speech—but *through* language: through his experiences of reading Virgil's Latin and hearing Beatrice's Italian, through his whole emotional and intellectual landscape embodied in words. The Word will come to him, if it comes, translated through words. If we as readers find ourselves touched by this poem, it will be because we, too, have tasted the language of delusion and recognize it to be soiled, rotten, or toughened as beef jerky.

Inferno has a full menu of such anti-communions. Francesca's hash of Guinizelli's *canzone* of courtly love is one: "Amor, ch'al cor gentil ratto s'apprende . . ." (Love, which is quickly kindled in a gentle heart . . . *Inf.* 5.100). The wrathful sinners burbling in the slime are another: "Quest'inno si gorgoglian ne la strozza, / ché dir nol posson con parola integra" (This hymn they gurgle in their throats, for they cannot speak it in full words, *Inf.* 7.125–26). So is Brunetto Latini's perversion of the rhetoric of learning. So are the desperate mechanics by which Ulysses and Guido da Montefeltro force human speech from the tongues of flames they inhabit. Language betrayed is the very medium of Hell: there's no dearth of examples. But one scene in particular has haunted me for years, perhaps since it so incarnates the conditions of struggling speech: Pier della Vigna, the suicide, imperial minister, ambassador, and poet trapped in a tree.

In the seventh circle where the violent are punished, the suicides suffer for violence against the self. At every level, the canto reminds us of the claustrophobia and self-entrapment that define suicide. Pier della Vigna seems imprisoned by the figurative force of his own name: Pier of the Grapevine, his soul now enclosed in a twisted thorn tree on which he will hang the rags of his body at the Last Judgment in a meaningless parody of the Crucifixion. He is entrapped, too, in the model of *Aeneid* 3, doomed to repeat the suffering of Polydorus from Virgil's poem; but whereas Polydorus is imprisoned in a mound beneath his bleeding thornbush in Thrace as a victim of murder, Pier has murdered himself, further tightening the circle in around the self. In yet another intensification of the Virgilian scene, Pier is embodied *within* his tree, not just under it. The violence with which Aeneas yanked at the bleeding bush in Thrace is repeated here as a consciously cruel experiment inflicted by the poet Dante through the agency of Virgil, as a way of educating the pilgrim. Virgil's apology to Pier for the violation seems oddly ambivalent in the script provided by Dante, sympathetic but at the same time competitive, demonstrating Dante's superior realism: " 'If he, O wounded spirit, had been able to believe before', replied my sage, 'what he had never seen save in my verses, he would not have stretched forth his hand against you; but the incredible thing made me prompt him to a deed that grieves me' " (*Inf.* 13.46–51).

And then there is the self-enclosure of Pier's own speech. Or-

nate as befits a court poet, minister, and counselor to Emperor
Frederick II, Pier's speech rounds in on itself in elaborate repeti-
tions, variations, and antitheses. The harlot envy, Pier says,

> infiammò contra me li animi tutti;
> e li 'nfiammati infiammar sì Augusto . . .
> (Inf. 13.67–68)

> inflamed all minds against me; and they, inflamed, did so in-
> flame Augustus . . .

Pier's chiastic description of his own suicidal impulse acts like an
architectural figure for self-destruction. His mind, he says,
"ingiusto fece me contra me giusto" (made me unjust against my
just self, *Inf.* 13.72). The Italian word order builds an arch:
paradoxically opposed and symmetrical, "inguisto" and "giusto"
sustain the foundations. The repeated first person singular pronoun "me," in the sadly objective case, flanks the keystone: the
self as object, multiplied and detached. In the center, holding
together the whole sorry structure, is poised the adversarial
preposition "contra," which in its own way embodies the spirit
of suicide.

A master of rhetoric in life, Pier della Vigna in Hell must struggle to enunciate. Only in Italian does this passage spit and whistle
as it must:

> Come d'un stizzo verde ch'arso sia
>   da l'un de' capi, che da l'altro geme
>   e cigola per vento che va via,
> sì de la scheggia rotta usciva insieme
>   parole e sangue; ond'io lasciai la cima
>   cadere, e stetti come l'uom che teme.
> (Inf. 13.40–45)

As from a green brand that is burning at one end, and drips
from the other, so from that broken twig came out words
and blood together; whereon I let fall the tip, and stood like
one who is afraid.

Here, the fallen word is made flesh in the onomatopoeia of the
doubled "z" of "stizzo," in the hissing "s's," "sc's," and "c's." It is
made drama in the enjambments: the broken bough spits words
and blood, "parole e sangue," out from the broken end of its line:
"si de la scheggia rotta usciva insieme / parole e sangue" The as-
tounded pilgrim lets the twig fall from one line to the next:
"ond'io lasciai la cima / cadere." The language of suffering issues,
physically, as blood, sizzling off the page.

Poetry is, by itself, a secular art. Dante has achieved in this passage
a piece of bravura mimesis, a phonetic, syntactic, and metrical rendi-
tion of the action he describes. Like the astonishingly lifelike paintings
and sculptures in *Purgatorio* (and their forebears in the *Aeneid*), Dante's
own figuration can take the breath away. Logically, however, nothing
requires a relation to be established between the injured, lowercase
words of human pain, and the uppercase incarnate Word of Christian
promise. We can recognize the truth of the symptoms described in *Inferno* without buying the prescriptions that follow: acceptance of
Christ's sacrifice, belief in the efficacy of penitence, redirection of desire from earthly objects to the Christian God. Theology, though,
presses to connect word and Word, arguing through analogy. Dante's
narrative will try to shape such a relation imaginatively, bringing into
hierarchical association the fallen word and the divine Word, Adam
and Christ. The trinitarian verse form and the triple rhymes of
"Cristo" with itself urge that association, and *Paradiso* takes us far toward its fulfillment before Dante's "alta fantasia" fails him.

Failure is, of course, written into the literary, if not the religious,
endeavor, as human and divine can never be commensurate, however analogous. Christ as human, as Word made flesh, uneasily con-

nects the two realms, but the poet's account, at the end of *Paradiso*, of gazing into the heart of light, absolute love, can only be made in the negative and imagistic terms suited to mortal cognition:

> Così la neve al sol si disigilla;
>
>   così al vento ne le foglie levi
>
>   si perdea la sentenza di Sibilla.
>
>   (*Par.* 33.64–66)

> Thus is the snow unsealed by the sun; thus in the wind, in the light leaves, the Sibyl's oracle was lost.

There is a far earlier scene, however, in the lower reaches of *Purgatorio*, that seems to me to dramatize convincingly the redemption of lowercase language in Christian terms, and to bring words into experiential relation to the Word. Like the episode of Pier della Vigna, it has to do with gargled and agonized speech. In the case of Buonconte da Montefeltro, however, the last strangled utterance in life is enough to save him. We find him near the base of the mountain of Purgatory, not even in Purgatory proper, among those who sinned up until the last moment and died violently. Buonconte compresses his life story into the few moments that matter to him:

> "Oh!" rispuos'elli, "a piè del Casentino
>
>   traversa un'acqua c'ha nome l'Archiano,
>
>   che sovra l'Ermo nasce in Apennino.
>
> Là've'l vocabol suo diventa vano,
>
>   arriva'io forato ne la gola,
>
>   fuggendo a piede e sanguinando il piano.
>
> Quivi perdei la vista e la parola;
>
>   nel nome di Maria fini', e quivi
>
>   caddi, e rimase la mia carne sola."
>
>   (*Purg.* 5.94–102)

"Oh!" he answered, "at the foot of the Casentino a stream crosses, named the Archiano, which rises in the Apennines above the Hermitage. To the place where its name is lost I came, wounded in the throat, flying on foot and bloodying the plain. There I lost my sight and speech. I ended on the name of Mary, and there I fell, and my flesh remained alone."

Buonconte's last-minute salvation balances his father's damnation; we had met Guido da Montefeltro with Ulysses among the false counselors in the speaking flames of *Inferno* 27. Whereas Guido had converted late in life, in outward form at least, thinking to assure his salvation, only to be brutally surprised at the outcome, his son dying at the Battle of Campaldino concludes with a prayer of a single name that saves him. Buonconte's story, the tale of a name choked out by a man wounded in the throat, occurs in a canto running with appalling liquids: blood, swamp water, torrents, an infernal rainstorm, the marshes of Maremma. Between Jacopo del Cassero dying in the mire in the pool of his own blood, and the sibylline La Pia whose life is concentrated in a one-line chiasmus of place—"Siena mi fe, disfecemi Maremma" (Siena made me, Maremma unmade me, *Purg.* 5.134)—Buonconte participates, through his wound, in his entire watery landscape. The place incarnates his story. There where the Archiano River loses its name in a densely alliterative line ("Là've'l vocabol suo diventa vano"), Buonconte also loses his "vocabol," wounded in the throat, making of his blood another tributary to the river. Though he loses speech, he saves the essential word, Maria, and the enjambment of his dying is not a prelude to damnation: "nel nome di Maria fini', e quivi / caddi . . ." (I ended on the name of Mary, and there I fell . . . , *Purg.* 5.101). In a touch of brilliant irony, the devil who feels cheated of the soul sneers that this salvation occurred "per una lagrimetta"—one tiny teardrop to be weighed against the rivers of blood, sin, and diabolical revenge, and, most astonishingly, against a lifetime of violence.

We may also weigh that teardrop, and that gurgled prayer, against the self-involuting language of Pier della Vigna. In both cases, Dante has made the language physically present. Ink, in both scenes, has become transubstantiated as blood. The question is, whether or not, in each case within the fiction, the blood will have sacrificial efficacy. A doctrine concerning damnation and grace takes on substance as drama. More than doctrine, it is Dante's dramatic psychology and embodied phonetics that allow us to sense in Pier della Vigna what a soul feels like, trapped in self-destruction, spitting out its painful account of itself like sap from a green bough in flame. It is the dramatized, imagistically embodied landscape of *Purgatorio* 5 that allows us to absorb the saving force of Buonconte's last gasped word.

The doctrine itself is shocking; a split-second repentance outweighs years of destruction. But does that intellectual and moral shock become an obstacle to apprehension of the poem by non-doctrinal readers? Modern readers have dashed themselves over and over at this question, and so forceful and provocative is Dante's theology that each new reader, I suspect, is drawn back to grapple with it personally in spite of Eliot's useful suspension of "both belief and disbelief," and Auerbach's bold assertion that in the *Divine Comedy* "the image of man eclipses the image of God." Eliot and Auerbach, each in his way, might have been thought to have settled certain matters of literature and belief. In fact, they settled very little. The *Comedy* continues to be a monumentally unsettling poem. For myself, I have found it indispensable to recognize that a vast, systematic theology undergirds the poem, while at the same time reminding myself not to read sclerotically; not to allow attention to congeal, in approval or indignation, around any particular theological point. This is, after all, a poem; a course of action, not a *summa*. In an important sense, the poem's reality overflows its doctrine. That reality is made present, substantial, and dynamic in many ways, but especially in language's corporeality: ono-matopoeia, lineation, and imagery. It appeals to the mind through the nervous system, and leaves us room to apprehend Pier della Vigna's and Buonconte's tortured syllables as universal examples of human speech.

When we try to tell the truth, whoever we are, of whatever faith or non-faith, the best we can do, often, is to sputter. We will be fortunate if the truth we spit out is not entirely self-concerned. Poetry heals nothing. But by placing its lowercase communion upon our tongues, it can draw us into imaginative relation with truths beyond our own, and can place the personal pronoun—subjective or objective—in the neighborhood of far greater words.

W. S. Di Piero

Our Sweating Selves

Several years ago, while visiting Lanciano, the major city in the province of Abruzzi, I saw a reliquary in the Church of San Francesco containing an opaque, brownish wafer said to be living tissue from the body of Christ. The priest in charge assured us that scientists have corroborated this "life." I was with my Abruzzese cousin, a pious, unquestioning man who whispered his awe to me explosively, as a child would. The priest was the kind of severe adult who would scold the child, a sour man who spoke with pinched, impatient aloofness, as if he knew we could not possibly understand the significance of what he was showing us. He seemed to me someone who, having miserably suffered a crisis of faith, emerges with a deepened belief inseparable from a deepened disdain for nonbelievers. Like my cousin, I felt awe in the presence of the relic, but for different reasons. That slice of flesh—it looked like sepia-stained amber—was a token of the Incarnation, which is the most elusive, terrifying, and melancholy mystery of Catholicism. The hypostatic union is Christ's grandeur. As a child, I was enthralled by the fact of the god in the flesh, the mortal able to bring himself back from the land of the dead. As an adult fallen from belief, I think more about the flesh of the god, and about our condition, as Hopkins says, of being bound to our bones, fastened to flesh.

Whenever I read the *Inferno* and the *Purgatorio*, I'm aware it's the story of a body of a certain voluminous substance tracking its destiny among substanceless shades. Every time Dante is made aware of himself as a solidity passing among those who are without solidity, aware of his own thingness (though he could not and would not have thought of himself or any human being in these terms), the poem is commemorating and celebrating the Incarnation. It is in imitation of Christ that Dante lives out what may be the most acute, finely calibrated awareness of the body in premodern literature. He was giving to the body in poetry the earthbound opacity and solidity that Giotto was giving it in painting. In the *Inferno*, when he follows Virgil into Phlegyas's boat to cross the river Styx, he notices that only then does the boat seem laden ("carca," 8.27). Dante is, first of all, following his powerful predecessor by imitating him: when Aeneas steps into the Stygian boat, it groans under his weight. But "carca" has shadow meanings: the boat, when this creature is in it, is loaded, weighted down, *charged*, as we speak of being charged with a duty or task. In that place of shades, the boat is charged with the presence of flesh and blood, of memory embodied. As they cross the river, Dante notices that the prow cuts the water more deeply than when it carries others. That channel is the first mark of embodiment in the underworld, where souls who have no substance suffer real physical pain. It is human presence carving its record into Hell's topography.

Whenever we are reminded of Dante's inspirited weightedness, we remember that this assigns him a particular position in the order of the universe. Beatrice will explain to him later that all things have order among themselves, and it is this orderliness, this form, that makes the universe like God. The more responsive he is to the world's physicality, to its proper weights and measures, the more the poet participates in and contributes to that godly order. His desire is expressed physically in the many different kinds of seeing that he does: he looks, stares, marvels, regards, peers. It's an act of piety for Dante to get things right, to present the consistency and stability of things in fine detail. To describe the exact degree of lightness of the big, fiery flakes falling on the heads of those who defied God, he says they fall "come di neve in alpe senza vento" (like windless mountain snow, *Inf.* 14.30).

Dante's journey in the *Inferno* is a series of recognitions of human wrongness, recognitions shaped by the different kinds of resistance his body meets. Once he breaks through the point of absolute gravity on the floor of Hell and emerges in the light of day—true sunlight, not the travesties of light he saw in Hell—he delivers himself of his weightedness. Now it is the body-as-stuff that matters. When the shades in Ante-Purgatory approach him in canto 3, anxious for memories received and transmitted, they suddenly stop and pull back because they (and Dante) see that the light on a rock is broken by Dante's shadow. The moment is so compelling because it's as if Dante has just now acquired a shadow, just now been given volume to define and articulate his weightedness. He is the thing that throws a shadow. Virgil's words to the shades, "What you're seeing is a human body" (*Purg.* 3.95), make that fact seem strange and marvelous. The shadow "l'ombra," the mortality print, becomes Dante's new companion in Purgatory, a memory print of the sinfulness whose horrific consequences he witnessed in Hell among the shades, "le ombre."

When the Hale-Bopp comet passed within view of the earth a few years ago, the memory of that Lanciano relic struck me with the kind of force Dante describes when he first sees Matelda on the opposite bank of the river Lethe: it was "a thing of such wonder that it drives away every other thought" (*Purg.* 28.38–39). I had never seen a comet; now there it was, framed in my window night after night, a lump of ice and space dirt coinciding, in ways I strongly felt but did not understand, with the reality of a small tissue of live flesh two millennia old.

This sort of coincidence is often the occasion of poems.

Crude, nebulously related material begins to take on a felt shape of meaning in my consciousness. But the more I wrote in answer to the occasion, the more inert and intractable that coincidence became. The two events existed in meaningful relation merely because they happened to occur to me. They were significant only because they were the accidental conjunction of unrelated celestial and earthly facts. I was trying to muscle the material into a meaningful pattern, to will poetry into existence out of atomized haphazardness. I think many poets now live in a vague Emersonian world of spiritual becoming, without a justifying, sponsoring cosmology created by God. "This one fact the world hates," Emerson says in "Self-Reliance," "that the soul *becomes*; for that forever degrades the past . . . confounds the saint with the rogue, shoves Jesus and Judas equally aside." I live with the conflicted belief that spirit or soul, that restless processal dynamic we live toward and into at the same time, is whatever consciousness conceives or imagines to be greater than itself. I think not so much about the soul's "eternality" as about its earthly self-definition.

My modest problem made me think of the *Comedy*, in which celestial and earthly realities are a bonded pattern of correspondences, alignments, and coincidings authored in and by Divine Mind. Dante, possessing "il ben dell'intelletto" (*Inf.* 3.18)—Good Mind, Godly Mind—dramatizes himself as part of that massive coherence. The poem and the universe it represents are beautifully rotund and complete. It is two hours before dawn on Easter Sunday in the year 1300 when Dante, under the morning star of Venus, arrives at the mountain of Purgatory, the southern pole precisely opposite the northern pole of Jerusalem. The poem is authorized to contain earthly history, celestial events, and divine interventions in one ordered, balanced structure. Dante had Agency (the pilgrim and his guides), Purpose (the beatific vision), and Process (education by bearing witness). He applied a mechanics of foreknowledge and remembrance by which everything that surprises us and Dante as he makes his way has already happened.

The journey is complete before the journey commences, complete, perhaps most of all, even when Dante seems most vulnerable to contingency. While we read it, the poem is jumpy with possibility and accident, yet at any time we can hold in our mind its finished, resolved structure. The poem is busily intimate—we are kept physically so close to Dante and his humanness—and shockingly remote. The certainties of the *Comedy* are so consistent that exactly while I'm engaged with the pilgrim's tense anxieties, the poem remains almost as "other" as the *Iliad*.

Many of us are the more or less deformed grandchildren of Thomas Hardy's belief that destiny is ruled by Crass Casualty, by accident and random coincidence, unreasonable, purposeless, unsponsored. Much of what I write is not only about contingency, it's grounded in it, rooted in a preoccupation with the "sweating selves" Gerard Manley Hopkins speaks of. Haphazard change, whatever its consequences, is a species of beauty, but it's not rounded and self-enfolding, it's angular and fragmentarily expansive. Lady Fortune, who occupies a fixed place in Dante's cosmos, thus becomes an unstable terrorist. According to the *Comedy*, the goddess's turning wheel determines what we experience as change, whether it be the sudden loss or acquisition of wealth, political tumult or peace, the death or good health of a child. Unchanging in her changefulness, Lady Fortune oversees the orderliness of accident as a manifestation of divine plan. What we experience on earth as terrifying uncertainty and irresoluteness exists by a perfectly ordered divine dispensation and sponsorship. The *Inferno* and *Purgatorio* are theaters of fortune, where the process and consequences of change are in a constant state of motion, of excited reenactment and disclosure. But they are also display cases in which all discrete actions are suspended and tableaued in the larger order of the poem.

Dante's journey plays out as discovery through instruction: his destiny is to happen upon what he needs to know but does not expect to find. Having "chanced upon" Brunetto Latini or Farinata or Belacqua or La Pia, he is somehow changed because his understanding of divine order and the human place in it has been enlarged. The poem's cosmology justifies the terror, anxiety, and uncertainty Dante experiences. The more each witnessed event seems like chance, the more divinely ordered it must be. Dante's poem offers us, whether we are believers or not, a fully articulated order that can account for the entire range of human experience, and the model of a human consciousness that has the power to imagine being at the same time indentured to chance and delivered eternally from it.

The *Comedy* is one of the most relentlessly subjective poems ever written, although it's not about subjectivity and certainly not about the kind of modern selfhood, self-analytical and self-ironizing, that Shakespeare invents in the characters of Hamlet, Prince Hal, and Macbeth. In his great book, *Dante, Poet of the Secular World*, Erich Auerbach says that even before the *Comedy*, in the *Vita Nuova*, Dante intensified his feeling "by raising it above the sphere of subjectivity to which feeling is ordinarily confined . . . by establishing it in the empyrean realm of the ultimate and absolute." Later poets did not need an ultimate, eschatological plan in order to perceive the self as a unified entity. "Sheer intuitive power seems to have enabled subsequent writers to combine inner and outward observation into a whole." He is describing, I think, the history of western European literature as a fall into pure contingency, into the recognition that human life turns on a series of accidents or uncontrollable events, only sometimes mediated (and even then vaguely or slightly) by supernatural agency. Knowledge of contingency is tragic knowledge.

Nothing happens by chance in the poem. Everything occurs in covenant with divine order. And yet Dante the seeker's experience is dramatized in such an exquisitely seamless and humanized way that he experiences events as we do, as chance occurrences. In the *Inferno* and *Purgatorio* especially, he happens upon whatever happens. We experience with him the anxiety and danger of being a child of contingency. Pound said that a poet's duty is to make accurate reports. Dante says that he wants to relate events "sì che dal fatto il dir non sia diverso" (so that what I say is exactly how it was, *Inf.* 32.12). Every encounter is coincidence, and he feels it to be so, but he knows—with a knowledge indistinguishable from feeling—that all coincidence is aligned and justified in the mind of God. This double knowledge accounts for what I often feel to be the remote, exotic strangeness of the poem, and at the same time, it accounts for the humane passion of Dante's imagination: every encounter where Dante is shown to be completely human is cannily webbed into the unquestionable presence of God's plan. The poem is both an intimacy and a decree, the open field of a hermetic system.

Certain lines in the *Comedy* are talismans. I recite them to myself when I'm distressed or anxious, or to protect me from writing badly, as if they could. In the Paolo and Francesca canto, when Dante describes the cranes flying single file, singing their love songs, the sound weave, the songfulness, the *taste* of "E come i gru van cantando lor lai" (*Inf.* 5.46)—those droning *n*'s and elegaic "lor lai"—express before the fact the mournful pity Dante will feel toward the two lovers. One of my favorite tercets hums a tricky, accurate fact. It comes in the Master Adam canto when Virgil scolds Dante for staring too amazedly at the grotesque scene of Sinon and Master Adam punching and vilifying each other. Dante, wanting to excuse himself but unable to form the words, describes himself thus: "Qual è colui che suo dannaggio sogna / che sognando desidera sognare / sì che quel ch'è, come non fosse, agogna" (Like someone who dreams he's being hurt / and while dreaming, wishes he were dreaming: he desires / what's already happening as if it weren't, *Inf.* 30.136–38). "Sogna/agogna" is an experiential rhyme: to dream/to desire. The language swoons and insinuates, and yet the lines have a cool, purposeful psychological precision. That word "agogna," which my Dante dictionary defines as "desiderare ardentemente" (to desire ardently) bears so much of what makes us human but which, according to doctrine, must be directed by the will only toward the good, so that a complex Thomistic dynamic is locked into the rhyme.

And there's this. On the second terrace of Purgatory, Dante sees the congregation of the envious, their eyes stitched shut with wire. They lean on each other, he says, like blind men begging alms ("bisogna"), whose very appearance craves ("agogna") pity. In the *Inferno*, Dante uses the "agogna" rhyme to describe dream desire, the illusion-making we practice in sleep. Here he uses it to fix a particular kind of waking wretchedness. These are the only two occurrences of the word in the poem (an irregular form with a different ending, "agugna," appears in *Inf.* 6.28). By repeating "agogna" (*Purg.* 26.9 and 30.138) while in Purgatory, Dante instantly makes the rhyme recall Hell to us and thus review his progress. It's as if he were rhyming two entire canticles.

The quickest bittersweet instant is the appearance of La Pia at the very end of *Purgatorio*'s fifth canto. She comes like an apparition and says to Dante: "Deh, quando tu sarai tornato al mondo . . . ricorditi di me" (Ah, when you're back in the world . . . remember me, *Purg.* 5. 130, 133). The prick of memory, "la puntura de la rimembranza" (*Purg.* 12.20), memory's *bite*, is expressed in that breathy, untranslatable particle "deh." She begs Dante to remember her when he returns to the life that *she* remembers. It's a charge to do what he is in the actual process of doing. Her "deh" contains a world of anxiety and neediness to be heard, witnessed, and reported. The lines have a terrible pity because they are so exact and, in their blunt brevity, summarize an entire life. "Siena gave me life, / Maremma gave me death, and the one who knows this best / with his ring betrothed and married me" (*Purg.* 5.134–36).

Dante himself utters the same cry when late in the *Purgatorio*, entering the Earthly Paradise, he asks Matelda to come closer to the river that separates them so that he can understand what he hears only as song-like sounds. For all that Dante says throughout the poem about his literary mentors, his ambitions, his own desire to make certain kinds of music from rough and screechy rhymes ("rime aspre e chiocce" [*Inf.* 32.1]) to "dolce stil nuovo" elegance, this is the scene that dramatizes the call to a life of poetry, much of which begins in impassioned but inarticulate music, pure in its way, then works toward clear meaning. Sheer sounds, especially for a poet trying to create a primal orchestration of the vernacular, are Siren songs, powerfully alluring and sensuous, which must be shaped into statements. To answer the call, Matelda instructs him, he must first step into two streams: Lethe, which washes away the memory of sin, and Eunoe, which restores to memory good deeds. The one is efficacious only with the other. The episode articulates the mechanic of memory that governs our knowledge of good and evil.

A poet's memory is a whispering gallery of other poets' voices. Who would not want as an early guide a great predecessor who does not get in the way, who launches the younger poet into the freedom of his own idiom? Dante's real traveling companion is the *Aeneid.* Apart from the grand *topos* of the descent into the underworld, the *Comedy* contains a multitude of imitations of that poem. When Virgil bathes Dante's face early in the *Purgatorio*, it's an image of an exemplary antiquated poem blessing and clarifying a modern poem's aspirations. On the many occasions where Virgil reads his mind ("You could cover your face / with a hundred masks and still not hide / even your slightest thoughts from me" [*Purg.* 15.127–29]), Dante dramatizes the cool but profound and peculiar intimacy that often exists between a master poet and an ambitious successor. Younger poets, especially, will say, or complain, that they have the music of some long-dead poet in their heads; or certain lines will haunt them only because of the idiosyncrasy of the music, the strange noise familiar words make.

Although it's Virgil who calls the pilgrim Dante to his journey, it's Dante, poet of the vernacular, who calls Virgil to sponsor and participate in his poem. In leading Dante, Virgil is in a sense remembering himself, living himself back into a version of his own greatest poem. When, as they approach the Earthly Paradise (with every step, Dante says, he feels more fledged for the flight), Virgil turns the poet over to Matelda and Beatrice, he is setting him loose into his own visionary independence. His happy announcement—"Your will is now free, upright, and whole . . . I crown and miter you to rule yourself" (*Purg.* 27.140, 142)—is the decree many poets sooner or later need to hear, or imagine they hear, or never hear at all.

Daniel Halpern

Dante in Perpignan

Why read the classics? I grew up in Southern California, avoiding pretty much everything that had to do with school, except sports. For my first eighteen years, I successfully avoided books, with the exception of my mother's poetry anthologies and a few novels given to me by trusted friends, which were able to catch and hold my transitory attention—the list would have included *Been Down So Long It Looks Like Up to Me* by Richard Fariña, Jack Kerouac's *On the Road*, *The Ginger Man* by J. P. Donleavy, Sybille Bedford's *A Legacy*, and what seemed to me even then a miracle of prose, a novel by a Scottish writer named Alan Sharp entitled *A Green Tree in Gedde*.

I began to read for real after my first year of college, when I spent a year traveling through Europe, North Africa, and the Middle East. My first encounter with Dante took place in a youth hostel on the outskirts of Perpignan, France. I'd been hitchhiking all day, coming down from Paris through Vichy, Lyon, and Avignon, heading south. South toward Africa. It was a late autumn month and the air was platinum and stiffly cold. The hostel where I was to spend the night was hard to find—I remember it now with clarity, thirty-five years later, placed well off the road out of Perpignan in a "dark wood," as it were. I found it, finally, by following the scent of wood smoke through the dark shadows of these woods.

The door opened onto a large square room with a huge fireplace at the far end. There were couches and easy chairs placed erratically around the room, and three young Frenchmen and two Danish women were smoking in front of the blazing fire. The light was orange from the flames, blue from the Gauloises. I am sure they all wore jeans and turtleneck sweaters and each had long dark hair. They greeted me in English (an obvious American, although I had a great deal invested in hiding this fact), as if they'd been awaiting my arrival, and immediately offered me a glass of their wine, a chunk of bread and cheese. They switched from French to English but continued talking among themselves—an exuberant and excited discussion of Dante's *Inferno*. One of the women asked if I had read it recently. I had not. In fact, I had never read it. Her name was Tove (pronounced "Tova") and she tossed me the copy sitting on her lap and said, "You should read this tonight." She said it sweetly. Her eyes were the color of teal and placed very far apart, which is what I remember of that night. Almost nothing of what they talked about remains, except that as they tossed about details of Dante's descent, I thought of the journey I'd set for myself: leaving the States, moving south from the cold north of Europe, Spain to Tangier—down to what seemed to me then exotic darkness, my descent toward whatever discovery I imagined to be awaiting me there.

That night in Perpignan, after a liter of bright Medoc, I took my inherited *Inferno* to bed—if not its owner, alas. It seemed to me, in its worn Penguin paperback cover, less "a classic" than a gift from the woman who gave it to me, something personal, the memento of a night talking about Dante's adventure, his metaphorical journey that would provide direction to my own somewhat awkward flight from what had been my life. Dante begins (I'm using Seamus Heaney's translation of canto 1 here because I no longer have that ancient Penguin):[1]

In the middle of the journey of our life,
I found myself astray in a dark wood
where the straight road had been lost sight of.

The text was now personal and immediate—a gift and a message from Tove, who, by the time I woke, had already departed. This would be true of many books I read—not departure but text as an extension of something personal.

I read the *Inferno* as an adventure story, an odyssey to the many dark places we are capable of finding our way to. A catalogue of dire dreams, a masquerade of altered states of being, as I read it then—room after room of misery, penance in the process of being paid out into an infinite future.

I had already begun to write a sort of poetry in my first year of college because I watched my college roommate (Samuel McElresh was his name) write love poems to his girlfriend in the dorm next to ours; he'd read them to her from the grass below her room, at midnight. This made a remarkable impression on me—it resonated of a journey very different from any I had imagined growing up in the San Fernando Valley of Los Angeles. For the first time, I could envision an itinerary I could shape and make my own.

When he wasn't writing poems to his Beatrice, Sam read chapters of *Don Quixote* out loud. So when I eventually began my descent with Dante and Virgil in Perpignan, I had as preparation and partner the bright voice and presence of Don Quixote, not to mention his pal Sancho and the horse Rocinante, who traveled a different journey, possessed a different vision. I was ready for Virgil and the road ahead:

"What you have said has turned my heart around
   so much that I am as ready to come now
   as I was before I started losing ground.
Go on, then, for one will inform us both.

You are my guide, my master and my teacher."
This is what I said, and when he moved
I entered on the deep and savage path.
            (*Inf.* 2.136–42, tr. Seamus Heaney)

I'm a slow reader—I read only a canto or two a night, beginning that night in Perpignan. By way of Dante, I was able to imagine the journey that became my own, away from my past in Los Angeles—thanks, in part, to Sam and the escapades of Cervantes' Knight of La Mancha—"one of those old-fashioned gentlemen who are never without a lance upon a rack, an old target, a lean horse, and a greyhound"—and of course to Tove and her edition of the *Inferno*, which became mine. And finally I arrived at the beginning of my own work. The territory I've been able to cover through language, I see these many years later, had rejected, early on, the abstract in favor of tracking the actual event. I leave for my daughter a collection of poems that marks her father's journey.

It was Dante, who along with Cervantes, mapped what seemed to me, as a young man, the extremes of human destiny, not to put too fine a point on this. Yet now when I read their books, they seem not extreme but simply two different visions of inherited worlds, two sensibilities of this one world. As texts, they are wonderful counselors to anyone mindful of the life to be led. The *Inferno* provides narrative and personality—a history brought to life by making it interactive the moment Dante steps onto that deep and savage path. I discovered upon reading other literary "classics" (the *Odyssey* or the stories of Chekhov) the ways in which I was engaged and guided by their episodic constructions, their ability to accommodate the formal requirements they set for themselves—adding the stamp of their distinctive voice, even through translation. Dante and Cervantes, in their modern works, made narratives out of the fabric of their lives and times, whether via fantasy, history, or an invented projection of both. They are writers who inhabit their writing, writers who recreate existing worlds, rewrite history and then extend it. Reading the *Inferno*, I was given an index to my own history and the chance to reshape that history, to make sense of it in this semi-fictional world we inherit—isn't life, as it's actually lived, random and chaotic?

Dante continued with me south, in Spain through Barcelona, Valencia—a night of reading in a Spanish prison converted into a youth hostel (how appropriate it seemed, how imitative this life!) in Alicante—deeper into Dante, deeper south: Málaga, Seville, Algeciras. And finally onto the continent of Africa, where I discovered, climbing up from the Port of Tangier, the city of Tangier, the city that would draw me back and alter the path my life would take. I finished the final canto of the *Inferno* my first night in Tangier, in the Hotel Carlton in the Socco Chico, an inferno of a hotel to be sure (life again caught imitating art), but a fitting end to Dante's journey and the beginning of mine. Just down the street, I could hear a group of local *gnoua* musicians playing for the tourists sipping mint tea from glass tumblers in the Cafe Central. Their music accompanied Dante and me as we burst back to this earth.

> My guide and I set out on that hidden path
>   to make our way into the bright world again,
>   and so we climbed with no thought of rest—
> He first and I second—until we reached ground
>   where I could see through a rounded opening
>   the night sky with the beautiful things it carries;
> And we came out and looked up at the stars.
>   (*Inf.* 34.133–39, tr. Robert Hass)

Note

1. Translations are from Daniel Halpern, ed., *Dante's Inferno: Translations by Twenty Contemporary Poets* (Hopewell, N.J.: Ecco Press, 1993).

Alan Williamson

The Tears of Cocytus

It is hard to put my relation to Dante into a few words, or even a few pages. Suffice it to say that I started reading him seriously, in the original, when I was near the midpoint of our life, and found myself in a dark wood. His experience that such a condition was escapable both interpreted and helped my own. He replaced Proust, and to some degree even Rilke, as the writer I was always referring back to, in refiguring my life. My Dante, then, is irrevocably a psychological Dante, and follows the pattern Jungians call the "night journey"—the descent into the darkest possibilities of our own selves and of collective human nature, that seems world-shattering when it comes on us out of the blue, but may paradoxically be the only way to true human growth.

For me, then, the *Inferno* is about the terrible stasis of this initial deadlock with darkness, as experienced in obsession or depression. The *Purgatorio* is the tremulous amazement (the sea "trembles" in its first lines) of recovery; the delight that, however much pain and incapacity persist, the light, the stars, the green hills are still there and can touch the soul. And the *Paradiso* is an attempt to describe happiness, and its relation to experiences of inter-identity with others, on a level that only our subtlest psychologists, writers like D. W. Winnicott or Jessica Benjamin, have begun to approximate.

Imagine my surprise and distress, then, to find just how far my way of reading Dante was from that standard in literature departments! The despised nineteenth century, it seemed, had been more willing to modernize and psychologize him than the Moderns were. Medieval literary studies, more than any other field, seemed afflicted with the notion that the literature of a time could only be understood legitimately in terms of that time's explicit ideology. Not only was any kind of psychological universalism anathema; only a few venturesome critics—V. A. Kolve, for instance—had even gone outside theology to popular culture for evidence that a more free-wheeling medieval imagination existed.

Yet my whole way of reading as a poet told me that Dante "was not for an age, but for all time"; that (like all great imaginative writers, I believe), he emits high frequencies in his metaphors and sounds that only later ages, informed by other experience, will be able to transcribe as conceptual thought. In that sense, I am no more "wrong" to read a psychological Dante than he was to read a Christian Virgil.

Canto 33 of the *Inferno* is the only passage in Dante I can point to as having specifically influenced my own work. It came back to me when I was trying to give shape to a very particular unpleasant feeling—the obsessive, haunted reaction that I, and I think many people, have to hearing about cruel or terrible events, and the odd feeling of complicity, as if becoming preoccupied with such acts proved one capable of performing them. Before it occurred to me that canto 33 could give me a structure for certain interrelated stories—as it did, eventually, in a poem called "Speakers from the Ice"—I knew it was the psychic atmosphere I was wandering in. An atmosphere, too, that called up some of the particular nightmares of the twentieth century—the Battle of Stalingrad, the terrible winters of Siberia and Auschwitz, naked prisoners lined up on their way to the gas chambers. For us, I believe, whatever specific crimes Dante chose to punish there, the ice is the place where a certain degree of atrocity has made the good of life unbelievable; where there is no emotion but a gnawing, useless, infinite rage. It is thus one of those symbols in literature that have outleapt their original intellectual framework to become parts of the collective imagination, Yeats's *anima mundi.*

I wrote the essay that follows some years after I wrote the poem, partly to clarify the moral assistance I had gotten from Dante, partly to explore a pattern of imagery which, as far as I know, no one else—except one poet friend in Berkeley, in private conversation—has noticed.

The finality of atrocity, the impossibility of living beyond it, haunts the late-twentieth-century mind. None of the normal human responses seem available. Grief is the usual way back to moral health, the way that keeps us open to empathy with all victims and fellow sufferers. But in mourning there is an element of acceptance; and how does one accept the unacceptable? Retaliatory rage may seem the preferable, the more virile response; but rage can never end, since the crime can never be undone. It locks victim and persecutor, prosecutor and defendant, into a terrible and eternal twinship.

And here, as elsewhere, we find that Dante has gone before us, and way in advance of the thinking of his own time. The Cocytus cantos center on a story of atrocity and permanent retaliation:

> We had left him, moving on
> When I saw two shades frozen in a single hole—
> Packed so close, one hooded the other one;
> The way the starving devour their bread, the one
> Above had clenched the other with his teeth
> Where the brain meets the nape.[1]
>
> (*Inf.* 32.124–29)

Count Ugolino has watched his children starve, and (as many readers take it) has been driven by hunger to cannibalize their dead bodies. Now, throughout eternity, he repeats the crime on its perpetrator, satisfying his hunger with Archbishop Ruggieri's brains.

Ugolino's story is so affecting that readers almost forget (as with Paolo and Francesca, or Ulysses) that he, too, is a sinner, and deserves to be in Hell. Modern commentators, unwilling to base their interpretations on a technicality which has no emotional weight in the poem (Ugolino, too, is a traitor; he did betray the Pisans' castles), have argued that Ugolino's real sin lies in his response to his fate. His children, John Freccero suggests, model for him the Christ-like response to undeserved suffering, one of empathy and self-sacrifice:

> "Father, our pain," they said,
> "Will lessen if you eat us—you are the one
> Who clothed us in this wretched flesh: we plead
> For you to be the one who strips it away."
> (*Inf.* 33.61–63)

Ugolino, Freccero writes,

> seems to be unaware of the Christological significance of the children's suffering and his own. As they die, they echo the words first of Job—"The Lord gave, and the Lord hath taken away"—and then of the Saviour on the Cross—"My God, why hast thou forsaken me?" Ugolino's response is simply to repress his own grief for fear of increasing theirs.
>
> The children's apparently naive offer of their flesh echoes Jesus' offer to the disciples in John 6: "Whoso eateth my flesh . . . hath eternal life." . . . Because Ugolino does not understand, there is no redemption.[2]

Ugolino, trapped by his anger and his terrible sense of responsibility, is incapable of a self-forgetful response like his children's; and the sign of his incapacity is *tears*. Ugolino asks the hearer to weep for him ("and if not now, then when do you shed a tear?"); and he himself weeps as he tells his story. But in the moment, the stoniness of despair makes any expression of emotion impossible:

> Inside me I was turned to stone, so hard
> I could not weep; the children wept.
> (*Inf.* 33.49–50)

Finally, his rage at his own powerlessness, lacking another outlet, turns on himself—in the same gesture with which, in eternity, it will turn on his enemy: "I bit my hands for grief." And this is the gesture which his children misunderstand, when they offer themselves as food.

What Freccero does not say—but it seems clear enough—is that Dante the character follows Ugolino, expressing grief only as rage. As the Canadian-American poet Peter Dale Scott, whose thinking in this area has influenced mine more than I can easily sort out, writes in an unpublished poem, Dante

> when invited to weep

> at the fate of Ugolino
>   cursed all Pisa and its children
>   until the sight of Beatrice

> released from his frozen heart
>   a great deluge of tears[3]

The curse is indeed one of startling ferocity:

> Ah, Pisa! You shamed the peoples of that fair land
>   Where sì is spoken: slow as your neighbors are
>   To punish you, may Gorgona shift its ground,

And Capraia, till those islands make a bar
　To dam the Arno, and drown your populace—
　Every soul in you!

(Inf. 33.79–84)

One might even say that Dante, as a character, is repeating the crime of Archbishop Ruggieri, sweeping up the innocent along with the guilty—Ugolino's "figliuoli," "every soul" in Pisa.

But this brings us to one of the great dividing points in Dante criticism. For historicist readers, including most modern dantisti, there is no question Dante belonged to an age with few scruples about moral vindictiveness. Burnings at the stake, breakings on the wheel were public entertainments; and Dante himself thought so well of the Albigensian Crusade that he put two of the chief persecutors in Paradise. Virgil commends Dante elsewhere—though not in Cocytus—for his anger against sinners.

But if one believes poets sometimes write better than they know; if one risks universalism by reading the Comedy as a journey through permanent states of the human psyche, then one will be particularly interested in the places where Dante the character seems to mirror the crimes he describes. Dante, like Ugolino and Ruggieri, is a good hater; and there is no question his inhumanity increases the closer he gets to the bottom of Cocytus. Already in canto 32, Dante compulsively ("I don't know whether by will or fate or chance") kicks one sinner in the face, then deliberately tears out the hair of another to force him to reveal his name. And, as I shall argue, the architecture of canto 33, both narrative and symbolic, forces the issue of Dante's behavior to the center of our attention.

For canto 33 is an extraordinarily broken-backed piece of work, unless one presumes some subtler thematic governing principle. Where the other great set pieces (Francesca, Ser Brunetto, Ulysses) all terminate with their respective cantos, Ugolino's story and the curse against Pisa bring us only to line 90. The rest of the canto tells a completely different story, bringing us round, however, to a precisely parallel curse against Genoa and all *its* inhabitants:

> Ah Genoese—to every accustomed good,
>   Strangers; with every corruption, amply crowned:
>   Why hasn't the world expunged you as it should?
>   (*Inf.* 33.151–53)

In between the two curses, Dante commits his own greatest act of treachery, promising, and then refusing, to clear the ice away from Fra Alberigo's eyes. He justifies the act by asserting a complete reversal, or suspension, of moral norms: "to be rude / To such a one as him was courtesy."

The equivocations surrounding Dante's broken promise are easy to catch and chuckle over; but their ultimate moral meaning is harder to assess. "[I]f I don't help you then, / May I be sent to the bottom of the ice" (*Inf.* 33.116–17). We know that he will go there—will have to haul himself up the tufts of hair on Satan's thighs—but only as a tourist. Or is it only as a tourist? "Oh souls so cruel that here, / Of all the stations, you're assigned the last" (110–11), Fra Alberigo addresses Dante and Virgil. It is a mistake other damned souls have made before; but Dante's behavior *is* "cruel," the cruelest we have seen from him in the poem. And it is at this very moment that he first feels the "wind" from the "bottom," from Satan's wings, though he hardly knows he feels it, because "as when a callus has grown numb, / The cold had sucked all feeling from my face"(100–2) — a physical insensibility it is hard not to give a moral meaning.

"E cortesia fu lui esser villano." I am sure many a medieval man, and many a medievalist, has clapped his hands in agreement with Dante, at this point. And still I suspect this parody of the moral norm, this absolute zero of human obligation, may *be* "the last station." For Primo Levi, a comparable statement, "Hier ist

kein warum" (Here there don't have to be reasons), was the very
motto of Auschwitz; but the utter lapse of empathy distressed him
more in his fellow prisoners even than in the Nazis themselves.

The ultimate argument of canto 33—its supreme, subterranean
genius—lies in the continued manipulation of the motif of tears.
The inability to weep, figurative or psychological in Ugolino, becomes literal in those more deeply damned:

> There, weeping keeps them from weeping—for as they do,
> Grief finds a barrier where the eyes would weep
>   But forced back inward, adds to their agonies;
>   A crystal visor of prior tears fills the cup
> Below the eyebrow with a knot of ice.
>
> (*Inf.* 33.94–99)

The tears that are not expressed are themselves the punishment;
they torment the inner self by isolation and constriction, as the
growing "crystal visor" would constrict the eyes. And these are the
tears that Dante refuses to clear away from Fra Alberigo's face.

Now look back at the curse against Pisa: the Arno, the two islands that will block it at its mouth, drowning all the inhabitants . . . It is the same figure! A flow, a blockage, and then the
backward turning of the same flow as an endless malignity, against
the self or against others. "They become what they behold,"
William Blake wrote. Dante's anger, concretized in Capraia and
Gorgona, *is* the punishment he witnesses, and will not sympathize
with, in Fra Alberigo.

And, of course, the two images repeat a third image, from earlier in the canto: the "nailing shut [of] the door" to Ugolino's
"fearful tower." The finality of atrocity, the boundless repercussions
of unbounded anger, resound in the figuration as in the story itself: Dante invents one more terrible metaphor for this finality, in
the strange fiction that makes up most of Fra Alberigo's story. "[A]s

soon as a soul commits betrayal / the way I did," Fra Alberigo says, it "falls headlong" into Hell, and "a devil displaces it / And governs inside the body until its toll / of years elapses" (*Inf.* 33.129–32). What Dante means, I think, is that certain acts prevent the soul from changing, from giving its life a new significance, as even the worst of ordinary sinners can. To be sure, this fiction serves Dante's need to put men like Fra Alberigo outside the moral pale. But my main reaction to this passage has always been horror and pity for the zombie-like body above, that "eats and drinks and sleeps and puts on clothes," but has no further moral life. I have felt the same watching Claude Lanzmann's *Shoah*, listening to the hollowed-out voices of death-camp guards, telling their stories to a narrator who, like Dante, breaks promises, because he feels no bond of reciprocal humanity.

In insisting as it does on the image of tears, canto 33 seems always to bring us back to the release of grief—grief that makes us vulnerable, since it admits that what is done can never be undone—as what moves us forward in life, whereas anger only breeds further anger. Grief restores our human brotherhood, as Ugolino's children always remain in empathetic contact with him, though he cannot be in contact with them. The drying or freezing up of these capacities is the *contrapasso*, the sin that is its own punishment. Expression in language is part of the same liquidity, as the imagery at the end of canto 32 tells us: "if that with which I speak does not go dry." And perhaps it is because Dante retains this power—continues to bear mindful witness to himself, as he plunges into the cul-de-sac of ultimate hatred—that he survives in spirit.

When my thinking had worked itself through to this point, I happened to come on some musings by Michael Mazur, the great illustrator of Robert Pinsky's great translation of *Inferno*:

I think that the most overriding element of the whole *Inferno* is not the horror of the *Inferno*. It is, in fact, the sadness of the *Inferno* . . . There is this strange rhythmic movement of water through the whole *Inferno* down to the ice field at the end. Sometimes it's blood; sometimes it's water; sometimes it's sewage. And in each case, it comes from one mysterious source, some old man who is shedding his tears in a faraway land, supposedly Crete. Those tears then turn into rivers and the rivers turn into large areas of ice.[4]

The old man of Crete appears in canto 14. Hidden inside Mount Ida, he is the mourner (and, perhaps, the former king) of the Golden Age, which the ancients located in Crete.

> Every part but the gold head bears a crack,
>   A fissure dripping tears that collect and force
>   Their passage down the cavern from rock to rock
> Into this valley's depth, where as a source
>   They form the Acheron, Styx, and Phlegethon,
>   Then their way down is by this narrow course
> Until, where all descending has been done,
>   They form Cocytus—and about that pool
>   I will say nothing, for you will see it soon.
>   (*Inf.* 14.112–20)

So the tears of Cocytus *are* the ice of Cocytus, and both another metamorphosis of the Virgilian "tears of things"—the tears that Dante, as Peter Dale Scott remarks, is finally able to weep, when he meets Beatrice in Purgatory. Or, as another of my master-guides, Rilke, put it, "Killing too is a form of our wandering mourning."[5] Marvelous!

Notes

1. This, and all subsequent quotations, are taken from Robert Pinsky, *The Inferno of Dante: A New Verse Translation* (New York: Farrar, Straus and Giroux, 1994), p. 347.

2. John Freccero, note to Robert Pinsky, *Inferno*, p. 424.

3. Peter Dale Scott, *Minding the Darkness* (unpublished poem), IV, xiii.

4. Robert Pinsky and Michael Mazur, *Image and Text* (Berkeley: Occasional Papers of the Doreen B. Townsend Center for the Humanities, 1994), p. 37.

5. Rainer Maria Rilke, *Sonnets to Orpheus*, 2.11 (my translation).

Mark Doty

Rooting for the Damned

I have never been especially comfortable with masterpieces of a grand scale, the heroic gesture, the cosmological scheme. Given the choice between the Sistine Chapel and Vermeer, I'd take the latter anytime. I prefer the precisely delineated light through one Northern window to a whole sea of writhing saints. Perhaps it's a distrust of some kinds of transcendence, the sort that seem public and institutional; perhaps it's simply a rebellious streak, which resists looking for meaning where it is well known to reside, and resists finding grandeur where grandeur is expected. Certain masterworks seem to come with a whole apparatus attached, like a cathedral wrapped in scaffolding: the structure of explanation, interpretation, and opinion makes it hard to see down to the architectural substance. It is easy to feel, in the face of such tradition, that one doesn't have much freedom or authority to like or dislike, or to discern when there is a whole canon of discernment before us.

Some texts can hardly be detached from their commentaries, since time has dimmed readers' acquaintance with circumstances and characters essential to the narrative—characters who seem to matter now primarily because they've been pickled in the brine and honey of the verse. This is more of an issue in the *Comedy* than it is in, say, Chaucer, whose characters need little in the way

of introduction, while Dante's huge cast of Guelphs and Ghibellines can't be told apart without a program.

Therefore, I bring to this universe of a poem a certain resistance, and I hadn't felt compelled to return to it for a while, until
the publication of Robert Pinsky's forceful and vital translation of
the *Inferno* drew me in. Following the muscular, supple progression
of the cantos, I found myself feeling a little guilty to be more interested in the details than in the whole picture. Had I forgotten,
or never really paid attention to, the way this big, crowded canvas—world upon world!—is crowded with local incident, with
particularity, details not really of the next life but of this one, the
sort that begin to endear the voice of the poem to the reader?

Here, for instance, the pilgrim narrator has just come across a
band of shades

> Who looked at us the way that men will look
> At one another at dusk, when daylight fails
> Under a new moon: knitting their brows at us
> The way old tailors do when threading needles.[1]
>
> (Inf. 15.18–21)

That simile has about it the unmistakable quality of observation;
to know this were true, you would need to have noticed not just
tailors at work, but long-experienced seamsters who were losing
their vision. As an instance of worldly knowledge, it achieves two
things for Dante's poem: it makes the speaker more credible, and it
makes the otherworldly seem more likely to us—more possible,
since the next life is full of resemblance to this one.

But I have to confess that my real pleasure lies in the recorded
act of witness itself, the notation of perception. In her book on
Dutch painting in the seventeenth century, *The Art of Describing*,
Svetlana Alpers draws a distinction between Italian art and the art
of the North. The former, she suggests, emphasizes narrative, the
painting as a window through which we see a world, while the art

of the North focuses on description, conceiving of the picture as more of a surface, like a map or a mirror. Dante's hurrying *terza rima* is the physical form of a great narrative motion, a long plunging look through a cosmic window, but all along the way, our attention is arrested by beautiful bits of detail, acts of seeing which humanize the whole.

Here is one that occurs a little earlier, in canto 14: "All over the sand / Distended flakes of fire drifted from aloft / Slowly as mountain snow without a wind." Just as the adjective that noted the tailors' years clinched that detail, making it alive, so an adjective here delivers the texture of actuality. The suggestion that snow falls differently in a windless mountain landscape than it does down on a windless plain implies a familiarity with landscape and weather, the fabric of the world. I begin to imagine Dante noticing, noticing— going to have clothing fitted, visiting a friend in the mountains. The poet indulges his eye for the particular, storing information, squirreling away details which become means of seeing.

Sometimes such detail seems offered less because it illuminates the actions and conditions of the next life than because it is interesting and valuable in itself. In canto 21, for instance, when the pilgrim traverses Malebolge, an abyss of boiling pitch makes Dante think of off-season activity in the vast spaces of the Arsenal in Venice:

> As is done
> In winter, when the sticky pitch is boiled
>   In the Venetian arsenal to caulk
>   Their unsound vessels while no ship can be sailed,
> And so instead one uses the time to make
>   His ship anew, another one repairs
>   Much-voyaged ribs, and some with hammers strike
> The prow, and some the stern; and this one makes oars
>   While that one might twist rope, another patch
>   The jib and mainsail—
>
> (Inf. 21.7–15)

That aside is not strictly necessary in order to suggest the boiling pitch of Hell. Dante is interested in telling us about Venice, and about what goes on in a particular realm of labor, the less familiar part of a sailor's working life. This sort of detail is here out of delight, perhaps out of that same impulse to make a crowded human canvas which Robert Browning, five hundred years later, ascribed to Fra Lippo Lippi.

Dante's poem is full of such instances of seeing, a world of evidence. He has firsthand knowledge of leaping dolphins, decamping soldiers, ducks fleeing from falcons, a dog attacking a hare, sluices of water turning mill wheels. He has watched a knife blade remove scales from a carp; he remarks how "wet hands smoke in winter"; he notes "the hour when the fly gives way / to the mosquito." Here he is watching paper burn: "as the track / of flame moves over paper, there is a shade / That moves before it that is not yet black, / And the white dies away." This is startlingly exact, and it reflects a catholic interest, taking all the stuff of the world as a set of instances to be studied, considered, examined for their own value as well as employed in description. He behaves, in these passages, more like a scientist than a metaphysician, but this observant turn of mind makes us far more likely to accept his visionary perceptions, since it suggests that all his seeing is of a piece—the roseate glories of Heaven observed with precisely the same acuity as that given to a burning sheet of paper, or the vapor rising from cold, wet hands.

Nonetheless, to my taste, Dante's worldly eye remains a greater source of pleasure than the orders of Heaven, or the horrors of Hell and the moral and political dramas, satirical or earnest, enacted there. I imagine this marks me as a twentieth-century reader, with a modern distrust of large claims; it may speak to an inability to quite imagine fixed theaters of eternity. But whether it is my failing or not, I can't be truthful without speaking in favor of the local, the unweighted, the quotidian plain. Here is perhaps my fa-

vorite passage in the *Inferno*, an extended metaphor for a rapid alternation of despair and hope.

> In that part of the young year when the sun
>   Goes under Aquarius to rinse his beams,
>   And the long nights already begin to wane
> Toward half the day, and when the hoarfrost mimes
>   The image of her white sister upon the ground—
>   But only a while, because her pen, it seems
> Is not sharp long—a peasant who has found
>   That he is running short of fodder might rise
>   And go outside and see the fields have turned
> To white, and slap his thigh, and back in the house
>   Pace grumbling here and there like some poor wretch
>   Who can't see what to do; and then he goes
> Back out, and finds hope back within his reach,
>   Seeing in how little time the world outside
>   Has changed its face, and takes his crook to fetch
> His sheep to pasture. I felt this way . . .
>   (*Inf.* 24.1–16)

It takes fifteen lines in Italian (fifteen and a half for Pinsky) to
come around to "Così mi fece"—"I felt this way"—fifteen lines
to arrive at the point of the comparison! Surely, this is because
these lines delineate, in themselves, something essential about the
world, as if Dante had sketched in the corner of his great manu-
script's page a little cartouche, like those small views which sometimes adorn the edges of old maps. Here is a miniature of hope;
here is a deeply attentive look at both frost and at the evanescence
of human feeling, how despair may melt as quickly as hoarfrost itself.

    Such a portrait of a singular moment is more what I want from
poetry than great schemes of moral cosmology or broad maps of
social life. If my pleasures belong to a minor category of art—as I

am not, of course, convinced they do—they are nonetheless sustaining ones.

But, of course, there is still more to my Dante problem. As a reader come of age in the twentieth century's second half, perched here on the rim of the twenty-first, I cannot muster much enthusiasm for a God who consigns his children the sodomites to a burning plain—even if you convince me he is a brilliant point of light, or that the sodomites' own failure to control their passions has isolated them from divine love, so it's their own fault they're getting doused with burning rain. I doubt that many contemporary readers feel at ease with Dante's judgments; who really condemns Paolo and Francesca, or the wrenching grief of Ugolino? Of course, one does not wish to transport the ethical standard of one's own time backward into everything one reads, but the *Inferno* begs the question by demanding that we consider the relative demerits of various sins; it requires our participation in a moral economy.

In canto 15—to my mind, one of the poem's strangest moments—Dante establishes a particularly troubling ambiguity. Our pilgrim narrator honors his beloved old teacher, Brunetto Latini, who is one of those ghosts with an old tailor's knotted brows. As they walk together—Latini at a lower level because he's down in the scorching sand—the pilgrim bends his head toward the older man "as if in reverence." Latini praises Dante's work, predicts a bright future for him; the pilgrim responds by praising his mentor as "dear, fatherly, benevolent."

But Latini, however kind and helpful he may have been to Dante, is forever confined to the Hell of those who have done violence against nature, and the pilgrim actually asks him to name names of the other shades who accompany him. Latini says he doesn't have time to name them all, since they're so numerous, but he does let on that they are all "clerics and men of letters," then goes ahead and names a few.

The ending of the canto is extraordinary. Latini asserts that he lives on in his work, the books he left behind on earth; by implication, his position in the realm of death is thus less important. "And he went off," Dante tells us,

> Seeming to me like one of those who run
>   Competing for the green cloth in the races
>   Upon Verona's field—and of them, like one
> Who gains the victory, not one who loses.
>   (*Inf.* 15.121–24)

This is a beautiful image of triumph, made especially poignant in that it describes the movement of a shade disappearing back into inescapable darkness. Latini's soul has, at least metaphorically, won, and the figure seems of a piece with the way the pilgrim has been speaking to him. For a moment, it seems as if the poet has inscribed here a remarkable act of rebellion, by affirming the dignity and victory of this writer and teacher despite his sin.

Oh, but it is the pilgrim Dante, the *character* who approves and lauds. The poet Dante has "outed" Latini—who was not known as a sodomite in his own time—and placed him in the depths of Hell. It is not an attractive gesture, and it raises inevitable questions: who is this poet who so energetically conjures a world of torture, an endlessly imaginative range of ways to exact revenge? Suddenly the pitying, awestruck pilgrim seems disingenuous, the ethical terms of the entire poem thrown in question. Doesn't he lament, with one side of his mouth, the cruelty of the universe, while with the other he—quite literally—makes it so? I'm not complaining merely about Christian condemnation of sexual behavior; Dante actually lets the sodomites off more easily than he does lots of other sinners. And he does place them in *Purgatorio* 26 on their way to Eden. But this canto raises questions of friendship and loyalty, the relations between students and teachers, between any of us and those we admire. How are we to reconcile the kindness of those lines with the cruelty which conceived this circumstance in the first place?

I do not have any specific answer to this question, which does not cease to trouble me in Dante, but perhaps I do have a general one. If the *Comedy* is a crowded map of human character—a costume show in which a vast earthly cast is got up as angels and devils— then it must contain generosity and cruelty, forgiveness and judgment. In a great poem, the conflicts and tensions in human character are reconciled simply by being yoked together. By "reconciled" I do not mean resolved, but only that the strains of the self may pull against one another, may exist in intense opposition, because they are held together by formal principles strong enough to contain them. Dante's poem is, of course, a vastly articulated formal strategy, a funnel-shaped extravaganza of infernal and celestial mathematics. However, it is on the local level that one most vividly experiences the power of that formality, in the supple strength and unifying form of the *terza rima*.

I used to know a window dresser—a profession containing enough sodomites to populate many a burning plain!—who was a talented practitioner of his art. He told me that he would never place an even number of objects in a display window; there was always one umbrella, three wineglasses, five bracelets, or seven umbrellas. Even numbers, he said, made things appear inert, at rest, while odd numbers produced in the viewer the subtle urge to complete the assemblage, to create unity by finding the missing piece.

Godhead, were it composed only of Father and Son, would feel likewise static; it's that third, the vital emanation that is the Holy Ghost, that makes the whole thing take flight. Dante's brilliant formal invention takes ultimate advantage of this momentum. The tercet seems forever unstable, tilting forward; each stanza compels us on to the next. Rhyme enhances this movement through the chiming across stanzas, the sense of a brief completion each stanza delivers to the one before while simultaneously refusing to complete entirely, requiring us to keep reading in order to "finish" the rhyme.

Two suggests opposition, duality. When a third element is introduced, relations are always more complicated. We can never have a simple resolution, in the victory of one part or the other, nor mere binary opposition. Instead, the presence of the third requires a blending, a harmonization of elements, or at least a constant dynamism.

The effect is mobile and liquid, and it binds together a great deal of disparate stuff. The verse becomes a medium in which hang suspended cruelty and grace, darkness and promise, the experience of being lost and the steady radiance of certainty.

Part of the effect of this seamless formal accomplishment is an astonishing sense of authority; combine that with the poem's visionary claims and one has the feeling that to argue with Dante is to argue with God himself. This returns me to my masterpiece problem: were Dante not so psychologically acute, I don't think I could stand this massive dose of authority, the poem as scripture. But over and over again, the text is enlivened by a kind of understanding that doesn't necessarily have to do with Christian cosmology. The circumstances of the pilgrim are everyone's, and their appeal, on a mythic level, is inexhaustible: we all awake lost in the wood; the world darkens for each of us; we descend, we grope through moral uncertainty, we look to be lifted. "In the bright life above," he says to Brunetto Latini,

> I came into a valley and lost my way,
> Before my age had reached its ripening time—
> (Inf. 15.50–51)

Who hasn't felt such a loss of certainty and direction? What is mid-life but a loss of the way? From this point of view, the clambering down the talus slopes of Hell and the winding climb up the slopes of Purgatory before the flowering into Paradise seem like a traversing of the possibilities of human character, as if a soul's possibilities could all be laid out, given form, and seen in themselves to equal a world.

Would it be, then, too much a modern imposition to suggest that what troubles me in *Inferno* 15 troubles Dante as well? That the canto feels so contradictory and unresolved because it oscillates between respect and judgment, gratitude and bitterness, reflecting the confusing mixtures of nobility and failure which human character must always reveal? Perhaps this is merely my rereading (or rewriting) of the poem. What it offers, however, is an interpretation that does justice to the image with which Dante leaves us, in the haunting conclusion of *Inferno* 15, as the old teacher—poet, encyclopedist, sodomite—disappears back into Hell's darkness, like one of those runners "who gains the victory, not one who loses." Certainly, I want him to win, whatever God—or Dante—proposes.

C. K. Williams

Souls

There are moments in the *Comedy* when figures appear before Dante and introduce themselves by saying, "I am the soul of . . ." Not I *am* so and so, but "I am the soul . . ." When I come across those moments, I always feel an edge of dismay, or envy, or something deeper than either. In my world, in the portion of the drama of history of which I partake, I've never found the place from which to regard myself or the world in a way that would allow me to use with any confidence such terms concerning the nature of, if not the human, then my own existence. When I use the word "soul," or the word "spirit," to refer to something in my life or anyone else's (and I have often enough), I realize I'm creating a space in myself for something to occur, but what does occur is a hope, an aspiration, toward wholeness, toward the comprehensive vision of self and the universe which the words imply but by no means entail. Neither word ever comes to my mind without evoking a rueful feeling of having deceived myself, and my language, and, in some sense, the truth of my life.

Still, when those beings called "souls" do come before Dante to complain or explain or, at the end, to exalt, I feel not skepticism but a terrific relief, as though a kind of consummation had been offered to me that never quite can be provided by anything else, in literature or life. Dante can deploy the concept of soul with a conviction I can share, not because I agree with his religious beliefs, but because he has elaborated a poetic vision that connects our conscious life to a personal idea of self and to a larger scheme of the human, as well as to what is beyond but accessible to humans and to which we are ultimately responsible.

And I think I can bring myself to believe in, to accept, Dante's "systems," because the poetical-ethical vision he elaborates has been shriven of any degree of synthetic innocence, of any moral pose which would have self-forgiveness assumed for it in advance. When we give ourselves to Dante, to the poetry he weaves and the cosmology he elaborates, we're ever afterward embedded in a realm in which ethic and act are sensually fused, and we experience the conclusions to which our ethical, spiritual meditations have committed us as though in the sensitive flesh of consciousness. Dante doesn't create a morality in which we can enclose and so protect ourselves; he convinces us that the conditions for an ethical existence are already entire within us, and, most importantly for me, he defines these conditions as complete, complete enough to contain all that humans can be or aspire to; it's up to us to bring ourselves into accord with that vision. Our falling away doesn't necessarily mean we are evil, but it does mean that we might be existing in the same ambiguity and indecisiveness from which the *Inferno* demonstrates that most evil is generated.

It is, of course, just that demonstration, or more precisely the poetry that embodies it, which is everything. Because the imaginative business of the poem is the fusion of the absolutely concrete with the wholly ineffable, of the indelibly physical with the moral, of value with code, passion with will, intention with outcome. Its genius gleams in its symbolizations of act and emotion, and the metaphoric transfigurations of both, and it makes of our world a material on which mind can and perhaps has to meditate as a function of its own structure and substance. So it may be that we have no terms other than "soul" and "spirit" to capture the complexities of what happens to us when we're drawn into such an exacting unity of sensibility and reflection.

At the end, although there is certainly much strictness in the ethical method of the *Comedy*, the cosmology it presents, even to a nonbeliever, is benevolent and rich with hope. So much so that sometimes I think that what we've lived through in our recent history has been too vile, too willfully cruel, for this benevolence to seem more than a wistful conceit. There has been too much mindless and mindful malignity, too many hecatombs and holocausts for even Dante's cosmos to contain. Sometimes it can seem as though Purgatory now would have to be a mountain of burnt flesh; would a consciousness creeping woefully across it be able then to proclaim itself the "soul" or "spirit," even of itself? Homer might have had the poetic language to show how we become, how perhaps we ever will be brutes who almost gleefully tear each other to pieces; and Shakespeare, our poet of eternal becoming, of the tenuousness of moral character, had the poetry to describe what we can make of ourselves—there have been so many Richards—but can we imagine the rose of holy love blooming from all this human ash? Our evils seem to be so much more *abashing* than Dante's; our entire world system is called into account by having beheld civilization degraded in ways even Dante couldn't imagine.

And yet . . . Recently I came across a passage in a book in which Franz Stangl, the commandant of the death camp at Treblinka, recounts his initial arrival at the camp, before he assumes command and before the last filament of humanity has been consumed in him. "Treblinka," Stangl says, "was the most awful thing I'd ever seen . . . It was Dante's Inferno, it was Dante come to life." That even a depraved criminal like Stangl could find no referent more apt to describe his revulsion makes us realize again just how capacious and compelling the metaphysical drama was which Dante, and Dante alone, elaborated for us.

Mary Baine Campbell

Wrath, Order, Paradise

And you mortals, keep yourselves restrained in judging; for we,

who see God, know not yet all the elect.

Paradiso 20.133–35

During the pre-apocalyptic summer of 1999, I reread Dante's *Comedy* for the first time without notes or commentary at hand. It was an interesting experiment, reading an old, old poem intended to exist outside of its time with neither commentary nor a *dantista*'s knowledge of Italian micropolitics. I felt stormy often, as many have before me: for Northrop Frye, the *Inferno* was "the greatest obscenity of the Middle Ages." After the mobility and eros and orient sapphire of *Purgatorio*, where everyone climbs the same mountain, passing through the same seven territories of reparation at varying speeds, it was raining hard in Heaven when I found again, harder to bear this time, the judgments, placing and fixing human souls in hierarchical order—the first of the blessed Dante meets begins immediately to explain for what fault she has been placed "in the slowest sphere" (*Par.* 3.51; tr. Charles Singleton).

The ordinal fixation of Dante's spiritual cosmos brings the image of his Paradise into close relation with the oppressive orders of the military, of racial caste (mulatto, quadroon, octoroon), of class. Ordination first, rationalization second. A colleague says to my objections: "But it's still important to keep the *ideal* of justice," and I say, perhaps insanely, "No: it is precisely that ideal which wreaks such systemic 'miscarriage' of itself in the world, where the ideal cannot be realized and its approximations cannot be just."

The *Comedy* can be read as a transcendental love story, but the texture of the *Paradiso* does not read as though energized by eros. Dante's writing energy pours into diatribes against various polities and politicians, temporal and spiritual, uttered by those engaged in "eyelocks" with the very fount of being. Cunizza explains, in the sphere of Venus, that "because her people [Guelphs] are stubborn against duty, Padua at the marsh will stain the waters that bathe Vicenza" (*Par.* 9.46–48). St. Peter rails, at the brink of the ninth heaven, "It was not our purpose that the keys that were committed to me should become the ensign on a banner for warfare against the baptized" (*Par.* 27.49–51), the literal sense an allusion to the papal troop sent against Frederick II in 1229. Into which ring of Hell would I put this compulsive point counter and grudge bearer? Into which ring of Hell would he put me?

Is poetry an institution of moral judgment?

Or is judgment just a phase of human consciousness this particular European poem must encompass in its wide Hell-mouth? I am curious—was personal and private judgment once more prevalent, honored, powerful, as an emotion supported by certain high levels of character, than it is now? Or was it just one of the temptations of *auctoritas*? If God was a judge, then so perhaps could Dante be, without shame. But: "judge not, lest ye be judged," saith the Lord. And "judgment is mine." The poet's judgments are consequential: consider the effect, on the reputations of his forebears Brunetto Latini and Priscian the Grammarian, of his unsubstantiated accusations of sodomy. Dante should have been singed not on the Cornice of Love but in the circle of Judges. But there isn't one.

If [the longitude and latitude of every place] were known, man would be able to know the characteristics of all things in the world and their natures and qualities which they contract from the force of this location. (Roger Bacon, *Opus majus*)

In the world that preceded print and large personal libraries, the arts of memory helped people manage knowledge by storing it internally on a spatial grid that inevitably saturated its data with hierarchy and allegorical significance. The *Comedy* is what Ignatius of Loyola later called a memory palace, a topographical map of spiritual knowledge like the Tibetan Kalachakra, or the fourteenth-century frescoes of Hell and Heaven in Florence's Santa Maria Novella (where Dante probably attended the *studium*). The memory palace invites long meditation on the structure and details of its depicted spaces and the beings who occupy them. It is rooted in the notion of the *topos* (Latin *locus*) or "place," as it is known in rhetoric. The architectonics which are the *Comedy*'s grandest effects are then a function of rhetoric, in the service of memory and spiritual experience. They are also, as Roger Bacon tells us, all we need to know to know about who and what is *in* the system of places they construct.

The medieval idea espoused above by Bacon assumes not only a belief in geography as helping to shape individual and ethnic character, but a belief in—or perhaps semiconscious reliance on—judicial astrology, then part of astronomy. Dante's (nondeterminist) belief in the shaping influence of the physical heavens went further than that of the theologians, despite his deep belief in free will. Ideas of geographical and zodiacal influence, understood in Macrobian zone theory to predispose one to certain characteristics or, in Foucault's term, "resemblances," make easy homologies with an aristocratic society's understanding that estate and social status predetermine, not only one's place (*topos*) at the table, but one's capacities and one's right to power.

This hierarchy of being and power is normatively repudiated by modern liberal democracies, in which individual or national relation to cash flow determines the distribution of rights. It would be easy to indulge in as much "rigid judgment" (*Inf.* 30.70) as Dante does in the *Inferno* if the representative personae of the cash nexus were considered for a moment, or their doppelgängers, the politicians they pay for, the shadows of the shadow puppets. The pleasure of imagining shelves of torment for top executives of the World Bank, for Rupert Murdoch, Steve Forbes, or the congressmen who keep Texas oil companies afloat by abolishing social welfare, is palpable. But indulgence of every kind is the name of our weary 2K game. Moralist indulgence is another shadow of the shadow puppetry of wild consumption, wild expansion. A puppetry already begun in the city-states of fourteenth-century Italy. We go to Dante for tact, for order.

Do we like order, then?

Apparently, I do not. This summer, Dante reads like a utopianist to me, sinless and omniscient, eager to represent an order that will exclude the messes caused by rebellion, ambition, restlessness, curiosity, desire, even by moral or cultural difference. I cannot bear to be told what is right and wrong in such specific detail, in the zestful context—even in Heaven—of graphically visualized punishments or subordinations. Why not? In part because I was a "Catholic girl"; like Dante, though unwillingly, I still secretly believe the Law is real, the order(s) invoked by its patriarchal operatives and beneficiaries valid, larger than I am, time-honored. I believe, deep down, in the Author, and that he is listening to me read. So it's not enough just to say "how medieval!" and get on with "the poetry."

But order is a difficult theme for diatribe. Start writing about it and it threatens to convert you, by means not only of its heavily armed police, but of its religious or supernatural charm, its sentimental charm—its promise to hold you. The famous autistic designer of slaughterhouse equipment, Temple Grandin, intensely empathetic with the cows and pigs she designs her guillotines for, has described the necessity that she be held not by a human, but in a confining place (a *topos*). She says she understands that cows need and want this too, and in her humanely engineered abattoirs, the cows are held tightly and guided individually to their ap-, pointed ends.

Dante's immortal and orderly abattoirs are less humane. George Santayana wrote, in *Three Philosophical Poets*, of the inscription over the gate of Dis: "The damned are damned for the glory of God. This doctrine, I cannot help thinking, is a great disgrace to human nature." Perhaps, but it was no human who inscribed it on that gate. Dante's Paradise represents *God's* fiction, a *didactic* fiction. The souls' inadvertent performance of it is for us—the living, the students; it confirms or enlivens our belief that sin's consequences, life's consequences, are enormous. The fiction therefore uses, and in so doing might figuratively be said to *abuse*, the blessed souls who must array themselves in the various *tableaux vivants* of the *Paradiso*'s light show. These formations may not be amenable to the inherently mobile nature of the soul. To explain the pain of purgatorial fire for the immaterial bodies of souls in Purgatory, Thomas Aquinas describes it as a jail: "fire of its nature is able to have an incorporeal spirit united to it as a thing is united to its place . . . as the instrument of Divine justice [the fire] is enabled to detain it enchained."

I do not look forward to participating eternally in a choreographed demonstration, a Busby Berkeley ballet of compelling but tiring force, for the benefit of occasional lost souls. I want joy, huge, heaping tons of joy, *compensation*. And I do not want it to be found in some outer ring of the blessed, where I helpfully indicate to tourists that even the Outer Rings are happy: "Our affections, which are kindled solely in the pleasure of the Holy Ghost, rejoice in being conformed to his order" (*Par.* 3.52–54). I want *all happiness*. I did not die under torture or in prison. I have experienced relatively ordinary levels of anguish. And still I want relief, and an apology, although in fact I expect nothing, not even silence.

Dante Alighieri did not live in postmodern America. Perhaps in his particular Italy, the rigid placements of social order and a perpetual readiness to judge were to be preferred over an always-threatening level of violent chaos we call an "emergency" when we see it now, in Kosovo or South Central L.A. It is probably better to read his *Inferno* and *Paradiso* as registers of horror at the approaching collapse of empire, papacy, and feudalism itself. The concept of order had not yet been corrupted by its associations with Fascism and apartheid. At any rate, I am being impossible. Order is a feature of poetry as well as of the cosmos and of the idea of justice. A world-encompassing allegorical poem is necessarily isomorphic with the avatar of world-encompassing order known as Justice, and if we are enjoying the placing, enclosing, and holding at one level, it is difficult to reject it at the level it mirrors. That's the magic trick of allegory.

No artist can inveigh forever against the "blessed rage for order"—though, *note well*, it is a *rage*. It is perhaps the meaning of social order as an object of approval or reverence, and especially the relation of human judgment to order, that have detained me all this long, hot summer. For here are issues of dominance and power, and Dante, whatever his powerlessness in the actual social realm of exile, has all the power in his poem—including the power of rhetoric to convince, to move, to terrify. Perhaps in Dante's Heaven and Hell, souls go precisely where they want to go, find their own places. ("What I was living, that am I dead!" yells Capaneus in Hell [*Inf.* 14.51], and Piccarda in "the slowest sphere" of Heaven asserts that "the power of love quiets our will and makes us wish only for that which we have" [*Par.* 3.70–72]). It's a wonderful idea; the present Pope has just reaffirmed it. But though it's declared often, it does not seem to me represented in the *Comedy*, only declared. Where it is absent, one can easily feel oneself in the presence of a hanging judge in border country, where "the law's whatever I say it is."

One reads the *Comedy* more literally without commentaries. Whatever else, the poem is a narrative fiction, narrated by an "I" who is the central character, the only character with whom a reader can "identify"—in whom we can place ourselves—as the others disappear continuously. Modern readers can identify with Virgil for about half of the poem—he is like us in being barred entrance to the territories of the true aristocrats, the Saved, but he is not "I," the poem rejects him with no formal leave-taking, and we keep reading. At any given moment, one can (and usually does) "identify" with a soul in torment. But the only consciousness to whom the whole narrative is as present as it must be to the reader is that of the "I"—not only a soul developing toward enlightenment, but also the representative of a soul in rage, a soul that defines and creates the states of torment which are our only alternative to identification with Dante the revenant narrator. This narrator is an implacable taxonomist, who knows exactly how much Heaven to dole out to whom, who can only imagine the sublime of transcendence as a set of gradations and promotions, of places we will know and keep.

The rage I feel against this narrator, against the idea of order itself, is hard to control: Justice, says Freud, begins in the nursery, and contemplation of it easily returns us there. I have been trained to honor Dante as both the most perfect poet of All Time and also the revenant, the man who has seen the country of Death and has deserved such a vision. For many Catholics, it is his Afterlife to which we are all headed. Where we can rest assured we will not have to sit next to a Jew on the strictly segregated bleachers, and that there will be very few Guelphs, whatever a Guelph is. But we will be held. Held in place, like a cow in an abattoir who never arrives at the blade itself.

I want to protect the dead and the to-be-dead from Dante, because atavistically I feel he has the power to hurt them, and that power must be the power of poetry, since he died banished and poor, in someone else's house. In my miserable millennial Nursery, I want to rearrange Heaven, so everyone will be as close to God as everyone else, and slow learners like Piccarda won't have to stand submissively in the back ("you will see a marvelous correspondence of greater to more, and of smaller to less, in each heaven with respect to its Intelligence" [*Par.* 28.76–78]), reading the eyes of God at a third-grade level. Or better—so that people can take a walk and get away from God, the Great and Powerful. I want to redesign God, so he has some of the enlightened compassion necessary to design a Heaven that will in fact, as Robert Thurman says of the Kalachakra, "nurture beings' development" (rather than "fix you," like Eliot's party guest, "sprawling on a pin"). So that he has enough of it to design a Hell that will at least not suffer from comparison with Temple Grandin's abattoirs. I want Dante's sister-in-law Piccarda, abducted from a convent and raped into marriage, to be forgiven for not "escaping" back to the imprisonment that preceded the marriage. I want Dante to spend several lifetimes as a woman, as a Jew, as a Muslim, as a Black Guelph, as a Ghibelline, as a Pope. I want him to burn and weep in the Circle of the Judges.

What an extraordinary matter, that such a poem, such an infinite thing, such a powerful story with so many consequences in the religious imaginations of "those who will call these times ancient," that a poem describing—as no European poem before and perhaps no European poem since has done—*Paradise*, should be so bitter, so desperate, so merely personal. What a disappointment, when one had wanted there to be the Poet, the Vision, the Cosmos, the Truth. A home. There's no place, unfortunately, like home. The exile knows that one way, the reader of Dante guesses it another. Home, that "world endlessly bitter" (*Par.* 17.112), is where if you have to go there, they don't have to take you in after all.

Middle-class modern people tend to respond defensively to the "judgmentalness" of Dante's spiritual world, sensing that Dante would probably at best assign them to the outer suburb of the meaningless, that monotonous crowd doomed to be harried by mosquitoes for eternity, rejected even by Satan. Late capitalist culture has made of us "consumers," an "audience," people who must be attracted, wooed, not threatened and shamed. People who are used to being as Special as Dante is (central focus of the Eternal World for a whole week!), but who are suspicious of merit, even a sense of their own, lest merit and demerit complicate their/our imagination of "democracy." It is not a heavy task to share the irate Dante's need to place us all on some ratty couch in the leaking Vestibule of Hell's fern bar.

But we are not completely worthless, I think. In a work that promises to introduce us to the "endless variety of goodness," as a friend of mine put it, we are properly disappointed to find instead a hierarchy of goodness, which can only rest justly on the premise of a single conception of goodness, a single axis of achievement. History excuses us from finding submission to the will of God the highest imaginable form of goodness: "God" has too often willed genocide as a response to the disorder of moral difference.

It is not the poet Dante's fault, of course, that those of later days who shared his imperialism, his love of order, his hierarchicalism, his ethical "objectivity," have provided some of history's most appalling monsters. Our world is one in which order has so triumphed that the very *conception* of goodness is in doubt, and many souls of moral dignity have deep ambivalence about the orderly production of beauty as well. After the efficient order of Auschwitz, Adorno feared, any poem—not just a spiritually eugenic poem like the *Comedy*—might be a sin by association with the unspeakable rhymes of the death camps. But Dante's world was closer than ours to being one of sheer, random willfulness. The life of a member of the global village, the global economy, the registry of motor vehicles, is a different matter, life now nearly extinguished by an excess of order.

And it is not Dante's fault that I was brought up to feel that order was good, and that art was not order but the subversion of order, and that I, too, was a misfit in the moral order that constitutes the world's real beauty. Not Dante's fault that so many boys of my generation died or were ruined for the institution of a "new world order," and that they are said to have found restitution now in the beautiful order of Maya Ying Lin's Vietnam Veterans Memorial in the nation's capital. Not Dante's fault that his *Comedy* was taught in colleges to generation after generation of the powerful, the political class, those for whom that God's-eye view had huge convenience in the necessarily pitiless pursuits of foreign policy, urban redevelopment, criminal justice systems, and the free market. Certainly not Dante's fault that aerial photography, mimicking his visual perspective on the blessed in Heaven, has revealed to the twentieth century the astonishing orderly beauty of mass destruction, whether military or industrial.

Dante himself when not designing God's fiction of Justice for him is flinching at it, weeping, trembling, fainting, disappearing in it. He is never angry at it, though—it is as if he has left that business to us, whoever he thought we might be. I don't feel guilty toward him for this rage, because his poem has invited it—indeed, invented it. For there is no God, no Afterlife, no three-ring circus of fixed destinies on display. There is only the rhetorician, Dante, and his grand design—a design that includes a suffering subject through whom we can feel the horrors and injustices of Justice, and a thousand objects in whom we can see ourselves—truly dead, like specimens—from the perspective of Justice. Could Dante's *Comedy* be an indictment, not of the human beings Frye commends for having the quiet courage, after this poem, to go on sinning, but of a world in which the greatest imaginable reparation must be this hard to distinguish from the madness of cruelty? Is the *Comedy* a cri de coeur, rather than an encyclopedia of the cosmos?

Dante slips easily through the Cornice of Wrath, despite the obvious wrath of his composition. In the poetic order of his poem, it is necessary for him to be stalled on the Cornice of Lust, where that sin is corrected which impersonates—and underesti-

mates—the fundamental physics of his cosmos. In the fecund disorder of reading it, however, his reader will do his penance for him
on the proper cornice. In the awful effectiveness of the poem, this
reader's own inadequate idea of "goodness" might even place her
in Hell, its fifth, wrathful ring, where Dante should be her company but isn't—because the magic power of Poetry protects him
as well as it does the pagan Poets, whose place in Hell is the very
Paradise they conceived for their own heroes.

Despite the problems of our resistance, to be in the story ourselves, as I have said above, we must be in it as Dante the protagonist is, because his is the only subjectivity there to inhabit—except
for the narrator's, also Dante. Dante trying to find out the particular shape of his own failure to be human, or simply rehearsing the
precise shape of his own terror of the world. Or Dante designing
an infinite that hurts us, "detains" us, shames us. Narrative entails
the danger of knowing through imaginative experience. Dante has
made me know, and utter, the utter wrath of the soul who refuses
to submit to another.

And in so doing, of course, I've let the Poet manhandle me,
dead though he is, imaginary though he is, enraged though I am at
his timidity in suppressing his own subliminal hatred of God. I've
let him make me his puppet. He's hurt me, detained me, shamed
me. He's brought me inside his imaginary world, though I am real
and he no longer is.

The first time I taught the *Comedy*, the sweetest and (I thought)
dumbest student in the class said on her course evaluation form
that she was grateful to me for having given her beautiful religion
back to her. I was curious about that for a long time. This summer,
I am wondering if it wasn't terror that yanked her back into place
as a good Catholic girl who could aim without sin for the outer,
"slowest" sphere of Blessedness, the terror of someone who had
courageously opened herself to Poetry and found it more powerful than Sunday school.

How much does this power have to do with the constantly enacted power of the liturgical word, the sacramental performatives: I baptize thee, I renounce thee, Satan, This is my body . . . ? Is the fiercely competitive Dante competing here with his hated popes, and winning? The liturgical is the extreme case of the performative, of language as literally creative, enactive. According to Allen Grossman, poets are always in competition, not with mere popes but with the gods, those fictioneers whose worlds we are doomed to die in. If the poets win, does that mean they have become as gods?

Charles Singleton's final note to the *Comedy* is touchingly but chillingly atavistic:

> No poet could have endured a greater tragedy than Dante, had exile and then death at the age of 56 forced him to leave his *Commedia* unfinished—which would have meant that a structure . . . designed to reflect God's work in *its* completeness and perfection, would have failed in its goal. But at some time before that fatal date of mid-September, 1321, that last verse, speaking of Love to the very end, had been conceived and penned, and that *Comedy* to which Heaven and earth had set hand, and had made its author lean through many years, *was done*, an "imitation" finished in its perfection.

"That which overcomes you is power against which naught defends itself" (*Par.* 23.35–36). Poetry's power is what Dada and L=A=N=G=U=A=G=E poets have renounced in fierce loathing. Like Procne, they are dicing up the corpse to serve the murderous Father in *contrapasso*, and are silenced and made to sing nonsense syllables. Their resistance is futile, as is that of any resister in Dante's finished, perfected world. They will perhaps go to my Heaven, but my Heaven is only make-believe. And in it, I will be found curled in a sudden arbor, beside a purling stream, my hair lifted by a breeze in which the distant notes of caroling angels drift, reading the *Comedy* and gnashing my teeth.

Edward Hirsch

Summoning Shades

Every writer has a date with the dead. There comes a time when each of us—psychologically, poetically—must enter the Stygian realm and cross the dark river, leaving the solid realm of the living behind, going down into the mournful land of the shades. It happens somewhere in the middle of your life. I can tell you, the air is thick and the ghosts swarm. Smoke burns your eyes; the stench is terrible. Voices cry out, as if from nowhere, and fade away. Death has undone so many. This place, if you can call it a place, is unspeakable, mute. It is below or beyond words. I wish this journey on no one. I wish luck to anyone who sails forth, who navigates the black waters; I hope you find your way back.

I was first sucked down into the underworld after my mother-in-law died and I dreamt of handing her birds-of-paradise in the vestibule to the afterlife. My grandmother was somewhere out there in the unnamed swamp, too. I went there again after my closest friend died from liver cancer. My most charmed friend— the luckiest in his personality, unluckiest in life. One night after his funeral, I dreamt that I was wandering around in a malignant fog searching for a wooden pier, which I could never find. I heard strange languages, horrible screams. I stood on a high bridge and peered intently down into the depth, but I could make out nothing there. When I woke up, I could still smell the smoke on my clothes. After that, I never quite read Dante in the same way again.

Dante was obsessively drawn into the smoky regions. He was called to them. He dramatized the desperate vulnerability of human beings caught up in an implacable world. He seems to have been able to split himself off; as an author, he was unwavering and even ruthless in his judgments, though as a pilgrim, his heart kept going out to "the disconsolate and mutilated shades" with whom he identified. His distress as a voyager in the world of the damned is everywhere palpable. There was a shocking and perhaps irreconcilable tension in him between the icy judgments of the administrator and the humane emotions of the pilgrim. The tension between the temporal and the transcendental orders is part of what gives the *Inferno* so much of its terrifying force.

The *Comedy* is at once a metaphysical adventure story (a pilgrim ventures forth to discover the fate of souls after death), a personal odyssey understood in allegorical terms ("Midway in the journey of our life," the poem famously begins, "I found myself in a dark wood"), an encyclopedic guide to the schematics of the otherworld (from the doomed in Hell to the atoning sinners in Purgatory to the blessed souls in Heaven), and a quest beyond the grave for a visionary beauty (Beatrice). I've been endlessly fascinated by Dante's notion of *contrapasso*, his imaginative map of the other side, his unabashed geography—a medieval mythology—of the psyche. He's a great systematizer whose humanity keeps transcending his own system as the shades come to surpass the sins—the functions—they embody, and thereby materialize as human beings in their own right. ("The beyond," as Erich Auerbach puts it, "becomes a stage for human beings and human passions.") It's as if by giving names to things, to places, to torments, even names which I cannot recognize as entirely accurate, Dante has helped give me access to the shadowy regions of my own psyche, my own churning heart, a place of suffering I could return to and explore. He has broken the silence:

Ruppemi l'alto sonno ne la testa
  un greve truono, sì ch'io mi riscossi
  come persona ch'è per forza desta;

A heavy thunderclap broke the deep sleep in my head, so
that I started like one who is awakened by force;[1]

(*Inf.* 4.1–3, tr. Charles Singleton)

I have been moved, over the years, by the radical audacity of
Dante's imagination, by the seriousness and gravity of his epic
task, by the utterly weird and heretically Christian landscape he
proposes beyond death, by the wondrous strangeness of the *Comedy*. I have been mostly unaffected by T. S. Eliot's idea of Dante as
a "classic," a universal figure of European literature. Dante as a
national bard, a canonical figure whose work is recited by school-
children and engraved on Italian monuments, leaves me un-
touched. But I have been overwhelmingly affected by Dante's
story of himself descending into the bowels of earth, into the region of demons and lost souls, and emerging, like Job, to tell the
story of his strange journey.

I believe that poetry is, in a profound way, a quest for the divine, and Dante is, for me, the first figure of that quest, a relentless
dreamer, an unremitting precisionist of the otherworld who took
the way down in order to find the way up. That dizzying infernal
path—fiery, windblown—still trembles with a sacred air. It radiates
heat. I am grateful to Dante for following Virgil, for following the
sixth book of the *Aeneid*, into the delirious landscape of the underworld, just as I am grateful to Hermann Broch for his heart-
breakingly beautiful and feverish immersion in Virgil's final hours,
final consciousness, in *The Death of Virgil*, a lyrical prose poem in
the guise of a novel. Rereading Broch, I am reminded of Dante's
full-scale immersion in Virgil—and his profoundly independent
response to the *Aeneid*—and I recognize how much I have come

to admire and engage Dante as a quirky grand master, a reckless singer of tales who flung himself into the abyss and represented himself as a bewildered pilgrim, an apprentice not only to Virgil, but also to Beatrice, to Love, to the entire Wisdom tradition. He was a spiritual seeker, a vehicle of his own mysterious visions. His grandly designed poem is a kind of Augustinian confession: a search for the Absolute under the sign of eternity.

I first read the *Inferno* seriously during my freshman year in college, and it spooked me no end. I've always been strangely susceptible to its landscape of death, a land of unlikeness. (It took me much longer to get to the *Purgatorio* and the *Paradiso*, mostly, I suppose, because I couldn't recognize my own world in them.) I connected immediately to the *Inferno* as an urban poem, like *The Waste Land*. I didn't make much of Dante's medieval cosmology or politics (his peculiar quasi-renegade Catholicism still baffles me), but I didn't have much trouble recognizing his portrait of Hell as a stand-in for a secular human city. I have walked that city, which is filled with Dostoyevskian sufferers, disenfranchised crowds, Sadean torments.

I also understood right away, I think, that Dante had high dreams of grandeur, but was really an outsider, an inner exile who had lost his footing in the middle of life. I recognized his confusion. Osip Mandelstam put his finger on this aspect of Dante's character, his psychological makeup, when he wrote: "One would have to be a blind mole not to notice that throughout the *Divina Commedia* Dante does not know how to behave, how to act, what to say, how to bow." It was easy for me to relate to the way that Dante portrayed himself as a social stumbler trying to figure things out. In fact, there's a sort of extended question-and-answer session operating throughout the poem between the diffident, eager apprentice and the mentor he has chosen to explain things to him— at first Virgil, then Beatrice. Mandelstam playfully continued: "If Dante had been sent forth alone, without his *dolce padre*, without Virgil, scandal would have inevitably erupted at the very start, and we would have had the most grotesque buffoonery rather than a journey amongst the torments and sights of the underworld!"

It was Dante who first demonstrated to me how poetry comes from other poetry, how poems beget poems. As an American poet, I've taken special note of the fact that Dante wrote the *Comedy* in Italian, which was still a nebulous national language, rather than in the customary literary language of Latin, so that he could be accessible to a wider audience. It was a little like reconceiving Lamentations in the language of *In the American Grain*. I've registered Dante's claim in *De vulgari eloquentia* (*On Eloquence in the Vernacular*) that "Our illustrious vernacular wanders like a stranger and finds hospitality in lowly refuges." This idea is so fresh—so democratic—it sounds almost Emersonian (Emerson was himself a great *dantista*), which is one reason, I suppose, Dante's handbook for "making it new" has had such powerful appeal for American poets from Longfellow to Pound. So, too, I've always liked that moment in section 30 of the *Vita Nuova* when Dante acknowledged the friendship—and the aesthetic dream—he shared with Guido Cavalcanti, saying, "I am well aware, too, that my closest friend, for whom I wrote this work, also desired that I should write it entirely in the vernacular." Dante turns that vernacular into an instrument of such dizzying verbal majesty, of such fully embodied imagination, that in his poem, souls become corporeal and words metamorphose into things.

There is something abject and beautiful about the way that Dante summons Virgil to his side to lead his pilgrim self through the Inferno and Purgatory to the gates of Paradise. (After that, love has to take over.) One could surmise that Dante's need for Virgil's guidance was so great that he summoned up the Latin poet out of the dust, as if by magic, across the centuries. As E. R. Curtius splendidly puts it, "The awakening of Virgil by Dante is an arc of flame which leaps from one great soul to another." Dante is in some sense rescuing Virgil, who appears in the dim light as "chi per lungo silenzio parea fioco" (one who seemed faint through long silence, *Inf.* 1.63), but, even more profoundly, he is himself being rescued and guided by the poet he evokes and addresses as "lo mio maestro e 'l mio autore" (my master and my author, 1.85).

"Then are you Virgil?" he cries out to the human shape who appears in the wasteland. He answers his own question, shamefaced that he had not recognized in person the poet who had meant so much to him:

> "The glory and light are yours,
> That poets follow—may the love that made me search
> Your book in patient study avail me, Master!
> You are my guide and author, whose verses teach
> The graceful style whose model has done me honor."
> (*Inf.* 1.82–87, tr. Robert Pinsky)

Dante dramatizes here a direct and intimate meeting of poets—one Christian, one pagan—across the centuries. He provides a spirited tale of mentorship. And he offers a model of poetic apprenticeship, a model of mutuality and presence, a place to turn to for antecedents, a way to write poetry that acknowledges our interdependence. I've tried to take note, too, of how Dante imagines a kind of literary Parnassus of pagan poets in a privileged place in Limbo, how he establishes for himself a direct line of poetic ancestry and even at one point compares himself to "the humble psalmist, David," how he engineers in *Purgatorio* 21 and 22 the moving reunion between Virgil and Statius, whom he elsewhere calls "dolce poeta" (sweet poet). It's startling—and wholly revealing—that Statius speaks of Virgil's masterwork in terms of maternity and nursing: "de l'Eneïda dico, la qual mamma / fummi, e fummi nutrice, poetando" (I mean the *Aeneid*, which in poetry was both mother and nurse to me, 21.97–98). Dante imbibed the poetry of his predecessors, especially the three Latin poets he recognized in Limbo (Horace, Ovid, and Lucan), as nourishing sustenance. The *Aeneid*, which he referred to as "alta tragedia," was mother's milk to him. He also singled out Linus, a mythical Greek poet whom Virgil describes in the *Eclogues* as "divino carmina pastor" (shepherd of immortal song) and linked him to Orpheus, who sings so divinely. Dante may have been powerfully drawn to Christian orthodoxy, but he was also eager to take his rightful place as a poet among the poets.

It was through a Dantesque lens that I read backward to the haunted and enabling story of a Thracian minstrel who sings so poignantly that he charms his way into the underworld to reclaim—and lose again—his dead bride. I have taken up the voice—the journey—of that singer, and I have enacted the role of that bride in my own poems. It was through a Dantesque lens that I read backward to book 11 of the *Odyssey*, in which Odysseus sails his ship into a country where the sun never shines, and then, pouring libations to the dead, summons up a swarm of ghosts, among them an unburied friend, his mother, and the seer Tiresias. This scene is echoed in book 6 of the *Aeneid*, when Aeneas persuades the Sybil of Cumae to guide him into Hades, so he can speak to his dead father about the future. I have read that scene so often I feel almost as if I have witnessed it. I have also come to recognize how as Homer's scene informs Virgil's, Virgil's account offers a prototype for the *Inferno*—the most entrancing, detailed, and audacious treatment of a human being's journey into Hell ever written.

How often I have used a Dante setting, the gait of Dante's verse form, to deliver me to my own emotional life, my own material. I have learned from Dante how fruitful it is to call upon poets from the past to guide you through the mired and foggy swamps of experience. I, too, have plumbed the shadows and summoned up the shades; I, too, have imagined long walks with my beloved immortals. When I can manage it, I also love the spiraling effect of *terza rima*, which seems to be both open-ended and con-

clusive, like moving through a series of interpenetrating rooms
or going down a set of winding stairs: you are always traveling forward while looking backward. This gives a poem a particular kind
of momentum—an urgency slowed by retrospection. I've tried to
learn from Dante the artistry that delivers a ferocious intensity.

Leonard Barkan identifies a key aspect of Dante's voyage for
me when he writes, "The figure of Dante, with his own che-
quered past, is partly in a mirror relationship to the sinners he
scrutinizes." He recognizes them. I have always been called to moments in the *Inferno* when Dante's action mirrors the sinners he is
encountering, such as in canto 5 when he swoons in the presence
of the swooning lovers Paolo and Francesca. I recognize the poet
in those moments of doomed recognition, doomed identification.
Such dizzying moments magnetize my own experience. They ob-
jectify it. They offer a mode of transformative thinking. Here,
then, is a recent poem—a one-sentence *terza rima* sonnet—in
which a lover addresses the beloved through the scrim of a classic
Dante text:

The Sentence
(*Inferno*, Canto Five)

When you read Canto Five aloud last night
in your naked, sing-song, fractured Italian,
my sweet compulsion, my carnal appetite,

I suspected we shall never be forgiven
for devouring each other body and soul,
and someday Minos, a connoisseur of sin,

will snarl himself twice around his tail
to sentence us to life in perpetual motion,
funneling us downward to the second circle

where we will never sleep or rest again
in turbulent air, like other ill–begotten
lovers who embraced passion beyond reason,

and yet I cannot turn from you, my wanton;
our heaven will always be our hell, a swoon.

Permissions